HISTORICAL VIEWPOINTS

VOLUME TWO SINCE 1865

D1406928

HISTORICAL VIEWPOINTS

Notable Articles from *American Heritage*

EIGHTH EDITION

VOLUME TWO SINCE 1865

EDITOR

John A. Garraty

Gouverneur Morris Professor of History
Columbia University

 LONGMAN

An imprint of Addison Wesley Longman, Inc.

New York • Reading, Massachusetts • Menlo Park, California • Harlow, England
Don Mills, Ontario • Sydney • Mexico City • Madrid • Amsterdam

Acquisitions Editor: Jay O'Callaghan
Development Manager: Betty Slack
Executive Marketing Manager: Sue Westmoreland
Project Coordination and Text Design: Ruttle, Shaw & Wetherill, Inc.
Cover Manager/Designer: Nancy Danahy
Cover Illustration: "The 12:09—On Time Again" by Jane Wooster Scott/SuperStock, Inc.
Full Service Production Manager: Joseph Vella
Photo Researcher: Photosearch, Inc.
Electronic Page Makeup: Ruttle, Shaw & Wetherill, Inc.
Senior Print Buyer: Hugh Crawford
Printer and Binder: The Maple-Vail Book Manufacturing Group
Cover Printer: The Lehigh Press, Inc.

For permission to use copyrighted material, grateful acknowledgment is made to the
copyright holders on pages 315–318, which are hereby made part of this copyright page.

Library of Congress Cataloging-in-Publication Data

Historical viewpoints : notable articles from American heritage /
    editor, John A. Garraty. — 8th ed.
        p.   cm.
    Includes bibliographical references.
    Contents: v. 1. To 1877 — v. 2. Since 1865.
    ISBN 0-321-00299-7 (v. 1). — ISBN 0-321-00301-2 (v. 2). —
    ISBN 0-321-00302-0 (free copy)
    1. United States—History.   I. Garraty, John Arthur, 1920–
II. American heritage.
E178.6.H67   1999
973—dc21   98-17549
                                                                            CIP

Copyright © 1999 by John A. Garraty

All rights reserved. No part of this publication may be reproduced, stored in a retrieval
system, or transmitted, in any form or by any means, electronic, mechanical, photocopying,
recording, or otherwise, without the prior written permission of the publisher. Printed in
the United States.

Please visit our website at http://longman.awl.com

ISBN 0-321-00301-2

2345678910—MA—010099

CONTENTS

INTRODUCTION

This eighth edition has been inspired by the encouraging reception afforded the earlier editions of *Historical Viewpoints* and by the fact that interesting new articles continue to appear in *American Heritage*. This volume contains five new essays. I have included these new selections because they seem ideally suited to current historical interests and because they present fresh viewpoints.

There are almost as many kinds of history as there are historians. In addition to the differences between political history and the social, economic, and cultural varieties, the discipline lends itself to such classifications as analytical, narrative, statistical, impressionistic, local, comparative, philosophical, and synthetic. Often the distinctions between one kind of history and another are overemphasized. No one can write good political history without some consideration of social, economic, and cultural questions; narrative history requires analysis to be meaningful; impressionistic treatments of past events are, in a way, statistical histories based on very tiny samples. Nevertheless, the different approaches exist and serve different purposes. Each focuses on part of the total human experience and sees it from a particular perspective; each, when well done, adds its own contribution to the total record.

Each perspective has its value for the introductory student. Some are perhaps more generally useful (that is, more interesting to a wider segment of the population) or more suggestive at a particular time and place than others, but the distinctions are like those between a miniature and a mural, a sonnet and an epic poem. No one would suggest that "The Moonlight Sonata" was a waste of Beethoven's time because he was capable of producing the *Choral* symphony, or that Mozart should not have written "Eine Kleine Nachtmusik" because he had within him *Don Giovanni*. In the same way, a monograph or an article of twenty pages can be as well worth doing and as satisfying to read as Edward Gibbon's *Decline and Fall of the Roman Empire*.

The terms "scholarly" and "popular" history came into existence during the latter half of the nineteenth century. Before that time, all history was popular in the sense that those who wrote it, viewing themselves as possessors of special information acquired through scholarship or through having observed firsthand the events they described, aimed to transmit that knowledge to anyone interested in the subject. But when history became "scientific" and professionalized, historians began to write primarily for other historians. They assumed that nonspecialists had no interest in their work or were incapable of understanding it, and even argued that to write history for the general reader was to prostitute one's talents. Therefore, although with many notable exceptions, the best-trained and most intelligent historians tended to forswear the task of transmitting their scholarly findings to ordinary readers.

Of course popular history continued to be written and read, but most of it was produced by amateurs. Its quality varied greatly. The scholarly prejudice against "popularizers" had a solid basis in fact. Too often popular history was—and still is—shallow, error ridden, out of date before publication, a mere rehash of already written books, or an exasperating mixture, as one critic has said, of "something we all knew before" and "something which is not so." Much of it was written by journalists and novelists who often lacked the patience, the professional skills, and the knowledge of sources that are as necessary for writing good history as narrative power, imagination, and lucidity of style.

It was chiefly with the hope of encouraging professional historians to broaden their perspectives that, beginning in the 1930s, a group of historians led by Professor Allan Nevins of Columbia University began to think of founding a general circulation magazine of American history. Their aim was to create a magazine in which solidly researched and significant articles would be presented in a way that would interest and educate readers who were not professional students of the past. Nevins himself, one of the great historians of the twentieth century, epitomized the combination they sought to produce. He was a prodigious scholar, author of dozens of learned volumes, and trainer of literally hundreds of graduate students, but he was also a fluent and graceful writer whose work was widely read and appreciated. Nevins's books won Pulitzer Prizes as well as academic renown.

The example provided by Nevins and a few other outstanding historians of his generation, such as Samuel Eliot Morison, undoubtedly influenced the gradual revival of concern for popular history that has occurred in recent times on the part of professional academic scholars. So did the increasing sophistication of the general reading public, which made it less difficult for these experts to write this type of history without sacrificing their intellectual standards. In any case, in 1954 the Nevins group—the Society of American Historians—joined the American Association for State and Local History in sponsoring the magazine they had envisioned: *American Heritage.*

The success of *American Heritage* was rapid and substantial. It achieved a wide circulation, and the best professional historians began to publish in its pages. Its articles, at their best, have been authoritative, interesting, significant, and a pleasure to read. They have ranged over the whole course of American history from the precolonial era to the present, and have dealt with every aspect of American development from politics to painting and from economics to architecture.

The present selection from among the hundreds of outstanding essays and book excerpts that have appeared in *American Heritage* since 1954 seeks to provide a balanced assortment of articles to supplement and enrich general college courses in American history. Keeping in mind the structure of these courses and the topics they tend to emphasize, I have reprinted here articles that, in my opinion, will add depth and breadth to the student's understanding. The articles new to this edition are Robert James Maddox, "Why We Had to Drop the Atomic Bomb"; Arthur Schlesinger, Jr., "FDR: The Man of the Century"; Richard Reeves, "The Education of John F. Kennedy"; Alexander O. Boulton, "Levittown: The Buy of the Century"; and Fergus M. Bordewich, "The New Indians."

This is—by definition—popular history, but it is also history written by experts. The articles differ in purpose and approach. Some present new findings, some reexamine old questions from a fresh point of view, others magisterially distill and synthesize masses of facts and ideas. From the total, readers may extract, along with the specifics of the individual essays, a sense of the variety and richness of historical literature. They will observe how different historians (not all of them academic scholars) have faced the task of presenting knowledge not to other historians alone but to an audience of intelligent and interested general readers.

Since most of the students enrolled in college history courses are not specialists—even those who intend to become professional historians stand at the very beginning of their training—this approach seems to me ideally adapted to their needs. Many, though by no means all, of the subjects treated in these essays have also been covered in articles in professional historical periodicals, often written by the same historians. But as presented here, without sacrifice of intellectual standards, the material is not so much easier to grasp as it is more meaningful. Details are clearly related to larger issues; historical characters are delineated in the round, not presented as stick figures or automatons; not too much previous knowledge is assumed.

Finally, at least some of the essays I have included here illustrate the truth that history is, at its best, an art as well as a science. After all, the ancients gave history its own Muse, Clio. I hope and expect that students, from reading the following pages, will come to realize that history is a form of literature, that it can be *enjoyed*, not merely assimilated. Even those who see college history courses exclusively as training grounds for future professionals surely will not object if their students enjoy these readings while they learn.

Needless to say, I hope the book will serve even better than its predecessors the needs and interests of students of American history.

John A. Garraty

HISTORICAL VIEWPOINTS

VOLUME TWO SINCE 1865

1

Reconstruction and Race Relations

In this 1897 photograph a black woman with her child and dog watches her husband, cane in hand, leave for work.

Why They Impeached Andrew Johnson

David Herbert Donald

The story of presidential Reconstruction after Lincoln is told in this essay by David Herbert Donald, Charles Warren Professor of American History at Harvard University. Lincoln's approach to restoring the Union was cautious, practical, thoughtful—humane in every sense of the word. Because of his assassination, however, the evaluation of his policy has to be a study in the might-have-beens of history. The Reconstruction policy of his successor, Andrew Johnson, superficially similar to Lincoln's, was reckless, impractical, emotional, and politically absurd. While historians have differed in evaluating his purposes, they have agreed unanimously that his management of the problem was inept and that his policy was a total failure.

Professor Donald's essay provides an extended character study of Johnson, and it is not an attractive portrait. Donald believes that Johnson "threw away a magnificent opportunity" to smoothly and speedily return the Confederate states to a harmonious place in the Union. But he also shows how difficult Johnson's task was and to how great an extent Southern white opinion was set against the full acceptance of black equality. Donald is the author of many books, including a Pulitzer Prize–winning biography of the Massachusetts senator, Charles Sumner.

■ ■ ■ ■ ■ ■ ■

Reconstruction after the Civil War posed some of the most discouraging problems that have ever faced American statesmen. The South was prostrate. Its defeated soldiers straggled homeward through a countryside desolated by war. Southern soil was untilled and exhausted; southern factories and railroads were worn out. The four billion dollars of southern capital invested in Negro slaves was wiped out by advancing Union armies, "the most stupendous act of sequestration in the history of Anglo-American jurisprudence." The white inhabitants of eleven states had somehow to be reclaimed from rebellion and restored to a firm loyalty to the United States. Their four million former slaves had simultaneously to be guided into a proper use of their newfound freedom.

For the victorious Union government there was no time for reflection. Immediate decisions had to be made. Thousands of destitute whites and Negroes had to be fed before long-range plans of rebuilding the southern economy could be drafted. Some kind of government had to be established in these former Confederate states, to preserve order and to direct the work of restoration.

A score of intricate questions must be answered: Should the defeated southerners be punished or pardoned? How should genuinely loyal southern Unionists be rewarded? What was to be the social, economic, and political status of the now free Negroes? What civil rights did they have? Ought they to have the ballot? Should they be given a freehold of property? Was Reconstruction to be controlled by the national government, or should the southern states work out their own salvation? If the federal government supervised the process, should the President or the Congress be in control?

Intricate as were the problems, in early April, 1865, they did not seem insuperable. President Abraham Lincoln was winning the peace as he had already won the war. He was careful to keep every detail of Reconstruction in his own hands; unwilling to be committed to any "exclusive, and inflexible plan," he was working out a pragmatic program of restoration not, perhaps, entirely satisfactory to any group, but reasonably acceptable to all sections. With his enormous prestige as commander of the victorious North and as victor in the 1864 election, he was able to promise freedom to the Negro, charity to the southern white, security to the North.

The blighting of these auspicious beginnings is one of the saddest stories in American history. The reconciliation of the sections, which seemed so imminent in 1865, was delayed for more than ten years. Northern magnanimity toward a fallen foe curdled into bitter distrust. Southern whites rejected moderate leaders, and inveterate racists spoke for the new South. The Negro, after serving as a political pawn for a decade, was relegated to a second-class citizenship, from which he is yet struggling to emerge. Rarely has democratic government so completely failed as during the Reconstruction decade.

The responsibility for this collapse of American statesmanship is, of course, complex. History is not a tale of deep-dyed villains or pure-as-snow heroes. Part of the blame must fall upon ex-Confederates who refused to recognize that the war was over; part upon freedmen who confused liberty with license and the ballot box with the lunch pail; part upon northern antislavery extremists who identified patriotism with loyalty to the Republican party; part upon the land speculators, treasury grafters, and railroad promoters who were unwilling to have a genuine peace lest it end their looting of the public till.

Yet these divisive forces were not bound to triumph. Their success was due to the failure of constructive statesmanship that could channel the magnanimous feelings shared by most Americans into a positive program of reconstruction. President Andrew Johnson was called upon for positive leadership, and he did not meet the challenge.

Andrew Johnson's greatest weakness was his insensitivity to public opinion. In contrast to Lincoln, who said, "Public opinion in this country is everything," Johnson made a career of battling the popular will. A poor white, a runaway tailor's apprentice, a self-educated Tennessee politician, Johnson was a living defiance to the dominant southern belief that leadership belonged to the plantation aristocracy.

As senator from Tennessee, he defied the sentiment of his section in 1861 and refused to join the secessionist movement. When Lincoln later appointed him military governor of occupied Tennessee, Johnson found Nashville "a furnace of treason," but he braved social ostracism and threats of assassination and discharged his duties with boldness and efficiency.

Such a man was temperamentally unable to understand the northern mood in 1865, much less to yield to it. For four years the northern people had been whipped into wartime frenzy by propaganda tales of Confederate atrocities. The assassination of Lincoln by a southern sympathizer confirmed their belief in southern brutality and heartlessness. Few northerners felt vindictive toward the South, but most felt that the rebellion they had crushed must never rise again. Johnson ignored this postwar psychosis gripping the North and plunged ahead with his program of rapidly restoring the southern states to the Union. In May, 1865, without any previous preparation of public opinion, he issued a proclamation of amnesty, granting forgiveness to nearly all the millions of former rebels and welcoming them back into peaceful fraternity. Some few Confederate leaders were excluded from his general amnesty, but even they could secure pardon by special petition. For weeks the White House corridors were thronged with exConfederate statesmen and former southern generals who daily received presidential forgiveness.

Ignoring public opinion by pardoning the former Confederates, Johnson actually entrusted the formation of new governments in the South to them. The provisional governments established by the President proceeded, with a good deal of reluctance, to rescind their secession ordinances, to abolish slavery, and to repudiate the Confederate debt. Then, with far more enthusiasm, they turned to electing governors, representatives, and senators. By December, 1865, the southern states had their delegations in Washington waiting for admission by Congress. Alexander H. Stephens, once vice president of the Confederacy, was chosen senator from Georgia; not one of the North Carolina delegation could take a loyalty oath; and all of South Carolina's congressmen had "either held office under the Confederate States, or been in the army, or countenanced in some way the Rebellion."

Johnson himself was appalled, "There seems in many of the elections something like defiance, which is all out of place at this time." Yet on December 5 he strongly urged the Congress to seat these southern representatives "and thereby complete the work of reconstruction." But the southern states were omitted from the roll call.

Such open defiance of northern opinion was dangerous under the best of circumstances, but in Johnson's case it was little more than suicidal. The President seemed not to realize the weakness of his position. He was the representative of no major interest and had no genuine political following. He had been considered for the vice presidency in 1864 because, as a southerner and a former slaveholder, he could lend plausibility to the Republican pretension that the old parties were dead and that Lincoln was the nominee of a new, nonsectional National Union party.

A political accident, the new Vice President did little to endear himself to his countrymen. At Lincoln's second inauguration Johnson appeared before the Senate in an obviously inebriated state and made a long, intemperate harangue about his plebeian origins and his hard-won success. President, Cabinet, and senators were humiliated by the shameful display, and Charles Sumner felt that "the Senate should call upon him to resign." Historians now know that Andrew Johnson was not a heavy drinker. At the time of his inaugural display, he was just recovering from a severe attack of typhoid fever. Feeling ill just before he entered the Senate chamber, he asked for some liquor to steady his nerves, and either his weakened condition or abnormal sensitivity to alcohol betrayed him.

Lincoln reassured Republicans who were worried over the affair: "I have known Andy for many years; he made a bad slip the other day, but you need not be scared.

Andy ain't a drunkard." Never again was Andrew Johnson seen under the influence of alcohol, but his reformation came too late. His performance on March 4, 1865, seriously undermined his political usefulness and permitted his opponents to discredit him as a pothouse politician. Johnson was catapulted into the presidency by John Wilkes Booth's bullet. From the outset his position was weak, but it was not necessarily untenable. The President's chronic lack of discretion made it so. Where common sense dictated that a chief executive in so disadvantageous a position should act with great caution, Johnson proceeded to imitate Old Hickory, Andrew Jackson, his political idol. If Congress crossed his will, he did not hesitate to defy it. Was he not "the Tribune of the People"?

Sure of his rectitude, Johnson was indifferent to prudence. He never learned that the President of the United States cannot afford to be a quarreler. Apprenticed in the rough-and-tumble politics of frontier Tennessee, where orators exchanged violent personalities, crude humor, and bitter denunciations, Johnson continued to make stump speeches from the White House. All too often he spoke extemporaneously, and he permitted hecklers in his audience to draw from him angry charges against his critics.

On Washington's birthday in 1866, against the advice of his more sober advisers, the President made an impromptu address to justify his Reconstruction policy. "I fought traitors and treason in the South," he told the crowd; "now when I turn around, and at the other end of the line find men—I care not by what name you call them—who will stand opposed to the restoration of the Union of these States, I am free to say to you that I am still in the field."

During the "great applause" which followed, a nameless voice shouted, "Give us the names at the other end. . . . Who are they?"

"You ask me who they are," Johnson retorted. "I say Thaddeus Stevens of Pennsylvania is one; I say Mr. Sumner is another; and Wendell Phillips is another." Applause urged him to continue. "Are those who want to destroy our institutions . . . not satisfied with the blood that has been shed? . . . Does not the blood of Lincoln appease the vengeance and wrath of the opponents of this government?"

The President's remarks were as untrue as they were impolitic. Not only was it manifestly false to assert that the leading Republican in the House and the most conspicuous Republican in the Senate were opposed to "the fundamental principles of this government" or that they had been responsible for Lincoln's assassination; it was incredible political folly to impute such actions to men with whom the President had to work daily. But Andrew Johnson never learned that the President of the United States must function as a party leader.

There was a temperamental coldness about this plain-featured, grave man that kept him from easy, intimate relations with even his political supporters. His massive head, dark, luxuriant hair, deep-set and piercing eyes, and cleft square chin seemed to Charles Dickens to indicate "courage, watchfulness, and certainly strength of purpose," but his was a grim face, with "no genial sunlight in it." The coldness and reserve that marked Johnson's public associations doubtless stemmed from a deep-seated feeling of insecurity; this self-educated tailor whose wife had taught him how to write could never expose himself by letting down his guard and relaxing.

A Harper's Weekly cartoon depicts Johnson (left) and Thaddeus Stevens (right) as engineers committed to a collision course.

Johnson knew none of the arts of managing men, and he seemed unaware that face-saving is important for a politician. When he became President, Johnson was besieged by advisers of all political complexions. To each he listened gravely and non-committally, raising no questions and by his silence seeming to give consent. With Radical Senator Sumner, already intent upon giving the freedmen both homesteads and the ballot, he had repeated interviews during the first month of his presidency. "His manner has been excellent, & even sympathetic," Sumner reported triumphantly. With Chief Justice Salmon P. Chase, Sumner urged Johnson to support immediate Negro suffrage and found the President was "welldisposed, & sees the rights & necessities of the case." In the middle of May, 1865, Sumner reassured a Republican caucus that the President was a true Radical; he had listened repeatedly to the Senator and had told him "there is no difference between us." Before the end of the month the rug was pulled from under Sumner's feet. Johnson issued his proclamation for the reconstruction of North Carolina, making no provisions for Negro suffrage. Sumner first learned about it through the newspapers.

While he was making up his mind, Johnson appeared silently receptive to all ideas; when he had made a decision, his mind was immovably closed, and he defended his course with all the obstinacy of a weak man. In December, alarmed by Johnson's Reconstruction proclamations, Sumner again sought an interview with the President. "No longer sympathetic, or even kindly," Sumner found, "he was harsh, petulant, and unreasonable." The Senator was depressed by Johnson's "prejudice, ignorance, and perversity" on the Negro suffrage issue. Far from listening amiably to Sumner's argument that the South was still torn by violence and not yet ready for readmission, Johnson attacked him with cheap analogies. "Are there no murders in Massachusetts?" the President asked.

"Unhappily yes," Sumner replied, "sometimes."

"Are there no assaults in Boston? Do not men there sometimes knock each other down, so that the police is obliged to interfere?"

"Unhappily yes."

"Would you consent that Massachusetts, on this account, should be excluded from Congress?" Johnson triumphantly queried. In the excitement the President unconsciously used Sumner's hat, which the Senator had placed on the floor beside his chair, as a spittoon!

Had Johnson been as resolute in action as he was in argument, he might conceivably have carried much of his party with him on his Reconstruction program. Promptness, publicity, and persuasion could have created a presidential following. Instead Johnson boggled. Though he talked boastfully of "kicking out" officers who failed to support his plan, he was slow to act. His own Cabinet, from the very beginning, contained members who disagreed with him, and his secretary of war, Edwin M. Stanton, was openly in league with the Republican elements most hostile to the President. For more than two years he impotently hoped that Stanton would resign; then in 1867, after Congress had passed the Tenure of Office Act, he tried to oust the Secretary. This belated firmness, against the letter of the law, led directly to Johnson's impeachment trial.

Instead of working with his party leaders and building up political support among Republicans, Johnson in 1866 undertook to organize his friends into a new party. In August a convention of white southerners, northern Democrats, moderate Republicans, and presidential appointees assembled in Philadelphia to endorse Johnson's policy. Union General Darius Couch of Massachusetts marched arm in arm down the convention aisle with Governor James L. Orr of South Carolina, to symbolize the states reunited under Johnson's rule. The convention produced fervid oratory, a dignified statement of principles—but not much else. Like most third-party reformist movements it lacked local support and grass-roots organization.

Johnson himself was unable to breathe life into his stillborn third party. Deciding to take his case to the people, he accepted an invitation to speak at a great Chicago memorial honoring Stephen A. Douglas. When his special train left Washington on August 28 for a "swing around the circle," the President was accompanied by a few Cabinet members who shared his views and by the war heroes Grant and Farragut.

At first all went well. There were some calculated political snubs to the President, but he managed at Philadelphia, New York, and Albany to present his ideas soberly and cogently to the people. But Johnson's friends were worried lest his tongue again get out of control. "In all frankness," a senator wrote him, do not "allow the excitement of the moment to draw from you any *extemporaneous speeches.*"

At St. Louis, when a Radical voice shouted that Johnson was a "Judas," the President flamed up in rage. "There was a Judas and he was one of the twelve apostles," he retorted. ". . . The twelve apostles had a Christ. . . . If I have played the Judas, who has been my Christ that I have played the Judas with? Was it Thad Stevens? Was it Wendell Phillips? Was it Charles Sumner?" Over mingled hisses and applause, he shouted, "These are the men that stop and compare themselves with the Saviour; and everybody that differs with them . . . is to be denounced as a Judas."

Johnson had played into his enemies' hands. His Radical foes denounced him as a "trickster," a "culprit," a man "touched with insanity, corrupted with lust, stimulated with drink." More serious in consequence was the reaction of northern moderates, such as James Russell Lowell, who wrote, "What an anti-Johnson lecturer we have in Johnson! Sumner has been right about the *cuss* from the first. . . ." The fall elections were an overwhelming repudiation of the President and his Reconstruction policy.

Johnson's want of political sagacity strengthened the very elements in the Republican party which he most feared. In 1865 the Republicans had no clearly defined attitude toward Reconstruction. Moderates like Gideon Welles and Orville Browning wanted to see the southern states restored with a minimum of restrictions; Radicals like Sumner and Stevens demanded that the entire southern social system be revolutionized. Some Republicans were passionately concerned with the plight of the freedmen; others were more interested in maintaining the high tariff and land grant legislation enacted during the war. Many thought mostly of keeping themselves in office, and many genuinely believed, with Sumner, that "the Republican party, in its objects, is identical with country and with mankind." These diverse elements came slowly to adopt the idea of harsh Reconstruction, but Johnson's stubborn persistency in his policy left them no alternative. Every step the President took seemed to provide "a new encouragement to (1) the rebels at the South, (2) the Democrats at the North and (3) the discontented elements everywhere." Not many Republicans would agree with Sumner that Johnson's program was "a defiance to God and Truth," but there was genuine concern that the victory won by the war was being frittered away.

The provisional governments established by the President in the South seemed to be dubiously loyal. They were reluctant to rescind their secession ordinances and to repudiate the Confederate debt, and they chose high-ranking ex-Confederates to represent them in Congress. Northerners were even more alarmed when these southern governments began to legislate upon the Negro's civil rights. Some laws were necessary—in order to give former slaves the right to marry, to hold property, to sue and be sued, and the like—but the Johnson legislatures went far beyond these immediate needs. South Carolina, for example, enacted that no Negro could pursue the trade "of an artisan, mechanic, or shopkeeper, or any other trade or employment besides that of husbandry" without a special license. Alabama provided that "any stubborn or refractory servants" or "servants who loiter away their time" should be fined $50 and, if they could not pay, be hired out for six months' labor. Mississippi ordered that every Negro under eighteen years of age who was an orphan or not supported by his parents must be apprenticed to some white person, preferably the former owner of the slave. Such southern laws indicated a determination to keep the Negro in a state of peonage.

It was impossible to expect a newly emancipated race to be content with such a limping freedom. The thousands of Negroes who had served in the Union armies and had helped conquer their former Confederate masters were not willing to abandon their new-found liberty. In rural areas southern whites kept these Negroes under control through the Ku Klux Klan. But in southern cities white hegemony was less secure, and racial friction erupted in mob violence. In May, 1866, a quarrel between a Memphis Negro and a white teamster led to a riot in which the city police and the poor whites raided the Negro quarters and burned and killed promiscuously. Far more serious was the disturbance in New Orleans two months later. The Republican party in Louisiana was split into pro-Johnson conservatives and Negro suffrage advocates. The latter group determined to hold a constitutional convention, of dubious legality, in New Orleans, in order to secure the ballot for the freedmen and the offices for themselves. Through imbecility in the War Department, the Federal troops occupying the city were left without orders, and the mayor of New Orleans, strongly opposed to Negro equality, had the responsibility for preserving order. There were acts of provocation on both sides, and finally, on July 30, a procession of Negroes marching toward the convention hall was attacked.

"A shot was fired . . . by a policeman, or some colored man in the procession," General Philip Sheridan reported. "This led to other shots, and a rush after the procession. On arrival at the front of the Institute [where the convention met], there was some throwing of brick-bats by both sides. The police . . . were vigorously marched to the scene of disorder. The procession entered the Institute with the flag, about six or eight remaining outside. A row occurred between a policeman and one of these colored men, and a shot was again fired by one of the parties, which led to an indiscriminate firing on the building, through the windows, by the policemen.

"This had been going on for a short time, when a white flag was displayed from the windows of the Institute, whereupon the firing ceased and the police rushed into the building. . . . The policemen opened an indiscriminate fire upon the audience until they had emptied their revolvers, when they retired, and those inside barricaded the doors. The door was broken in, and the firing again commenced when many of the colored and white people either escaped out of the door, or were passed out by the policemen inside, but as they came out, the policemen who formed the circle nearest the building fired upon them, and they were again fired upon by the citizens that formed the outer circle."

Thirty-seven Negroes and three of their white friends were killed; 119 Negroes and seventeen of their white sympathizers were wounded. Of their assailants, ten were wounded and but one killed. President Johnson was, of course, horrified by these outbreaks, but the Memphis and New Orleans riots, together with the Black Codes, afforded a devastating illustration of how the President's policy actually operated. The southern states, it was clear, were not going to protect the Negroes' basic rights. They were only grudgingly going to accept the results of the war. Yet, with Johnson's blessing, these same states were expecting a stronger voice in Congress than ever. Before 1860, southern representation in Congress had been based upon the white population plus three fifths of the slaves; now the Negroes, though not permitted to vote, were to be counted like all other citizens, and southern states would be entitled to at least nine additional congressmen. Joining with the northern Copperheads, the southerners could easily regain at the next presidential election all that had been lost on the Civil War battlefield.

It was this political exigency, not misguided sentimentality nor vindictiveness, which united Republicans in opposition to the President.

Johnson's defenders have pictured Radical Reconstruction as the work of a fanatical minority, led by Sumner and Stevens, who drove their reluctant colleagues into adopting coercive measures against the South. In fact, every major piece of Radical legislation was adopted by the nearly unanimous vote of the entire Republican membership of Congress. Andrew Johnson had left them no other choice. Because he insisted upon rushing Confederate-dominated states back into the Union, Republicans moved to disqualify Confederate leaders under the Fourteenth Amendment. When, through Johnson's urging, the southern states rejected that amendment, the Republicans in Congress unwillingly came to see Negro suffrage as the only counterweight against Democratic majorities in the South. With the Reconstruction Acts of 1867 the way was open for a true Radical program toward the South, harsh and thorough.

Andrew Johnson became a cipher in the White House, futilely disapproving bills which were promptly passed over his veto. Through his failure to reckon with public opinion, his unwillingness to recognize his weak position, his inability to function as a party leader, he had sacrificed all influence with the party which had elected him and had turned over its control to Radicals vindictively opposed to his policies. In March, 1868, Andrew Johnson was summoned before the Senate of the United States to be tried on eleven accusations of high crimes and misdemeanors. By a narrow margin the Senate failed to convict him, and historians have dismissed the charges as flimsy and false. Yet perhaps before the bar of history itself Andrew Johnson must be impeached with an even graver charge—that through political ineptitude he threw away a magnificent opportunity.

■　■　■　■　■　■　■

Ride-In: A Century of Protest Begins

Alan F. Westin

The last quarter of the nineteenth century—after the federal government relaxed its pressure on the southern states to deal fairly with their black citizens—has been called "the nadir" of the history of black Americans after emancipation. Some historians argue that the low point came somewhat later, during the early twentieth century, but few would disagree with the thesis that the period in question was indeed disastrous for American blacks. Although never really treated decently (in the North as well as in the South), they had made important gains during Reconstruction; the Fourteenth and Fifteenth amendments "guaranteed" their political and civil rights, and Congress passed stiff laws protecting these rights, including the Civil Rights Act of 1875, which outlawed discrimination in places of public accommodation.

After the so-called Compromise of 1877, however, these gains were gradually stripped away by a combination of southern pressure, northern indifference, and a series of crippling legal interpretations by the Supreme Court. In this essay Professor Alan F. Westin of Columbia University, an expert on constitutional history, describes one of the first and most significant of the Supreme Court decisions of the era, one that emasculated the Civil Rights Act of 1875. His story reads in some ways like an account of the civil rights struggles of the 1950s and 1960s, but with the terrible difference that freedom and justice were in this instance the losers, not the winners, of the fight.

■　■　■　■　■　■　■

It began one day early in January when a Negro named Robert Fox stepped aboard a streetcar in Louisville, Kentucky, dropped his coin into the fare box, and sat down in the white section of the car. Ordered to move, he refused, and the driver threw him off the car. Shortly after, Fox filed a charge of assault and battery against the streetcar company in the federal district court, claiming that separate seating policies were illegal and the driver's actions were therefore improper. The district judge instructed the jury that under federal law common carriers must serve all passengers equally without regard to race. So instructed, the jury found the company rules to be invalid and awarded damages of fifteen dollars (plus $72.80 in legal costs) to Mr. Fox.

Immediately there was sharp criticism of the Fox decision from the city and state administrations, both Democratic; the company defied the court's ruling and continued segregated seating. After several meetings with local federal officials and white attorneys co-operating with them, Louisville Negro leaders decided to launch a full-scale "ride-in." At 7 P.M. on May 12, a young Negro boy boarded a streetcar near the Willard Hotel, walked past the driver, and took a seat among the white passengers. The driver, under new company regulations, did not attempt to throw him off but simply stopped the car, lit a cigar, and refused to proceed until the Negro moved to "his place." While the governor, the Louisville chief of police, and other prominent citizens looked on from the sidewalks, a large crowd which included an increasingly noisy mob of jeering white teen-agers gathered around the streetcar.

Before long, there were shouts of "Put him out!" "Hit him!" "Kick him!" "Hang him!" Several white youths climbed into the car and began yelling insults in the face of the young Negro rider. He refused to answer—or to move. The youths dragged him from his seat, pulled him off the car, and began to beat him. Only when the Negro started to defend himself did the city police intervene: they arrested him for disturbing the peace and took him to jail.

This time the trial was held in Louisville city court, not the federal court. The magistrate ruled that streetcar companies were not under any obligation to treat Negroes exactly as they treated whites, and that any federal measures purporting to create such obligations would be "clearly invalid" under the constitutions of Kentucky and the United States. The defendant was fined, and the judge delivered a warning to Louisville Negroes that further ride-ins would be punished.

But the ride-in campaign was not halted that easily. In the following days, streetcar after streetcar was entered by Negroes who took seats in the white section. Now the drivers got off the cars entirely. On several occasions, the Negro riders drove the cars themselves, to the sound of cheers from Negro spectators. Then violence erupted. Bands of white youths and men began to throw Negro riders off the cars: windows were broken, cars were overturned, and for a time a general race riot threatened. Moderate Kentucky newspapers and many community leaders deplored the fighting; the Republican candidate for governor denounced the streetcar company's segregation policies and blamed the violence on Democratic encouragement of white extremists.

By this time, newspapers across the country were carrying reports of the conflict, and many editorials denounced the seating regulations. In Louisville, federal marshals and the United States attorney backed the rights of the Negro riders and stated that federal court action would be taken if necessary. There were even rumors that the President might send troops.

Under these threats, the streetcar company capitulated. Soon, all the city transit companies declared that "it was useless to try to resist or evade the enforcement by the United States authorities of the claim of Negroes to ride in the cars." To "avoid serious collisions," the company would thereafter allow all passengers to sit where they chose. Although a few disturbances took place in the following months, and some white intransigents boycotted the streetcars, mixed seating became a common practice. The Kentucky press soon pointed with pride to the spirit of conciliation and harmony which prevailed in travel facilities within the city, calling it a model for good race relations. Never again would Louisville streetcars be segregated.

The event may have a familiar ring, but it should not, for it occurred almost one hundred years ago, in 1871. The streetcars were horse-drawn. The President who considered ordering troops to Louisville was ex-General Grant, not ex-General Eisenhower. The Republican gubernatorial candidate who supported the Negro riders, John Marshall Harlan, was not a post–World War II leader of the G.O.P. but a former slaveholder from one of Kentucky's oldest and most famous political families. And the "new" Negroes who waged this ride-in were not members of the Congress of Racial Equality and the National Association for the Advancement of Colored People, or followers of Dr. Martin Luther King, but former slaves who were fighting for civil rights in their own time, and with widespread success.

And yet these dramatic sit-ins, ride-ins, and walk-ins of the 1870's are almost unknown to the American public today. The standard American histories do not mention them, providing only thumbnail references to "bayonet-enforced" racial contacts during Reconstruction. Most commentators view the Negro's resort to direct action as an invention of the last decade. Clearly, then, it is time that the civil-rights struggle of the 1870's and 1880's was rescued from newspaper files and court archives, not only because it is historically important but also because it has compelling relevance for our own era.

Contrary to common assumptions today, no state in the Union during the 1870's, including those south of the Mason-Dixon line, required separation of whites and Negroes in places of public accommodation. Admission and arrangement policies were up to individual owners. In the North and West, many theatres, hotels, restaurants, and public carriers served Negro patrons without hesitation or discrimination. Some accepted Negroes only in second-class accommodations, such as smoking cars on railroads or balconies in theatres, where they sat among whites who did not have first-class tickets. Other northern and western establishments, especially the more exclusive ones, refused Negro patronage entirely.

The situation was similar in the large cities of the southern and border states. Many establishments admitted Negroes to second-class facilities. Some gave first-class service to those of privileged social status—government officials, army officers, newspapermen, and clergymen. On the other hand, many places of public accommodation, particularly in the rural areas and smaller cities of the South, were closed to Negroes whatever their wealth or status.

From 1865 through the early 1880's, the general trend in the nation was toward wider acceptance of Negro patronage. The federal Civil Rights Act of 1866, with its guarantee to Negroes of "equal benefit of the laws," had set off a flurry of enforcement suits—for denying berths to Negroes on a Washington-New York train; for refusing to sell theatre tickets to Negroes in Boston; and for barring Negro women from the waiting rooms and parlor cars of railroads in Virginia, Illinois, and California. Ratification of the Fourteenth Amendment in 1868 had spurred more challenges. Three northern states, and two southern states under Reconstruction regimes, passed laws making it a crime for owners of public-accommodation businesses to discriminate. Most state and federal court rulings on these laws between 1865 and 1880 held in favor of Negro rights, and the rulings built up a steady pressure on owners to relax racial bars.

Nevertheless, instances of exclusion and segregation continued throughout the 1870's. To settle the issue once and for all (thereby reaping the lasting appreciation of the Negro voters), congressional Republicans led by Senator Charles Sumner pressed for a federal statute making discrimination in public accommodations a crime. Democrats and conservative Republicans warned in the congressional debates that such a law would trespass on the reserved powers of the states and reminded the Sumner supporters that recent Supreme Court decisions had taken a narrow view of federal power under the Civil War amendments.

Cartoonist Thomas Nast mocked the provision of the Civil Rights Act of 1875 that allowed African Americans to collect $500 from those who barred them from places of public accommodation.

After a series of legislative compromises, however, Sumner's forces were able to enact the statute; on March 1, 1875, "An Act to Protect all Citizens in their Civil and Legal Rights" went into effect. "It is essential to just government," the preamble stated, that the nation "recognize the equality of all men before the law, and . . . it is the duty of government in its dealings with the people to mete out equal and exact justice to all, of whatever nativity, race, color, or persuasion, religious or political. . ."

Section 1 of the act declared that "All persons within the jurisdiction of the United States shall be entitled to the full and equal enjoyment of the accommodations . . . of inns, public conveyances on land or water, theaters and other places of public amusement; subject only to the conditions and limitations established by law, and applicable alike to citizens of every race or color. . . ." Section 2 provided that any person violating the act could be sued in federal district court for a penalty of $500, could be fined $500 to $1,000, or could be imprisoned from thirty days to one year. (A separate section forbade racial discrimination in the selection of juries.)

Reaction to the law was swift. Two Negro men were admitted to the dress circle of Macauley's Theatre in Louisville and sat through the performance without incident. In Washington, Negroes were served for the first time at the bar of the Willard Hotel, and a Negro broke the color line when he was seated at McVicker's Theatre in Chicago. But in other instances, Negroes were rejected despite "Sumner's law." Several hotels in Chattanooga turned in their licenses, became private boardinghouses, and accepted whites only. Restaurants and barber shops in Richmond turned away Negro customers.

Suits challenging refusals were filed en masse throughout the country. Perhaps a hundred were decided in the federal district courts during the late 1870's and early 1880's. Federal judges in Pennsylvania, Texas, Maryland, and Kentucky, among others, held the law to be constitutional and ruled in favor of Negro complainants. In North Carolina, New Jersey, and California, however, district judges held the law invalid. And when other courts in New York, Tennessee, Missouri, and Kansas put the issue to the federal circuit judges, the judges divided on the question, and the matter was certified to the United States Supreme Court.

But the Supreme Court did not exactly rush to make its ruling. Though two cases testing the 1875 act reached it in 1876 and a third in 1877, the Justices simply held them on their docket. In 1879, the Attorney General filed a brief defending the constitutionality of the law, but still the Court reached no decisions. In 1880, three additional cases were filed, but two years elapsed before the Solicitor General presented a fresh brief supporting the statute. It was not until late in 1883 that the Supreme Court passed upon the 1875 act, in what became famous as the *Civil Rights Cases* ruling. True, the Court was badly behind in its work in this period, but clearly the Justices chose to let the civil-rights cases "ripen" for almost eight years.

When they finally came to grips with the issue, six separate test suits were involved. The most celebrated had arisen in New York City in November of 1879. Edwin Booth, the famous tragedian and brother of John Wilkes Booth, had opened a special Thanksgiving week engagement at the Grand Opera House. After playing *Hamlet, Othello,* and *Richelieu* to packed houses, he was scheduled to perform Victor Hugo's *Ruy Blas* at the Saturday matinee on November 22.

One person who had decided to see Booth that Saturday was William R. Davis, Jr., who was later described in the press as a tall, handsome, and well-spoken Negro of twenty-six. He was the business agent of the *Progressive-American,* a Negro weekly published in New York City. At 10 o'clock Saturday morning, Davis' girl friend ("a bright octoroon, almost white," as the press put it), purchased two reserved seats at the box office of the Grand Opera House. At 1:30 P.M., Davis and his lady presented themselves at the theatre, only to be told by the doorkeeper, Samuel Singleton, that "these tickets are no good." If he would step out to the box office, Singleton told Davis, his money would be refunded.

It is unlikely that Davis was surprised by Singleton's action, for this was not the first time he had encountered such difficulties. Shortly after the passage of the 1875 act, Davis had been refused a ticket to the dress circle of Booth's Theatre in New York. He had sworn out a warrant against the ticket seller, but the failure of his witnesses to appear at the grand jury proceedings had led to a dismissal of the complaint. This earlier episode, as well as Davis' activity as a Negro journalist, made it probable that this appearance at the Opera House in 1879 was a deliberate test of the management's discriminatory policies.

Though Davis walked out of the lobby at Singleton's request, he did not turn in his tickets for a refund. Instead, he summoned a young white boy standing near the theatre, gave him a dollar (plus a dime for his trouble), and had him purchase two more tickets. When Davis and his companion presented these to Singleton, only the lady was allowed to pass. Again Davis was told that his ticket was "no good." When he now refused to move out of the doorway, Singleton called a policeman and asked that Davis be escorted off the theatre property. The officer told Davis that the Messrs. Poole and Donnelly, the managers of the Opera House, did not admit colored persons. "Perhaps the managers do not," Davis retorted, "but the laws of the country [do]."

The following Monday, November 24, Davis filed a criminal complaint; on December 9, this time with witnesses in abundance, Singleton was indicted in what the press described as the first criminal proceeding under the 1875 act to go to trial in New York. When the case opened on January 14, 1880, Singleton's counsel argued that the 1875 law was unconstitutional. "It interferes," he said, "with the right of the State of New York to provide the means under which citizens of the State have the power to control and protect their rights in respect to their private property." The assistant United States attorney replied that such a conception of states' rights had been "exploded and superseded long ago." It was unthinkable, he declared, that "the United States could not extend to one citizen of New York a right which the State itself gave to others of its citizens—the right of admission to places of public amusement."

The presiding judge decided to take the constitutional challenge under advisement and referred it to the circuit court, for consideration at its February term. This left the decision up to Justice Samuel Blatchford of the Supreme Court, who was assigned to the circuit court for New York, and District Judge William Choate. The two judges reached opposite conclusions and certified the question to the United States Supreme Court.

Davis' case, under the title of *United States* v. *Singleton*, reached the Supreme Court in 1880. Already lodged on the Court's docket were four similar criminal prosecutions under the act of 1875. *U.S.* v. *Stanley* involved the refusal of Murray Stanley in 1875 to serve a meal at his hotel in Topeka, Kansas, to a Negro, Bird Gee. *U.S.* v. *Nichols* presented the refusal in 1876 of Samuel Nichols, owner of the Nichols House in Jefferson City, Missouri, to accept a Negro named W. H. R. Agee as a guest. *U.S.* v. *Ryan* involved the conduct of Michael Ryan, door-keeper of Maguire's Theatre in San Francisco, in denying a Negro named George M. Tyler entry to the dress circle on January 4, 1876. In *U.S.* v. *Hamilton,* James Hamilton, a conductor on the Nashville, Chattanooga, and St. Louis Railroad, had on April 21, 1879, denied a Negro woman with a first-class ticket access to the ladies' car.

There was a fifth case, with a somewhat different setting. On the evening of May 22, 1879, Mrs. Sallie J. Robinson, a twenty-eight-year-old Negro, purchased two first-class tickets at Grand Junction, Tennessee, for a trip to Lynchburg, Virginia, on the Memphis and Charleston Railroad. Shortly after midnight she and her nephew, Joseph C. Robinson, described as a young Negro "of light complexion, light hair, and light blue eyes," boarded the train and started into the parlor car. The conductor, C. W. Reagin, held Mrs. Robinson back ("bruising her arm and jerking her roughly around," she alleged) and pushed her into the smoker.

A few minutes later, when Joseph informed the conductor that he was Mrs. Robinson's nephew and was a Negro, the conductor looked surprised. In that case, he said, they could go into the parlor car at the next stop. The Robinsons finished the ride in the parlor car but filed complaints with the railroad about their treatment and then sued for $500 under the 1875 act. At the trial, Reagin testified that he had thought Joseph to be a white man with a colored woman, and his experience was that such associations were "for illicit purposes."

Counsel for the Robinsons objected to Reagin's testimony, on the ground that his actions were based on race and constituted no defense. Admitting the constitutionality of the 1875 law for purposes of the trial, the railroad contended that the action of its conductor did not fall within the statute. The district judge ruled that the motive for excluding persons was the decisive issue under the act: if the jury believed that the conductor had acted because he thought Mrs. Robinson "a prostitute travelling with her paramour," whether "well or ill-founded" in that assumption, the exclusion was not because of race and the railroad was not liable. The jury found for the railroad, and the Robinsons appealed.

These, with William Davis' suit against the doorkeeper of New York's Grand Opera House, were the six cases to which the Supreme Court finally turned in 1882. The Justices were presented with a learned and eloquent brief for the United States submitted by Solicitor General Samuel F. Phillips, who reviewed the leading cases, described the history of the Civil War amendments to the Constitution, and stressed the importance to the rights of citizens of equal access to public accommodation. Four times since 1865, Phillips noted, civil-rights legislation had been enacted by a Congress filled with men who had fought in the Civil War and had written the war amendments. These men understood that "every rootlet of slavery has an individual vitality, and, to its minutest hair, should be anxiously followed and plucked up. . . ." They also knew that if the federal government allowed Negroes to be denied accommodation "by persons who notably were sensitive registers of local public opinion," then "what upon yesterday was only 'fact' will become 'doctrine' tomorrow."

The Supreme Court Justices who considered Phillips' brief and the six test cases were uncommonly talented, among them being Chief Justice Morrison R. Waite, a man underrated today; Joseph P. Bradley, that Court's most powerful intellect; and Stephen J. Field, a *laissez-faire* interpreter of American constitutional law. John Marshall Harlan, the youngest man on the Court, had already started on the course which was to mark him as the most frequent and passionate dissenter in the Gilded Age.

As a whole, the Court might have appeared to be one which would have looked favorably on the 1875 act. All were Republicans except Justice Field, and he was a Democrat appointed by Abraham Lincoln. All except Justice Harlan, who was the Court's only southerner, had made their careers primarily in the northern and western states. Without exception, all had supported the northern cause in the war, and none had any hostility toward Negroes as a class.

Yet on the afternoon of October 15, 1883, Justice Bradley announced that the Court found Sections 1 and 2 of the Civil Rights Act of 1875 to be unconstitutional. (This disposed of five of the cases; the sixth, *U.S.* v. *Hamilton,* was denied review on a procedural point.) There was added irony in the fact that Bradley delivered the majority opinion for eight of the Justices. A one-time Whig, Bradley had struggled for a North-South compromise in the darkening months of 1860–61, then had swung to a strong Unionist position after the firing on Fort Sumter. He had run for Congress on the Lincoln ticket in 1862 and in 1868 headed the New Jersey electors for Grant. When the Thirteenth and Fourteenth Amendments were adopted, he had given them firm support, and his appointment to the Supreme Court by Grant in 1870 had drawn no criticism from friends of the Negro, as had the appointment of John Marshall Harlan seven years later.

Bradley's opinion had a tightly reasoned simplicity. The Thirteenth Amendment forbade slavery and involuntary servitude, he noted, but protection against the restoration of bondage could not be stretched to cover federal regulation of "social" discriminations such as those dealt with in the 1875 statute. As for the Fourteenth Amendment, that was addressed only to deprivations of rights by the *states;* it did not encompass *private* acts of discrimination. Thus there was no source of constitutional authority for "Sumner's law"; it had to be regarded as an unwarranted invasion of an area under state jurisdiction. Even as a matter of policy, Bradley argued, the intention of the war amendments to aid the newly freed Negro had to have some limits. At some point, the Negro must cease to be "the special favorite of the law" and take on "the rank of a mere citizen."

At the Atlanta Opera House on the evening of the Court's decision, the end man of Haverly's Minstrels interrupted the performance to announce the ruling. The entire orchestra and dress circle audience rose and cheered. Negroes sitting in the balcony kept their seats, "stunned," according to one newspaper account. A short time earlier, a Negro denied entrance to the dress circle had filed charges against the Opera House management under the 1875 act. Now his case—their case—was dead.

Of all the nine Justices, only John Marshall Harlan, a Kentuckian and a former slaveholder, announced that he dissented from the ruling. He promised to give a full opinion soon.

Justice Harlan's progress from a supporter of slavery to a civil-rights dissenter makes a fascinating chronicle. Like Bradley, he had entered politics as a Whig and had tried to find a middle road between secessionist Democrats and antislavery Republicans. Like Bradley, he became a Unionist after the firing on Fort Sumter. But there the parallels ended. Although Harlan entered the Union Army, he was totally opposed to freeing the slaves, and his distaste for Lincoln and the Radicals was complete. Between 1863 and 1868, he led the Conservative party in Kentucky, a third-party movement which supported the war but opposed pro-Negro and civil-rights measures as "flagrant invasions of property rights and local government."

By 1868, however, Harlan had become a Republican. The resounding defeat of the Conservatives in the 1867 state elections convinced him that a third party had no future in Kentucky. His antimonopoly views and his general ideas about economic progress conflicted directly with state Democratic policies, and when the Republicans nominated his former field commander, Ulysses S. Grant, for President, in 1868, Harlan was one of the substantial number of Conservatives who joined the G.O.P.

His views on Negro rights also changed at this time. The wave of vigilante activities against white Republicans and Negroes that swept Kentucky in 1868–70, with whippings and murders by the scores, convinced Harlan that federal guarantees were essential. He watched Negroes in Kentucky moving with dignity and skill toward useful citizenship, and his devout Presbyterianism led him to adopt a "brotherhood-of-man" outlook in keeping with his church's national position. Perhaps he may have been influenced by his wife, Mallie, whose parents were New England abolitionists. As a realistic Republican politician, he was also aware that 60,000 Kentucky Negroes would become voters in 1870.

Thus a "new" John Harlan took the stump as Republican gubernatorial candidate in 1871, the year of the Louisville streetcar ride-ins. He opened his rallies by confessing that he had formerly been anti-Negro. But "I have lived long enough," he said, "to feel that the most perfect despotism that ever existed on this earth was the institution of African slavery." The war amendments were necessary "to place it beyond the power of any State to interfere with . . . the results of the war. . . ." The South should stop agitating the race issue, and should turn to rebuilding itself on progressive lines. When the Democrats laughed at "Harlan the Chameleon" and read quotations from his earlier anti-Negro speeches, Harlan replied: "Let it be said that I am right rather than consistent."

Harlan soon became an influential figure in the Republican party and, when President Rutherford B. Hayes decided to appoint a southern Republican to the Supreme Court in 1877, he was a logical choice. Even then, the Negro issue rose to shake Harlan's life again. His confirmation was held up because of doubts by some senators as to his "real" civil-rights views. Only after Harlan produced his speeches between 1871 and 1877 and party leaders supported his firmness on the question was he approved.

Once on the Supreme Court, Harlan could have swung back to a conservative position on civil rights. Instead, he became one of his generation's most intense and uncompromising defenders of the Negro. Perhaps his was the psychology of the convert who defends his new faith more passionately, even more combatively, than the born believer. Harlan liked to think that he had changed because he knew the South and realized that any relaxation of federal protection of the rights of Negroes would encourage the "white irreconcilables" first to acts of discrimination and then to violence, which would destroy all hope of accommodation between the races.

When Harlan sat down in October of 1883 to write his dissent in the *Civil Rights Cases,* he hoped to set off a cannon of protest. But he simply could not get his thoughts on paper. He worked late into the night, and even rose from half-sleep to write down ideas that he was afraid would elude him in the morning. "It was a trying time for him," his wife observed. "In point of years, he was much the youngest man on the Bench; and standing alone, as he did in regard to a decision which the whole nation was anxiously awaiting, he felt that . . . he must speak not only forcibly but wisely." After weeks of drafting and discarding, Harlan seemed to reach a dead end. The dissent would not "write." It was at this point that Mrs. Harlan contributed a dramatic touch to the history of the *Civil Rights Cases.*

When the Harlans had moved to Washington in 1877, the Justice had acquired from a collector the inkstand which Chief Justice Roger Taney had used in writing all his opinions. Harlan was fond of showing this to guests and remarking that "it was the very inkstand from which the infamous *Dred Scott* opinion was written." Early in the 1880's, however, a niece of Taney's, who was engaged in collecting her uncle's effects, visited the Harlans. When she saw the inkstand she asked Harlan for it, and the Justice agreed. The next morning Mrs. Harlan, noting her husband's re-luctance to part with his most prized possession, quietly arranged to have the ink-stand "lost." She hid it away, and Harlan was forced to make an embarrassed excuse to Taney's niece.

Now, on a Sunday morning, probably early in November of 1883, after Harlan had spent a sleepless night working on his dissent, Mallie Harlan remembered the inkstand. While the Justice was at church, she retrieved it from its hiding place, filled it with a fresh supply of ink and pen points, and placed it on the blotter of his desk. When her husband returned from church, she told him, with an air of mys-tery, that he would find something special in his study. Harlan was overjoyed to re-cover his symbolic antique. Mrs. Harlan's gesture was successful, for as she relates:

> The memory of the historic part that Taney's inkstand had played in the Dred Scott decision, in temporarily tightening the shackles of slavery upon the negro race in those ante-bellum days, seemed, that morning, to act like magic in clarify-ing my husband's thoughts in regard to the law . . . intended by Sumner to protect the recently emancipated slaves in the enjoyment of equal "civil rights." His pen fairly flew on that day and, with the running start he then got, he soon finished his dissent.

How directly the recollection of Dred Scott pervaded Harlan's dissent is appar-ent to anyone who reads the opinion. He began by noting that the pre–Civil War Supreme Court had upheld congressional laws forbidding individuals to interfere with recovery of fugitive slaves. To strike down the act of 1875 meant that "the rights of freedom and American citizenship cannot receive from the Nation that ef-ficient protection which heretofore was unhesitatingly accorded to slavery and the rights of masters."

Harlan argued that the Civil Rights Act of 1875 was constitutional on any one of several grounds. The Thirteenth Amendment had already been held to guaran-tee "universal civil freedom"; Harlan stated that barring Negroes from facilities li-censed by the state and under legal obligation to serve all persons without discrimi-nation restored a major disability of slavery days and violated that civil freedom. As for the Fourteenth Amendment, its central purpose had been to extend national citizenship to the Negro, reversing the precedent upheld in the Dred Scott deci-sion; its final section gave Congress power to pass appropriate legislation to enforce that affirmative grant as well as to enforce the section barring any state action which might deny liberty or equality. Now, the Supreme Court was deciding what legislation was appropriate and necessary for those purposes, although that deci-sion properly belonged to Congress.

Even under the "State action" clause of the Fourteenth Amendment, Harlan continued, the 1875 act was constitutional; it was well established that "railroad cor-porations, keepers of inns and managers of places of public accommodation are agents or instrumentalities of the State." Finally, Harlan attacked the unwillingness of the Court's majority to uphold the public-carrier section of the act under Con-gress' power to regulate interstate trips. That was exactly what was involved in Mrs.

Robinson's case against the Memphis and Charleston Railroad, he reminded his colleagues; it had not been true before that Congress had had to cite the section of the Constitution on which it relied.

In his peroration, Harlan replied to Bradley's comment that Negroes had been made "a special favorite of the law." The war amendments had been passed not to "favor" the Negro, he declared, but to include him as "part of the people for whose welfare and happiness government is ordained."

> Today, it is the colored race which is denied, by corporations and individuals wielding public authority, rights fundamental in their freedom and citizenship. At some future time, it may be that some other race will fall under the ban of race discrimination. If the constitutional amendments be enforced, according to the intent with which, as I conceive, they were adopted, there cannot be in this republic, any class of human beings in practical subjection to another class. . . .

The *Civil Rights Cases* ruling did two things. First, it destroyed the delicate balance of federal guarantee, Negro protest, and private enlightenment which was producing a steadily widening area of peacefully integrated public facilities in the North and South during the 1870's and early 1880's. Second, it had an immediate and profound effect on national and state politics as they related to the Negro. By denying Congress power to protect the Negro's rights to equal treatment, the Supreme Court wiped the issue of civil rights from the Republican party's agenda of national responsibility. At the same time, those southern political leaders who saw anti-Negro politics as the most promising avenue to power could now rally the "poor whites" to the banner of segregation.

If the Supreme Court had stopped with the *Civil Rights Cases* of 1883, the situation of Negroes would have been bad but not impossible. Even in the South, there was no immediate imposition of segregation in public facilities. During the late 1880's, Negroes could be found sharing places with whites in many southern restaurants, streetcars, and theatres. But increasingly, Democratic and Populist politicians found the Negro an irresistible target. As Solicitor General Phillips had warned the Supreme Court, what had been tolerated as the "fact" of discrimination was now being translated into "doctrine": between 1887 and 1891, eight southern states passed laws requiring railroads to separate all white and Negro passengers. The Supreme Court upheld these laws in the 1896 case of *Plessy* v. *Ferguson*. Then in the Berea College case of 1906, it upheld laws forbidding private schools to educate Negro and white children together. Both decisions aroused Harlan's bitter dissent. In the next fifteen or twenty years, the chalk line of Jim Crow was drawn across virtually every area of public contact in the South.

Today, as this line is slowly and painfully being erased, we may do well to reflect on what might have been in the South if the Civil Rights Act of 1875 had been upheld, in whole or in part. Perhaps everything would have been the same. Perhaps forces at work between 1883 and 1940 were too powerful for a Supreme Court to hold in check. Perhaps "Sumner's law" was greatly premature. Yet it is difficult to believe that total, state-enforced segregation was inevitable in the South after the

1880's. If in these decades the Supreme Court had taken the same *laissez-faire* attitude toward race relations as it took toward economic affairs, voluntary integration would have survived as a countertradition to Jim Crow and might have made the transition of the 1950's less painful than it was. At the very least, one cannot help thinking that Harlan was a better sociologist than his colleagues and a better southerner than the "irreconcilables." American constitutional history has a richer ring to it because of the protest that John Marshall Harlan finally put down on paper from Roger Taney's inkwell in 1883.

■ ■ ■ ■ ■ ■ ■

Reluctant Conquerors: American Army Officers and the Plains Indians

Thomas C. Leonard

The post–Civil War decades saw the tragic completion of the destruction of the cultures of the American Indian that began when Columbus first set foot in the New World. Previously, at least some of the tribes that inhabited what was to become the United States had been able to maintain their cultural integrity more or less intact by falling back before the white juggernaut into the western wilderness. After 1865 further retreat became impossible, and in a few years the free Indians were crushed and the survivors compelled to settle on reservations where their conquerors expected them to become "civilized Americans."

The role of the Army in the destruction of the Indians has frequently been described. What is unique about Thomas C. Leonard's treatment of the subject is its focus on the thoughts and feelings of the soldiers rather than on their deeds—on their appreciation of the Indians, not on their efforts to exterminate them. That professional soldiers should respect a foe so clever, so steadfast, so courageous, so dignified in defeat is not difficult to understand. Yet Leonard does not oversimplify or romanticize the American military reactions to the Indians and their way of life. His essay presents a complex and fascinating picture of a part of American history usually depicted in grossly oversimplified terms. Professor Leonard, who teaches at the University of California at Berkeley, is the author of *Above the Battle: War-Making in America from Appomattox to Versailles*.

▪ ▪ ▪ ▪ ▪ ▪ ▪

The white man's peace at Appomattox in 1865 meant war for the Plains Indians. In the next quarter century six and a half million settlers moved west of the Missouri River, upsetting a precarious balance that had existed between two million earlier pioneers and their hundred thousand "hostile" red neighbors. The industrial energy that had flowed into the Civil War now pushed rail lines across traditional hunting grounds. Some twenty-five thousand soldiers were sent west to meet insistent demands for protection coming from stockmen and miners spread out between the Staked Plains of Texas and the Montana lands watered by the Powder, Bighorn, and Yellowstone rivers.

It is ironic that the men who carried the wounds of the struggle to maintain the union of their own society now were ordered to dismember the culture of the native Americans. These Indian fighters today have been knocked out of that false gallery of heroes created by western novels and movies. On the centennial of the Battle of the Little Bighorn a granite mountain outside of Custer, South Dakota, is being carved into the shape of the Sioux warrior leader Crazy Horse. Times have changed, and a second look at the Army's Indian fighters is in order. They have a complex story to tell, one filled with an ambivalence about their enemy as well as about the civilians who sent them to fight.

The officer corps did not relish their double assignment of pushing Indians back from lands claimed by whites and, for good measure, "redeeming" native Americans from "barbarism"—for Christian civilization. In the letter books and official reports that these men kept so meticulously on the frontier there is a continual lament: civilian officials and opinion makers only cut budgets and issued contradictory directions. The rules of war demanded restraint and a fine regard for the enemy's rights, but it seemed as if the same civilians who interpreted these rules wanted quick work on the battlefield. The United States government itself broke the treaties that promised the Indians land, yet expected the Army to keep the peace through mutual trust.

At the same time that western settlers were clamoring for protection, their land grabs were provoking Indian retaliation. Not incidentally, army officers endured the torture of the annual congressional debate over how much their pay should be cut and seethed as western bankers charged 12 to 40 per cent to convert their government paper into the coin they needed on the frontier. "Friends" of the Indian— with their talk of a "conquest by kindness"—were a special annoyance. Eastern philanthropists like Edward A. Lawrence damned the officers when blood was shed and were among those who chillingly approved the "swift retribution" meted out to General Custer by the Sioux. Frontier forts rarely had the long, timbered stockades beloved by Hollywood set designers—but perhaps many officers longed for a massive wall, high enough to repel civilians as well as Indians.

By 1870 General William T. Sherman doubted he could fight with honor on the plains; from the west and the east, he wrote, "we are placed between two fires." But Sherman may have been envied by another proud Civil War hero, General Philip H. Sheridan, who mused upon a shattered reputation as he watched whole frontier towns—wanting the extermination of Indians—turn out to hang him in effigy.

To officers so provoked, action seemed the thing to sweep away the complications of the Indian problem; to strike at the red man again and again appeared not only the quickest way to dry up civilian complaints but the just way to punish an incomprehensibly wild enemy. Sheridan pleaded with Sherman for authority to act upon the appalling reports that crossed his desk each week:

> Since 1862 at least 800 men, women, and children have been murdered within the limits of my present command, in the most fiendish manner; the men usually scalped and mutilated, their [he omits the word] cut off and placed in their mouth; women ravished sometimes fifty and sixty times in succession, then killed and scalped, sticks stuck in their persons, before and after death.

Sheridan said it was now a question of who was to remain alive in his district, red or white. As for himself: "I have made my choice." It was, in fact, Sheridan who first enunciated the judgment that would become the epitaph of so many native Americans: "The only good Indians I ever saw were dead."

Sheridan's choice, made in passion, proved extraordinarily complicated to carry out, for the fact is that the Indian fighters were troubled by various kinds of respect for their enemy. In the first place, no commander in the West could con-

Starting in 1867, Phillip Henry Sheridan, pictured here, was responsible for Indian campaigns in the West. In 1883, he succeeded William T. Sherman as Army commander in chief.

ceal his admiration for the red man's fighting skill. "Experience of late years," one reported to his colleagues, "has most conclusively shown that our cavalry cannot cope with the Indian man for man." Though these seasoned veterans and heroes reported a very favorable official casualty ratio, in more candid moments they pronounced that Indian fighting was the most difficult combat American soldiers had ever faced.

It followed that so high an estimate of the enemy's ability undermined the Army's pride in its own competence. Sheridan berated the inefficiency that made campaigns in the West "a series of forlorn hopes," and Sherman wrote in so many words to the Secretary of War what had silently haunted his fellow officers: ". . . it seems to be impossible to force Indians to fight at a disadvantage in their own country. Their sagacity and skill surpasses that of the white race." It further followed that victory against such valiant opponents was bittersweet. Both Sheridan and Sherman confessed to pity and compassion for the native Americans they had set out to destroy. As Sheridan wrote:

> We took away their country and their means of support, broke up their mode of living, their habits of life, introduced disease and decay among them and it was for this and against this they made war. Could anyone expect less?

Few officers escaped a sort of wistful appreciation of their primitive enemy in what they took to be his insatiable appetite for war—and not a few admired precisely this unrestrained aggressiveness. Indeed, peaceful assimilation seemed not good enough for the Indians. One of Sheridan's favorite generals sought a large audience to explain the temptations of the Indian culture:

> To me, Indian life, with its attendant ceremonies, mysteries, and forms, is a book of unceasing interest. Grant that some of its pages are frightful, and, if possible, to be avoided, yet the attraction is none the weaker. Study him, fight him, civilize him if you can, he remains still the object of your curiosity, a type of man peculiar and undefined, subjecting himself to no known law of civilization, contending determinedly against all efforts to win him from his chosen mode of life.
>
> If I were an Indian, I often think I would greatly prefer to cast my lot among those of my people who adhered to the free open plains rather than submit to the confined limits of a reservation, there to be the recipient of the blessed benefits of civilization, with its vices thrown in without stint or measure.

Two years after he published this gratuitous advice, General George A. Custer met the object of his interest for the last time at the Little Bighorn.

General Nelson A. Miles, one of the officers who chased the Sioux after Custer's fall, had a personal reason for revenge: an Indian had taken a pointblank shot at him during an awkward moment in a peace parley. But Miles's reflections show the remarkable extent to which men like him overcame their anger with the enemy. The general spoke of the Indian's "courage, skill, sagacity, endurance, fortitude, and self-sacrifice of a high order" and of "the dignity, hospitality, and gentleness of his demeanor toward strangers and toward his fellow savages." Miles was inclined to think that lapses from this standard meant only that Indians had "degenerated through contact with the white man." Writing on this subject, he did not show the personal arrogance and pride that was the despair of his military superiors. Miles viewed Custer's fall in 1876 as a chastising message for the nation's centennial. He quoted Longfellow: ". . . say that our broken faith / wrought all this ruin and scathe, / In the Year of a Hundred Years."

Miles was not an eccentric in the sympathies he expressed. Colonel John Gibbon, for example, the man who discovered the mutilated bodies of the soldiers who had fallen with Custer at the Little Bighorn, seemed, during his subsequent chase of the Sioux, more angry at the "human ghouls" in the Army who had disturbed some Sioux graves than at the warriors who had killed his colleagues. Such desecrations, he thundered, "impress one with the conviction that in war barbarism stands upon a level only a little lower than our boasted civilization." By Gibbon's lights, the record of white hostility and treachery would force any man to fight: "Thus would the savage in us come to the surface under the oppression which we know the Indian suffers." Like so many Indian fighters who addressed the perennial "Indian question," Gibbon raised more questions about his own culture than he answered about his enemy's.

To these soldiers the courage and bearing of the red man suggested a purer way of life before the coming of the white man, and the military frequently searched for Greek and Roman analogies to suggest the virtues of its enemies. Heathens though they were, they had nobility. Even the Indians' faults might be excused by their manifestly lower stage of cultural evolution.

General George Crook was in a good position to speak of the red men's virtues, for as a fighting man he resembled them. In the field he dispensed with the army uniform and seemed only at ease when he was free of all cumbersome marks of civilization. Crook left one post, he tells us, "with one change of underclothes, toothbrush, etc., and went to investigate matters, intending to be gone a week. But I got interested after the Indians and did not return there again for over two years."

In the harsh campaigns in the Southwest, Crook taught his men to move over the land like Apaches, and when white men failed him, he was adept in recruiting Indians for army service. Frederic Remington observed Crook's methods and saw they made officers less "Indian fighters" than "Indian thinkers." "He's more of an Indian than I am," marveled one Apache. Crook repaid such compliments; back at West Point to deliver a graduation address, he may have shocked many with this observation:

> With all his faults, and he has many, the American Indian is not half so black as he has been painted. He is cruel in war, treacherous at times, and not over cleanly. But so were our forefathers. His nature, however, is responsive to treatment which assures him that it is based upon justice, truth, honesty, and common sense. . . .

Crook hesitated to condemn even the most ferocious Apaches, because he respected their spirit and believed that "we are too culpable as a nation, for the existing condition of affairs."

In the view of many officers the weaknesses of their own culture were more glaring than the faults of their enemy. "Barbarism torments the body; civilization torments the soul," one colonel concluded. "The savage remorselessly takes your scalp, your civilized friend as remorselessly swindles you out of your property." Indeed, many of the officers who led the fight for civilization seemed to accept Indian culture on its own terms. Colonel Henry B. Carrington—one of the field officers who supplied Sheridan with maddening accounts of Indian outrages—was an interesting case study. Carrington's official report of the eighty fallen soldiers under his command in the Fetterman fight in Wyoming in 1866 provided grisly reading:

> Eyes torn out and laid on the rocks; teeth chopped out; joints of fingers cut off; brains taken out and placed on rocks, with members of the body; entrails taken out and exposed; hands and feet cut off; arms taken out from sockets; eyes, ears, mouth, and arms penetrated with spearheads, sticks, and arrows; punctures upon every sensitive part of the body, even to the soles of the feet and the palms of the hand.

Yet Carrington's own response to this carnage was not vengeful but reflective, even scholarly. A year later Margaret Carrington, the colonel's wife, published *Absa-ra-ka,* a study of the region the Army had fought to control. In her book she treated this Indian act of warfare with impressive open-mindedness, never directly condemning it. She did note that "the noblest traits of the soldiers were touchingly developed as they carefully handled the mutilated fragments" from the battlefield—but she also praised the Indian: "In ambush and decoy, *splendid.*" Close observers, she wrote, overcame anger to become reconciled, even sympathetic, to "the bold warrior in his great struggle."

As he took charge of enlarged sections of *Ab-sa-ra-ka* in the 1870's Colonel Carrington expanded on this theme of noble resistance. To him the barbarities of the *whites,* in their "irresponsible speculative emigration," overshadowed the red "massacre" of Fetterman's men. Carrington confessed, like Custer, "if I had been a red man as I was a white man, I should have fought as bitterly, if not as brutally, as the Indian fought." And standing before the American Association for the Advancement of Science in 1880 to read his official report of the Fetterman mutilations again, Carrington explained to the scientists that the Indian's disposition of enemies was intended to disable his foe in the afterlife, and so was quite understandable. Nor did he disparage the red man's values, but rather closed his address by suggesting some inadequacies on the other—his own—side: "From 1865 until the present time, there has not been a border campaign which did not have its impulse in the aggressions of a white man."

Few men in the West raised more unusual questions about both cultures than Captain John Bourke. He entered the campaigns, he wrote later, "with the sincere conviction that the only good Indian was a dead Indian, and that the only use to make of him was that of a fertilizer." But the notebooks of this odd, inquiring soul reveal a man haunted by the details of the enemy's life. Mastering several Indian languages, Bourke produced an impressive series of monographs on native religious ceremonies, and in 1895 he became president of the American Folklore Society. Learning proved corrosive to his early cultural pride, and at the end of his army service he was willing to admit that "the American aborigine is not indebted to his pale-faced brother, no matter what nation or race he may be, for lessons in tenderness and humanity."

Admittedly, Captain Bourke's appreciation of native culture was more complex than the respect paid by other Indian fighters. Acknowledging the red man's fighting prowess and noble character, Bourke was more deeply interested in Indian snake ceremonies and scatological rites—mysteries thoroughly repulsive to most white sensibilities. Indeed, his interest in these ceremonies was as intense and sustained as were his protestations of "horror" during each "filthy" and "disgusting" rite. He put all this scholarship and his rather prurient curiosity to work in *Scatologic Rites of All Nations,* where he observed such "orgies" throughout the development of Western civilization, even surviving in nations of what he called "high enlightenment." Here was no sentimental accommodation with Indian culture but a panoramic reminder to the white race of its own barbaric past. Thus the Indians' vices, no less than their virtues, set up a mirror before the advancing Christian whites.

It did not, of course, deter the whites. However noble their image of the savage may have been, it is important to recognize in all of these Indian fighters a fundamental conviction that the price of civilization was not too high. Aware as they were of the ambiguities of their mission, their sympathies and remorse never swayed them from their duty, and no officer of tender conscience was provoked to resign his commission.

How were such mixed emotions sustained? In point of fact, the military's apologia for the red man answered certain professional and psychological needs of the workaday Army. The Army, for both noble and ignoble reasons, wanted to assume control of the administration of Indian affairs that had been held by civilians—a few good words for the long-suffering red man smoothed the way to this goal. Further, by praising the Plains Indians as relentless and efficient warriors the military justified its own ruthless strategy—and setbacks. Nor was frontier ethnology exactly disinterested; close study of the Indians often yielded military advantage for white men. And while empathy for the enemy clearly made the assignment to "redeem" the Indian more painful, there were some emotional satisfactions to be derived from even the most generous attitudes toward the Indians' way of life.

In some instances an officer's respect for the primitive's unfettered aggressiveness happily loosened his own. Thus General George Schofield, commander of the Department of the Missouri, could confess that "civilized man . . . never feels so happy as when he throws off a large part of his civilization and reverts to the life of a semi-savage." When Schofield acted on his own advice on a long hunting trip, he returned invigorated, recording that "I wanted no other occupation in life than to ward off the savage and kill off his food until there should no longer be an Indian frontier in our beautiful country." One of Sherman's aides reached a similar ominous conclusion after saluting the red man's way of life. This officer was deeply impressed by his colleagues' glowing reports of the nobility of Indian religion, and, he mused,

> There is no doubt the Indians have, at times, been shamefully treated. . . . And there is no doubt a man of spirit would rebel. . . . However, it is useless to moralize about the Indians. Their fate is fixed, and we are so near their end, it is easy to see what that fate is to be. That the Indian might be collected, and put out of misery by being shot deliberately, (as it would be done to a disabled animal), would seem shocking, but something could be said in favor of such procedure.

This puzzling mixture of aggression and regret is less surprising if we take into account the ways, according to contemporary psychologists, that anger and frustration can give rise to these contrasting emotions. The officer corps was enraged by much of what it saw happening to America. The Indians' tactics seemed horrible yet ingenious. Their culture was repellent, but also alluring for its integrity. At the same time, evident in the reports and memoirs of these officers is a disturbing sense of having been abandoned by their own unworthy civilization. Army training and experience prevented these men from acting out their anger, and some anger was instead internalized and expressed in the mourning and guilt they exhibited so frequently. Their appreciation of the native Americans for what they had been was combined with a determination to punish a society for what it refused to become. Their fight for civilized settlement as it should be was troubled by their anger that some virtues, retained by the Indians, were slipping away from the white man.

If we appreciate the military's doubts—of its mandate, of its justice, of its ability, as well as of its commitments to civilization, duty, and progress—the tragedy of the West does not go away. It deepens. Was there an escape from the emotional trap in which the Army found itself? To refuse to win the West would have required a conversion to primitivism hard to imagine inside the ranks of army life and scarcely imaginable in ordinary men living ordinary lives outside of the Army. But the career of one lieutenant in the Nez Perce war illustrates that such a transformation was possible.

Charles Erskine Scott Wood (1852–1944) served on General O. O. Howard's staff, and it was he who took down the very moving speech of the defeated Chief Joseph. Wood's reflections on the Nez Perce campaign, published in the early 1880's, struck the conventional balance between remorse and pride. Surveying the shameful record of white treaty violations, he warned his army colleagues that retribution might follow. Yet there seemed to be no other possible outcome—"forces" were "silently at work, beyond all human control," against the red man's survival. Wood, a gifted literary man, proceeded to join the somewhat crowded celebration of the culture he had worked to destroy, hymning the vividness and nobility of the Indian, qualities that seemed poignant by their passing. But in all this he declined to attack directly the civilization that had corrupted and supplanted the Indians', and his fashionable sympathy sounded much like General Custer's.

But Wood was, in time, to change greatly. He quit the Army, entered the Columbia Law School, and began to cause trouble. Not satisfied with the state of letters or the law in his time, Wood allied himself with the radical Industrial Workers of the World and searched for a literary form to express his increasingly anarchistic temperament. The fruit of this veteran's singular rehabilitation was a long experimental poem, *The Poet in the Desert,* an affecting personal renunciation of "civilization" and a call for the revolt of the masses against privilege. Wood, with booming voice and flowing white beard, was in the twentieth century rather like Father Time—reminding Americans of sins against the Indians. He knew:

I have lain out with the brown men
And know they are favored.
Nature whispered to them her secrets,
But passed me by.

I sprawled flat in the bunch-grass, a target
For the just bullets of my brown brothers betrayed.
I was a soldier, and, at command,
Had gone out to kill and be killed.

We swept like fire over the smoke-browned tee-pees;
Their conical tops peering above the willows.
We frightened the air with crackle of rifles,
Women's shrieks, children's screams,
Shrill yells of savages;

Curses of Christians.
The rifles chuckled continually.
A poor people who asked nothing but freedom,
Butchered in the dark.

Wood's polemic is more straightforward than many that are asserted today on behalf of the native Americans. He learned—and his colleagues in the Army demonstrated—that respect and compassion for another culture are very unsure checks on violence. And Wood's life points out one of the costs of war that Americans have generally been spared: in a prolonged campaign the victor can emerge attracted to his enemy's faith. Our frontier officers had put a civil war behind them and were not ready to turn against their society to save the red man. But their thoughtfully expressed ambivalence toward their task of winning the West throws a revealing light on a history that is still too often falsified with glib stereotypes.

■ ■ ■ ■ ■ ■ ■

2

Impact of Industrialism

Pennsylvania coal miners, their gas lamps burning, prepare to descend into the pit.

John D. Rockefeller: America's First Billionaire

Robert L. Heilbroner

The driving force behind late nineteenth-century economic growth, social change, and the thousand new developments that heralded the birth of modern America was the rapid expansion of industry. Industrialization made the United States the richest nation in the world and placed some of its citizens among the world's richest. At one and the same time it fostered the belief that individuals could rise from rags to riches in a generation and the fear that great extremes between the wealthy and the poor would destroy opportunity, even democracy. It lent credence to the idea that Americans were gross materialists, but it also produced a philanthropic outpouring of unprecedented dimensions.

If any one person epitomized the industrialization of the United States to the average late nineteenth-century citizen, it was certainly John D. Rockefeller, the master of Standard Oil. To critics, Rockefeller was the robber baron par excellence, the greedy monopolist who crushed competitors ruthlessly and ruled the oil-refining business like an oriental monarch. Yet to others he typified the perfect industrial statesman, the efficient, imaginative organizer who provided cheaper and better products than his competitors and who, having amassed a great fortune as a result of his ability, devoted his mature years to equally beneficial philanthropic activities.

Professor Robert L. Heilbroner, an economist at the New School for Social Research, the author of this essay, has written extensively in the field of economic history and thought. In works such as *The Worldly Philosophers, The Great Ascent,* and *The Limits of American Capitalism* he has repeatedly demonstrated that it is possible to write history that is at once popular and scholarly even when dealing with highly technical material.

■ ■ ■ ■ ■ ■ ■

The incredibly shrunken face of an animate mummy, grotesque behind enormous black-rimmed glasses; the old boy tottering around the golf course, benign and imperturbable, distributing his famous dimes; the huge foundation with its medical triumphs; the lingering memory of the great trust and the awed contemplation of the even greater company; and over all, the smell of oil, endlessly pumping out of the earth, each drop adding its bit to the largest exaction ever levied on any society by a private individual—with such associations it is no wonder that the name has sunk into the American mind to an extraordinary degree. From his earliest days the spendthrift schoolboy is brought to his senses with: "Who do you think you are, John D. Rockefeller?"

Yet for all the vivid associations, the man himself remains a shadowy presence. Carnegie, Morgan, or Ford may not have entered so decisively into the American parlance, but they are full-blooded figures in our memory: Carnegie, brash, bustling, proselytizing; Morgan, imperious, choleric, aloof; Ford, shrewd, small-town, thing-minded. But what is John D. Rockefeller, aside from the paper silhouettes of very old age and the aura of immense wealth?

Even his contemporaries did not seem to have a very clear impression of Rockefeller as a human being. For forty years of his active career, he was commonly regarded as an arch economic malefactor—La Follette called him the greatest criminal of the age—and for twenty years, as a great benefactor—John Singer Sargent, painting his portrait, declared himself in the presence of a medieval saint—but neither judgment tells us much about the man. Nor do Ida Tarbell or Henry Demarest Lloyd, both so skillful in portraying the company, succeed in bringing to life its central figure; he lurks in the background, the Captain Nemo of Standard Oil. Similarly, in the reminiscences of his associates we catch only the glimmer of a person—a polite, reserved man, mild in manner, a bit of a stickler for exactitude, totally unremarkable for anything he says or for any particular style of saying it. Surely there must be more to John D. than this! What sort of man was this greatest of all acquisitors? What was the secret of his incredible success?

His mother came of a prosperous Scottish farming family, devout, strait-laced, uncompromising. She springs out at us from her photographs: a tired, plain face, deep-set eyes, and a straight, severe mouth announce Eliza Davison Rockefeller's tired, straight, severe personality. Rockefeller later recalled an instance when he was being whipped by her and finally managed to convince her that he was innocent of a supposed misdemeanor. "Never mind," she said, "we have started in on this whipping and it will do for the next time." Her approach to life made an indelible impression—even in his old age Rockefeller could hear her voice enjoining: "Willful waste makes woeful want."

His father, William Avery Rockefeller, was cut from a different bolt of cloth. Big, robust, and roistering, he treated his sons with a curious mixture of affection and contempt. "I trade with the boys," he boasted to a neighbor, "and skin 'em and I just beat 'em every time I can. I want to make 'em sharp." Sharp himself, he was in and out of a dozen businesses in John's youth and, we have reason to suspect, as many beds. Later, when his son was already a prominent businessman, we can still follow his father's erratic career, now as "Doctor" William A. Rockefeller, "the Celebrated Cancer Specialist," peddling his cures on the circuit. Still later, when John D. had become a great eminence in New York, the father drops into obscurity—only to materialize from time to time in the city, where he is shown around by an embarrassed Standard Oil underling. At the very end he simply disappears. Joseph Pulitzer at one time offered a prize of $8,000 for news of his whereabouts, and the rumor spread that for thirty-five years old William had led a double life, with a second wife in Illinois. No one knows.

It was an unpleasantly polarized family situation, and it helps us understand the quiet, sober-sided boy who emerged. His schoolmates called John "Old pleased-because-I'm-sad," from the title of a school declamation that fitted him to perfection; typically, when the boys played baseball, he kept score. Yet, if it was subdued, it was not an unhappy boyhood. At home he milked the cow and drove the horse and did the household chores that were expected of a boy in upstate New York, but af-

Three faces of John D. Rockefeller: (top) the earnest young man at 18, a clerk who would become a partner in his own firm; (bottom left) at 35, the commanding businessman; (bottom right) at 91, the "shrunken face of an animate mummy," still active in retirement.

ter hours he indulged with his brothers, William and Frank, in the usual boyhood escapades and adventures. A favorite pastime, especially savored since it was forbidden, was to go skating at night on the Susquehanna. On one occasion William and John saved a neighbor's boy from drowning, whereupon their evening's sally had to be admitted. Eliza Rockefeller praised their courage—and whipped them soundly for their disobedience.

Always in the Rockefeller home there was the stress on gainful work. Their father may have worked to make them sharp, but their mother worked to make them industrious. John was encouraged to raise turkeys, and he kept the money from their sale in a little box on the mantel until he had accumulated the sum of $50. A neighboring farmer asked to borrow the amount at seven per cent for a year, and his mother approved. During that summer John dug potatoes at thirty-seven and a half cents a day. When the farmer repaid the loan with $3.50 in interest, the lesson was not lost on John: the earning power of capital was much to be preferred to that of labor.

He was then only in his teens—he was born in 1839—but already, frugal ways, a deliberate manner, and a strong sense of planning and purposefulness were in evidence. As his sister Lucy said: "When it's raining porridge, you'll find John's dish right side up." But now the time for summer jobs was coming to an end. The family had moved from Moravia and Oswego, where John had grown up, to Cleveland, where he went to the local high school in his fifteenth and sixteenth years. For a few months he attended Folsom's Commercial College, where he learned the elements of bookkeeping—and then began the all-important search for the first real job.

That search was performed with a methodical thoroughness that became a hallmark of the Rockefeller style. A list of promising establishments was drawn up—nothing second-rate would do—and each firm was hopefully visited. Rebuffed on the first go-round, John went the rounds again undaunted, and then a third time. Eventually his perseverance was rewarded. He became a clerk in the office of Hewitt & Tuttle, commission merchants and produce shippers. Typically, he took the job without inquiring about salary, hung his coat on a peg, climbed onto the high bookkeeper's stool, and set to work. It was a red-letter day in his life; later, when he was a millionaire many times over, the flag was regularly hoisted before his house to commemorate September 26, 1855.

Work came naturally, even pleasurably to John Rockefeller. He was precise, punctual, diligent. "I had trained myself," he wrote in his memoirs, ". . . that my check on a bill was the executive act which released my employer's money from the till and was attended with more responsibility than the spending of my own funds."

With such model attitudes, Rockefeller quickly advanced. By 1858 his salary (which turned out to be $3.50 a week) had more than tripled, but when Hewitt & Tuttle were unable to meet a request for a further raise, he began to look elsewhere. A young English acquaintance named Maurice Clark, also a clerk, was similarly unhappy with his prospects, and the two decided to form a produce-shipping firm of their own. Clark had saved up $2,000, and John Rockefeller had saved $900; the question was, where to get the last necessary $1,000. John knew that at age twenty-one he was entitled to a patrimony of this amount under his father's will, and he turned to William Rockefeller for an advance. His father listened with mingled approval and suspicion, and finally consented to lend his son the money if John would pay interest until he was twenty-one. "And John," he added, "the rate is ten."

Rockefeller accepted the proposition, and Clark & Rockefeller opened its doors in 1859. The Cleveland *Leader* recommended the principals to its readers as "experienced, responsible, and prompt," and the venture succeeded from the start. In its first year the firm made a profit of $4,400; in the second year, $17,000; and when the Civil War began, profits soared. Rockefeller became known as an up-and-coming young businessman, a man to be watched. Even his father agreed. From time to time he would come around and ask for his loan back, just to be sure the money was really there, but then, unable to resist ten per cent interest, he would lend it back again.

Meanwhile an adult personality begins to emerge. A picture taken just before he married Laura Spelman in 1864 shows a handsome man of twenty-five with a long, slightly mournful visage, a fine straight nose, a rather humorless mouth. Everyone who knew him testified to his virtues. He was industrious, even-tempered, generous, kind; and if it was not a sparkling personality, it was not a dour one. Yet there is something not quite attractive about the picture as a whole. Charitable from his earliest days, he itemized each contribution—even the tiniest—in his famous Ledger A, with the result that his generosity, of which there was never any doubt, is stained with self-observance and an over-nice persnicketiness. Extremely self-critical, he was given to intimate "pillow talks" at night in which he took himself to task for various faults, but the words he recalled and later repeated—"Now a little success, soon you will fall down, soon you will be overthrown. . . " smack not so much of honest self-search as of the exorcising of admonitory parental voices. He was above all orderly and forethoughted, but there is a compulsive, and sometimes a faintly repellent quality about his self-control. He recounts that when he was travelling as a commission merchant, he would never grab a bite in the station and wolf it down, like the others on the train, but "if I could not finish eating properly, I filled my mouth with as much as it would hold, then went leisurely to the train and chewed it slowly before swallowing it."

Yet the faults, far from constituting major traits in themselves, were minor flaws in an essentially excellent character. Rockefeller forged ahead by his merits, not by meanness—and among his merits was a well-developed capacity to size up a business situation coolly and rationally. Living in Cleveland, he could scarcely fail to think about one such situation virtually under his nose. Less than a day's journey by train were the Oil Regions of Pennsylvania, one of the most fantastic locales in America. A shambles of mud, dying horses (their skins denuded by petroleum), derricks, walking beams, chugging donkey engines, and jerry-built towns, the Regions oozed oil, money, and dreams. Bits of land the size of a blanket sold on occasion for three and four hundred dollars, pastures jumped overnight into fortunes (one pasture rose from $25,000 to $1,600,000 in three months), whole villages bloomed into existence in a matter of months. Pithole, Pennsylvania, an aptly named pinprick on the map, became the third largest center for mail in Pennsylvania and boasted a $65,000 luxury hotel. Within a few years it was again a pinprick, and the hotel was sold for $50.

It is uncertain whether Rockefeller himself visited the Oil Regions in the halcyon early 1860's. What is certain is that he sniffed oil in Cleveland itself, where the crude product was transported by barge and barrel for distillation and refining. In any event, the hurly-burly, the disorganization, and above all the extreme riskiness of the Oil Regions would never have appealed to Rockefeller's temperament. Let someone else make a million or lose it by blindly drilling for an invisible reservoir—a surer and far steadier route to wealth was available to the refiner who bought the crude oil at thirty-one or thirty-two cents a gallon and then sold the refined product at eighty to eighty-five cents.

The chance to enter the refining business came to Clark and Rockefeller in the person of an enterprising and ingenious young engineer named Sam Andrews. Andrews, recently come from England (by coincidence, he was born in the same town as Clark), was restive in his job in a land refinery and eager to try his hand at oil refining. He talked with his fellow townsman and through Clark met Rockefeller. The three agreed to take a fling at the business. Andrews, together with Clark's brothers, took on the production side, and Maurice Clark and Rockefeller the financial side. Thus in 1863 Andrews, Clark & Company was born. Rockefeller, content behind the anonymity of the "Company," had contributed, together with his partner, half the total capital, but he retained his interest in the produce business. The investment in oil was meant to be no more than a side venture.

But the side venture prospered beyond all expectation. The demand for refined oil increased by leaps and bounds. As Allan Nevins has written: "A commodity that had been a curiosity when Lincoln was nominated, had become a necessity of civilization, the staple of a vast commerce, before he was murdered." And the supply of oil, despite a thousand warnings, auguries, and dire prophecies that the mysterious underground springs would dry up, always matched and overmatched demand.

As the business boomed, so did the number of refineries. One could go into the refinery business for no more capital than it took to open a well-equipped hardware store, and Cleveland's location with its favoring rivers and fortunately placed rail lines made it a natural center for the shipment of crude oil. Hence by 1866, only two years after Andrews, Clark & Company had opened its doors, there were over thirty refineries along the Cleveland Flats, and twenty more would be added before the year was out.

The Rockefeller refinery was among the largest of these. In Sam Andrews had been found the perfect plant superintendent; in Clark and Rockefeller, the perfect business management. From half-past six in the morning, when Andrews and Clark would burst in on their partner at breakfast, until they parted company just before supper, the three talked oil, oil, oil. Slowly, however, Andrews and Rockefeller found themselves at odds with Clark. They had become convinced that oil was to be a tremendous and permanent business enterprise; Clark was more cautious and less willing to borrow to expand facilities. Finally, in 1865, it was decided to put the firm up for auction among themselves, the seller to retain the produce business. "It was the day that determined my career," Rockefeller recalled long afterward. "I felt the bigness of it, but I was as calm as I am talking to you now." When at last Maurice Clark bid $72,000, Rockefeller topped him by $500. Clark threw up his hands. "The business is yours," he declared.

From the beginning Rockefeller & Andrews, as the new firm was called, was a model of efficiency. Even before acquiring the firm, Rockefeller had become interested in the economies of plant operation. When he found that plumbers were expensive by the hour, he and Sam Andrews hired one by the month, bought their own pipes and joints, and cut plumbing costs in half. When cooperage grew into a formidable item, they built their own shop where barrels cost them only forty per cent of the market price, and soon costs were cut further by the acquisition of a stand of white oak, a kiln, and their own teams and wagons to haul the wood from kiln to plant. The emphasis on cost never ceased; when Rockefeller & Andrews had long since metamorphosed into the Standard Oil Company and profits had grown into the millions, cost figures were still carried to three decimal places. One day Rockefeller was watching the production line in one of his plants, where cans of finished oil were being soldered shut. "How many drops of solder do you use on each can?" he inquired. The answer was forty. "Have you ever tried thirty-eight? No? Would you mind having some sealed with thirty-eight and let me know?" A few cans leaked with thirty-eight, but with thirty-nine all were perfect. A couple of thousand dollars a year were saved.

The zeal for perfection of detail was from the beginning a factor in the growth of Rockefeller's firm. More important was his meeting in 1866 with Henry M. Flagler, the first of a half-dozen associates who would bring to the enterprise the vital impetus of talent, enthusiasm, and a hard determination to succeed. Flagler, a quick, ebullient, bold businessman who had fought his way up from the poverty of a small-town parsonage, was a commission merchant of considerable prominence when Rockefeller met him. The two quickly took a liking to one another, and Rockefeller soon induced Flagler to join the fast-expanding business. Flagler brought along his own funds and those of his father-in-law, Stephen Harkness, and this fresh influx of capital made possible even further expansion. Rockefeller, Andrews & Flagler—soon incorporated as the Standard Oil Company—rapidly became the biggest single refinery in Cleveland.

Flagler brought to the enterprise an immense energy and a playfulness that Rockefeller so egregiously lacked. The two main partners now had a code word in their telegrams—AMELIA—which meant "Everything is lovely and the goose hangs high." And everything *was* lovely. One of Flagler's first jobs was to turn his considerable bargaining skills to a crucial link in the chain of oil-processing costs. All the major refineries bought in the same market—the Oil Regions—and all sold in the same markets—the great cities—so that their costs of purchase and their prices at the point of sale were much alike. In between purchase and sale, however, lay two steps: the costs of refining and the costs of transportation. In the end it was the latter that was to prove decisive in the dog-eat-dog struggle among the refineries.

For the railroads needed a steady flow of shipments to make money, and they were willing to grant rebates to the refiners if they would level out their orders. Since there were a number of routes by which to ship oil, each refiner was in a position to play one road against another, and the Standard, as the biggest and strongest refiner in Cleveland, was naturally able to gain the biggest and most lucrative discounts on its freight. This was a game that Flagler played with consummate skill. Advantageous rebates soon became an important means by which the Standard pushed ahead of its competitors—and in later years, when there were no more competitors, an important source of revenue in themselves. By 1879, when the Rockefeller concern had become a giant, a government investigatory agency estimated that in a period of five months the firm had shipped some eighteen million barrels of oil, on which rebates ran from eleven per cent on the B&O to *forty-seven* per cent on the Pennsylvania Railroad. For the five months, rebates totalled over ten million dollars.

This is looking too far ahead, however. By 1869, a scant three years after Flagler had joined it, the company was worth about a million dollars, but it was very far from being an industrial giant or a monopoly. Indeed, the problem which constantly plagued Rockefeller and his associates was the extreme competition in the oil business. As soon as business took a downturn—as it did in 1871—the worst kind of cutthroat competition broke out; prices dropped until the Titusville *Herald* estimated that the average refiner lost seventy-five cents on each barrel he sold.

As the biggest refiner, Rockefeller naturally had the greatest stake in establishing some kind of stability in the industry. Hence he set about to devise a scheme— the so-called South Improvement Company—which would break the feast-and-famine pattern that threatened to overwhelm the industry. In its essence the South Improvement Company was a kind of cartel aimed at holding up oil prices—by arranging "reasonable" freight rates for its own members while levying far higher ones on "outsiders." Since the scheme was open to all, presumably there would soon be no outsiders, and once all were within the fold, the refiners could operate a single, powerful economic unit.

The plan might have worked but for the inability of such headstrong and individualistic groups as the railroads and the producers to cooperate for more than a passing moment. When the producers in the Oil Regions rose in wrath against a plan which they (quite rightly) saw as a powerful buying combination against them, the scheme simply collapsed.

The idea of eliminating competition did not, however, collapse with it. Instead, Rockefeller turned to a plan at once much simpler and much more audacious. If he could not eliminate competition, then perhaps he could eliminate his competitors by buying them up one by one—and this he set out to do. The plan was set in motion by a meeting with Colonel Oliver Payne, the chief stockholder in Rockefeller's biggest competitor. Briefly Rockefeller outlined the ruinous situation which impended if competition were permitted to continue unbridled; equally briefly, he proposed a solution. The Standard would increase its capitalization, the Payne plant would be appraised by impartial judges, and its owners would be given stock in proportion to their equity. As for Payne himself, Rockefeller suggested he should take an active part in the management of the new, bigger Standard Oil.

Payne quickly assented; so did Jabez Bostwick, the biggest refiner in New York, and one after another the remaining refiners sold out. According to Rockefeller, they were only too glad to rid themselves of their burdensome businesses at fair prices; according to many of the refiners, it was a question of taking Rockefeller's offer or facing sure ruin. We need not debate the point here; what is certain is that by the end of 1872 the Standard was the colossus of Cleveland. There remained only the United States to conquer.

Rockefeller himself was in his mid-thirties. The slightly melancholy visage of the younger man had altered; a thick mustache trimmed straight across the bottom hid his lips and gave to his face a commanding, even stern, aspect. In a family portrait we see him standing rather stiffly, carefully dressed as befits a man in his station. For he was already rich—even his non-oil investments, as he wrote to his wife, were enough to give him independence, and his style of life had changed as his fortune had grown. He and his wife now lived in Forest Hill, a large, gaunt house on eighty acres just east of Cleveland. He had begun to indulge himself with snappy trotters, and on a small scale commenced what was to become in time a Brobdingnagian pastime—moving landscape around.

In town, in his business pursuits, he was already the reserved, colorless, almost inscrutable personality who baffled his business contemporaries; at home, he came as close as he could to a goal he sought assiduously—relaxation. His children were his great delight: he taught them to swim and invented strange and wonderful contraptions to keep them afloat; he bicycled with them; he played daring games of blindman's bluff—so daring in fact that he once had to have stitches taken in his head after running full tilt into a doorpost.

It was, in a word, the very model of a Victorian home, affectionate, dutiful, and, of course, rich. An air of rectitude hung over the establishment, not so much as to smother it, but enough to give it a distinctive flavor. Concerts (aside from the performances of their children), literature, art, or theatre were not Rockefeller amusements; in entertaining, their tastes ran to Baptist ministers and business associates. An unpretentious and earnest atmosphere hid—or at least disguised—the wealth; until they were nearly grown up the children had no idea of "who they were."

And of course the beneficences continued and grew: $23,000 for various charities in 1878, nearly $33,000 in 1880, over $100,000 in 1884. But the nice preciseness of giving was maintained; a pledge card signed in 1883 for the Euclid Avenue Baptist Church reads:

Mrs. Rockefeller	$10.00 each week
Self	30.00 each week
Each of our four children	00.20 each week

How rich was Rockefeller by 1873, a mere ten years after Andrews, Clark & Company had opened its doors? We cannot make an accurate estimate, but it is certain that he was a millionaire several times over. In another ten years his Standard Oil holdings alone would be worth a phenomenal twenty million dollars—enough, with his other investments, to make him one of the half-dozen richest men in the country.

But now a legal problem began to obtrude. The Standard Oil Company was legally chartered in Ohio, and it had no right to own plants in other states. Not until 1889 would New Jersey amend its incorporation laws to allow a corporation chartered within the state to hold the stock of corporations chartered elsewhere. Hence the question: how was the Standard legally to control its expanding acquisitions in other states?

The problem was solved by one of Rockefeller's most astute lieutenants—Samuel Dodd, a round little butterball of a man with an extraordinarily clear-sighted legal mind and an unusually high and strict sense of personal integrity. Because he believed that he could render the best advice to the Standard if he was above any suspicion of personal aggrandizement, he repeatedly refused Rockefeller's offers to make him a director or to buy for him stock which would have made him a multimillionaire.

The sword which Dodd applied to the Gordian knot of interstate control was the device of the trust. In brief, he proposed a single group of nine trustees, with headquarters in New York, who would hold "in trust" the certificates of all Standard's operating companies, including the major company in Ohio itself. In 1882 the Standard Oil Trust was formally established, with John and his brother William Rockefeller, Flagler, Payne Bostwick, John D. Archbold, Charles Pratt, William G. Warden, and Benjamin Brewster as trustees. (Sam Andrews had sold the last of his stock to Rockefeller four years before, saying the business had grown too big). In fact, though not in law, one enormous interstate corporation had been created.

Few people even at this time appreciated quite how great the company was. By the 1880's the Standard was the largest and richest of all American manufacturing organizations. It had eighty-five per cent of a business which took the output of 20,000 wells and which employed 100,000 people. And all this before the advent of the automobile. The colossus of the Standard was built not on the internal combustion engine but on the kerosene lamp.

With the creation of the Trust the center of gravity of the concern moved to New York. Rockefeller himself bought a $600,000 brownstone on West Fifty-fourth Street, where the round of teas and dinners for temperance workers, church people, and Standard executives soon went on. The Trust itself occupied No. 26 Broadway, an eleven-story "skyscraper" with gay striped awnings shading its large windows. It was soon known as the most famous business address in the world. There Rockefeller appeared daily, usually in high silk hat, long coat, and gloves—the accepted costume for the big business executive of the time.

At 26 Broadway Rockefeller was the commanding figure. But his exercise of command, like his personality, was notable for its lack of color, dash, and verve. Inquiring now of this one, now of that, what he thought of such and such a situation, putting his questions methodically and politely in carefully chosen words, never arguing, never raising his voice, Rockefeller seemed to govern his empire like a disembodied intelligence. He could be, as always, a stickler for detail; an accountant recalls him suddenly materializing one day, and with a polite "Permit me," turning over the ledger sheets, all the while murmuring, "Very well kept, very indeed," until he stopped at one page: "A little error here; will you correct it?" But he could also be decisive and absolutely determined. "He saw strategic points like a Napoleon, and he swooped down on them with the suddenness of a Napoleon," wrote Ida Tarbell. Yet even that gives too much of the impression of dash and daring. She was closer to the mark when she wrote: "If one attempts to analyse what may be called the legitimate greatness of Mr. Rockefeller's creation in distinction to its illegitimate greatness, he will find at the foundation the fact that it is as perfectly centralized as the Catholic Church or the Napoleonic government." It was true. By 1886 the Standard had evolved a system of committees, acting in advisory roles to the active management, which permitted an incalculably complex system to function with extraordinary ease. It is virtually the same system that is used today. Rockefeller had created the great Trust on which the eyes of the whole world were fastened, but behind the Trust, sustaining it, operating it, maintaining it, he had created an even greater Organization.

"It's many a day since I troubled you with a letter," wrote William Warden, a onetime independent Cleveland refiner who had been bought out and was now a trustee and major official in the Standard, "and I would not do so now could I justify myself in being silent. . . . We have met with a success unparalleled in commercial history, our name is known all over the world, and our public character is not one to be envied. We are quoted as representative of all that is evil, hard hearted, oppressive, cruel (we think unjustly), but men look askance at us, we are pointed at with contempt, and while some good men flatter us, it's only for our money . . . This is not pleasant to write, for I had longed for an honored position in commercial life. None of us would choose such a reputation; we all desire a place in the honor & affection of honorable men."

It was a cry of anguish, but it was amply justified. By the 1880's the Standard was not only widely known—it was notorious. In part its increasingly bad business reputation originated in the business community itself. Stories began to circulate of the unfair advantage taken by the colossus when it bid for smaller properties: the case of the Widow Backus, whose deceased husband's refinery was supposedly bought for a pittance, was much talked about. Many of these tales—the Backus case in particular—were simply untrue. But as the Standard grew in size and visibility, other business practices came to light which *were* true, and which were hardly calculated to gain friends for the company.

Foremost among these practices was an evil device called the drawback. Not content with enjoying a large competitive advantage through its special rebates, Standard also forced the railroads to pay it a portion of the freight charges paid by non-Standard refiners! Thus Daniel O'Day, a particularly ruthless Standard official, used his local economic leverage to get a small railroad to carry Standard's oil at ten cents a barrel, to charge all independents thirty-five cents, *and to turn over the twenty-five cent differential to a Standard subsidiary.* Another Standard agent, finding that a competitor's car had slipped through without paying the Standard exaction, wrote the road to collect the amount owing, adding: "Please turn another screw."

Such incidents and practices—always denied by the company and never admitted by Rockefeller—plagued the Standard for years. And the impression of high-handedness was not much improved by the behavior of the Standard's officials when they went on public view. John D. Archbold, a key executive called to testify before New York State's Hepburn Committee in 1879, was a typical bland witness. When pressed hard, he finally admitted he was a stockholder of the Standard. What was his function there? "I am a clamorer for dividends. That is the only function I have in connection with the Standard Oil Company." Chairman Alonzo Hepburn asked how large dividends were. "I have no trouble transporting my share," answered Archbold. On matters of rebates he declined to answer. Finally Hepburn asked him to return for further questioning the next day. "I have given today to the matter," replied Archbold politely. "It will be impossible for me to be with you again."

Not least, there was the rising tide of public protest against the monopoly itself. In 1881 Henry Demarest Lloyd, a journalist of passionate reformist sentiments, wrote for the *Atlantic Monthly* an article called "The Story of a Great Monopoly." Editor William Dean Howells gave it the lead in the magazine, and overnight it was a sensation (that issue of the *Atlantic* went through seven printings). "The family that uses a gallon of kerosene a day pays a yearly tribute to the Standard of $32...," wrote Lloyd. "America has the proud satisfaction of having furnished the world with the greatest, wisest, and meanest monopoly known to history."

Standard's profits were nothing so great as described by Lloyd, but that hardly mattered. If the article was imprecise or even downright wrong in detail, it was right in its general thrust. What counted was Lloyd's incontrovertible demonstration that an individual concern had grown to a position of virtual impregnability, a position which made it in fact no longer subordinate to the states from which it drew its legal privilege of existence, but their very peer or better in financial strength and even political power. Before Lloyd wrote his article, the Standard was the source of rage or loss to scattered groups of producers, businessmen, or consumers. When he was through with his indictment, it was a national scandal.

That it should be a scandal was totally incomprehensible to John D. The mounting wave of protest and obloquy perplexed him more than it irritated him. Ida Tarbell's famous—and generally accurate—*History of the Standard Oil Company* he dismissed as "without foundation." The arrogance of an Archbold he merely chuckled at, recounting the Hepburn testimony in his *Random Reminiscences of Men and Events* with the comment that Archbold had a "well-developed sense of humor." With his own passion for order, he understood not a whit the passions of those whose demise was required that order might prevail. On one occasion when he was testifying in court, he spied in the courtroom George Rice, an old adversary (against whom, as a matter of fact, the famous screw had been turned, and whom Rockefeller had once offered to buy out). As he left the witness stand, Rockefeller walked over to Rice and, putting out his hand, said: "How do you do, Mr. Rice? You and I are getting to be old men, are we not?"

Rice ignored the hand. "Don't you think, Mr. Rice," pursued Rockefeller, "it might have been better if you had taken my advice years ago?"

"Perhaps it would," said Rice angrily. "You said you would ruin my business and you have done so."

"Pshaw! Pshaw!" rejoined Rockefeller.

"Don't you pooh-pooh me," said Rice in a fury. "I say that by the power of your great wealth you have ruined me."

"Not a word of truth in it," Rockefeller answered, turning and making his way through the crowd. "Not a word of truth in it."

He could not in fact bring himself to believe that there was a word of truth in any of it. There was nothing to argue about concerning the need for giant enterprise, or "industrial combinations" as they were called. They were simply a necessity, a potentially dangerous necessity admittedly, but a necessity nonetheless. All the rest was ignorance or willful misunderstanding. "You know," he wrote to a university president who offered to prepare a scholarly defense of Standard's policies, "that great prejudice exists against all successful business enterprise—the more successful, the greater the prejudice."

It was common, during the early 1900's, to read thunderous accusations against the Standard Oil Company and its sinister captain, but the fact was that John D. Rockefeller had severed all connection with the business as early as 1897. When news came to him, ten years later, that the great Trust had been heavily fined by the government, he read the telegram and without comment went on with his game of golf. At the actual dissolution of the Trust in 1911, he was equally unconcerned. For already his interests were turning away from business management toward another absorbing role—the disposition of the wealth which was now beginning to accumulate in truly awesome amounts.

Here enters the last of those indispensable subordinates through whom Rockefeller operated so effectively. Frederick T. Gates, onetime minister, now a kind of Baptist minister-executive, met Rockefeller when Gates played a crucial role in the studies that established the need for a great new university in Chicago. Shortly he became the catalytic figure in instituting the university with a Rockefeller gift of $600,000. (Before he was done, Rockefeller would give it 80 million dollars.) Then one morning in 1889, when the two were chatting, Rockefeller suddenly said: "I am in trouble, Mr. Gates." He told him of the flood of appeals which now came by the sackful, and of his inability to give away money with any satisfaction until he had made the most thorough investigation into the cause. Rockefeller continued: "I want you to come to New York and open an office here. You can aid me in my benefactions by taking interviews and inquiries and reporting the results for action. What do you say?"

Gates said yes, and it was under his guidance, together with that of Rockefeller's son, John D., Jr., that the great philanthropies took root: the General Education Board, which pioneered in the educational, social, and medical development of our own South; the Rockefeller Institute for Medical Research, quickly famous for its campaign against yellow fever; the Rockefeller Foundation with its far-ranging interests in the promotion of research. Not that the giving was done hastily. Gates had a meticulousness of approach which suited his employer perfectly. It was not until 1900 that more than 2 million dollars was given away, not until 1905 that the total of annual giving exceeded 10 million dollars, not until 1913 that the great climactic disbursements began to be made: 45 million dollars that year and 65 million the next, to establish the Rockefeller Foundation; finally 138 million dollars in 1919 to support the philanthropies already endowed.

Gates took his philanthropic duties with ministerial zeal and profound seriousness. Raymond Fosdick, president of the Rockefeller Foundation, recalls Gates' last meeting as a trustee. Shaking his fist at the startled board, he boomed: "When you die and come to approach the judgment of Almighty God, what do you think He will demand of you? Do you for an instant presume to believe He will inquire into your petty failures or your trivial virtues? No! He will ask just one question: *'What did you do as a Trustee of the Rockefeller Foundation?'*"

Gates was more than just a philanthropic guide. Rapidly he became a prime business agent for Rockefeller in the large business deals which inevitably continued to arise. When Rockefeller came into immense iron properties along the

Mesabi Range, it was Gates who superintended their development and the creation of a giant fleet of ore carriers, and it was Gates who carried through their eventual sale to Morgan and Frick at the huge price of 88.5 million dollars. It was the only time in Gates' long association with John D. that he indicated the slightest desire to make money for himself. When the immense iron deal was complete and Gates had made his final report, Rockefeller, as usual, had no words of praise, but listened attentively and without objection and then said, with more emphasis than usual, "Thank you, Mr. Gates!" Gates looked at him with an unaccustomed glint in his eye. "Thank you is not enough, Mr. Rockefeller," he replied. Rockefeller understood and promptly saw to it that Gates was remunerated handsomely.

John D. was becoming an old man now. His face, sharper with age, took on a crinkled, masklike appearance, in the midst of which his small eyes twinkled. Golf had become a great passion and was performed in the deliberate Rockefeller manner. A boy was hired to chant: "Keep your head down," useless steps were saved by bicycling between shots, and even when he was playing alone, every stroke was remorselessly counted. (John D. was once asked to what he owed the secret of the success of Standard Oil; he answered: "To the fact that we never deceived ourselves.")

To the outside world the old man more and more presented a quaint and benevolent image. By the 1920's the antitrust passions of the 1890's and early 1900's had been transmuted into sycophancy of big business; there were no more cries of "tainted money," but only a hopeful queuing up at the portals of the great foundations. The man who had once been denounced by Theodore Roosevelt and Tolstoy and William Jennings Bryan was now voted, in a popular poll, one of the Greatest Americans. Cartoonists and feature writers made the most of his pith helmet and his paper vest, his monkishly plain food, his beaming, almost childlike expression. To the outside world he seemed to live in a serene and admirable simplicity, which indeed he did, in a purely personal sense. But the reporters who told of his afternoon drives did not report that the seventy miles of road over his estate at Pocantico Hills were built by himself, that the views he liked so well were arranged by moving hills around as an interior decorator moves chairs. The perfection of Pocantico became an obsession: some railway tracks that were in the way were relocated at the cost of $700,000, a small college that spoiled a view was induced to move for $1,500,000, a distant smokestack was camouflaged. It was, to repeat George Kaufman's famous line, an example of what God could have done if He'd only had the money.

In the midst of it all was the never-failingly polite, always slightly disengaged old man, somehow disappointing in close view, somehow smaller than we expect. There are mannerisms and eccentricities, of course, which, when viewed under the magnification of 900 million dollars, take on a certain prominence, but they are peccadilloes rather than great flaws. There is the enormous industrial generalship, to be sure, but it is a generalship of logic and plan, not of dash and daring. There is the generosity on a monumental scale, but then again, not on such a scale as to cut the Rockefeller fortune by ninety per cent, as was the case with Carnegie. Rockefeller gave away over half a billion, but probably he kept at least that much for his family.

In short, the more we look into the life of John D. Rockefeller, the more we look into the life of an incredibly successful—and withal, very unremarkable—

man. It is a curious verdict to pass on the greatest acquisitor of all time, and yet it is difficult to avoid the conclusion that John Flynn has perfectly phrased: "Rockefeller in his soul was a bookkeeper." We can see the bookkeeperishness in unexpected but telling places, such as in his *Random Reminiscences,* where he dilates on the importance of friendship, but cites as a dubious friend the man who protests, "I can't indorse your note, because I have an agreement with my partners not to. . . "; or again, when he expands on the nonmaterial pleasures of life, such as gardening, but adds as a clincher: "We make a small fortune out of ourselves, selling to our New Jersey place at $1.50 and $2.00 each, trees which originally cost us only five or ten cents at Pocantico." Whether he turns to friendship or to nature, money is the measure.

These are surely not the sentiments of greatness—but then John D. was not a great man. Neither was he, needless to say, a bad man. In most ways he was the very paragon of the business virtues of his day, and at the same time the perfect exemplar of the unvirtues as well. It is likely that he would have made his mark in any field, but unlikely that any commodity other than oil would have offered such staggering possibilities for industrial growth and personal aggrandizement. He personified in ideas the typical business thought of his day—very Christian, very conventional, very comfortable.

Yet as the image of John D. recedes, we realize the pointlessness of such personal appraisals. We study Rockefeller not so much as a person but as an agent—an agent for better and worse in the immense industrial transformation of America. Viewed against this stupendous process of change, even the largest lives take on a subordinate quality, and personal praise and blame seem almost irrelevant. And Rockefeller was not one of the largest lives—only one of the luckiest.

In the end there was only the frail ghost of a man, stubbornly resisting the inevitable. His son, John D., Jr., whom he had fondly called "my greatest fortune," had long since taken over the reins of the great foundations and had begun to refashion the Rockefeller image in his own way: Rockefeller Center, The Cloisters, the restoration of Williamsburg. His grandsons, among them one who would one day aspire to the Presidency of the United States, were already young men, carefully imbued with the family style: determination, modesty on the grand scale, a prudent balance between self-interest and altruism. And the Standard itself, now split and resplit into a handful of carefully noncollusive (and equally carefully noncompetitive) companies, was bigger and more powerful than ever. All in all, it was an extraordinary achievement, and the old man must have enjoyed it to the hilt. For it had indeed rained porridge, and his dish had surely been kept right side up.

■ ■ ■ ■ ■ ■ ■

The Diaspora in America: A Study of Jewish Immigration

David Boroff

Except for Indians, all Americans are themselves at least the descendants of immigrants; thus, it is perhaps not surprising that "native born" citizens have often displayed a kind of love–hate attitude toward newcomers. They recognize in these newcomers their own successes and failures, their pride in what they have forgotten or rejected in their heritage. This ambivalence has been exacerbated by the very real conflicts that immigration has caused. On the one hand, immigrants have always been a national asset—their labor and intelligence add to the productivity and wealth of society; their culture enriches and diversifies American civilization. On the other hand, the immigrant has represented competition, strangeness, unsettling change. Most immigrants have been poor and many upon arrival have been ill-adjusted to American values and habits. Social and economic problems have frequently resulted, especially when large numbers have flooded into the country in relatively short periods of time. This last point explains why the late nineteenth and early twentieth centuries produced the movement to restrict immigration, for the influx was greater then than at any other time.

In this essay the late David Boroff of New York University discusses the impact of Jewish immigrants on the United States and the impact of the nation on these immigrants. He focuses chiefly on the period after 1880, when Jewish immigration was heaviest. His account provides a vivid picture of the life of these people and helps explain both why they, as well as other immigrants, were sometimes disliked and why they were themselves at times ambivalent in their reactions to America.

■ ■ ■ ■ ■ ■ ■

It started with a tiny trickle and ended in a roaring flood. The first to come were just twenty-three Jews from Brazil who landed in New Amsterdam in 1654, in flight from a country no longer hospitable to them. They were, in origin, Spanish and Portuguese Jews (many with grandiloquent Iberian names) whose families had been wandering for a century and a half. New Amsterdam provided a chilly reception. Governor Peter Stuyvesant at first asked them to leave, but kinder hearts in the Dutch West India Company granted them the right to stay, "provided the poor among them ... be supported by their own nation." By the end of the century, there were perhaps one hundred Jews; by the middle of the eighteenth century, there were about three hundred in New York, and smaller communities in Newport, Philadelphia, and Charleston.

Because of their literacy, zeal, and overseas connections, colonial Jews prospered as merchants, though there were artisans and laborers among them. The

Jewish community was tightly knit, but there was a serious shortage of trained religious functionaries. There wasn't a single American rabbi, for example, until the nineteenth century. Jews were well regarded, particularly in New England. Puritan culture leaned heavily on the Old Testament, and Harvard students learned Hebrew; indeed, during the American Revolution, the suggestion was advanced that Hebrew replace English as the official language of the new country. The absence of an established national religion made it possible for Judaism to be regarded as merely another religion in a pluralistic society. The early days of the new republic were thus a happy time for Jews. Prosperous and productive, they were admitted to American communal life with few restrictions. It is little wonder that a Jewish spokesman asked rhetorically in 1820: "On what spot in this habitable Globe does an Israelite enjoy more blessings, more privileges?"

The second wave of immigration during the nineteenth century is often described as German, but that is misleading. Actually, there were many East European Jews among the immigrants who came in the half century before 1870. However, the German influence was strong, and there was a powerful undercurrent of Western enlightenment at work. These Jews came because economic depression and the Industrial Revolution had made their lot as artisans and small merchants intolerable. For some there was also the threatening backwash of the failure of the Revolution of 1848. Moreover, in Germany at this time Jews were largely disfranchised and discriminated against. During this period, between 200,000 and 400,000 Jews emigrated to this country, and the Jewish population had risen to about half a million by 1870.

This was the colorful era of the peddler and his pack. Peddling was an easy way to get started—it required little capital—and it often rewarded enterprise and daring. Jewish peddlers fanned out through the young country into farmland and mining camp, frontier and Indian territory. The more successful peddlers ultimately settled in one place as storekeepers. (Some proud businesses—including that of Senator Goldwater's family—made their start this way.) Feeling somewhat alienated from the older, settled Jews, who had a reputation for declining piety, the new immigrants organized their own synagogues and community facilities, such as cemeteries and hospitals. In general, these immigrants were amiably received by native Americans, who, unsophisticated about differences that were crucial to the immigrants themselves, regarded all Central Europeans as "Germans."

Essentially, the emigration route was the same between 1820 and 1870 as it would be in the post-1880 exodus. The travellers stayed in emigration inns while awaiting their ship, and since they had all their resources with them, they were in danger of being robbed. The journey itself was hazardous and, in the days of the sailing vessels when a good wind was indispensable, almost interminable. Nor were the appointments very comfortable even for the relatively well to do. A German Jew who made the journey in 1856 reported that his cabin, little more than six feet by six feet, housed six passengers in triple-decker bunks. When a storm raged, the passengers had to retire to their cabins lest they be washed off the deck by waves. "Deprived of air," he wrote, "it soon became unbearable in the cabins in which six seasick persons breathed." On this particular journey, sea water began to trickle into the cabins, and the planks had to be retarred.

Still, the emigration experience was a good deal easier than it would be later. For one thing, the immigrants were better educated and better acquainted with modern political and social attitudes than the oppressed and bewildered East European multitudes who came after 1880. Fewer in number, they were treated courteously by ships' captains. (On a journey in 1839, described by David Mayer, the ship's captain turned over his own cabin to the Jewish passengers for their prayers and regularly visited those Jews who were ill.) Moreover, there was still the bloom of adventure about the overseas voyage. Ships left Europe amid the booming of cannon, while on shore ladies enthusiastically waved their handkerchiefs. On the way over, there was a holiday atmosphere despite the hazards, and there was great jubilation when land was sighted.

There were, however, rude shocks when the voyagers arrived in this country. The anguish of Castle Garden and Ellis Island was well in the future when immigration first began to swell. But New York seemed inhospitable, its pace frantic, the outlook not entirely hopeful. Isaac M. Wise, a distinguished rabbi who made the journey in 1846, was appalled. "The whole city appeared to me like a large shop," he wrote, "where everyone buys or sells, cheats or is cheated. I had never before seen a city so bare of all art and of every trace of good taste; likewise I had never witnessed anywhere such rushing, hurrying, chasing, running. . . . Everything seemed so pitifully small and paltry; and I had had so exalted an idea of the land of freedom." Moreover, he no sooner landed in New York than he was abused by a German drayman whose services he had declined. "Aha! thought I," he later wrote, "you have left home and kindred in order to get away from the disgusting Judaeophobia and here the first German greeting that sounds in your ears is hep! hep!" (The expletive was a Central European equivalent of "Kike.") Another German Jew who worked as a clothing salesman was affronted by the way customers were to be "lured" into buying ("I did not think this occupation corresponded in any way to my views of a merchant's dignity").

After 1880, Jewish immigration into the United States was in flood tide. And the source was principally East Europe, where by 1880 three quarters of the world's 7.7 million Jews were living. In all, over two million Jews came to these shores in little more than three decades—about one third of Europe's Jewry. Some of them came, as their predecessors had come, because of shrinking economic opportunities. In Russia and in the Austro-Hungarian empire, the growth of large-scale agriculture squeezed out Jewish middlemen as it destroyed the independent peasantry, while in the cities the development of manufacturing reduced the need for Jewish artisans. Vast numbers of Jews became petty tradesmen or even *luftmenschen* (men without visible means of support who drifted from one thing to another). In Galicia, around 1900, there was a Jewish trader for every ten peasants, and the average value of his stock came to only twenty dollars.

Savage discrimination and pogroms also incited Jews to emigrate. The Barefoot Brigades—bands of marauding Russian peasants—brought devastation and bloodshed to Jewish towns and cities. On a higher social level, there was the "cold pogrom," a government policy calculated to destroy Jewish life. The official hope was that one third of Russia's Jews would die out, one third would emigrate, and one third would be converted to the Orthodox Church. Crushing restrictions were imposed. Jews were required to live within the Pale of Settlement in western Russia, they could not Russify their names, and they were subjected to rigorous quotas for schooling and professional training. Nor could general studies be included in the curriculum of Jewish religious schools. It was a life of poverty and fear.

Nevertheless, the *shtetl*, the typical small Jewish town, was a triumph of endurance and spiritual integrity. It was a place where degradation and squalor could not wipe out dignity, where learning flourished in the face of hopelessness, and where a tough, sardonic humor provided catharsis for the tribulations of an existence that was barely endurable. The abrasions and humiliations of everyday life were healed by a rich heritage of custom and ceremony. And there was always Sabbath—"The Bride of the Sabbath," as the Jews called the day of rest—to bring repose and exaltation to a life always sorely tried.

To be sure, even this world showed signs of disintegration. Secular learning, long resisted by East European Jews and officially denied to them, began to make inroads. Piety gave way to revolutionary fervor, and Jews began to play a heroic role in Czarist Russia's bloody history of insurrection and suppression.

This was the bleak, airless milieu from which the emigrants came. A typical expression of the Jewish attitude toward emigration from Russia—both its hopefulness and the absence of remorse—was provided by Dr. George Price, who had come to this country in one of the waves of East European emigration:

> Should this Jewish emigrant regret his leave-taking of his native land which fails to appreciate him? No! A thousand times no! He must not regret fleeing the clutches of the blood-thirsty crocodile. Sympathy for this country? How ironical it sounds! Am I not despised? Am I not urged to leave? Do I not hear the word *Zhid* constantly? . . . Be thou cursed forever my wicked homeland, because you remind me of the Inquisition . . . May you rue the day when you exiled the people who worked for your welfare.

After 1880, going to America—no other country really lured—became the great drama of redemption for the masses of East European Jews. (For some, of course, Palestine had that role even in the late nineteenth century, but these were an undaunted Zionist cadre prepared to endure the severest hardships.) The assassination of Czar Alexander II in 1881, and the subsequent pogrom, marked the beginning of the new influx. By the end of the century, 700,000 Jews had arrived, about one quarter of them totally illiterate, almost all of them impoverished. Throughout East Europe, Jews talked longingly about America as the "goldene medinah" (the golden province), and biblical imagery—"the land of milk and honey"—came easily to their lips. Those who could write were kept busy composing letters to distant kin—or even to husbands—in America. (Much of the time, the husband went first, and by abstemious living saved enough to fetch wife and children from the old country.) Children played at "emigrating games," and for the entire *shtetl* it was an exciting moment when the mail-carrier announced how many letters had arrived from America.

German steamship companies assiduously advertised the glories of the new land and provided a one-price rate from *shtetl* to New York. Emigration inns were established in Brody (in the Ukraine) and in the port cities of Bremen and Hamburg, where emigrants would gather for the trip. There were rumors that groups of prosperous German Jews would underwrite their migration to America; and in fact such people often did help their co-religionists when they were stranded without funds in the port cities of Germany. Within Russia itself, the government after 1880 more or less acquiesced in the emigration of Jews, and connived in the vast business of "stealing the border" (smuggling emigrants across). After 1892, emigration was legal—except for those of draft age—but large numbers left with forged papers, because that proved to be far easier than getting tangled in the red tape of the Czarist bureaucracy. Forged documents, to be sure, were expensive—they cost twenty-five rubles, for many Jews the equivalent of five weeks' wages. Nor was the departure from home entirely a happy event. There were the uncertainties of the new life, the fear that in America "one became a gentile." Given the Jewish aptitude for lugubriousness, a family's departure was often like a funeral, lachrymose and anguished, with the neighbors carting off the furniture that would no longer be needed.

For people who had rarely ventured beyond the boundaries of their own village, going to America was an epic adventure. They travelled with pitifully little money; the average immigrant arrived in New York with only about twenty dollars. With their domestic impedimenta—bedding, brass candlesticks, samovars—they would proceed to the port cities by rail, cart, and even on foot. At the emigration inns, they had to wait their turn. Thousands milled around, entreating officials for departure cards. There were scenes of near chaos—mothers shrieking, children crying; battered wicker trunks, bedding, utensils in wild disarray. At Hamburg, arriving emigrants were put in the "unclean" section of the *Auswandererhallen* until examined by physicians who decided whether their clothing and baggage had to be disinfected. After examination, Jews could not leave the center; other emigrants could.

The ocean voyage provided little respite. (Some elected to sail by way of Liverpool at a reduction of nine dollars from the usual rate of thirty-four dollars.) Immigrants long remembered the "smell of ship," a distillation of many putrescences. Those who went in steerage slept on mattresses filled with straw and kept their clothes on to keep warm. The berth itself was generally six feet long, two feet wide, and two and a half feet high, and it had to accommodate the passenger's luggage. Food was another problem. Many Orthodox Jews subsisted on herring, black bread, and tea which they brought because they did not trust the dietary purity of the ship's food. Some ships actually maintained a separate galley for kosher food, which was coveted by non-Jewish passengers because it was allegedly better.

Unsophisticated about travel and faced by genuine dangers, Jewish emigrants found the overseas trip a long and terrifying experience. But when land was finally sighted, the passengers often began to cheer and shout. "I looked up at the sky," an immigrant wrote years later. "It seemed much bluer and the sun much brighter than in the old country. It reminded me on [*sic*] the Garden of Eden."

Unhappily, the friendly reception that most immigrants envisioned in the new land rarely materialized. Castle Garden in the Battery, at the foot of Manhattan—and later Ellis Island in New York Harbor—proved to be almost as traumatic as the journey itself. "Castle Garden," an immigrant wrote, "is a large building, a Gehenna, through which all Jewish arrivals must pass to be cleansed before they are considered worthy of breathing freely the air of the land of the almighty dollar. . . . If in Brody, thousands crowded about, here tens of thousands thronged about; if there they were starving, here they were dying; if there they were crushed, here they were simply beaten."

One must make allowances for the impassioned hyperbole of the suffering immigrant, but there is little doubt that the immigration officials were harassed, overworked, and often unsympathetic. Authorized to pass on the admissibility of the newcomers, immigration officers struck terror into their hearts by asking questions designed to reveal their literacy and social attitudes. "How much is six times six?" an inspector asked a woman in the grip of nervousness, then casually asked the next man, "Have you ever been in jail?"

There were, of course, representatives of Jewish defense groups present, especially from the Hebrew Immigrant Aid Society. But by this time, the immigrants, out of patience and exhausted, tended to view them balefully. The Jewish officials tended to be highhanded, and the temporary barracks which they administered on Ward's Island for those not yet settled became notorious. Discontent culminated in a riot over food; one day the director—called The Father—had to swim ashore for his life, and the police were hastily summoned.

Most immigrants went directly from Castle Garden or Ellis Island to the teeming streets of Manhattan, where they sought relatives or *landsleit* (fellow townsmen) who had gone before them. Easy marks for hucksters and swindlers, they were overcharged by draymen for carrying their paltry possessions, engaged as strikebreakers, or hired at shamelessly low wages.

"Greenhorn" or "greener" was their common name. A term of vilification, the source of a thousand cruel jokes, it was their shame and their destiny. On top of everything else, the immigrants had to abide the contempt of their co-religionists who had preceded them to America by forty or fifty years. By the time the heavy East European immigration set in, German Jews had achieved high mercantile status and an uneasy integration into American society. They did not want to be reminded of their kinship with these uncouth and impoverished Jews who were regarded vaguely as a kind of Oriental influx. There was a good deal of sentiment against "aiding such paupers to emigrate to these shores." One charitable organization declared: "Organized immigration from Russia, Roumania, and other semi-barbarous countries is a mistake and has proved to be a failure. It is no relief to the Jews of Russia, Poland, etc., and it jeopardizes the well-being of the American Jews."

A genuine uptown-downtown split soon developed, with condescension on one side and resentment on the other. The German Jews objected as bitterly to the rigid, old-world Orthodoxy of the immigrants as they did to their new involvement in trade unions. They were fearful, too, of the competition they would offer in the needle trades. (Indeed, the East Europeans ultimately forced the uptown Jews out of the industry.) On the other side of the barricades, Russian Jews complained that at the hands of their uptown brethren, "every man is questioned like a criminal, is looked down upon . . . just as if he were standing before a Russian official." Nevertheless, many German Jews responded to the call of conscience by providing funds for needy immigrants and setting up preparatory schools for immigrant children for whom no room was yet available in the hopelessly overcrowded public schools.

Many comfortably settled German Jews saw dispersion as the answer to the problem. Efforts were made to divert immigrants to small towns in other parts of the country, but these were largely ineffective. There were also some gallant adventures with farming in such remote places as South Dakota, Oregon, and Louisiana. Though the Jewish pioneers were brave and idealistic, drought, disease, and ineptitude conspired against them. (In Oregon, for example, they tried to raise corn in cattle country, while in Louisiana they found themselves in malarial terrain.) Only chicken farming in New Jersey proved to be successful to any great degree. Farm jobs for Jews were available, but as one immigrant said: "I have no desire to be a farm hand to an ignorant Yankee at the end of the world. I would rather work here at half the price in a factory; for then I would at least be able to spend my free evenings with my friends."

It was in New York, then, that the bulk of the immigrants settled—in the swarming, tumultuous Lower East Side—with smaller concentrations in Boston, Philadelphia, and Chicago. Far less adaptable than the German Jews who were now lording it over them, disoriented and frightened, the East European immigrants constituted a vast and exploited proletariat. According to a survey in 1890, sixty per cent of all immigrant Jews worked in the needle trades. This industry had gone through a process of decentralization in which contractors carried out the bulk of production, receiving merely the cut goods from the manufacturer. Contracting establishments were everywhere in the Lower East Side, including the contractors' homes, where pressers warmed their irons on the very stove on which the boss's wife was preparing supper. The contractors also gave out "section" work to families and *landsleit* who would struggle to meet the quotas at home. The bondage of the sewing machine was therefore extended into the tenements, with entire families enslaved by the machine's voracious demands. The Hester Street "pig market," where one could buy anything, became the labor exchange; there tailors, operators, finishers, basters, and pressers would congregate on Saturday in the hope of being hired by contractors.

Life in the sweatshops of the Lower East Side was hard, but it made immigrants employable from the start, and a weekly wage of five dollars—the equivalent of ten rubles—looked good in immigrant eyes. Moreover, they were among their own kin and kind, and the sweatshops, noisome as they were, were still the scene of lively political and even literary discussions. (In some cigar-making shops, in fact, the bosses hired "readers" to keep the minds of the workers occupied with classic and Yiddish literature as they performed their repetitive chores.) East European Jews, near the end of the century, made up a large part of the skilled labor force in New York, ranking first in twenty-six out of forty-seven trades, and serving, for example, as bakers, building-trade workers, painters, furriers, jewellers, and tinsmiths.

Almost one quarter of all the immigrants tried their hands as tradesmen—largely as peddlers or as pushcart vendors in the madhouse bazaar of the Lower East Side. For some it was an apprenticeship in low-toned commerce that would lead to more elegant careers. For others it was merely a martyrdom that enabled them to subsist. It was a modest enough investment—five dollars for a license, one

dollar for a basket, and four dollars for wares. They stocked up on pins and needles, shoe laces, polish, and handkerchiefs, learned some basic expressions ("You
wanna buy somethin'?"), and were on their hapless way.

It was the professions, of course, that exerted the keenest attraction to Jews,
with their reverence for learning. For most of them it was too late; they had to reconcile themselves to more humble callings. But it was not too late for their children, and between 1897 and 1907, the number of Jewish physicians in Manhattan
rose from 450 to 1,000. Of all the professions it was medicine that excited the greatest veneration. (Some of this veneration spilled over into pharmacy, and "druggists"
were highly respected figures who were called upon to prescribe for minor—and
even major—ills, and to serve as scribes for the letters that the immigrants were unable to read and write themselves.) There were Jewish lawyers on the Lower East
Side and by 1901 over 140 Jewish policemen, recruited in part by Theodore Roosevelt, who, as police commissioner, had issued a call for "the Maccabee or fighting
Jewish type."

The Lower East Side was the American counterpart of the ghetto for Jewish immigrants, as well as their glittering capital. At its peak, around 1910, it packed over
350,000 people into a comparatively small area—roughly from Canal Street to
Fourteenth Street—with as many as 523 people per acre, so that Arnold Bennett
was moved to remark that "the architecture seemed to sweat humanity at every window and door." The most densely populated part of the city, it held one sixth of
Manhattan's population and most of New York's office buildings and factories. "Up-
towners" used to delight in visiting it (as a later generation would visit Harlem) to
taste its exotic flavor. But the great mass of Jews lived there because the living was
cheap, and there was a vital Jewish community that gave solace to the lonely and
comfort to the pious.

A single man could find lodgings of a sort, including coffee morning and
night, for three dollars a month. For a family, rent was about ten dollars a month,
milk was four cents a quart, kosher meat twelve cents a pound, bread two cents a
pound, herring a penny or two. A kitchen table could be bought for a dollar, chairs
at thirty-five cents each. One managed, but the life was oppressive. Most families
lived in the notorious "dumbbell" flats of old-law tenements (built prior to 1901).
Congested, often dirty and unsanitary, these tenements were six or seven stories
high and had four apartments on each floor. Only one room in each three or four
room apartment received direct air and sunlight, and the families on each floor
shared a toilet in the hall.

Many families not only used their flats as workshops but also took in boarders
to make ends meet. Jacob Riis tells of a two-room apartment on Allen Street which
housed parents, six children, and six boarders. "Two daughters sewed clothes at
home. The elevator railway passed by the window. The cantor rehearses, a train
passes, the shoemaker bangs, ten brats run around like goats, the wife putters. . . .
At night we all try to get some sleep in the stifling, roach-infested two rooms." In
the summer, the tenants spilled out into fire escapes and rooftops, which were converted into bedrooms.

Nevertheless, life on the Lower East Side had surprising vitality. Despite the
highest population density in the city, the Tenth Ward had one of the lowest death

The immigrants' new home: a crowded, noisy, but friendly street on New York's Lower East Side.

rates. In part, this was because of the strenuous personal cleanliness of Jews, dictated by their religion. Though only eight per cent of the East European Jews had baths, bathhouses and steam rooms on the Lower East Side did a booming business. There was, of course, a heavy incidence of tuberculosis—"the white plague." Those who were afflicted could be heard crying out, "*Luft! Gib mir luft!*" ("Air! Give me air!"). It was, in fact, this terror of "consumption" that impelled some East Side Jews to become farmers in the Catskills at the turn of the century, thus forerunning the gaudy career of the Catskill Borscht Belt resort hotels. The same fear impelled Jews on the Lower East Side to move to Washington Heights and the Bronx, where the altitude was higher, the air presumably purer.

Alcoholism, a prime afflication of most immigrant groups, was almost unknown among Jews. They drank ritualistically on holidays but almost never to excess. They were, instead, addicted to seltzer or soda water—Harry Golden's "2¢ plain"—which they viewed as "the worker's champagne." The suicide rate was relatively low, though higher than in the *shtetl,* and there was always a shudder of sympathy when the Yiddish press announced that someone had *genumen di ges* (taken gas).

The Lower East Side was from the start the scene of considerable crime. But its inhabitants became concerned when the crime rate among the young people seemed to rise steeply around 1910. There was a good deal of prostitution. The dancing academies, which achieved popularity early in this century, became recruiting centers for prostitutes. In 1908–9, of 581 foreign women arrested for prostitution, 225 were Jewish. There was the notorious Max Hochstim Association, which actively recruited girls, while the New York Independent Benevolent Association—an organization of pimps—provided sick benefits, burial privileges, bail, and protection money for prostitutes. The membership was even summoned to funerals with a two-dollar fine imposed on those who did not attend. Prostitution was so taken for granted that Canal Street had stores on one side featuring sacerdotal articles, while brothels were housed on the other.

Family life on the Lower East Side was cohesive and warm, though there was an edge of shrillness and hysteria to it. Marriages were not always happy, but if wives were viewed as an affliction, children were regarded as a blessing. The kitchen was the center of the household, and food was almost always being served to either family or visitors. No matter how poor they were, Jewish families ate well—even to excess—and mothers considered their children woefully underweight unless they were well cushioned with fat.

It was a life with few conventional graces. Handkerchiefs were barely known, and the Yiddish newspapers had to propagandize for their use. Old men smelled of snuff, and in spite of bathing, children often had lice in their hair and were sent home from school by the visiting nurse for a kerosene bath. Bedbugs were considered an inevitability, and pajamas were viewed as an upper-class affectation. Parents quarrelled bitterly—with passionate and resourceful invective—in the presence of their children. Telephones were virtually unknown, and a telegram surely meant disaster from afar.

The zeal of the immigrants on behalf of their children was no less than awe-inspiring. Parents yearned for lofty careers for their offspring, with medicine at the pinnacle. In better-off homes, there was always a piano ("solid mahogany"), and parents often spent their precious reserves to arrange a "concert" for their precocious youngsters, followed by a ball in one of the Lower East Side's many halls.

To be sure, the children inspired a full measure of anxiety in their parents. "Amerikane kinder" was the rueful plaint of the elders, who could not fathom the baffling new ways of the young. Parents were nervous about their daughters' chastity, and younger brothers—often six or seven years old—would be dispatched as chaperones when the girls met their boy friends. There was uneasiness about Jewish street gangs and the growing problem of delinquency. The old folks were vexed by the new tides of secularism and political radicalism that were weaning their children from traditional pieties. But most of all, they feared that their sons would not achieve the success that would redeem their own efforts, humiliations, and failures in the harsh new land. Pressure on their children was relentless. But on the whole the children did well, astonishingly well. "The ease and rapidity with which they learn," Jacob Riis wrote, "is equalled only by their good behavior and close attention while in school. There is no whispering and no rioting at these desks." Samuel Chotzinoff, the music critic, tells a story which reveals the attitude of the Jewish schoolboy. When an altercation threatened between Chotzinoff and a classmate, his antagonist's reaction was to challenge him to spell "combustible."

The Lower East Side was a striking demonstration that financial want does not necessarily mean cultural poverty. The immigrant Jews were nearly always poor and often illiterate, but they were not culturally deprived. In fact, between 1890 and World War I, the Jewish community provides a remarkable chapter in American cultural history. Liberated from the constrictions of European captivity, immigrant Jews experienced a great surge of intellectual vitality. Yiddish, the Hebrew-German dialect which some people had casually dismissed as a barbarous "jargon," became the vehicle of this cultural renascence. Between 1885 and 1914, over 150 publications of all kinds made their appearance. But the new Yiddish journalism reached its apogee with the *Jewish Daily Forward* under the long editorial reign of Abraham Cahan. The *Forward* was humanitarian, prolabor, and socialistic. But it was also an instrument for acclimatizing immigrants in the new environment. It provided practical hints on how to deal with the new world, letters from the troubled *(Bintel Brief),* and even, at one time, a primer on baseball ("explained to non-sports"). The *Forward* also published and fostered an enormous amount of literature in Yiddish—both original works by writers of considerable talent, and translations of classic writers.

In this cultural ferment, immigrants studied English in dozens of night schools and ransacked the resources of the Aguilar Free Library on East Broadway. "When I had [a] book in my hand," an immigrant wrote, "I pressed it to my heart and wanted to kiss it." The Educational Alliance, also on East Broadway, had a rich program designed to make immigrant Jews more American and their sons more Jewish. And there were scores of settlement houses, debating clubs, ethical societies, and literary circles which attracted the young. In fact, courtships were carried on in a rarefied atmosphere full of lofty talk about art, politics, and philosophy. And though there was much venturesome palaver about sexual freedom, actual behavior tended to be quite strait-laced.

But the most popular cultural institution was the café or coffee house, which served as the Jewish saloon. There were about 250 of them, each with its own following. Here the litterateurs sat for hours over steaming glasses of tea; revolutionaries and Bohemians gathered to make their pronouncements or raise money for causes; actors and playwrights came to hold court. For immigrant Jews, talk was the breath of life itself. The passion for music and theatre knew no bounds. When Beethoven's Ninth Symphony was performed one summer night in 1915, mounted police had to be summoned to keep order outside Lewisohn Stadium, so heavy was the press of crowds eager for the twenty-five-cent stone seats. Theatre (in Yiddish) was to the Jewish immigrants what Shakespeare and Marlowe had been to the groundlings in Elizabethan England. Tickets were cheap—twenty-five cents to one dollar—and theatregoing was universal. It was a raucous, robust, and communal experience. Mothers brought their babies (except in some of the "swellest" theatres, which forbade it), and peddlers hawked their wares between the acts. There were theatre parties for trade unions and *landsmanschaften* (societies of fellow townsmen), and the audience milled around and renewed old friendships or argued the merits of the play. The stage curtain had bold advertisements of stores or blown-up portraits of stars.

There was an intense cult of personality in the Yiddish theatre and a system of claques not unlike that which exists in grand opera today. The undisputed monarch was Boris Thomashefsky, and a theatre program of his day offered this panegyric:

Thomashefsky! Artist great!
No praise is good enough for you!
Of all the stars you remain the king
You seek no tricks, no false quibbles;
One sees truth itself playing.
Your appearance is godly to us
Every movement is full of grace
Pleasing is your every gesture
Sugar sweet your every turn
You remain the king of the stage
Everything falls to your feet.

Many of the plays were sentimental trash—heroic "operas" on historical themes, "greenhorn" melodramas full of cruel abandonments and tearful re-unions, romantic musicals, and even topical dramas dealing with such immediate events as the Homestead Strike, the Johnstown Flood, and the Kishinev Pogrom of 1903. Adaptability and a talent for facile plagiarism were the essence of the play-wright's art in those days, and "Professor" Moses Horwitz wrote 167 plays, most of them adaptations of old operas and melodramas. The plays were so predictable that an actor once admitted he didn't even have to learn his lines; he merely had to have a sense of the general situation and then adapt lines from other plays.

There was, of course, a serious Yiddish drama, introduced principally by Jacob Gordin, who adapted classical and modernist drama to the Yiddish stage. Jewish in-tellectuals were jubilant at this development. But the process of acculturation had its amusing and grotesque aspects. Shakespeare was a great favorite but "*verbessert and vergrossert*" (improved and enlarged). There was the Jewish *King Lear* in which Cordelia becomes Goldele. (The theme of filial ingratitude was a "natural" on the Lower East Side, where parents constantly made heroic sacrifices.) *Hamlet* was also given a Jewish coloration, the prince becoming a rabbinical student who returns from the seminary to discover treachery at home. And *A Doll's House* by Ibsen was transformed into *Minna,* in which a sensitive and intelligent young woman, mar-ried to an ignorant laborer, falls in love with her boarder and ultimately commits suicide.

Related to the Jewish love of theatre was the immigrant's adoration of the can-tor, a profession which evoked as much flamboyance and egotistical preening as acting did. (In fact, actors would sometimes grow beards before the high holy-days and find jobs as cantors.) Synagogues vied with each other for celebrated cantors, sometimes as a way of getting out of debt, since tickets were sold for the high-holy-day services.

The Lower East Side was a vibrant community, full of color and gusto, in which the Jewish immigrant felt marvelously at home, safe from the terrors of the alien city. But it was a setting too for fierce conflict and enervating strain. There were three major influences at work, each pulling in a separate direction: Jewish Ortho-doxy, assimilationism, and the new socialist gospel. The immigrants were Ortho-dox, but their children tended to break away. *Cheders* (Hebrew schools) were every-where, in basements and stores and tenements, and the old custom of giving a child a taste of honey when he was beginning to learn to read—as symbolic of the sweetness of study—persisted. But the young, eager to be accepted into American society, despised the old ways and their "greenhorn" teachers. Fathers began to view their sons as "freethinkers," a term that was anathema to them. Observance of the Law declined, and the Saturday Sabbath was ignored by many Jews. A virulent antireligious tendency developed among many "enlightened" Jews, who would hold profane balls on the most sacred evening of the year—Yom Kippur—at which they would dance and eat nonkosher food. (Yom Kippur is a fast day.) And the trade-union movement also generated uneasiness among the pious elders of the Lower East Side. "Do you want us to bow down to your archaic God?" a radical newspaper asked. "Each era has its new Torah. Ours is one of freedom and justice."

But for many immigrants the basic discontent was with their American experience itself. The golden province turned out to be a place of tenements and sweatshops. A familiar cry was "*a klug af Columbus!*" ("a curse on Columbus") or, "Who ever asked him, Columbus, to discover America?" Ellis Island was called *Trernindzl* (Island of Tears), and Abraham Cahan, in his initial reaction to the horrors of immigration, thundered: "Be cursed, immigration! Cursed by those conditions which have brought you into being. How many souls have you broken, how many courageous and mighty souls have you shattered." The fact remains that most Jewish immigrants, in the long run, made a happy adjustment to their new land.

After 1910, the Lower East Side went into a decline. Its strange glory was over. New areas of Jewish settlement opened up in Brooklyn, the Bronx, and in upper Manhattan. By the mid-twenties, less than ten per cent of New York's Jews lived on the Lower East Side, although it still remained the heartland to which one returned to shop, to see Yiddish theatre, and to renew old ties. By 1924 Jewish immigration into the United States was severely reduced by new immigration laws, and the saga of mass immigration was done. But the intensities of the Jewish immigrant experience had already made an indelible mark on American culture and history that would endure for many years.

The Age of the Bosses

William V. Shannon

The rapid industrialization of the United States after the Civil War, which produced great tycoons such as Andrew Carnegie and encouraged millions of work-hungry Europeans to migrate, changed the shape of society in a variety of ways. One of the most obvious and important of these was industrialization's effect on where and how people lived. Huge industrial concerns brought together masses of workers in one place; commercial and service enterprises sprang up alongside the factories; in short, great cities rapidly developed and America was on its way to becoming an urban nation.

The advantages of urbanization were great—new wealth, better educational opportunities, a wide range of amusements; soon a more refined and complex culture emerged. But great problems also appeared—crowded, unhealthy living conditions, crime and vice, and countless others. Not the least of these was the problem of how to govern these gigantic agglomerations. More government was essential to run a city, yet the nation had lived for the better part of a century by the motto: "that government is best which governs least." New kinds of government were necessary—building and sanitary codes, social services, a system of representation suited to a mass but atomized society—for which no precedents existed.

It was this situation, as William V. Shannon explains, that produced the big-city political machines and the bosses who ran them. Shannon shows that the bosses served a function; they filled a gap in the political system created by the changes resulting from swift industrialization and urban growth. Eventually better machinery than the "machine" was devised to perform that function, although the proper government of cities still eludes us today. As a former editor of the *New York Times,* Mr. Shannon brings to this subject a thorough knowledge of modern urban politics and, as the author of *The American Irish,* an equally solid understanding of the old boss system.

■ ■ ■ ■ ■ ■ ■

The big cities and the political bosses grew up together in America. Bossism, with all its color and corruption and human drama, was a natural, perhaps even a necessary accompaniment to the rapid development of cities. The new urban communities did not grow slowly and according to plan; on the contrary, huge conglomerations of people from all over the world and from widely varying backgrounds came together suddenly, and in an unplanned, unorganized fashion fumbled their way toward communal relationships and a common identity. The political bosses emerged to cope with this chaotic change and growth. Acting out of greed, a ruthless will for mastery, and an imperfect understanding of what they were about, the bosses imposed upon these conglomerations called cities a certain feudal order and direction.

By 1890 virtually every sizable city had a political boss or was in the process of developing one. By 1950, sixty years later, almost every urban political machine was in an advanced state of obsolescence and its boss in trouble. The reason is not hard to find. Some of the cities kept growing and all of them kept changing, but the bosses, natural products of a specific era, could not grow or change beyond a certain point. The cities became essentially different, and as they did, the old-style organizations, like all organisms which cannot adapt, began to die. The dates vary from city to city. The system began earlier and died sooner in New York. Here or there, an old-timer made one last comeback. In Chicago, the organization and its boss still survive. But exceptions aside, the late nineteenth century saw the beginning, and the middle twentieth, the end, of the Age of the Bosses. What follows is a brief history of how it began, flourished, and passed away.

Soft-spoken Irish farmers from County Mayo and bearded Jews from Poland, country boys from Ohio and sturdy peasants from Calabria, gangling Swedes from near the Arctic Circle and Chinese from Canton, laconic Yankees from Vermont villages and Negro freedmen putting distance between themselves and the old plantation—all these and many other varieties of human beings from every national and religious and cultural tradition poured into America's cities in the decades after the Civil War.

Rome and Alexandria in the ancient world had probably been as polyglot, but in modern times the diversity of American cities was unique. Everywhere in the Western world, cities were growing rapidly in the late nineteenth century; but the Germans from the countryside who migrated to Hamburg and Berlin, the English who moved to Birmingham and London, and the French who flocked to Paris stayed among fellow nationals. They might be mocked as country bumpkins and their clothes might be unfashionable, but everyone they met spoke the same language as themselves, observed the same religious and secular holidays, ate the same kind of food, voted—if they had the franchise at all—in the same elections, and shared the same sentiments and expectations. To move from farm or village to a big European city was an adventure, but one still remained within the reassuring circle of the known and the familiar.

In American cities, however, the newcomers had nothing in common with one another except their poverty and their hopes. They were truly "the up-rooted." The foreign-born, unless they came from the British Isles, could not speak the language of their new homeland. The food, the customs, the holidays, the politics, were alien. Native Americans migrating to the cities from the countryside experienced their own kind of cultural shock: they found themselves competing not with other Americans but with recently arrived foreigners, so that despite their native birth they, too, felt displaced, strangers in their own country.

It was natural for members of each group to come together to try to find human warmth and protection in Little Italy or Cork Hill or Chinatown or Harlem. These feelings of clannish solidarity were one basis of strength for the political bosses. A man will more readily give his vote to a candidate because he is a neighbor from the old country or has some easily identifiable relationship, if only a similar name or the same religion, than because of agreement on some impersonal issue. Voters can take vicarious satisfaction from his success: "One of our boys is making good."

With so many different races and nationalities living together, however, mutual antagonisms were present, and the opportunity for hostility to flare into open violence was never far away. Ambitious, unscrupulous politicians could have exploited these antagonisms for their own political advantage, but the bosses and the political organizations which they developed did not function that way. If a man could vote and would "vote right," he was accepted, and that was the end of the matter. What lasting profit was there in attacking his religion or deriding his background?

Tammany early set the pattern of cultivating every bloc and faction and making an appeal as broad-based as possible. Of one precinct captain on the Lower East Side it was said: "He eats corned beef and kosher meat with equal nonchalance, and it's all the same to him whether he takes off his hat in the church or pulls it down over his ears in the synagogue."

Bosses elsewhere instinctively followed the same practice. George B. Cox, the turn-of-the-century Republican boss of Cincinnati, pasted together a coalition of Germans, Negroes, and old families like the Tafts and the Longworths. James M. Curley, who was mayor of Boston on and off for thirty-six years and was its closest approximation to a political boss, ran as well in the Lithuanian neighborhood of South Boston and the Italian section of East Boston as he did in the working-class Irish wards. In his last term in City Hall, he conferred minor patronage on the growing Negro community and joined the N.A.A.C.P.

The bosses organized neighborhoods, smoothed out antagonisms, arranged ethnically balanced tickets, and distributed patronage in accordance with voting strength as part of their effort to win and hold power. They blurred divisive issues and buried racial and religious hostility with blarney and buncombe. They were not aware that they were actually performing a mediating, pacifying function. They did not realize that by trying to please as many people as possible they were helping to hold raw new cities together, providing for inexperienced citizens a common meeting ground in politics and an experience in working together that would not have been available if the cities had been governed by apolitical bureaucracies. Bossism was usually corrupt and was decidedly inefficient, but in the 1960's, when antipoverty planners try to stimulate "community action organizations" to break through the apathy and disorganization of the slums, we can appreciate that the old-style machines had their usefulness.

When William Marcy Tweed, the first and most famous of the big-city bosses, died in jail in 1878, several hundred workingmen showed up for his funeral. The *Nation* wrote the following week:

> Let us remember that he fell without loss of reputation among the bulk of his supporters. The bulk of the poorer voters of this city today revere his memory, and look on him as the victim of rich men's malice; as, in short, a friend of the needy who applied the public funds, with as little waste as was possible under the circumstances, to the purposes to which they ought to be applied—and that is to the making of work for the working man. The odium heaped on him in the pulpits last Sunday does not exist in the lower stratum of New York society.

This split in attitude toward political bosses between the impoverished many and the prosperous middle classes lingers today and still colors historical writing. To respectable people, the boss was an exotic, even grotesque figure. They found it hard to understand why anyone would vote for him or what the sources of his popularity were. To the urban poor, those sources were self-evident. The boss ran a kind of ramshackle welfare state. He helped the unemployed find jobs, interceded in court for boys in trouble, wrote letters home to the old country for the illiterate; he provided free coal and baskets of food to tide a widow over an emergency, and organized parades, excursions to the beach, and other forms of free entertainment. Some bosses, such as Frank Hague in Jersey City and Curley in Boston, were energetic patrons of their respective city hospitals, spending public funds lavishly on new construction, providing maternity and children's clinics, and arranging medical care for the indigent. In an era when social security, Blue Cross, unemployment compensation, and other public and private arrangements to cushion life's shocks did not exist, these benefactions from a political boss were important.

In every city, the boss had his base in the poorer, older, shabbier section of town. Historians have dubbed this section the "walking city" because it developed in the eighteenth and early nineteenth centuries, when houses and businesses were jumbled together, usually near the waterfront, and businessmen and laborers alike had to live within walking distance of their work. As transportation improved, people were able to live farther and farther from their place of work. Population dispersed in rough concentric circles: the financially most successful lived in the outer ring, where land was plentiful and the air was clean; the middle classes lived in intermediate neighborhoods; and the poorest and the latest arrivals from Europe crowded into the now-rundown neighborhoods in the center, where rents were lowest. Politics in most cities reflected a struggle between the old, boss-run wards downtown and the more prosperous neighborhoods farther out, which did not need a boss's services and which championed reform. The more skilled workingmen and the white-collar workers who lived in the intermediate neighborhoods generally held the balance of power between the machine and the reformers. A skillful boss could hold enough of these swing voters on the basis of ethnic loyalty or shared support of a particular issue. At times, he might work out alliances with business leaders who found that an understanding with a boss was literally more businesslike than dependence upon the vagaries of reform.

But always it was the poorest and most insecure who provided the boss with the base of his political power. Their only strength, as Professor Richard C. Wade of the University of Chicago has observed, was in their numbers.

> These numbers were in most cases a curse; housing never caught up with demand, the job market was always flooded, the breadwinner had too many mouths to feed. Yet in politics such a liability could be turned into an asset. If the residents could be mobilized, their combined strength would be able to do what none could do alone. Soon the "boss" and the "machine" arose to organize this potential. The boss system was simply the political expression of inner city life.

At a time when many newcomers to the city were seeking unskilled work, and when many families had a precarious economic footing, the ability to dispense jobs was crucial to the bosses. First, there were jobs to be filled on the city payroll. Just as vital, and far more numerous, were jobs on municipal construction projects. When the machine controlled a city, public funds were always being spent for more schools, hospitals, libraries, courthouses, and orphanages. The growing cities had to have more sewer lines, gas lines, and waterworks, more paved streets and trolley tracks. Even if these utilities were privately owned, the managers needed the good-will of city hall and were responsive to suggestions about whom to hire.

The payrolls of these public works projects were often padded, but to those seeking a job, it was better to be on a padded payroll than on no payroll. By contrast, the municipal reformers usually cut back on public spending, stopped projects to investigate for graft, and pruned payrolls. Middle- and upper-income taxpayers welcomed these reforms, but they were distinctly unpopular in working-class wards.

Another issue that strengthened the bosses was the regulation of the sale of liquor. Most women in the nineteenth century did not drink, and with their backing, the movement to ban entirely the manufacture and sale of liquor grew steadily stronger. It had its greatest support among Protestants with a rural or small-town background. To them the cities, with their saloons, dance halls, cheap theatres, and red-light districts, were becoming latter-day versions of Sodom and Gomorrah.

Many of the European immigrants in the cities, however, had entirely different values. Quite respectable Germans took their wives to beer gardens on Sundays. In the eyes of the Irish, keeping a "public house" was an honorable occupation. Some Irish women drank beer and saw no harm in going to the saloon or sending an older child for a bucketful—"rushing the growler," they called it. Poles, Czechs, Italians, and others also failed to share the rage of the Prohibitionists against saloons. Unable to entertain in their cramped tenements, they liked to congregate in neighborhood bars.

The machine also appealed successfully on the liquor issue to many middle-class ethnic voters who had no need of the machine's economic assistance. Thus, in New York in 1897, Tammany scored a sweeping victory over an incumbent reform administration that had tried to enforce a state law permitting only hotels to sell liquor on Sundays. As one of the city's three police commissioners, Theodore Roosevelt became famous prowling the tougher neighborhoods on the hunt for saloon violations, but on the vaudeville stage the singers were giving forth with the hit song, "I Want What I Want When I Want It!" As a character in Alfred Henry Lewis' novel *The Boss* explained it, the reformers had made a serious mistake: "They got between the people and its beer!"

In 1902, Lincoln Steffens, the muckraker who made a name for himself writing about political bossism, visited St. Louis to interview Joseph W. Folk, a crusading district attorney. "It is good businessmen that are corrupting our bad politicians," Folk told him. "It is good business that causes bad government in St. Louis." Thirty-five years later, Boss Tom Pendergast was running the entire state of Missouri on that same reciprocal relationship.

Although many factory owners could be indifferent to politics, other business-men were dependent upon the goodwill and the efficiency of the municipal government. The railroads that wanted to build their freight terminals and extend their lines into the cities, the contractors who erected the office buildings, the banks that held mortgages on the land and loaned money for the construction, the utility and transit companies, and the department stores were all in need of licenses, franchises, rights of way, or favorable rulings from city inspectors and agencies. These were the businesses that made the big pay-offs to political bosses in cash, blocks of stock, or tips on land about to be developed.

In another sense, profound, impersonal, and not corrupt, the business community needed the boss. Because the Industrial Revolution hit this country when it was still thinly populated and most of its cities were overgrown towns, American cities expanded with astonishing speed. For example, in the single decade from 1880 to 1890, Chicago's population more than doubled, from a half million to over a million. Minneapolis and St. Paul tripled in size. New York City increased from a million to a million and a half; Detroit, Milwaukee, Columbus, and Cleveland grew by sixty to eighty per cent.

Municipal governments, however, were unprepared for this astonishing growth. Planning and budgeting were unknown arts. City charters had restrictive provisions envisaged for much smaller, simpler communities. The mayor and the important commissioners were usually amateurs serving a term or two as a civic duty. Authority was dispersed among numerous boards and special agencies. A typical city would have a board of police commissioners, a board of health, a board of tax assessors, a water board, and many others. The ostensible governing body was a city council or board of aldermen which might have thirty, fifty, or even a hundred members. Under these circumstances, it was difficult to get a prompt decision, harder still to coordinate decisions taken by different bodies acting on different premises, and easy for delays and anomalies to develop.

In theory, the cities could have met their need for increased services by municipal socialism, but the conventional wisdom condemned that as too radical, although here and there a city did experiment with publicly owned utilities. In theory also, the cities could have financed public buildings and huge projects such as water and sewer systems by frankly raising taxes or floating bonds. But both taxes and debt were no more popular then than they are now. Moreover, the laissez-faire doctrine which holds that "that government is best which governs least" was enshrined orthodoxy in America from the 1870's down to the 1930's.

As men clung to such orthodox philosophies, the structures of government became obsolete; they strained to meet unexpected demands as a swelling number of citizens in every class clamored for more services. In this climate the bosses emerged. They had no scruples about taking shortcuts through old procedures or manipulating independent boards and agencies in ways that the original city fathers had never intended. They had no inhibiting commitment to any theory of limited government. They were willing to spend, tax, and build—and to take the opprobrium along with the graft. Sometimes, like Hague in Jersey City, Curley in Boston, and Big Bill Thompson in Chicago, they got themselves elected mayor and openly assumed responsibility. More often, like Pendergast in Kansas City, Cox in Cincinnati, the leaders of Tammany, and the successive Republican bosses of Philadelphia, they held minor offices or none, stayed out of the limelight, and ran city government through their iron control of the party organization. In ruling Memphis for forty years, Ed Crump followed one pattern and then the other. Impeached on a technicality after being elected three times as mayor, Crump retreated to the back rooms and became even more powerful as the city's political boss.

What manner of men became political bosses? They were men of little education and no social background, often of immigrant parentage. A college-educated boss like Edward Flynn of The Bronx was a rarity. Bosses often began as saloonkeepers, because the saloon was a natural meeting place in poorer neighborhoods in the days before Prohibition. They were physically strong and no strangers to violence. Seventy-five years ago, most men made their living with brawn rather than brain, and a man who expected to be a leader of men had to be tough as well as shrewd. Open violence used to be common at polling places on Election Day, and gangs of repeaters roamed from one precinct to another. Although the typical boss made his way up through that roughneck system, the logic of his career led him to suppress violence. Bloody heads make bad publicity, and it is hard for any political organization to maintain a monopoly on violence. Bosses grew to prefer quieter, more lawful, less dangerous methods of control. Ballot-box stuffing and overt intimidation never disappeared entirely, but gradually they receded to weapons of last resort.

Political bosses varied in their idiosyncrasies and styles. A few, like Curley, became polished orators; others, like the legendary Charles Murphy of Tammany Hall, never made speeches. They were temperate, businesslike types; among them a drunk was as rare as a Phi Beta Kappa. If they had a generic failing it was for horses and gambling. Essentially they were hardheaded men of executive temper and genuine organizing talents; many, in other circumstances and with more education, might have become successful businessmen.

They have disappeared now, most of them. Education has produced a more sophisticated electorate; it has also encouraged potential bosses to turn away from politics toward more secure, prestigious, and profitable careers. A young man who had the energy, persistence, and skill in 1899 to become a successful political boss would in 1969 go to college and end up in an executive suite.

The urban population has also changed. The great flood of bewildered foreigners has dwindled to a trickle. In place of the European immigrants of the past, today's cities receive an influx of Negroes from the rural South, Puerto Ricans, Mexicans, and the white poor from Appalachia. As they overcome the language barrier and widen their experience, the Puerto Ricans are making themselves felt in urban politics. New York City, where they are most heavily concentrated, may have a Puerto Rican mayor in the not too distant future.

But the other groups are too isolated from the rest of the community to put together a winning political coalition of have-nots. The Mexicans and the ex-hillbillies from Appalachia are isolated by their unique cultural backgrounds, the Negroes by the giant fact of their race. Inasmuch as they make up a quarter to a third of the population in many cities, are a cohesive group, and still have a high propor-

In this contemporary cartoon, Michael Ramus has pictured Chicago Mayor Richard J. Daley as "The Last Leaf" on the blasted tree of old-style urban bosses.

tion of poor who have to look to government for direct help, the Negroes might have produced several bosses and functioning political machines had they been of white European ancestry. But until Negroes attain a clear numerical majority, they find it difficult to take political power in any city because various white factions are reluctant to coalesce with them.

Regardless of the race or background of the voters, however, there are factors which work against the old-style machines. Civil service regulations make it harder to create a job or pad a payroll. Federal income taxes and federal accounting requirements make it more difficult to hide the rewards of graft. Television, public relations, and polling have created a whole new set of political techniques and undermined the personal ties and neighborhood loyalties on which the old organizations depended.

The new political style has brought an increase in municipal government efficiency and probably some decline in political corruption and misrule. But the politics of the television age puts a premium on hypocrisy. Candor has gone out the window with the spoils system. There is still a lot of self-seeking in politics and always will be. But gone are the days of Tammany's Boss Richard Croker, who when asked by an investigating committee if he was "working for his own pocket," shot back: "All the time—same as you." Today's politicians are so busy tending their images that they have become incapable of even a mildly derogatory remark such as Jim Curley's: "The term 'codfish aristocracy' is a reflection on the fish."

Curley entitled his memoirs *I'd Do It Again.* But the rough-and-tumble days when two-fisted, rough-tongued politicians came roaring out of the slums to take charge of America's young cities are not to come again.

■ ■ ■ ■ ■ ■ ■

The Myth of the Happy Yeoman

Richard Hofstadter

The following essay, like Oliver La Farge's essay on the American Indian in Volume One, is a study in the differences between reality and people's view of reality. Usually the historian seeks only for the reality and discards the myths that surround it in the records of the past. But in some contexts the myths themselves are vitally important and thus the proper subject of historical analysis.

The concept of the yeoman farmer had, as the late Professor Richard Hofstadter of Columbia University demonstrates, a solid basis in fact in early America. Farming was for many a way of life, not primarily a way of making a living. But national growth and development changed this steadily, and after the rapid expansion of industrialization the true yeoman practically disappeared. Why the myth persisted is the subject of Hofstadter's inquiry. The tale is part of the larger story of the impact of the Industrial Revolution on American thought, a subject Hofstadter developed at greater length in his Pulitzer Prize–winning history, *The Age of Reform.*

▪ ▪ ▪ ▪ ▪ ▪ ▪

The United States was born in the country and has moved to the city. From the beginning its political values as well as ideas were of necessity shaped by country life. The early American politician, the country editor, who wished to address himself to the common man, had to draw upon a rhetoric that would touch the tillers of the soil; and even the spokesman of city people knew that his audience had been in very large part reared upon the farm.

But what the articulate people who talked and wrote about farmers and farming—the preachers, poets, philosophers, writers, and statesmen—liked about American farming was not, in every respect, what the typical working farmer liked. For the articulate people were drawn irresistibly to the noncommercial, non-pecuniary, self-sufficient aspect of American farm life. To them it was an ideal.

Writers like Thomas Jefferson and Hector St. John de Crèvecœur admired the yeoman farmer not for his capacity to exploit opportunities and make money but for his honest industry, his independence, his frank spirit of equality, his ability to produce and enjoy a simple abundance. The farmer himself, in most cases, was in fact inspired to make money, and such self-sufficiency as he actually had was usually forced upon him by a lack of transportation or markets, or by the necessity to save cash to expand his operations.

For while early American society was an agrarian society, it was fast becoming more commercial, and commercial goals made their way among its agricultural classes almost as rapidly as elsewhere. The more commercial this society became, however, the more reason it found to cling in imagination to the noncommercial agrarian values. The more farming as a self-sufficient way of life was abandoned for farming as a business, the more merit men found in what was being left behind. And the more rapidly the farmers' sons moved into the towns, the more nostalgic the whole culture became about its rural past. Throughout the nineteenth and even in the twentieth century, the American was taught that rural life and farming as a vocation were something sacred.

This sentimental attachment to the rural way of life is a kind of homage that Americans have paid to the fancied innocence of their origins. To call it a "myth" is not to imply that the idea is simply false. Rather the "myth" so effectively embodies men's values that it profoundly influences their way of perceiving reality and hence their behavior.

Like any complex of ideas, the agrarian myth cannot be defined in a phrase, but its component themes form a clear pattern. Its hero was the yeoman farmer, its central conception the notion that he is the ideal man and the ideal citizen. Unstinted praise of the special virtues of the farmer and the special values of rural life was coupled with the assertion that agriculture, as a calling uniquely productive and uniquely important to society, had a special right to the concern and protection of government. The yeoman, who owned a small farm and worked it with the aid of his family, was the incarnation of the simple, honest, independent, healthy, happy human being. Because he lived in close communion with beneficent nature, his life was believed to have a wholesomeness and integrity impossible for the depraved populations of cities.

His well-being was not merely physical, it was moral: it was not merely personal, it was the central source of civic virtue; it was not merely secular but religious, for God had made the land and called man to cultivate it. Since the yeoman was believed to be both happy and honest, and since he had a secure propertied stake in society in the form of his own land, he was held to be the best and most reliable sort of citizen. To this conviction Jefferson appealed when he wrote: "The small land holders are the most precious part of a state."

In origin the agrarian myth was not a popular but a literary idea, a preoccupation of the upper classes, of those who enjoyed a classical education, read pastoral poetry, experimented with breeding stock, and owned plantations or country estates. It was clearly formulated and almost universally accepted in America during the last half of the eighteenth century. As it took shape both in Europe and America, its promulgators drew heavily upon the authority and the rhetoric of classical writers—Hesiod, Xenophon, Cato, Cicero, Virgil, Horace, and others—whose works were the staples of a good education. A learned agricultural gentry, coming into conflict with the industrial classes, welcomed the moral strength that a rich classical ancestry brought to the praise of husbandry.

Chiefly through English experience, and from English and classical writers, the agrarian myth came to America, where, like so many other cultural importations, it eventually took on altogether new dimensions in its new setting. So appealing were the symbols of the myth that even an arch-opponent of the agrarian interest like Alexander Hamilton found it politic to concede in his *Report on Manufactures* that "the cultivation of the earth, as the primary and most certain source of national supply . . . has intrinsically a strong claim to pre-eminence over every other kind of industry." And Benjamin Franklin, urban cosmopolite though he was, once said that agriculture was "the only *honest way*" for a nation to acquire wealth, "wherein man receives a real increase of the seed thrown into the ground, a kind of continuous miracle, wrought by the hand of God in his favour, as a reward for his innocent life and virtuous industry."

Among the intellectual classes in the eighteenth century the agrarian myth had virtually universal appeal. Some writers used it to give simple, direct, and emotional expression to their feelings about life and nature; others linked agrarianism with a formal philosophy of natural rights. The application of the natural rights philosophy to land tenure became especially popular in America. Since the time of Locke it had been a standard argument that the land is the common stock of society to which every man has a right—what Jefferson called "the fundamental right to labor the earth"; that since the occupancy and use of land are the true criteria of valid ownership, labor expended in cultivating the earth confers title to it; that since government was created to protect property, the property of working landholders has a special claim to be fostered and protected by the state.

At first the agrarian myth was a notion of the educated classes, but by the early nineteenth century it had become a mass creed, a part of the country's political folklore and its nationalist ideology. The roots of this change may be found as far back as the American Revolution, which, appearing to many Americans as the victory of a band of embattled farmers over an empire, seemed to confirm the moral and civic superiority of the yeoman, made the farmer a symbol of the new nation, and wove the agrarian myth into his patriotic sentiments and idealism.

Still more important, the myth played a role in the first party battles under the Constitution. The Jeffersonians appealed again and again to the moral primacy of the yeoman farmer in their attacks on the Federalists. The family farm and American democracy became indissolubly connected in Jeffersonian thought, and by 1840 even the more conservative party, the Whigs, took over the rhetorical appeal to the common man, and elected a President in good part on the strength of the fiction that he lived in a log cabin.

The Jeffersonians, moreover, made the agrarian myth the basis of a strategy of continental development. Many of them expected that the great empty inland regions would guarantee the preponderance of the yeoman—and therefore the dominance of Jeffersonianism and the health of the state—for an unlimited future. The opening of the trans-Allegheny region, its protection from slavery, and the purchase of the Louisiana Territory were the first great steps in a continental strategy designed to establish an internal empire of small farms. Much later the Homestead Act was meant to carry to its completion the process of continental settlement by small homeowners. The failure of the Homestead Act "to enact by statute the fee-simple empire" was one of the original sources of Populist grievances, and one of the central points at which the agrarian myth was overrun by the commercial realities.

Above all, however, the myth was powerful because the United States in the first half of the nineteenth century consisted predominantly of literate and politically enfranchised farmers. Offering what seemed harmless flattery to this numerically dominant class, the myth suggested a standard vocabulary to rural editors and politicians. Although farmers may not have been much impressed by what was said about the merits of a noncommercial way of life, they could only enjoy learning about their special virtues and their unique services to the nation. Moreover, the editors and politicians who so flattered them need not in most cases have been insincere. More often than not they too were likely to have begun life in little villages or on farms, and what they had to say stirred in their own breasts, as it did in the breasts of a great many townspeople, nostalgia for their early years and perhaps relieved some residual feelings of guilt at having deserted parental homes and childhood attachments. They also had the satisfaction in the early days of knowing that in so far as it was based upon the life of the largely self-sufficient yeoman the agrarian myth was a depiction of reality as well as the assertion of an ideal.

Oddly enough, the agrarian myth came to be believed more widely and tenaciously as it became more fictional. At first it was propagated with a kind of genial candor, and only later did it acquire overtones of insincerity. There survives from the Jackson era a painting that shows Governor Joseph Ritner of Pennsylvania standing by a primitive plow at the end of a furrow. There is no pretense that the Governor has actually been plowing—he wears broadcloth pants and a silk vest, and his tall black beaver hat has been carefully laid in the grass beside him—but the picture is meant as a reminder of both his rustic origin and his present high station in life. By contrast, Calvin Coolidge posed almost a century later for a series of photographs that represented him as haying in Vermont. In one of them the President sits on the edge of a hay ring in a white shirt, collar detached, wearing highly polished black shoes and a fresh pair of overalls; in the background stands his Pierce Arrow, a secret service man on the running board, plainly waiting to hurry the President away from his bogus rural labors. That the second picture is so much more pretentious and disingenuous than the first is a measure of the increasing hollowness of the myth as it became more and more remote from the realities of agriculture.

Throughout the nineteenth century hundreds upon hundreds of thousands of farm-born youths sought their careers in the towns and cities. Particularly after 1840, which marked the beginning of a long cycle of heavy country-to-city migration, farm children repudiated their parents' way of life and took off for the cities where, in agrarian theory if not in fact, they were sure to succumb to vice and poverty.

When a correspondent of the *Prairie Farmer* in 1849 made the mistake of praising the luxuries, the "polished society," and the economic opportunities of the city, he was rebuked for overlooking the fact that city life "*crushes, enslaves,* and *ruins so many thousands of our young men* who are insensibly made the victims of *dissipation,* of *reckless speculation,* and of *ultimate crime.*" Such warnings, of course, were futile. "Thousands of young men," wrote the New York agriculturist Jesse Buel, "who annually forsake the plough, and the honest profession of their fathers, if not to win the fair, at least form an opinion, too often confirmed by mistaken parents, that agriculture is not the road to wealth, to honor, nor to happiness. And such will continue to be the case, until our agriculturists become qualified to assume that rank in society to which the importance of their calling, and their numbers, entitle them, and which intelligence and self-respect can alone give them."

Rank in society! That was close to the heart of the matter, for the farmer was beginning to realize acutely not merely that the best of the world's goods were to be

According to this 1869 engraving from The Prairie Farmer, *each occupation has its uses, but the farmer alone foots all the bills.*

had in the cities and that the urban middle and upper classes had much more of them than he did but also that he was losing in status and respect as compared with them. He became aware that the official respect paid to the farmer masked a certain disdain felt by many city people. "There [is] . . . a certain class of individuals grown up in our land," complained a farm writer in 1835, "who treat the cultivators of the soil as an inferior caste . . . whose utmost abilities are confined to the merit of being able to discuss a boiled potato and a rasher of bacon." The city was symbolized as the home of loan sharks, dandies, fops, and aristocrats with European ideas who despised farmers as hayseeds.

The growth of the urban market intensified this antagonism. In areas like colonial New England, where an intimate connection had existed between the small town and the adjacent countryside, where a community of interests and even of occupations cut across the town line, the rural-urban hostility had not developed so sharply as in the newer areas where the township plan was never instituted and where isolated farmsteads were more common. As settlement moved west, as urban markets grew, as self-sufficient farmers became rarer, as farmers pushed into commercial production for the cities they feared and distrusted, they quite correctly thought of themselves as a vocational and economic group rather than as members of a neighborhood. In the Populist era the city was totally alien territory to many farmers, and the primacy of agriculture as a source of wealth was reasserted with much bitterness. "The great cities rest upon our broad and fertile prairies," declared Bryan in his "Cross of Gold" speech. "Burn down your cities and leave our farms, and your cities will spring up again as if by magic; but destroy our farms, and the grass will grow in the streets of every city in the country." Out of the beliefs nourished by the agrarian myth there had arisen the notion that the city was a parasitical growth on the country. Bryan spoke for a people raised for generations on the idea that the farmer was a very special creature, blessed by God, and that in a country consisting largely of farmers the voice of the farmer was the voice of democracy and of virtue itself.

The agrarian myth encouraged farmers to believe that they were not themselves an organic part of the whole order of business enterprise and speculation that flourished in the city, partaking of its character and sharing in its risks, but rather the innocent pastoral victims of a conspiracy hatched in the distance. The notion of an innocent and victimized populace colors the whole history of agrarian controversy.

For the farmer it was bewildering, and irritating too, to think of the great contrast between the verbal deference paid him by almost everyone and the real economic position in which he found himself. Improving his economic position was always possible, though this was often done too little and too late; but it was not within anyone's power to stem the decline in the rural values and pieties, the gradual rejection of the moral commitments that had been expressed in the early exaltations of agrarianism.

It was the fate of the farmer himself to contribute to this decline. Like almost all good Americans he had innocently sought progress from the very beginning, and thus hastened the decline of many of his own values. Elsewhere the rural classes had usually looked to the past, had been bearers of tradition and upholders of stability. The American farmer looked to the future alone, and the story of the American land became a study in futures.

In the very hours of its birth as a nation Crèvecœur had congratulated America for having, in effect, no feudal past and no industrial present, for having no royal, aristocratic, ecclesiastical, or monarchial power, and no manufacturing class, and had rapturously concluded: "We are the most perfect society now existing in the world." Here was the irony from which the farmer suffered above all others: the United States was the only country in the world that began with perfection and aspired to progress.

To what extent was the agrarian myth actually false? During the colonial period, and even well down into the nineteenth century, there were in fact large numbers of farmers who were very much like the yeomen idealized in the myth. They were independent and self-sufficient, and they bequeathed to their children a strong love of craftsmanlike improvisation and a firm tradition of household industry. These yeomen were all too often yeomen by force of circumstance. They could not become commercial farmers because they were too far from the rivers or the towns, because the roads were too poor for bulky traffic, because the domestic market for agricultural produce was too small and the overseas markets were out of reach. At the beginning of the nineteenth century, when the American population was still living largely in the forests and most of it was east of the Appalachians, the yeoman farmer did exist in large numbers, living much as the theorists of the agrarian myth portrayed him.

But when the yeoman practiced the self-sufficient economy that was expected of him, he usually did so not because he wanted to stay out of the market but because he wanted to get into it. "My farm," said a farmer of Jefferson's time, "gave me and my family a good living on the produce of it; and left me, one year with another, one hundred and fifty dollars, for I have never spent more than ten dollars a year, which was for salt, nails, and the like. Nothing to wear, eat, or drink was purchased, as my farm provided all. With this saving, I put money to interest, bought cattle, fatted and sold them, and made great profit." Great profit! Here was the significance of self-sufficiency for the characteristic family farmer. Commercialism had already begun to enter the American Arcadia.

For, whatever the spokesman of the agrarian myth might have told him, the farmer almost anywhere in early America knew that all around him there were examples of commercial success in agriculture—the tobacco, rice, and indigo, and later the cotton planters of the South, the grain, meat, and cattle exporters of the middle states.

The farmer knew that without cash he could never rise above the hardships and squalor of pioneering and log-cabin life. So the savings from his self-sufficiency went into improvements—into the purchase of more land, of herds and flocks, of better tools; they went into the building of barns and silos and better dwellings. Self-sufficiency, in short, was adopted for a time in order that it would eventually be unnecessary.

Between 1815 and 1860 the character of American agriculture was transformed. The rise of native industry created a home market for agriculture, while demands arose abroad for American cotton and foodstuffs, and a great network of turnpikes, canals, and railroads helped link the planter and the advancing western farmer to the new markets. As the farmer moved out of the forests onto the flat, rich prairies, he found possibilities for machinery that did not exist in the forest. Before long he was cultivating the prairies with horse-drawn mechanical reapers, steel plows, wheat and corn drills, and threshers.

The farmer was still a hardworking man, and he still owned his own land in the old tradition. But no longer did he grow or manufacture almost everything he needed. He concentrated on the cash crop, bought more and more of his supplies from the country store. To take full advantage of the possibilities of mechanization, he engrossed as much land as he could and borrowed money for his land and machinery. The shift from self-sufficient to commercial farming varied in time throughout the West and cannot be dated with precision, but it was complete in Ohio by about 1830 and twenty years later in Indiana, Illinois, and Michigan. All through the great Northwest, farmers whose fathers might have lived in isolation and self-sufficiency were surrounded by jobbers, banks, stores, middlemen, horses, and machinery.

This transformation affected not only what the farmer did but how he felt. The ideals of the agrarian myth were competing in his breast, and gradually losing ground, to another, even stronger ideal, the notion of opportunity, of career, of the self-made man. Agrarian sentiment sanctified labor in the soil and the simple life; but the prevailing Calvinist atmosphere of rural life implied that virtue was rewarded with success and material goods. Even farm boys were taught to strive for achievement in one form or another, and when this did not take them away from the farms altogether, it impelled them to follow farming not as a way of life but as a *career*—that is, as a way of achieving substantial success.

The sheer abundance of the land—that very internal empire that had been expected to insure the predominance of the yeoman in American life for centuries—gave the *coup de grâce* to the yeomanlike way of life. For it made of the farmer a speculator. Cheap land invited extensive and careless cultivation. Rising land values in areas of new settlement tempted early liquidation and frequent moves. Frequent and sensational rises in land values bred a boom psychology in the American farmer and caused him to rely for his margin of profit more on the appreciation in the value of his land than on the sale of crops. It took a strong man to resist the temptation to ride skyward on lands that might easily triple or quadruple their value in one decade and then double in the next.

What developed in America, then, was an agricultural society whose real attachment was not, like the yeoman's, to the land but to land values. The characteristic product of American rural society, as it developed on the prairies and the plains, was not a yeoman or a villager, but a harassed little country businessman who worked very hard, moved all too often, gambled with his land, and made his way alone.

While the farmer had long since ceased to act like a yeoman, he was somewhat slower in ceasing to think like one. He became a businessman in fact long before he began to regard himself in this light. As the nineteenth century drew to a close, however, various things were changing him. He was becoming increasingly an employer of labor, and though he still worked with his hands, he began to look with suspicion upon the working classes of the cities, especially those organized in trade unions, as he had once done upon the urban fops and aristocrats. Moreover, when good times returned after the Populist revolt of the 1890's, businessmen and bankers and the agricultural colleges began to woo the farmer, to make efforts to persuade him to take the businesslike view of himself that was warranted by the nature of his farm operations. "The object of farming," declared a writer in the *Cornell Countryman* in 1904, "is not primarily to make a living, but it is to make money. To this end it is to be conducted on the same business basis as any other producing industry."

The final change, which came only with a succession of changes in the twentieth century, wiped out the last traces of the yeoman of old, as the coming first of good roads and rural free delivery, and mail order catalogues, then the telephone, the automobile, and the tractor, and at length radio, movies, and television largely eliminated the difference between urban and rural experience in so many important areas of life. The city luxuries, once so derided by farmers, are now what they aspire to give to their wives and daughters.

In 1860 a farm journal satirized the imagined refinements and affections of a city girl in the following picture:

Slowly she rises from her couch. . . . Languidly she gains her feet, and oh! what vision of human perfection appears before us: Skinny, bony, sickly, hipless, thighless, formless, hairless, teethless. What a radiant belle! . . . The ceremony of enrobing commences. In goes the dentist's naturalization efforts; next the witching curls are fashioned to her "classically molded head." Then the womanly proportions are properly adjusted; hoops, bustles, and so forth, follow in succession, then a profuse quantity of whitewash, together with a "permanent rose tint" is applied to a sallow complexion; and lastly the "killing" wrapper is arranged on her systematical and matchless form.

But compare this with these beauty hints for farmers' wives from the *Idaho Farmer,* April, 1935:

Hands should be soft enough to flatter the most delicate of the new fabrics. They must be carefully manicured, with none of the hot, brilliant shades of nail polish. The lighter and more delicate tones are in keeping with the spirit of freshness. Keep the tint of your fingertips friendly to the red of your lips, and check both your powder and your rouge to see that they best suit the tone of your skin in the bold light of summer.

Nothing can tell us with greater finality of the passing of the yeoman ideal than these light and delicate tones of nail polish.

■ ■ ■ ■ ■ ■ ■

3

Age of Reform

Unemployed white and black workers parade in New York City in 1909 to protest discriminatory hiring practices.

Jane Addams: Urban Crusader

Anne Firor Scott

As the reputations of Progressive political leaders have declined, those of some of the social reformers of the era have risen. This is particularly true of social workers such as Jane Addams and other founders of the settlement house movement, who in modern eyes seem to have had a more profound grasp of the true character of the problems of their age and to have worked more effectively and with greater dedication in trying to solve those problems than did any of the politicians.

These social workers were quite different from those of today—they were more personally involved and far less professionally oriented. Many were also, it is true, somewhat patronizing in their approach to those they sought to help, and they took a rather romantic and thus unrealistic view of the potentialities both of the poor and of their own capacity to help the poor. This essay by Professor Anne Firor Scott of Duke University makes clear, however, that Jane Addams of Chicago's Hull-House was neither patronizing nor a romantic. Professor Scott is the author of *The Southern Lady: From Pedestal to Politics* and *The American Woman: Who Was She?*

■ ■ ■ ■ ■ ■ ■

If Alderman Johnny Powers of Chicago's teeming nineteenth ward had only been prescient, he might have foreseen trouble when two young ladies not very long out of a female seminary in Rockford, Illinois, moved into a dilapidated old house on Halsted Street in September, 1889, and announced themselves "at home" to the neighbors. The ladies, however, were not very noisy about it, and it is doubtful if Powers was aware of their existence. The nineteenth ward was well supplied with people already—growing numbers of Italians, Poles, Russians, Irish, and other immigrants—and two more would hardly be noticed.

Johnny Powers was the prototype of the ward boss who was coming to be an increasingly decisive figure on the American political scene. In the first place, he was Irish. In the second, he was, in the parlance of the time, a "boodler": his vote and influence in the Chicago Common Council were far from being beyond price. As chairman of the council's finance committee and boss of the Cook County Democratic party he occupied a strategic position. Those who understood the inner workings of Chicago politics thought that Powers had some hand in nearly every corrupt ordinance passed by the council during his years in office. In a single year, 1895, he was to help to sell six important city franchises. When the mayor vetoed Powers' measures, a silent but significant two-thirds vote appeared to override the veto.

Ray Stannard Baker, who chanced to observe Powers in the late nineties, recorded that he was shrewd and silent, letting other men make the speeches and bring upon their heads the abuse of the public. Powers was a short, stocky man, Baker said, "with a flaring gray pompadour, a smooth-shaven face [*sic*], rather heavy features, and a restless eye." One observer remarked that "the shadow of sympathetic gloom is always about him. He never jokes; he has forgotten how to smile. . . ." Starting life as a grocery clerk, Powers had run for the city council in 1888 and joined the boodle ring headed by Alderman Billy Whalen. When Whalen died in an accident two years later, Powers moved swiftly to establish himself as successor. A few weeks before his death Whalen had collected some thirty thousand dollars—derived from the sale of a city franchise—to be divided among the party faithful. Powers alone knew that the money was in a safe in Whalen's saloon, so he promptly offered a high price for the furnishings of the saloon, retrieved the money, and divided it among the gang—at one stroke establishing himself as a shrewd operator and as one who would play the racket fairly.

From this point on he was the acknowledged head of the gang. Charles Yerkes, the Chicago traction tycoon, found in Powers an ideal tool for the purchase of city franchises. On his aldermanic salary of three dollars a week, Powers managed to acquire two large saloons of his own, a gambling establishment, a fine house, and a conspicuous collection of diamonds. When he was indicted along with two other corrupt aldermen for running a slot machine and keeping a "common gambling house," Powers was unperturbed. The three appeared before a police judge, paid each other's bonds, and that was the end of that. Proof of their guilt was positive, but convictions were never obtained.

On the same day the Municipal Voters League published a report for the voters on the records of the members of the city council. John Powers was described as "recognized leader of the worst element in the council . . . [who] has voted uniformly for bad ordinances." The League report went on to say that he had always opposed securing any return to the city for valuable franchises, and proceeded to document the charge in detail.

To his constituents in the nineteenth ward, most of whom were getting their first initiation into American politics, Powers turned a different face. To them, he was first and last a friend. When there were celebrations, he always showed up: if the celebration happened to be a bazaar, he bought freely, murmuring piously that it would all go to the poor. In times of tragedy he was literally Johnny on the spot. If the family was too poor to provide the necessary carriage for a respectable funeral, it appeared at the doorstep—courtesy of Johnny Powers and charged to his standing account with the local undertaker. If the need was not so drastic, Powers made his presence felt with an imposing bouquet or wreath. "He has," said the Chicago *Times-Herald*, "bowed with aldermanic grief at thousands of biers."

Christmas meant literally tons of turkeys, geese, and ducks—each one handed out personally by a member of the Powers family, with good wishes and no questions asked. Johnny provided more fundamental aid, too, when a breadwinner was out of work. At one time he is said to have boasted that 2,600 men from his ward (about one third of the registered voters) were working in one way or another for the city of Chicago. This did not take into account those for whom the grateful holders of traction franchises had found a place. When election day rolled around, the returns reflected the appreciation of job-holders and their relatives.

The two young ladies on Halsted Street, Jane Addams and Ellen Starr, were prototypes too, but of a very different kind of figure: they were the pioneers of the social settlement, the original "social workers." They opposed everything Johnny Powers stood for.

Jane Addams' own background could hardly have been more different from that of John Powers. The treasured daughter of a well-to-do small-town business-man from Illinois, she had been raised in an atmosphere of sturdy Christian prin-ciples.

From an early age she had been an introspective child concerned with justify-ing her existence. Once in a childhood nightmare she had dreamed of being the only remaining person in a world desolated by some disaster, facing the responsi-bility for rediscovering the principle of the wheel! At Rockford she shared with some of her classmates a determination to live to "high purpose," and decided that she would become a doctor in order to "help the poor."

After graduation she went to the Woman's Medical College of Philadelphia, but her health failed and she embarked on the grand tour of Europe customary among the wealthy. During a subsequent trip to Europe in 1888, in the unlikely set-ting of a Spanish bull ring, an idea that had long been growing in her mind sud-denly crystallized: she would rent a house "in a part of the city where many primi-tive and actual needs are found, in which young women who had been given over too exclusively to study, might restore a balance of activity along traditional lines and learn something of life from life itself. . . ." So the American settlement-house idea was born. She and Ellen Starr, a former classmate at the Rockford seminary who had been with her in Europe, went back to Chicago to find a house among the victims of the nineteenth century's fast-growing industrial society.

The young women—Jane was twenty-nine and Ellen thirty in 1889—had no blueprint to guide them when they decided to take up residence in Mr. Hull's de-cayed mansion and begin helping "the neighbors" to help themselves. No school of social work had trained them for this enterprise: Latin and Greek, art, music, and "moral philosophy" at the seminary constituted their academic preparation. Toyn-bee Hall in England—the world's first settlement house, founded in 1884 by Samuel A. Barnett—had inspired them. Having found the Hull house at the corner of Polk and Halsted—in what was by common consent one of Chicago's worst wards—they leased it, moved in, and began doing what came naturally.

Miss Starr, who had taught in an exclusive girls' preparatory school, inaugu-rated a reading party for young Italian women with George Eliot's *Romola* as the first book. Miss Addams, becoming aware of the desperate problem of working mothers, began at once to organize a kindergarten. They tried Russian parties for the Russian neighbors, organized boys' clubs for the gangs on the street, and of-fered to bathe all babies. The neighbors were baffled, but impressed. Very soon children and grownups of all sorts and conditions were finding their way to Hull-House—to read Shakespeare or to ask for a volunteer midwife; to learn sewing or discuss socialism; to study art or to fill an empty stomach. There were few formali-ties and no red tape, and the young ladies found themselves every day called upon to deal with some of the multitude of personal tragedies against which the condi-tions of life in the nineteenth ward offered so thin a cushion.

Before long, other young people feeling twinges of social conscience and seek-ing a tangible way to make their convictions count in the world of the 1890's came

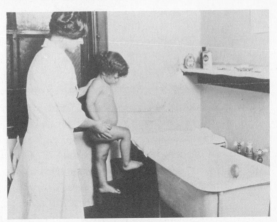

Children were Hull-House's first
concern. Infants were bathed (right)
and moppets put into nursery school
(below).

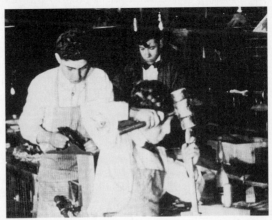

Older boys (right) took shop lessons
to prepare them to become successful artisans.

to live at Hull-House. These "residents," as they were called, became increasingly interested in the personal histories of the endless stream of neighbors who came to the House each week. They began to find out about the little children sewing all day long in the "sweated" garment trade, and about others who worked long hours in a candy factory. They began to ask why there were three thousand more children in the ward than there were seats in its schoolrooms, and why the death rate was higher there than in almost any other part of Chicago. They worried about youngsters whose only playground was a garbage-spattered alley that threatened the whole population with disease. (Once they traced a typhoid epidemic to its source and found the sewer line merging with the water line.) In the early days Hull-House offered bathtubs and showers, which proved so popular a form of hospitality that the residents became relentless lobbyists for municipal baths.

Hull-House was not the only American settlement house—indeed, Jane Addams liked to emphasize the validity of the idea by pointing out that it had developed simultaneously in several different places. But Hull-House set the pace, and in an astonishingly short time its founder began to acquire a national reputation. As early as 1893 Jane Addams wrote to a friend: "I find I am considered the grandmother of social settlements." She was being asked to speak to gatherings of learned gentlemen, sociologists and philosophers, on such subjects as "The Subjective Necessity for Social Settlements." When the Columbian Exposition attracted thousands of visitors to Chicago in 1893, Hull-House became—along with the lake front and the stockyards—one of the things a guest was advised not to miss. By the mid-nineties, distinguished Europeans were turning up regularly to visit the House and examine its workings. W. T. Stead, editor of the English *Review of Reviews*, spent much time there while he gathered material for his sensational book, *If Christ Came to Chicago*. By that time two thousand people a week were coming to Hull-House to participate in some of its multifarious activities, which ranged from philosophy classes to the Nineteenth Ward Improvement Association.

Neither her growing reputation nor the increasing demand for speeches and articles, however, distracted Jane Addams from what was to be for forty years the main focus of a many-sided life: Hull-House and the nineteenth ward. Much of her early writing was an attempt to portray the real inner lives of America's proliferating immigrants, and much of her early activity, an effort to give them a voice to speak out against injustice.

The Hull-House residents were becoming pioneers in many ways, not least in the techniques of social research. In the *Hull-House Maps and Papers,* published in 1895, they prepared some of the first careful studies of life in an urban slum, examining the details of the "homework" system of garment making and describing tumble-down houses, overtaxed schools, rising crime rates, and other sociological problems. The book remains today an indispensable source for the social historian of Chicago in the nineties.

Jane Addams' own interest in these matters was far from academic. Her concern for the uncollected garbage led her to apply for—and receive—an appointment as garbage inspector. She rose at six every morning and in a horse-drawn buggy followed the infuriated garbage contractor on his appointed rounds, making sure that every receptacle was emptied. Such badgering incensed Alderman Powers, in whose hierarchy of values cleanliness, though next to godliness, was a good bit below patronage—and he looked upon garbage inspection as a job for one of his henchmen. By now John Powers was becoming aware of his new neighbors; they were increasingly inquisitive about things close to Johnny Powers' source of power. By implication they were raising a troublesome question: Was Johnny Powers really "taking care of the poor"?

For a while, as one resident noted, the inhabitants of the House were "passive though interested observers of their representative, declining his offers of help and co-operation, refusing politely to distribute his Christmas turkeys, but feeling too keenly the smallness of their numbers to work against him." They were learning, though, and the time for passivity would end.

In company with many other American cities, Chicago after 1895 was taking a critical look at its political life and at the close connections that had grown up between politics and big business during the explosive era of industrial expansion following the Civil War. "The sovereign people may govern Chicago in theory," Stead wrote; "as a matter of fact King Boodle is monarch of all he surveys. His domination is practically undisputed."

The Municipal Voters League, a reform organization that included many of Jane Addams' close friends, was founded in 1896 in an effort to clean up the Common Council, of whose sixty-eight aldermen fifty-eight were estimated to be corrupt. The League aimed to replace as many of the fifty-eight as possible with honest men. But it was not easy: in 1896, as part of this campaign, a member of the Hull-House Men's Club ran for the second aldermanic position in the ward and against all expectations was elected. Too late, his idealistic backers found that their hero had his price: Johnny Powers promptly bought him out.

Jane Addams was chagrined but undiscouraged. By the time Powers came up for re-election in 1898, she had had time to observe him more closely and plan her attack. Her opening gun was a speech—delivered, improbably enough, to the Society for Ethical Culture—with the ponderous and apparently harmless title, "Some Ethical Survivals in Municipal Corruption." But appearances were deceptive: once under way, she took the hide off Powers and was scarcely easier on his opponents among the so-called "better elements."

She began by pointing out that for the immigrants, who were getting their first initiation in self-government, ethics was largely a matter of example: the office-holder was apt to set the standard and exercise a permanent influence upon their views. An engaging politician whose standards were low and "impressed by the cynical stamp of the corporations" could debauch the political ideals of ignorant men and women, with consequences that might, she felt, take years to erase.

Ethical issues were further complicated, she said, by habits of thought brought to the New World from the Old. Many Italians and Germans had left their respective fatherlands to escape military service; the Polish and Russian Jews, to escape government persecution. In all these cases, the government had been cast in the role of oppressor. The Irish, in particular, had been conditioned by years of resentment over English rule to regard any successful effort to feed at the public crib as entirely legitimate, because it represented getting the better of their bitterest enemies.

On the other hand, Miss Addams continued, there was nothing the immigrants admired more than simple goodness. They were accustomed to helping each other out in times of trouble, sharing from their own meager store with neighbors who were even more destitute. When Alderman Powers performed on a large scale the same good deeds which they themselves were able to do only on a small scale, was it any wonder that they admired him?

Given this admiration, and their Old World resentments toward government, the immigrants' developing standards of political morality suffered when Powers made it clear that he could "fix" courts or find jobs for his friends on the city payroll. It cheapened their image of American politics when they began to suspect that the source of their benefactor's largess might be a corrupt bargain with a traction tycoon, or with others who wanted something from the city of Chicago and were willing to pay for it.

Hull-House residents, Miss Addams said, very early found evidence of the influence of the boss's standards. When the news spread around the neighborhood that the House was a source of help in time of trouble, more and more neighbors came to appeal for aid when a boy was sent to jail or reform school, and it was impossible to explain to them why Hull-House, so ready to help in other ways, was not willing to get around the law as the Alderman did.

Removing Alderman Powers from office, Jane Addams told the sober gentlemen of the Society for Ethical Culture, would be no simple task. It would require a fundamental change in the ethical standards of the community, as well as the development of a deeper insight on the part of the reformers. These latter, she pointed out, with all their zeal for well-ordered, honest politics, were not eager to undertake the responsibilities of self-government 365 days a year. They were quite willing to come into the nineteenth ward at election time to exhort the citizenry, but were they willing to make a real effort to achieve personal relationships of the kind that stood Johnny Powers in such good stead?

On this last point, Hull-House itself had some experience. As Florence Kelley—a Hull-House resident who was to become a pioneer in the Illinois social reform movement—subsequently wrote:

> The question is often asked whether all that the House undertakes could not be accomplished without the wear and tear of living on the spot. The answer, that it could not, grows more assured as time goes on. You must suffer from the dirty streets, the universal ugliness, the lack of oxygen in the air you daily breathe, the endless struggle with soot and dust and insufficient water supply, the hanging from a strap of the overcrowded street car at the end of your day's work; you must send your children to the nearest wretchedly crowded school, and see them suffer the consequences, if you are to speak as one having authority and not as the scribes . . .

By 1898, after nine years of working with their neighbors, the Hull-House residents were ready to pit their influence against that of Powers. Jane Addams' philosophical address to the Ethical Culture society was followed by others in which she explained more concretely the relationships between Yerkes, Chicago's traction czar, and the city council, relationships in which Johnny Powers played a key role.

With several important deals in the making, 1898 would be a bad year for Yerkes to lose his key man in the seats of power.

The election was scheduled for April. The reformers—led by Hull-House and supported by independent Democrats, the Cook County Republicans, and the Municipal Voters League—put up a candidate of their own, Simeon Armstrong, to oppose Powers, and undertook to organize and underwrite Armstrong's campaign. By the end of January, the usually imperturbable Powers suddenly began paying attention to his political fences. The newspapers noted with some surprise that it was the first time he had felt it necessary to lift a finger more than two weeks in advance of election day.

His first move was an attack on Amanda Johnson, a Hull-House resident who had succeeded Miss Addams as garbage inspector. A graduate of the University of Wisconsin and described by the papers as blond, blue-eyed, and beautiful, she had taken the civil service examination and duly qualified for the position. Alderman Powers announced to the world that Miss Johnson, shielded by her civil service status, was telling his constituents not to vote for him. The Chicago *Record* dropped a crocodile tear at the sad picture of the martyred alderman:

> General sympathy should go out to Mr. Powers in this, his latest affliction. Heretofore he has been persecuted often by people opposed to bad franchise ordinances. He has been hounded by the upholders of civil service reform. He has suffered the shafts of criticism directed at his career by disinterested citizens. A grand jury has been cruel to him. Invidious comments have been made in his hearing as to the ethical impropriety of gambling institutions. . . . It is even believed that Miss Johnson in her relentless cruelty may go so far as to insinuate that Mr. Powers' electioneering methods are no better than those attributed to her—that, indeed, when he has votes to win, the distinctions of the civil service law do not deter him from going after those votes in many ways.

Powers' next move was to attempt a redistricting that would cut off the eastern, or Italian, end of his ward, which he took to be most seriously under Hull-House influence. It was reported that he also felt this area had been a "large source of expense to him through the necessity of assisting the poor that are crowded into that district." "These people," the Chicago *Record* reported, "formerly tied to him by his charities are said to be turning toward Hull-House and will vote solidly against him next spring."

Neither of Powers' first efforts was notably successful. A few days after his attack on Miss Johnson the *Tribune* reported:

> Trouble sizzled and boiled for Alderman John Powers in his own bailiwick last night. The Nineteenth Ward Independent club raked over the Alderman's sins . . . and . . . much indignation was occasioned by Alderman Powers' opposition to Miss Amanda Johnson. One Irish speaker says Johnny is a disgrace to the Irish race now that he has descended to fighting "poor working girls."

Meantime, Powers' colleagues on the council redistricting committee had no intention of saving his skin at the expense of their own, and stood solidly against his gerrymandering effort. Now the shaken boss began to show signs of losing his temper. He told reporters that if Miss Addams didn't like the nineteenth ward she should move out. Later, still more infuriated, he announced that Hull-House should be driven out. "A year from now there will be no such institution," he said flatly, adding that the women at Hull-House were obviously jealous of his charities. The *Record* published a cartoon showing Powers pushing vainly against the wall of a very substantial house.

The news of the campaign soon spread beyond the bounds of Chicago. The New York *Tribune* commented that Powers

> wouldn't mind Miss Addams saying all those things about him if he didn't begin to fear that she may succeed in making some of his well-meaning but misled constituents believe them. She is a very practical person, and has behind her a large volunteer staff of other practical persons who do not confine their efforts to "gassin' in the parlors," but are going about to prove to the plain people of the nineteenth ward that a corrupt and dishonest man does not necessarily become a saint by giving a moiety of his ill-gotten gains to the poor.

By March the campaign was waxing warm, and Powers resorted to an attempt to stir up the Catholic clergy against Miss Addams and the reform candidate. One of the Hull-House residents, a deputy factory inspector and a Catholic herself, went directly to the priests to find out why they were supporting Powers. When she reported, Jane Addams wrote to a friend:

> As nearly as I can make out, the opposition comes from the Jesuits, headed by Father Lambert, and the parish priests are not in it, and do not like it. Mary talked for a long time to Father Lambert and is sure it is jealousy of Hull-House and money obligations to Powers, that he does not believe the charges himself. She cried when she came back.

In another letter written about the same time, Miss Addams said that Powers had given a thousand dollars to the Jesuit "temperance cadets," who had returned the favor with a fine procession supporting Powers' candidacy. "There was a picture of your humble servant on a transparency and others such as 'No petticoat government for us. . . .' We all went out on the corner to see it, Mr. Hinsdale carefully shielding me from the public view."

By now the battle between Hull-House and Johnny Powers was sharing headlines in Chicago newspapers with the blowing up of the *Maine* in Havana's harbor and the approach of the war with Spain. "Throughout the nineteenth ward," said the *Tribune,* "the one absorbing topic of conversation wherever men are gathered is the fight being made against Alderman Powers." It was rumored that Powers had offered a year's free rent to one of the opposition leaders if he would move out of the ward before election day, and the Hull-House group let it be known that the Alderman was spending money freely in the ward, giving his lieutenants far more cash to spread around than was his custom. "Where does the money come from?" Jane Addams asked, and answered her own question: "From Mr. Yerkes." Powers was stung, and challenged her to prove that he had ever received one dollar from any corporation.

"Driven to desperation," said the *Tribune,* "Ald. Powers has at last called to his aid the wives and daughters of his political allies." Determined to fight fire with fire, he dropped his opposition to "petticoat politicians" and gave his blessing to a Ladies Auxiliary which was instructed to counteract the work of the women of Hull-House. An enterprising reporter discovered that few of the ladies had ever seen Miss Addams or been to Hull-House, but all were obediently repeating the charge that she had "blackened and maligned the whole ward" by saying that its people were ignorant, criminal, and poor.

As the campaign became more intense, Jane Addams received numbers of violent letters, nearly all of them anonymous, from Powers' partisans, as well as various communications from lodginghouse keepers quoting prices for votes they were ready to deliver! When the Hull-House residents discovered evidence of ties between banking, ecclesiastical, and journalistic interests, with Powers at the center, they proceeded to publicize all they knew. This brought upon their heads a violent attack by the Chicago *Chronicle,* the organ of the Democratic ring.

Suddenly a number of nineteenth-ward businessmen who had signed petitions for the reform candidate came out for Powers. They were poor and in debt; Powers gave the word to a landlord here, a coal dealer there, and they were beaten. The small peddlers and fruit dealers were subjected to similar pressure, for each needed a license to ply his trade, and the mere hint of a revocation was enough to create another Powers man.

When Alderman John M. Harlan, one of the stalwarts of the Municipal Voters League, came into the ward to speak, Powers supplied a few toughs to stir up a riot. Fortunately Harlan was a sturdy character, and offered so forcefully to take on all comers in fisticuffs that no volunteers appeared. Allowed to proceed, he posed some embarrassing questions: Why did nineteenth-ward residents have to pay ten-cent trolley fares when most of the city paid five? Why, when Powers was head of the city council's free-spending committee on street paving, were the streets of the ward in execrable condition? Why were the public schools so crowded, and why had Powers suppressed a petition, circulated by Hull-House, to build more of them?

Freely admitting Powers' reputation for charity, Harlan made the interesting suggestion that the councilman's motives be put to the test: Would he be so generous as a private citizen? "Let us retire him to private life and see."

Powers was pictured by the papers as being nearly apoplectic at this attack from Miss Addams' friend. He announced that he would not be responsible for Harlan's safety if he returned to the nineteenth ward. (Since no one had asked him to assume any such responsibility, this was presumed to be an open threat.) Harlan returned at once, telling a crowd well-laced with Powers supporters that he would "rather die in my tracks than acknowledge the right of John Powers to say who should and who should not talk in this ward." Summoning up the memory of Garibaldi, he urged the Italians to live up to their tradition of freedom and not allow their votes to be "delivered."

In a quieter vein, Miss Addams too spoke at a public meeting of Italians, where, it was reported, she received profound and respectful attention. "Show that you do not intend to be governed by a boss," she told them. "It is important not only for yourselves but for your children. These things must be made plain to them."

As the campaign progressed, the reformers began to feel they had a real chance of defeating Powers. Jane Addams was persuaded to go in search of funds with which to carry out the grand finale. "I sallied forth today and got $100," she wrote, and "will have to keep it up all week; charming prospect, isn't it?" But on about the twentieth of March she began to have serious hopes, too, and redoubled her efforts.

As election day, April 6, approached, the Chicago *Tribune* and the Chicago *Record* covered the campaign daily, freely predicting a victory for the reformers. Alas for all predictions. When election day came, Powers' assets, which Jane Addams had so cogently analyzed in that faraway speech to the Society for Ethical Culture, paid off handsomely. It was a rough day in the nineteenth ward, with ten saloons open, one man arrested for drawing a gun, and everything, as Miss Addams wrote despondently when the count began to come in, "as bad as bad can be." Too many election judges were under Powers' thumb. The reform candidate was roundly defeated. Hull-House went to court to challenge the conduct of the election, but in the halls of justice Powers also had friends. It was no use.

Even in victory, however, Powers was a bit shaken. Hull-House had forced him, for the first time, to put out a great effort for re-election. It was obviously *not* going to move out of the nineteenth ward; indeed, if the past was any portent, its influence with his constituents would increase.

Powers decided to follow an ancient maxim, "If you can't lick 'em, join 'em." Early in the 1900 aldermanic campaign, several Chicago papers carried a straight news story to the effect that Hull-House and Johnny Powers had signed a truce, and quoted various paternally benevolent statements on the Alderman's part. In the *Chronicle,* for example, he was reported to have said: "I am not an Indian when it comes to hate . . . let bygones be bygones." A day or two later another rash of stories detailed a number of favors the Alderman was supposed to have done for Hull-House.

Jane Addams was furious, and after considerable deliberation she decided to reply. It was one of the few times in her long public career when she bothered to answer anything the newspapers said about her. She knew that with his eye on the campaign, the master politician was trying to give the appearance of having taken his most vigorous enemy into camp. She had been observing him too long not to realize what he was up to, and she could not possibly let him get away with it.

On February 20, 1900, a vigorous letter from Miss Addams appeared in nearly all the Chicago papers, reaffirming the attitude of Hull-House toward Mr. Powers. "It is needless to state," she concluded, "that the protest of Hull-House against a man who continually disregards the most fundamental rights of his constituents must be permanent."

Permanent protest, yes, but as a practical matter there was no use waging another opposition campaign. Powers held too many of the cards. When all was said and done, he had proved too tough a nut to crack, though Hull-House could—and did—continue to harass him. An observer of the Municipal Voters League, celebrating its success in the *Outlook* in June, 1902, described the vast improvement in the Common Council, but was forced to admit that a few wards were "well-nigh hopeless." He cited three: those of "Blind Billy" Kent, "Bathhouse John" Coughlin, and Johnny Powers.

From a larger standpoint, however, the battle between "Saint Jane" (as the neighbors called Jane Addams when she was not around) and the Ward Boss was not without significance. It was one of numerous similar battles that would characterize the progressive era the country over, and many of them the reformers would win. Because of her firsthand experience, because she lived *with* the immigrants instead of coming into their neighborhood occasionally to tell them what to do, Jane Addams was perhaps the first of the urban reformers to grasp the real pattern of bossism, its logic, the functions it performed, and the reason it was so hard to dislodge. Years later political scientists, beginning to analyze the pattern, would add almost nothing to her speech of 1898. If copies of *The Last Hurrah* have reached the Elysian fields, Jane Addams has spent an amused evening seeing her ideas developed so well in fictional form.

The campaign of 1898 throws considerable light on Jane Addams' intensely practical approach to politics, and upon a little-known aspect of the settlement-house movement. If anyone had told her and Ellen Starr in 1889 that the logic of what they were trying to do would inevitably force them into politics, they would have hooted. But in due time politics, in many forms, became central to Hull-House activity. For Jane Addams herself, the campaign against Powers was the first in a long series of political forays, all essentially based on the same desire—to see that government met the needs of the "other half."

The regulation of child labor, for example, was one political issue in which Hull-House residents became involved because of their knowledge of the lives of the neighbors. The first juvenile court in Chicago was set up as a result of their efforts; it was a direct response to the anxious mothers who could not understand why Hull-House would not help get their boys out of jail. The first factory inspection law in Illinois was also credited to Hull-House, and Florence Kelley became the first inspector. Another Hull-House resident—Dr. Alice Hamilton—pioneered in the field of industrial medicine. Because of their intimate acquaintance with the human cost of industrialization, settlement workers became vigorous advocates of promoting social justice through law.

It was a long jump but not an illogical one from the campaign against Powers to the stage of the Chicago Coliseum in August, 1912, when Jane Addams arose to second the nomination of Teddy Roosevelt by the Progressive party on a platform of social welfare. More remarkable than the ovation—larger than that given to any other seconder—was the fact that the huge audience seemed to listen carefully to what she had to say.

Some newspapers grandly estimated her value to T.R. at a million votes. "Like the report of Mark Twain's death," she commented, "the report is greatly exaggerated." But she campaigned vigorously, in the face of criticism that this was not a proper role for a woman, and when the Bull Moose cause failed, she did not believe it had been a waste of time. It had brought about, she wrote Roosevelt, more discussion of social reform than she had dared to hope for in her lifetime. Alderman Powers was still in office—as were many like him—but the sources of his power were being attacked at the roots.

When the 1916 campaign came around, Democrats and Republicans alike made bids for Jane Addams' support. The outbreak of war in Europe had turned her attention, however, in a different direction. As early as 1907, in a book called *Newer Ideals of Peace,* she had begun to elaborate William James's notion of a "moral equivalent of war," and had suggested that the experience of polyglot immigrant populations in learning to live together might be laying the foundations for a true international order. Like her ideals of social justice, those that she conceived on international peace had their beginning in the nineteenth ward.

To her, as to so many idealistic progressives, world war came as a profound shock. Her response was a vigorous effort to bring together American women and women from all the European countries to urge upon their governments a negotiated peace. In Europe, where she went in 1915 for a meeting of the Women's International Peace Conference, she visited prime ministers; at the end of that year she planned to sail on Henry Ford's peace ship, but illness forced her to withdraw at the last moment. At home she appealed to President Wilson. Unshaken in her pacifism, she stood firmly against the war, even after the United States entered it.

Her popularity seemed to melt overnight. Many women's clubs and social workers, who owed so much to her vision, deserted her. An Illinois judge who thought it dangerous for her to speak in wartime was widely supported in the press. For most of 1917 and 1918 she was isolated as never before or again. But she did not waver.

When the war ended she began at once to work for means to prevent another. Through the twenties she was constantly active in searching for ways in which women could cut across national lines in their work for peace. In 1931, in her seventy-first year, she received the Nobel Peace Prize—the second American to be so recognized. She died, full of honors, in 1935.

As for Johnny Powers, he had lived to a ripe old age and died in 1930, remaining alderman almost to the end, still fighting reform mayors, still protesting that he and Miss Addams were really friends, after all. From whichever department of the hereafter he ended up in, he must have looked down—or up—in amazement at the final achievements of his old enemy, who had been so little troubled by his insistence that there should be "no petticoats in politics."

■ ■ ■ ■ ■ ■ ■

Reforming College Football

John S. Watterson

It is no coincidence that during the Progressive Era the game of football was both re-formed in the sense of being cleansed of some of the dangerous and unsporting elements that had infected it in earlier years and re-formed, given new rules that made it quite a different game from the one that occurred in 1869 when Princeton and Rutgers clashed in what traditionally has been called the first intercollegiate "football" contest. Football in 1910 was of course somewhat different from the game played in the 1990s but far closer to the modern game in form and tactics than to the game played in 1870 or even in 1900. Nor is it coincidental that Theodore Roosevelt, a man famous both as a reformer in the political sense and as a believer in the importance of physical fitness and physical competition, was president of the United States at the time and in the middle of the "progressive" changes that transformed the sport.

In the following pages, John S. Watterson describes the two "reformations" that affected collegiate football during the first decade of the twentieth century and places them in context. His essay is indeed a brief and fascinating history of football from its origin in the games of rugby and soccer to the complex (and still frequently scandal-ridden) sport we know today.

■ ■ ■ ■ ■ ■ ■

During October of 1905, President Theodore Roosevelt, who had recently intervened in a national coal strike and the Russo-Japanese War, turned his formidable attention to another kind of struggle. The President, a gridiron enthusiast who avidly followed the fortunes of his alma mater, Harvard, summoned representatives of the Eastern football establishment—Harvard, Yale, and Princeton—to the White House. He wanted to discuss brutality and the lack of sportsmanship in college play.

Theodore Roosevelt believed strongly that football built character, and he believed just as strongly that roughness was a necessary—even a desirable—feature of the game. "I have no sympathy whatever," he declared, "with the over-wrought sentimentality that would keep a young man in cotton wool. I have a hearty contempt for him if he counts a broken arm or collarbone as of serious consequences when balanced against the chance of showing that he possesses hardihood, physical prowess, and courage."

But now Roosevelt was worried that the brutality of the prize ring had invaded college football and might end up destroying it.

In an article in *McClure's Magazine*, the journalist Henry Beach Needham recounted an injury in the Dartmouth-Princeton game in which the star for Dartmouth—a black man—had his collarbone broken early in the game. A prep school friend of the Princeton quarterback who had inflicted the injury, himself black and a member of the Harvard team, confronted the offender: "You put him out because he is a black man."

"We didn't put him out because he is a black man," the Princeton quarterback replied indignantly. "We're coached to pick out the most dangerous man on the opposing side and put him out in the first five minutes of play." The author was a close friend of the President, and Roosevelt no doubt read Needham's two-part series. Soon after the first article had appeared, Roosevelt criticized flagrant disregard for the rules in his June commencement address at Harvard, and on his return trip he met with Needham.

By the fall of 1905 Roosevelt had more reason than ever to pay attention to college football. His son Ted was playing for the Harvard freshmen, and Roosevelt and other grads were concerned that the school's president, Charles Eliot, an opponent of football, might use gridiron conduct to argue for the abolition of the game at Harvard.

When Roosevelt's friend Endicott Peabody of Groton School, on behalf of an association of Eastern and Midwestern headmasters, suggested a meeting with Eastern college representatives, the President immediately sprang into action. Having ended the Russo-Japanese War and dealt with several major issues, *The New York Times* commented, Roosevelt "today took up another question of vital interest to the American people. He started a campaign of reform of football."

To the inner circle of football advisers and coaches who met with Roosevelt at the White House on October 9, 1905, the President first expressed general concerns about the game. Then he made a few remarks "on what he remembered of each college's unfair play from several things that had happened in previous years." Perhaps the examples hit too close to home; not everyone at the meeting concurred. Nevertheless, Roosevelt asked his guests to frame an agreement condemning brutality and disregard for the rules. The six men dutifully drew up a statement and pledged that their teams would honor it.

Unfortunately for Roosevelt the brief campaign did little more than draw attention to the evils of college play. The White House meeting came at the beginning of an injury-ridden season that plunged football into the worst crisis in its history. Twice more in 1905 the President intervened, behind the scenes, when lack of sportsmanship appeared to violate the spirit of the White House agreement. In the Harvard-Yale game, Harvard nearly withdrew its team from the field after a Yale tackler had hurled himself into a Harvard punt receiver who was calling for a fair catch and the referees refused to assess a penalty. Even Roosevelt's son Ted was battered in the Yale-Harvard freshman game, some said by Yale players out to ambush him.

By the end of November the protest had reached a fever pitch, and the future of college football—professional football barely existed—was more clouded than ever before. Columbia University abolished football play at the end of the season, President Nicholas Murray Butler declaring it an "academic nuisance." Professor Shailer Mathews of the University of Chicago Divinity School was more emphatic: "From the President of the United States to the humblest member of a school and college faculty there arises a general protest against this boy-killing, man-mutilating, money-making, education-prostituting, gladiatorial sport."

The crisis had been building for decades, and some of the problems that inflamed it were inherent in the American version of football, which had emerged from British rugby a generation earlier.

From its earliest years American football received mixed reviews as an entertaining sport but also a rough and sometimes dangerous one. In 1876 Yale and Harvard substituted rugby for the soccer-style version of football played in the first college matches. The British game was popular because it allowed players to run with the ball; but the rules prohibited members of the team with the ball to be in front of the ballcarrier, and the characteristic scrummage by which the ball was put in play was a far cry from the modern American system of four downs to make ten yards. In the rugby "scrum" the players gathered around the ball, their arms and bodies interlocked, and then kicked the ball until it came out of the pack. Before long the Eastern teams agreed to adopt a system of yards and downs—three downs to make five yards or lose ten yards—and devised a system of numerical scoring (a field goal counted five points, and by 1884, a touchdown counted four). The rule against interference in front of the ballcarrier, although often ignored by players and referees alike, was not repealed until 1888.

As early as 1884 a committee of Harvard faculty set about investigating the new game, and the members reported savage fistfights in which players had to be separated by the judges, the referees, and even the police. The bloodlust of the spectators also shocked the committee. While one player pushed a ballcarrier out of bounds, knocked him down, stole the ball, and returned in triumph to the field, the audience shouted, "Kill him," "Slug him," and "Break his neck." The Harvard

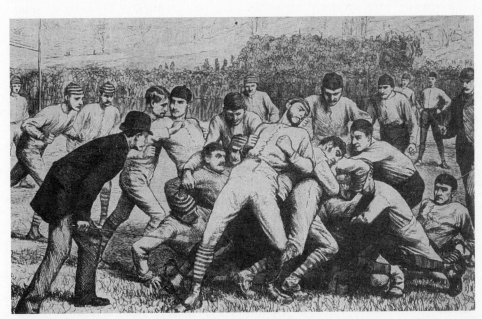

A drawing by A. B. Frost depicts one of the early struggles between Princeton and Yale, 1879.

faculty decided to ban football in 1888 but reneged after a year of angry student protest.

By the early 1890s college football had overtaken college baseball in popularity, but it still was regarded with distrust by faculty, newspaper editors, and clergy; changes in the rules had ushered in an era of team violence.

In 1888 the rules committee moved to permit blocking and tackling below the waist, and the game became less individual and more team-oriented. The open-field running and kicking of rugby had given way to a regimented sport based on force and momentum. Teams concentrated their offenses near the ball rather than spread them soccer-style across the field, and now six or more men could go into motion before the ball was put into play. Working from a variety of wedge-shaped formations (the notorious flying wedge was allowed only at the start of the half or after a score, in place of today's kickoff return), players interlocked their arms—and sometimes clung to straps on the backs of fellow players' uniforms—to push, pull, or even catapult the carrier through the defense.

Violence and physical danger were not the sole complaints. President Eliot, in his 1892–93 annual report to the Harvard Corporation, denounced the training by youthful coaches, intent on winning at any cost, who, he argued, had transformed the players into "powerful animals" and thereby dulled their minds. He charged that football gave the impression that universities were little more than "places of mere physical sport and not of intellectual training" and that the sometimes hefty gate receipts from college athletics had turned amateur contests into major commercial spectacles. But Eliot's views were not yet shared by most college presidents or, for that matter, many faculty.

From the 1880s until his death in 1925, the best-known and most respected figure in college football circles was the "father of American football," Walter Camp. Camp once wrote: "Coaching a football team is the most engrossing thing in the world. It is playing chess with human pawns." He played for Yale and continued to coach there after going into business in New Haven; his teams racked up one national championship after another. As secretary of the Intercollegiate Football Rules Committee, Camp persuaded the committee to adopt the rules that converted what remained of rugby into team-oriented American football, and he kept his name before the football public by editing the annual football rules book and writing widely on the sport for newspapers and magazines. An able diplomat, Camp deftly steered football around the shoals of public criticism and intercollegiate squabbling without hampering its phenomenal growth. At the request of the Harvard Corporation, Camp assembled a committee that surveyed players and coaches, both past and present, to determine the extent of the injury problem. Most praised football and reported few problems with injuries; one player fondly recalled the "humanities dinged into me on the football field."

In 1894 the rules committee bowed to public pressure by abolishing the flying wedge and proclaiming that "no momentum mass plays shall be allowed." Such plays were defined, however, as more than three men going into motion before the ball was put in play. Ingenious coaches merely brought guards and tackles into the backfield and put their backs in motion before the ball was snapped. It seemed that no minor adjustments in the rules could contain the potential for difficulties in this crude and often violent sport. Not long after the adoption of the rules changes, Harvard broke gridiron relations with Yale when the Yale captain, Frank Hinkey, near the end of an injury-plagued game, landed on the Harvard ballcarrier while the man was down and broke his collarbone. In a violent grudge match between Georgetown University and the Columbia Athletic Club of Washington, halfback George ("Shorty") Bahen was fatally injured, and three years later the Georgia legislature tried to ban football after the University of Georgia's Richard Von Gammon was killed in a game against the University of Virginia. Despite pleas by the dead boy's mother to save football, the Georgia legislature voted to abolish the game, and when the governor refused to sign the bill, the House of Representatives tried to pass it over his veto. Only a controversial interpretation of the legislative rules by the Speaker of the House saved football from the wrath of the legislators.

There were problems besides the violence. As football spread rapidly through the country, eligibility violations spread with it. In 1894 seven players of the University of Michigan's starting eleven were not even enrolled as students. At Ann Arbor two years later a talented halfback appeared at the season's start, never registered, attended only two courses, and dropped out after the end of the season. These "tramp" athletes became notorious for casually moving from school to school, as in the case of the Pennsylvania State College player who showed up so well in a loss to the University of Pennsylvania that he was practicing with the University of Pennsylvania team the following week. The Springfield *Republican* complained that the game had veered so far from its simple beginnings as to require an "armored eleven, twenty substitutes, a brass band, and a field telegraph."

Nevertheless, college presidents and their faculties continued to overlook many infractions because they believed football was a healthy outlet for pent-up schoolboy energies. President William H. P. Faunce of Brown University said the critics had forgotten "the old drinking and carousing of a generation ago . . . the smashing of windowpanes and destruction of property characteristic of that time." Football also provided an outlet for the faculty. Professor Woodrow Wilson's wife, Ellen, described her husband as so depressed by Princeton's first-ever loss to the University of Pennsylvania that only the election of Gover Cleveland as President that same week had relieved his gloom. "Really I think Woodrow would have had some sort of collapse if we had lost in politics, too," she wrote.

But the undercurrent of discontent evident in the 1890s continued into the early years of the new century. In the reformist tide of the Progressive Era college athletics suddenly found itself under attack along with political corruption and industrial monopolies. Taking aim at the practices in Eastern colleges, Henry Needham depicted, besides brutality, a system of laxity bordering on corruption in which prep schools such as Andover and Exeter groomed athletes for Eastern colleges and then bent the rules to allow the players to take entrance exams a year before they were eligible. "The only conclusion to be drawn," he wrote, "is that, thanks to the influence of the colleges, there is growing up a class of students tainted with commercialism."

He described the football career of an athlete named James J. Hogan, who entered Exeter in his early twenties and then went on to Yale. Though from a poor family, Hogan lived in the finest dormitory, took a free trip to Cuba with the Yale trainer Mike Murphy, and was given the lucrative franchise of representing the American Tobacco Company on campus. According to an official of the company, the player talked up the cigarettes to his friends. "They appreciate and like him; they realize that he is a poor fellow, working his way through college, and they want to help him. So they buy our cigarettes, knowing that Hogan gets a commission on every box sold in New Haven."

Even with the Needham articles and Roosevelt's concern, the public might have lost interest in the problem if the 1905 season had not brought its rash of casualties. There were twenty-three football deaths. Only a handful took place in intercollegiate play, but one in particular set in motion the movement to reform the game. In a match between Union College and New York University, Harold Moore of Union died after being kicked in the head. Chancellor Henry M. MacCracken of NYU seized the opportunity to summon a reform conference.

He invited the presidents of thirteen schools to confer in New York on December 5. Meeting less than two weeks after Columbia had dropped football, the conference came within a single vote of passing a resolution to abolish the game as then played but instead decided to hold a general convention of football-playing institutions later in the month.

The intercollegiate conference opened on December 28 with delegates from more than sixty schools attending. Some, like the representative from Columbia, wanted football done away with altogether, yet many delegates still hoped for a solution short of abolition. The pro-football forces grouped around Capt. Palmer Pierce of West Point and, according to a delegate from the University of Kansas, were the "best organized and came with a well-defined plan and a determination to save the game." The result was a proposal to appoint a rules committee to negotiate with the Intercollegiate Football Rules Committee in a final effort at joint action.

By early January the two committees were holding exploratory meetings followed by simultaneous but separate sessions at the Hotel Netherlands in New York City. Then, in a dramatic, though carefully orchestrated, move, the Harvard coach, Bill Reid, who after the White House meeting had met twice more with President Roosevelt, left the old committee to join the new group. Despite some grumbling by members of the old committee, a merger was arranged, and, symbolic of the transfer of power, Reid replaced Walter Camp as secretary of the joint rules committee. During the next months rules changes were hammered out in a series of tumultuous meetings.

As rules reform swung into motion, other complaints about football's role in college life were being hotly debated in the Midwestern "Big Nine" conference. Frederick Jackson Turner of the University of Wisconsin, best known for his essays on the American frontier, introduced a motion to suspend football for two years. An angry gathering of students marched on Turner's house. When he emerged, the students shouted, "When can we have football?" Amid hisses and shouts of "Put him in the lake!" Turner tried to reason with the students; they burned him in effigy.

In the end only Northwestern University dropped football. Many critics still wanted to give the rules committee a chance to make changes, although a few in the football world, such as Amos Alonzo Stagg, the University of Chicago coach and the only rules committee member from outside the East, feared that his fellow committee members might turn football into a "parlor game." The possibility of radical changes disturbed the old guard. Someone wrote to Walter Camp, troubled by rumors that "forward passes and other dream-like things have been brought into the realm of possibilities, even probabilities."

Already the rules committee had enacted the most sweeping changes since football had emerged from rugby a quarter-century before. In an attempt to strengthen the open-field features and to steer away from the grinding line play, a ten-yard rule was adopted. It would allow a team to have three opportunities to gain ten yards, rather than five yards as before. Walter Camp, who had proposed the change in 1904, believed that teams would have to play a more open offense to gain the extra five yards. Less palatable to older members was the "dream-like" forward pass that had been approved by the rules committee (before this change, the ball could only be lateraled).

The football world heaved a sigh of relief as all the major Eastern schools except Columbia embraced the new rules. In the 1906 season and for two years following, the verdict on the "new football" was generally favorable. In spite of fluctuations in the injury count, the number of deaths dropped to fourteen, fifteen, and ten.

Then, in the fall of 1909, the trend toward a safer game abruptly reversed itself. In a match between Harvard and West Point, the Army captain, Eugene Byrne, exhausted by continual plays to his side of the line, was fatally injured. Earl Wilson of the Naval Academy was paralyzed and later died as a result of a flying tackle. And the University of Virginia's halfback Archer Christian died after a game against Georgetown, probably from a cerebral hemorrhage suffered in a plunge through the line. "Does the public need any more proof," wrote the *Washington Post,* "that football is a brutal, savage, murderous sport? Is it necessary to kill many more promising young men before the game is revised or stopped altogether?" At both Georgetown and Virginia, football was suspended for the remainder of the season, and the District of Columbia school system banned it altogether. Even Col. John Mosby, the old Confederate raider, used Christian's death to rail against football as "murder" and said that the presence of a team doctor demonstrated that the game was tantamount to "war."

Stunned by the death of Christian, the University of Virginia's president, Eugene Alderman, who a decade earlier had declared, "I should rather see a boy of mine on the rush line fighting for his team than on the sideline smoking a cigarette," warned that the outcry was more than hysteria on the part of the press. President David Starr Jordan of Stanford referred to football as "Rugby's American pervert" and said that the "farce of football reform" that was slipped by the public in 1905 and 1906 could not be repeated. Even the presidents of the powerful triumvirate of Yale, Princeton, and Harvard, whose schools had not joined the conference of 1905, which was now known as the National Collegiate Athletic Association (NCAA), held special meetings to seek remedies.

As various sets of proposals were voted on, the forward pass loomed as the chief obstacle to settlement. By April 30, with the proceedings reaching a decisive point, opponents of the pass had collected enough votes to approve a motion to confine its reception to the area behind the line of scrimmage. While a three-man subcommittee put together a report, the Harvard coach Percy Haughton feverishly worked behind the scenes to save the apparently doomed forward pass. "To my mind," he wrote Amos Alonzo Stagg, "unless we retain the forward pass it will be the death of football."

On Friday, May 13, 1910, the committee adopted the new rules—seven men on the line of scrimmage, no pushing or pulling, no interlocking interference (arms linked or hands on belts and uniforms), and four fifteen-minute quarters—and it readopted the forward pass. Unable to invent a new formula for yards and downs, the committee stuck for the time with ten yards in three downs. Although the forward pass was narrowly saved, it still was not given a full vote of confidence; it had to be thrown at least five yards behind the line of scrimmage and was limited to twenty yards past it.

The adoption of these rules eliminated the cruder versions of nineteenth-century football and established the groundwork for a sleeker, faster, wide-open game. Two years later, in 1912, the committee added a fourth down to make ten yards, raised the value of the touchdown to six points, and reduced the field goal to three points. The twenty-yard restriction on forward passes was also eliminated, though the pass still had to be thrown from five yards behind the line of scrimmage. With the lifting of the most restrictive rules, the forward pass quickly became a potent offensive weapon, as illustrated by the brilliant performance of Knute Rockne and Gus Dorais in Notre Dame's 35–13 airborne upset of Army in 1913. In the sports-crazy 1920s the new open football proved to be entertainment as well as to have cash value, and mammoth stadiums were erected to accommodate the swelling attendance.

In the years since 1912 the size and speed of the athletes have changed the hazards of the game, but the form of football had remained much the same as it was when it emerged from the crisis of 1910. Although the upstart forward pass quickly proved itself, the rule requiring the ball to be thrown from five yards behind the line of scrimmage was not removed from college rules until 1945. Perhaps the rule change that altered the game the most was the adoption in the 1940s of free substitution, which ushered in two-platoon football. In 1954 the football solons tried to restore the old style of football, in which the same players had to play offense and defense, but this rear-guard action was abandoned in the early 1960s.

Football is safer today than in the early 1900s. Carefully engineered and tested equipment, especially headgear, has reduced the life-threatening injuries that plagued football before 1920. Early headgear, seldom worn consistently, shielded the ears and surface of the head but gave inadequate protection to the skull and brain. After World War I a sponge-rubber lining was added to the crown of the helmet, and by the late 1930s a sturdy leather helmet with an inner felt lining was being used. But it was not until 1943 that all players were required to wear headgear. The plastic helmet, which distributes shock more evenly, was introduced in the 1940s amid objections reminiscent of those that accompanied the original solely leather helmets. Some critics argued—and still do—that the hard plastic helmet, used as an offensive weapon, has as much potential for causing as for preventing serious injuries. So the game remains the subject of periodic debate requiring a battery of experts to keep it in balance between offense and defense, bodily contact and safety.

In spite of success in reforming the rules, criticism of commercial abuses of football and other sports has lingered, and the complaints of commercialism in big-time college sports are reminiscent of the criticisms in the early 1900s. Although the NCAA was in the 1940s given broader investigative and enforcement powers, problems have persisted. Professors and coaches do not love one another, and some college presidents face pressures—and quandaries—similar to those of their counterparts in the era of Charles Eliot and Frederick Jackson Turner.

Unlike turn-of-the-century crises, violence plays a comparatively minor role in today's turmoils. Rather, it is illegal payments to athletes, violations of academic standards, and drug abuse that bedevil athletic programs.

■ ■ ■ ■ ■ ■ ■

The Fight for Women's Suffrage:
An Interview with Alice Paul

Robert S. Gallagher

An increasingly popular technique being used by students of recent history, a kind of technological advance made possible by the tape recorder, is the personal interview. "Oral history," a term coined by Allan Nevins, who founded the great oral history archive at Columbia University, provides a method of preserving the recollections of participants in historical events. Superficially it resembles autobiography, an ancient literary form, but it has the great advantage of drawing out the speaker, prodding his or her memory, forcing him or her to confront contradictions and respond to criticism. The interviewer is able to direct the subject's thoughts toward the most significant and important aspects of the topic, matters an autobiographer might ignore out of modesty or embarrassment. This type of research requires that the interviewer be thoroughly familiar with the interviewee's career and with the events surrounding it and also that the interviewer be able to establish a rapport with the subject.

The following interview with Alice Paul, a leader in the early twentieth-century women's suffrage movement, is a fine example of the value of the interview technique. Ms. Paul is both frank and unprepossessing; she does not hesitate to speak her mind, yet she is perfectly capable of admitting sometimes that she no longer remembers all the details of her career. The interviewer, Robert S. Gallagher, formerly a contributing editor of *American Heritage,* had done his "homework" well and, as the reader will quickly recognize, had gained Ms. Paul's confidence. Her responses tell us a great deal about the fight for women's suffrage and also about the mood and spirit of the suffragists.

■ ■ ■ ■ ■ ■ ■

American women won the right to vote in 1920 largely through the controversial efforts of a young Quaker named Alice Paul. She was born in Moorestown, New Jersey, on January 11, 1885, seven years after the woman-suffrage amendment was first introduced in Congress. Over the years the so-called Susan B. Anthony amendment had received sporadic attention from the national legislators, but from 1896 until Miss Paul's dramatic arrival in Washington in 1912 the amendment had never been reported out of committee and was considered moribund. As the Congressional Committee chairman of the National American Woman Suffrage Association, Miss Paul greeted incoming President Woodrow Wilson with a spectacular parade down Pennsylvania Avenue. Congress soon began debating the suffrage amendment again. For the next seven years—a tumultuous period of demonstrations, picketing, politicking, street violence, beatings, jailings, and hunger strikes—Miss Paul led a determined band of suffragists in the confrontation tactics she had learned from the militant British feminist Mrs. Emmeline

Pankhurst. This unrelenting pressure on the Wilson administration finally paid off in 1918, when an embattled President Wilson reversed his position and declared that woman suffrage was an urgently needed "war measure."

The woman who, despite her modest disclaimers, is accorded major credit for adding the Nineteenth Amendment to the Constitution is a 1905 graduate of Swarthmore College. She received her master's degree (1907) and her Ph.D. (1912) from the University of Pennsylvania. Miss Paul combined her graduate studies in 1908 and 1909 at the London School of Economics with volunteer work for the British suffrage movement. Together with another American activist, Lucy Burns, she was jailed several times in England and Scotland and returned to this country in 1910 with a reputation as an energetic and resourceful worker for women's rights. She promptly enlisted in the American suffrage movement, and opponents and friends alike soon were—and still are—impressed by her unflinching fearlessness. "Alice Paul is tiny and her hair has turned gray," a sympathetic feminist writer recently observed, "but she is not a sweet little gray-haired lady."

Miss Paul's single-minded devotion to The Cause is, of course, legendary in the women's movement. . . .

How did you first become interested in woman suffrage?

It wasn't something I had to think about. When the Quakers were founded in England in the 1600's, one of their principles was and is equality of the sexes.

This striking portrait of Alice Paul was taken at the same time as this interview was conducted. She was 87.

So I never had any other idea. And long before my time the Yearly Meeting in Philadelphia, which I still belong to, formed a committee to work for votes for women. The principle was always there.

Then you had your family's encouragement in your work?

My father—he was president of the Burlington County [New Jersey] Trust Company—died when I was quite young, but he and Mother were both active in the Quaker movement. Mother was the clerk of the Friend's Meeting in our hometown. I would say that my parents supported all the ideals that I had.

In 1912 wasn't it a bit unusual for a woman to receive a Ph.D. degree?

Oh, no. There were no women admitted, of course, to the undergraduate school at the University of Pennsylvania, but there were a number of women graduate students.

When did you actually become involved in suffrage work?

Well, after I got my master's in 1907, my doctoral studies took me to the School of Economics in London. The English women were struggling hard to get the vote, and everyone was urged to come in and help. So I did. That's all there was to it. It was the same with Lucy Burns.

You met Miss Burns in London?

Yes, we met in a police station after we were both arrested. I had been asked to go on a little deputation that was being led by Mrs. [Emmeline] Pankhurst to interview the Prime Minister. I said I'd be delighted to go, but I had no idea that we'd be arrested. I don't know what the charge was. I suppose they hadn't made all the preparations for the interview with the Prime Minister or something. At any rate, I noticed that Miss Burns had a little American flag pin on her coat, so I went up to her, and we became great friends and allies and comrades. Well, we got out of that, and, of course, afterwards we were immediately asked to do something else. And that way you sort of get into the ranks.

What sort of things were you asked to do?

The next thing I was asked to do was to go up to Norwich and "rouse the town," as they say. Winston Churchill was in the British cabinet and was going to make a speech there. Well, the English suffragists knew that the government was completely opposed to suffrage, and they conceived this plan to publicly ask all the cabinet members what they were going to do about votes for women. For that moment at least, the whole audience would turn to the subject of suffrage. We considered it an inexpensive way of advertising our cause. I thought it was a very successful method.

What happened at Norwich?

I went to Norwich with one other young woman, who was as inexperienced as I was, and we had street meetings in the marketplace, where everyone assembled for several nights before Mr. Churchill's speech. I don't know whether we exactly "roused the town," but by the time he arrived, I think Norwich was pretty well aware of what we were trying to do. The night he spoke, we had another meeting outside the hall. We were immediately arrested. You didn't have to be a good speaker, because the minute you began, you were arrested.

Were you a good speaker?

Not particularly. Some people enjoyed getting up in public like that, but I didn't. I did it, though. On the other hand, Lucy Burns was a very good speaker—she had what you call that gift of the Irish—and she was extremely courageous, a thousand times more courageous than I was. I was the timid type, and she was just naturally valiant. Lucy became one of the pillars of our movement. We never, never, never could have had such a campaign in this country without her.

In her book about the suffrage movement Inez Haynes Irwin tells about your hiding overnight on the roof of St. Andrew's Hall in Glasgow, Scotland, in order to break up a political rally the next day.

Did Mrs. Irwin say that? Oh, no. I never hid on any roof in my life. In Glasgow I was arrested, but it was at a street meeting we organized there. Maybe Mrs. Irwin was referring to the Lord Mayor's banquet in London. I think it was in December of 1909, and Miss Burns and I were asked to interrupt the Lord Mayor. I went into the hall, not the night before but early in the morning when the charwomen went to work, and I waited up in the gallery all day. That night Lucy went in down below with the banquet guests. I don't remember whether she got up and interrupted the mayor. I only remember that I did.

What happened?

I was arrested, of course.

Was this the time you were imprisoned for thirty days and forcibly fed to break your hunger strike?

I can't remember how long I was in jail that time. I was arrested a number of times. As for forcible feeding, I'm certainly not going to describe that.

The whole concept of forcible feeding sounds shocking.

Well, to me it was shocking that a government of men could look with such extreme contempt on a movement that was asking nothing except such a simple little thing as the right to vote. Seems almost unthinkable now, doesn't it? With all these millions and millions of women going out happily to work today, and nobody, as far as I can see, thinking there's anything unusual about it. But, of course, in some countries woman suffrage is still something that has to be won.

Do you credit Mrs. Pankhurst with having trained you in the militant tactics you subsequently introduced into the American campaign?

That wasn't the way the movement was, you know. Nobody was being trained. We were just going in and doing the simplest little things that we were asked to do. You see, the movement was very small in England, and small in this country, and small everywhere, I suppose. So I got to know Mrs. Pankhurst and her daughter, Christabel, quite well. I had, of course, a great veneration and admiration for Mrs. Pankhurst, but I wouldn't say that I was very much trained by her. What happened was that when Lucy Burns and I came back, having both been imprisoned in England, we were invited to take part in the campaign over here; otherwise nobody would have ever paid any attention to us.

That was in 1913?

I came back in 1910. It was in 1912 that I was appointed by the National American Woman Suffrage Association to the chairmanship of their Congressional Committee in Washington, which was to work for the passage of the amendment that Susan B. Anthony had helped draw up. And Lucy Burns was asked to go with me. Miss Jane Addams, who was on the national board, made the motion for our appointments. They didn't take the work at all seriously, or else they wouldn't have entrusted it to us, two young girls. They did make one condition, and that was that we should never send them any bills, for as much as one dollar. Everything we did, we must raise the money ourselves. My predecessor, Mrs. William Kent, the wife of the congressman from California, told me that she had been given ten dollars the previous year by the national association, and at the end of her term she gave back some change.

Weren't you discouraged by the national association's attitude?

Well, when we came along, we tried to do the work on a scale which we thought, in our great ignorance, might bring some success. I had an idea that it might be a one year's campaign. We would explain it to every congressman, and the amendment would go through. It was so clear. But it took us seven years. When you're young, when you've never done anything very much on your own, you imagine that it won't be so hard. We probably wouldn't have undertaken it if we had known the difficulties.

How did you begin?

I went down to Washington on the seventh of December, 1912. All I had at the start was a list of people who had supported the movement, but when I tried to see them, I found that almost all of them had died or moved, and nobody knew much about them. So we were left with a tiny handful of people.

With all these obstacles how did you manage to organize the tremendous parade that greeted President-elect Wilson three months later?

Well, it wasn't such a tremendous parade. We called it a procession. I don't know whether there were five thousand or ten thousand marchers, maybe, but it wasn't a very big one. The idea for such a parade had been discussed at the 1912 suffrage convention, although some of the delegates thought it was too big an undertaking. It was unusual. There had never been a procession of women for any cause under the sun, so people did want to go and see it.

The press estimated the crowd at a half million. Whose idea was it to have the parade the day before Wilson's inaugural?

That was the only day you could have it if you were trying to impress the new President. The marchers came from all over the country at their own expense. We just sent letters everywhere, to every name we could find. And then we had a hospitality committee headed by Mrs. Harvey Wiley, the wife of the man who put through the first pure-food law in America. Mrs. Wiley canvassed all her friends in Washington and came up with a tremendous list of people who were willing to entertain the visiting marchers for a day or two. I mention these names to show what a wonderful group of people we had on our little committee. . . .

Didn't the parade start a riot?

The press reports said that the crowd was very hostile, but it wasn't hostile at all. The spectators were practically all tourists who had come for Wilson's inauguration. We knew there would be a large turnout for our procession, because the company that put up the grandstands was selling tickets and giving us a small percentage. The money we got—it was a gift from heaven—helped us pay for the procession. I suppose the police thought we were only going to have a couple of hundred people, so they made no preparations. We were worried about this, so another member of our committee, Mrs. John Rogers, went the night before to see her brother-in-law, Secretary of War [Henry L.] Stimson, and he promised to send over the cavalry from Fort Myer if there was any trouble.

Did you need his help?

Yes, but not because the crowd was hostile. There were just so many people that they poured into the street, and we were not able to walk very far. So we called Secretary Stimson, and he sent over the troops, and they cleared the way for us. I think it took us six hours to go from the Capitol to Constitution Hall. Of course, we did hear a lot of shouted insults, which we always expected. You know, the usual things about why aren't you home in the kitchen where you belong. But it wasn't anything violent. Later on, when we were actually picketing the White House, the people did become almost violent. They would tear our banners out of our hands and that sort of thing.

Were you in the front ranks of the 1913 parade?

No. The national board members were at the head of it. I walked in the college section. We all felt very proud of ourselves, walking along in our caps and gowns. One of the largest and loveliest sections was made up of uniformed nurses. It was very impressive. Then we had a foreign section, and a men's section, and a Negro women's section from the National Association of Colored Women, led by Mary Church Terrell. She was the first colored woman to graduate from Oberlin, and her husband was a judge in Washington. Well, Mrs. Terrell got together a wonderful group to march, and then, suddenly, our members from the South said they wouldn't march. Oh, the newspapers just thought this was a wonderful story and developed it to the utmost. I remember that that was when the men's section came to the rescue. The leader, a Quaker I knew, suggested that the men march between the southern delegations and the colored women's section, and that finally satisfied the southern women. That was the greatest hurdle we had.

If the parade didn't cause any real trouble, why was there a subsequent congressional investigation that resulted in the ouster of the district police chief?

The principal investigation was launched at the request of our women delegates from Washington, which was a suffrage state. These women were so indignant about the remarks from the crowd. And I remember that Congressman Kent was very aroused at the things that were shouted at his daughter, Elizabeth, who was riding on the California float, and he was among the first in Congress to demand an investigation into why the police hadn't been better prepared. As I said, the police just didn't take our little procession seriously. I don't think it was anything intentional. We didn't testify against the police, because we felt it was just a miscalculation on their part.

What was your next move after the parade?

A few weeks after Mr. Wilson became President, four of us went to see him. And the President, of course, was polite and as much of a gentleman as he always was. He told of his own support, when he had been governor of New Jersey, of a state referendum on suffrage, which had failed. He said that he thought this was the way suffrage should come, through state referendums, not through Congress. That's all we accomplished. We said we were going to try and get it through Congress, that we would like to have his help and needed his support very much. And then we sent him another delegation and another and another and another and another and another and another—

every type of women's group we could get. We did this until 1917, when the war started and the President said he couldn't see any more delegations.

So you began picketing the White House?

We said we would have a perpetual delegation right in front of the White House, so he wouldn't forget. Then they called it picketing. We didn't know enough to know what picketing was, I guess.

How did you finance all this work?

Well, as I mentioned, we were instructed not to submit any bills to the National American. Anything we did, we had to raise the money for it ourselves. So to avoid any conflict with them we decided to form a group that would work exclusively on the Susan B. Anthony amendment. We called it the Congressional Union for Woman's Suffrage. You see, the Congressional Committee was a tiny group, so the Congressional Union was set up to help with the lobbying, to help with the speechmaking, and especially to help in raising money. The first year we raised $27,000. It just came from anybody who wanted to help. Mostly small contributions. John McLean, the owner of the Washington Post, I think, gave us a thousand dollars. That was the first big gift we ever got.

The records indicate that you raised more than $750,000 over the first eight years. Did your amazing fund-raising efforts cause you any difficulties with the National American?

I know that at the end of our first year, at the annual convention of the National American, the treasurer got up—and I suppose this would be the same with any society in the world—she got up and made a speech, saying, "Well, this group of women has raised a tremendous sum of money, and none of it has come to my treasury," and she was very displeased with this. Then I remember that Jane Addams stood up and reminded the convention that we had been instructed to pay our own debts, and so that was all there was to it. Incidentally, the Congressional Union paid *all* the bills of that national convention, which was held in Washington that year. I remember we paid a thousand dollars for the rent of the hall. If you spend a hard time raising the money, you remember about it.

Were you upset about not being reappointed chairman of the Congressional Committee?

No, because they asked me to continue. But they said if I were the committee chairman, I would have to drop the Congressional Union. I couldn't be chairman of both. Some of the members on the National American board felt that all the work being put into the federal amendment wasn't a good thing for the entire suffrage campaign. I told them I had formed this Congressional Union and that I wanted to keep on with it.

Was it true, as some historians of the movement maintain, that the National Ameri-can's president, Dr. Anna Shaw, was "suspicious" of unusual activity in the ranks?

No, I don't think she was. She came down to Washington frequently and spoke at our meetings, and she walked at the head of our 1913 procession. But I think we did make the mistake perhaps of spending too much time and energy just on the campaign. We didn't take enough time, probably, to go and explain to all the leaders why we thought [the federal amendment] was something that could be accomplished. You see, the National American took the posi-tion—not Miss Anthony, but the later people—that suffrage was something that didn't exist anywhere in the world, and therefore we would have to go more slowly and have endless state referendums to indoctrinate the men of the country.

Obviously you didn't agree with this. Was this what caused the Congressional Union to break with the National American?

We didn't break with the National American. In a sense we were expelled. At the 1913 convention they made lots and lots of changes in the association's constitution. I don't recall what they were, and I didn't concern myself with the changes at the time. At any rate, the Congressional Union was affiliated with the National American under one classification, and they wrote to us and said if we would resign from that classification and apply for another classifica-tion, there would be a reduction in our dues. So we did what they told us, and then when we applied for the new classification, they refused to accept us, and we were out.

Why did the National American do this to your group?

The real division was over the Shafroth-Palmer amendment that the National American decided to substitute for the Anthony amendment in the spring of 1914. Under this proposal each state would hold a referendum on woman suf-frage *if* more than 8 per cent of the legal voters in the last preceding elec-tion—males, of course—signed a petition for it. This tactic had been tried without much success before, and with all the time and money such cam-paigns involve, I don't think many women would have ever become voters. Our little group wanted to continue with the original amendment, which we called the Susan B. Anthony because the women of the country, if they knew anything about the movement, had heard the name Susan B. Anthony. Now the great part of the American women were very loyal to this amendment, and when the National American suddenly switched to Shafroth-Palmer, we thought that the whole movement was going off on a sidetrack. And that is the reason we later formed the National Woman's Party, because if we hadn't con-tinued, there would have been nobody in Washington speaking up for the original amendment.

You didn't have much faith in state referendums?

The first thing I ever did—after I graduated from Swarthmore, I did some social work in New York City—one of the suffragists there asked me to go with her to get signatures for a suffrage referendum in New York State. So I went with her, and she was a great deal older and much more experienced than I was. I remember going into a little tenement room with her, and a man there spoke almost no English, but he could vote. Well, we went in and tried to talk to this man and ask him to vote for equality for women. And almost invariably these men said, "No, we don't think that it is the right thing. We don't do that in Italy, women don't vote in Italy." You can hardly go through one of those referendum campaigns and not think what a waste of the strength of women to try and convert a majority of men in the state. From that day on I was convinced that the way to do it was through Congress, where there was a smaller group of people to work with.

Then the National Woman's Party was formed to continue the work on the federal amendment?

We changed our name from the Congressional Union to the National Woman's Party in 1916, when we began to get so many new members and branches. Mainly people who disagreed with the National American's support of the Shafroth-Palmer. And the person who got us to change our name was Mrs. [Alva E.] Belmont.

Would you tell me about Mrs. Belmont?

She was, of course, a great supporter of the suffrage movement financially, and we didn't even know her the first year we were in Washington. People said to me that she was a wonderfully equipped person who was very fond of publicity, and they suggested that I invite her to come down and sit on one of the parade floats. Well, I didn't know who she was at all, but I wrote her an invitation, and I remember thinking what a queer person she must be to want to sit on a float. She turned out to be anything but the type she was described, and, of course, she didn't sit on any float. Anyway, a year later, after we had been expelled from the National American and couldn't have been more alone and more unpopular and more unimportant, one of our members, Crystal Eastman [Benedict], contacted Mrs. Belmont. And Mrs. Belmont invited me to come have dinner and spend the night at her home in New York City. Well, I like to go to bed early, but Mrs. Belmont was the type that liked to talk all night. So all night we talked about how we could probably get suffrage. A little later Mrs. Belmont withdrew entirely from the old National American and threw her whole strength into our movement. The first thing she did was give us five thousand dollars. We had never had such a gift before.

Why do you think Mrs. Belmont crossed over to your group?

She was entirely in favor of our approach to the problem. She wanted to be immediately put on our national board, so she could have some direction. And then, after suffrage was won, she became the president of the Woman's Party, and at that time she gave us most of the money to buy the house in Washington that is still the party's headquarters. Over the years Mrs. Belmont did an enormous amount for the cause of women's equality. She was just one of those people who were born with the feeling of independence for herself and for women.

Did Mrs. Belmont have something to do with the decision to campaign against the Democrats in the November, 1914, elections?

Yes. You see, here we had an extremely powerful and wonderful man—I thought Woodrow Wilson was a very wonderful man—the leader of his party, in complete control of Congress. But when the Democrats in Congress caucused, they voted against suffrage. You just naturally felt that the Democratic Party was responsible. Of course, in England they were up against the same thing. They couldn't get this measure through Parliament without getting the support of the party that was in complete control.

Didn't this new policy of holding the party in power responsible represent a drastic change in the strategy of the suffrage movement?

Up to this point the suffrage movement in the United States had regarded each congressman, each senator, as a friend or a foe. It hadn't linked them together. And maybe these men were individual friends or foes in the past. But we deliberately asked the Democrats to bring it up in their caucus, and they did caucus against us. So you couldn't regard them as your allies anymore. I reported all this to the National American convention in 1913, and I said that it seemed to us that we must begin to hold this party responsible. And nobody objected to my report. But when we began to put it into operation, there was tremendous opposition, because people said that this or that man has been our great friend, and here you are campaigning against him.

Would you have taken the same position against the Republicans if that party had been in power in 1914?

Of course. You see, we tried very hard in 1916—wasn't it [Charles Evans] Hughes running against Wilson that year?—to get the Republicans to put federal suffrage in their platform, and we failed. We also failed with the Democrats. Then we tried to get the support of Mr. Hughes himself. Our New York State committee worked very hard on Mr. Hughes, and they couldn't budge him. So we went to see former President [Theodore] Roosevelt at his home at Oyster Bay to see if *he* could influence Mr. Hughes. And I remember so vividly what Mr. Roosevelt said. He said, "You know, in political life you must always remember that you not only must be on the right side of a measure, but you must be on the right side at the right time." He told us that that was the great trouble with Mr. Hughes, that Mr. Hughes is certainly for suffrage, but he can't seem to know that he must do it in time. So Mr. Hughes started on his campaign around the country, and when he came to Wyoming, where women were already voting, he couldn't say he was for the suffrage amendment. And he went on and on, all around the country. Finally, when he came to make his final speech of the campaign in New York, he had made up his mind, and he came out strongly for the federal suffrage amendment. So it was true what Mr. Roosevelt had said about him. . . .

In the 1914 elections women voted for forty-five members of Congress, and the Democrats won only nineteen of these races, often by drastically reduced pluralities. Weren't you at all concerned about defeating some of your strongest Democratic supporters in Congress?

Not really. Whoever was elected from a suffrage state was going to be prosuffrage in Congress anyway, whether he was Republican or Democrat. But how else were we going to demonstrate that women could be influential, independent voters? One of the men we campaigned against was Representative—later Senator—Carl Hayden of Arizona, and he finally became a very good friend of the movement, I thought. But it is true that most of them really did resent it very much. . . .

You were once quoted to the effect that in picking volunteers you preferred enthusiasm to experience.

Yes. Well, wouldn't you? I think everybody would. I think every reform movement needs people who are full of enthusiasm. It's the first thing you need. I was full of enthusiasm, and I didn't want any lukewarm person around. I still am, of course.

One of your most enthusiastic volunteers was Inez Milholland Boissevain, wasn't she?

Inez Milholland actually gave her life for the women's movement. I think Inez was our most beautiful member. We always had her on horseback at the head of our processions. You've probably read about this, but when Inez was a student at Vassar, she tried to get up a suffrage meeting, and the college president refused to let her hold the meeting. So she organized a little group, and they jumped over a wall at the edge of the college and held the first suffrage meeting at Vassar in a cemetery. Imagine such a thing happening at a women's college so short a time ago. You can hardly believe such things occurred. But they did.

Inez Milholland in a demonstration parade. She was driving her own automobile, a most unusual thing for a woman at that time.

How did Miss Milholland give her life for the movement?

After college Inez wanted to study law, but every prominant law school refused to admit a girl. She finally went to New York University, which wasn't considered much of a university then, and got her law degree. Then she threw her whole soul into the suffrage movement and really did nothing else but that. Well, in 1916, when we were trying to prevent the re-election of Woodrow Wilson, we sent speakers to all the suffrage states, asking people not to vote for Wilson, because he was opposing the suffrage which they already had. Inez and her sister, Vita, who was a beautiful singer, toured the suffrage states as a team. Vita would sing songs about the women's movement, and then Inez would speak. Their father, John Milholland, paid all the expenses for their tour, which began in Wyoming. Well, when they got to Los Angeles, Inez had just started to make her speech when she suddenly collapsed and fell to the floor, just from complete exhaustion. Her last words were "Mr. President, how long must women wait for liberty?" We used her words on picket banners outside the White House. I think she was about twenty-eight or twenty-nine. . . . She was brought back and buried near her family home in New York State. We decided to have a memorial service for her in Statuary Hall in the Capitol on Christmas Day. . . .

Did you invite President Wilson and his family?

Oh, no. We did send a delegation to him from the meeting, but he wouldn't receive them. Finally on January 9, 1917, he agreed to meet with women from all over the country who brought Milholland resolutions. The women asked him once more to lend the weight and influence of his great office to the federal amendment, but the President rejected the appeal and continued to insist that he was the follower, not the leader, of his party. The women were quite disappointed when they returned to Cameron House, where we had established our headquarters across Lafayette Square from the White House. That afternoon we made the decision to have a perpetual delegation, six days a week, from ten in the morning until half past five in the evening, around the White House. We began the next day.

And this perpetual delegation, or picketing, continued until the President changed his position?

Yes. Since the President had made it clear that he wouldn't see any more delegations in his office, we felt that pickets outside the White House would be the best way to remind him of our cause. Every day when he went out for his daily ride, as he drove through our picket line he always took off his hat and bowed to us. We respected him very much. I always thought he was a great President. Years later, when I was in Geneva [Switzerland] working with the World Woman's Party, I was always so moved when I would walk down to the League of Nations and see the little tribute to Woodrow Wilson. . . .

Do you want to talk about the violence that occurred on the White House picket line?

Not particularly. It is true that after the United States entered the war [April 6, 1917], there was some hostility, and some of the pickets were attacked and had their banners ripped out of their hands. The feeling was—and some of our own members shared this and left the movement—that the cause of suffrage should be abandoned during wartime, that we should work instead for peace. But this was the same argument used during the Civil War, after which they wrote the word "male" into the Constitution. Did you know that "male" appears three times in the Fourteenth Amendment? Well, it does. So we agreed that suffrage came *before* war. Indeed, if we had universal suffrage throughout the world, we might not even have wars. So we continued picketing the White House, even though we were called traitors and pro-German and all that. . . .

It is true, isn't it, that you were arrested outside the White House on October 20, 1917, and sentenced to seven months in the District of Columbia jail?

Yes.

And that when you were taken to the cell-block where the other suffragists were being held, you were so appalled by the stale air that you broke a window with a volume of Robert Browning's poetry you had brought along to read?

No. I think Florence Boeckel, our publicity girl, invented that business about the volume of Browning's poetry. What I actually broke the window with was a bowl I found in my cell.

Was this the reason you were transferred to solitary confinement in the jail's psychopathic ward?

I think the government's strategy was to discredit me. That the other leaders of the Woman's Party would say, well, we had better sort of disown this crazy person. But they didn't.

During the next three or four weeks you maintained your hunger strike. Was this the second or third time you underwent forcible feeding?

Probably, but I'm not sure how many times.

Is this done with liquids through a tube put down through your mouth?

I think it was done through the nose, if I remember right. And they didn't use the soft tubing that is available today.

While you were held in solitary confinement your own lawyer, Dudley Field Malone, could not get in to see you. And yet one day David Lawrence, the journalist, came in to interview you. How do you explain this?

I think he was a reporter at that time, but anyway he was a very great supporter of and, I guess, a personal friend of President Wilson's. I didn't know then what he was, except that he came in and said he had come to have an interview with me. Of course, a great many people thought that Lawrence, because of his close connection with the White House, had been encouraged to go look into what the women were doing and why they were making all this trouble and so on.

You and all the other suffragist prisoners were released on November 27 and 28, just a few days after Lawrence's visit. Could this action have been based on his report to the President?

I wouldn't know about that. Of course, the only way we could be released would be by act of the President.

And on January 9, 1918, President Wilson formally declared for federal suffrage. The next day the House passed the amendment 274–136, and the really critical phase of the legislative struggle began.

Yes. Well, when we began, Maud Younger, our congressional chairman, got up this card catalogue, which is now on loan to the Library of Congress. We had little leaflets printed, and each person who interviewed a congressman would write a little report on where this or that man stood. We knew we had the task of winning them over, man by man, and it was important to know what our actual strength was in Congress at all times. These records showed how, with each Congress, we were getting stronger and stronger, until we finally thought we were at the point of putting the Anthony amendment to a vote. And of course this information was very helpful to our supporters in Congress.

Yet when the Senate finally voted on October 1, 1918, the amendment failed by two votes of the necessary two thirds. What happened?

We realized that we were going to lose a few days before the vote. We sat there in the Senate gallery, and they talked on and on and on, and finally Maud Younger and I went down to see what was going on, why they wouldn't vote. People from all over the country had come. The galleries were filled with suffragists. We went to see Senator Curtis, the Republican whip, and the Republican leader, Senator Gallinger. It was then a Republican Senate. And there they stood, each with a tally list in their hands. So we said, why don't you call the roll. And they said, well, Senator Borah has deserted us, he has decided to oppose the amendment, and there is no way on earth we can change his mind. . . .

Was it about this time that your members began burning the President's statements in public?

I'm not sure when it started. We had a sort of perpetual flame going in an urn outside our headquarters in Lafayette Square. I think we used rags soaked in kerosene. It was really very dramatic, because when President Wilson went to Paris for the peace conference, he was always issuing some wonderful, idealistic statement that was impossible to reconcile with what he was doing at home. And we had an enormous bell—I don't recall how we ever got such an enormous bell—and every time Wilson would make one of these speeches, we would toll this great bell, and then somebody would go outside with the Presi-

dent's speech and, with great dignity, burn it in our little caldron. I remember
that Senator Medill McCormick lived just down the street from us, and we
were constantly getting phone calls from him saying they couldn't sleep or
conduct social affairs because our bell was always tolling away.

You had better results from the next Congress, the Sixty-sixth, didn't you?

Yes. President Wilson made a magnificent speech calling for the amendment
as a war measure back in October, 1918, and on May 20, 1919, the House
passed the amendment. Then on June 4 the Senate finally passed it.

Did you go to hear the President?

I don't believe we were there, because when the President spoke, everybody
wanted tickets, and the Woman's Party has never asked for tickets, because we
still don't want to be in any way under any obligation. I know we were in the
gallery when the Senate actually voted, because nobody wanted tickets then.
Our main concern was that the Senate might try to reinstate the seven-year
clause that had been defeated in the House.

The seven-year clause?

This clause required the amendment to be ratified by the states within seven
years or else the amendment would be defeated. We got the clause eliminated
on the suffrage amendment, but we were unable to stop Congress from attach-
ing it to the present equal rights amendment.

Were you relieved when the Anthony amendment finally passed?

Yes, for many reasons. But we still had to get it ratified. We went to work on
that right away and worked continuously for the fourteen months it took. But
that last state . . . we thought we never would get that last state. And, you know,
President Wilson really got it for us. What happened was that Wilson went to
the governor of Tennessee, who was a Democrat. The President asked him to
call a special session of the state legislature so the amendment could be ratified in time for women to vote in the 1920 Presidential election.

*That was on August 18, 1920, and there is a well-known photograph of you, on the
balcony of your headquarters, unfurling the suffrage flag with thirty-six stars. What
were your feelings that day?*

You know, you are always so engrossed in the details that you probably don't
have all the big and lofty thoughts you should be having. I think we had this
anxiety about how we would pay all our bills at the end. So the first thing we
did was to just do nothing. We closed our headquarters, stopped all our expenses, stopped publishing our weekly magazine, *The Suffragist*, stopped everything and started paying off the bills we had incurred. Maud Younger and I

got the tiniest apartment we could get, and she took over the housekeeping, and we got a maid who came in, and we just devoted ourselves to raising this money. . . .

Then the following year, on February 15, 1921, we had our final convention to decide what to do. Whether to disband or whether to continue and take up the whole equality program—equality for women in all fields of life—that had been spelled out at the Seneca Falls convention in 1848. We decided to go on, and we elected a whole new national board, with Elsie Hill as our new chairman. We thought we ought to get another amendment to the Constitution, so we went to many lawyers—I remember we paid one lawyer quite a large sum, for us, at least—and asked them to draw up an amendment for equal rights. We had another meeting up in Seneca Falls on the seventy-fifth anniversary of the original meeting, and there we adopted the program we have followed ever since on the equal-rights amendment. That was 1923. So that is when we started.

Was that the year the first equal-rights amendment was introduced?

We hadn't been able to get any lawyer to draft an amendment that satisfied us, so I drafted one in simple ordinary English, not knowing anything about law, and we got it introduced in Congress. But at the first hearing our little group was the only one that supported it. All these other organizations of women that hadn't worked to get the vote, these professional groups and so on, opposed the amendment on the grounds that it would deprive them of alimony and force them to work in the mines, and they would lose these special labor laws that protect women. So it was obvious to us—and to the Congress—that we were going to have to change the thinking of American women first. So we began going to convention after convention of women, trying to get them to endorse E.R.A. It took many years. The American Association of University Women just endorsed it in 1972. Imagine, all the years and years that women have been going to universities. But the new generation of college women were so hopeless on this subject.

It was like forty years in the wilderness, wasn't it?

Yes, more or less. But during that time we opened—and by "we" I mean the whole women's movement—we opened a great many doors to women with the power of the vote, things like getting women into the diplomatic service. And don't forget we were successful in getting equality for women written into the charter of the United Nations in 1945.

Do you think the progress of the equal-rights amendment has been helped by the women's liberation movement?

I feel very strongly that if you are going to do anything, you have to take one thing and do it. You can't try lots of reforms and get them all mixed up together. Now, I think the liberation movement has been a good thing, because it has aroused lots of women from their self-interest, and it has made everyone more aware of the inequalities that exist. But the ratification of the equal-rights amendment has been made a bit harder by these people who run around advocating, for instance, abortion. As far as I can see, E.R.A. has nothing whatsoever to do with abortion.

How did abortion become involved with equal rights?

At the 1968 Republican convention our representative went before the platform committee to present our request for a plank on equal rights, and as soon as she finished, up came one of the liberation ladies, a well-known feminist, who made a great speech on abortion. So then all the women on the platform committee said, well, we're not going to have the Republican Party campaigning for abortion. So they voted not to put *anything* in the party platform about women's rights. That was the first time since 1940 that we didn't get an equal-rights plank in the Republican platform. And then that feminist showed up at the Democratic convention, and the same thing happened with their platform. It was almost the same story at the 1972 conventions, but this time we managed to get equal rights back into the platforms.

It's really the principle of equal rights that you're concerned with, isn't it, not the specific applications?

I have never doubted that equal rights was the right direction. Most reforms, most problems are complicated. But to me there is nothing complicated about ordinary equality. Which is a nice thing about our campaign. It really is true, at least to my mind, that only good will come to everybody with equality. If we get to the point where everyone has equality of opportunity—and I don't expect to see it, we have such a long, long way ahead of us—then it seems to me it is not our problem how women use their equality or how men use their equality.

Miss Paul, how would you describe your contribution to the struggle for women's rights?

I always feel . . . the movement is a sort of mosaic. Each of us puts in one little stone, and then you get a great mosaic at the end.

■   ■   ■   ■   ■   ■   ■

Gifford Pinchot: Father of the Forests

T. H. Watkins

Gifford Pinchot is best known for his role in the so-called "Ballinger-Pinchot Controversy," a heated and in part politically motivated conflict he had as Chief Forester of the U.S. Department of Agriculture with Richard Ballinger, President William Howard Taft's Secretary of the Interior about the disposition of certain coal-rich lands in Alaska. Actually, as T. H. Watkins explains in this essay, Pinchot was an important political leader, a three-term governor of Pennsylvania, one of the first professional foresters in America, and a lifelong supporter of conservationist causes of all types. His career in conservation is summarized and evaluated in these pages.

T. H. Watkins, editor of *Wilderness,* the magazine of the Wilderness Society, is also the author of *Righteous Pilgrim: The Life and Times of Harold L. Ickes.*

■ ■ ■ ■ ■ ■

Gifford Pinchot passed through nearly six decades of American public life like a Jeremiah, the flames of certitude seeming to dance behind his dark eyes. "Gifford Pinchot is a dear," his good friend and mentor Theodore Roosevelt once said of him, "but he is a fanatic, with an element of hardness and narrowness in his temperament, and an extremist."

The complaint was legitimate, but the zealot in question also was the living expression of an idea shared by much of an entire generation (indeed, shared by Roosevelt himself): the conviction that men and women could take hold of their government and shape it to great ends, great deeds, lifting all elements of American life to new levels of probity, grace, freedom, and prosperity. The urge was not entirely selfless; the acquisition and exercise of power have gratifications to which Pinchot and his kind were by no means immune. But at the forefront was a solemn and utterly earnest desire that the lot of humanity should be bettered by the work of those who were equipped by circumstance, talent, and training to change the world. It had something to do with duty and integrity and honesty, and if it was often marred by arrogance, at its best it was just as often touched by compassion.

And the world, in fact, was changed.

"I have . . . been a Governor, every now and then, but I am a forester all the time—have been, and shall be, all my working life." Gifford Pinchot made this pronouncement in a speech not long before his death at the age of eighty-one, and repeated it in *Breaking New Ground,* his account of the early years of the conservation movement and his considerable place in it. It was true enough, but it could just as legitimately be said of him that he had been a forester every now and then but was a politician, had been and would be, all his working life.

. . . From childhood Pinchot had been active in the outdoors, fond of hiking, camping, and, especially, trout fishing. Since there was nowhere yet in the United

States to study his chosen profession, after graduating from Yale he took himself back to Europe, where for more than a year he studied forest management at the French Forestry School in Nancy and put in a month of fieldwork under Forstmeister ("Chief Forester") Ulrich Meister in the city forest of Zurich, Switzerland.

Back in this country he was hired by George W. Vanderbilt in 1892 to manage the five-thousand-acre forest on his Biltmore estate in North Carolina, a ragged patchwork of abused lands purchased from numerous individual farmers. While nursing this wrecked acreage back to health, the young forester persuaded Vanderbilt to expand his holdings by an additional one hundred thousand acres of nearly untouched forest land outside the estate. This new enterprise became known as the Pisgah Forest, and it was there in 1895 that Pinchot introduced what were almost certainly the first scientific logging operations ever undertaken in this country.

By then the young man had made a secure reputation in the field; indeed, he *was* the field. In December 1893 he opened an office in Manhattan as a "consulting forester." Over the next several years, while continuing his work for Vanderbilt in North Carolina, he provided advice and research work on forest lands in Michigan, Pennsylvania, and New York State—including the six-million-acre Adirondack Park and Forest Preserve, established in 1895 as the largest state-owned park in the nation. . . .

It would be difficult to find a more convenient symbol for the dark side of American enterprise than the state of the nation's forest lands in the last quarter of the nineteenth century. Restrained only by the dictates of the marketplace, the timber industry had enjoyed a free hand for generations, and the wreckage was considerable. Most of the best forest land east of the Mississippi had long since been logged out—sometimes twice over—and while generally humid conditions had allowed some of the land to recover in second and third growth, erosion had permanently scarred many areas. Unimpeded runoff during seasonal rains had caused such ghastly floods as that leading to the destruction of Johnstown, Pennsylvania, in 1889.

The land of the Mississippi and Ohio valleys was almost entirely privately owned; west of the Mississippi most of the land belonged to the nation. It was called the public domain, its steward was the federal government, as represented by the General Land Office, and for years it had been hostage to the careless enthusiasm of a tradition that looked upon land as a commodity to be sold or an opportunity to be exploited, not a resource to be husbanded. About two hundred million acres of this federal land were forested, and much of it, too, had been systematically mutilated. In addition to legitimate timber companies that consistently misused the various land laws by clear-cutting entire claims without even bothering to remain around long enough to establish final title, many "tramp" lumbermen simply marched men, mules, oxen, and sometimes donkey engines onto an attractive (and vacant) tract of public forest land, stripped it, and moved out, knowing full well that apprehension and prosecution were simply beyond the means or interest of the understaffed, over-committed, and largely corrupt General Land Office. As early as 1866 such instances of cheerful plunder had gutted so many forests of the public domain that the surveyors general of both Washington Territory and Colorado Territory earnestly recommended to the General Land Office that the forest lands in their districts be sold immediately, while there was something left to sell.

The forests were not sold, nor did they vanish entirely, but they did remain vulnerable to regular depredation. It was not until 1891 and passage of an obscure legislative rider called the Forest Reserve Clause that the slowly growing reform element in the executive branch was enabled to do anything about it. Armed with the power of this law, President Benjamin Harrison withdrew thirteen million acres of public forest land in the West from uses that would have been permitted by any of the plethora of lenient land laws then on the books, and at the end of his second term, President Grover Cleveland added another twenty-one million acres. Since there was virtually no enforcement of the new law, however, withdrawal provided little protection from illegal use; at the same time, it specifically disallowed legitimate use of public timber and grasslands. In response to the howl that arose in the West and to give some semblance of protection and managed use, Congress passed the Forest Organic Act of June 1897, which stipulated that the forest reserves were intended "to improve and protect the forest . . . for the purpose of securing favorable conditions of water flow, and to furnish a continuous supply of timber for the use and necessities of citizens of the United States."

Gifford Pinchot, the young "consulting forester," was the author of much of the language of the act. In the summer of 1896 he had distinguished himself as the secretary of the National Forest Commission, a body formed by President Cleveland to investigate conditions in the nation's public forests and to recommend action for their proper use and protection, and it was the commission that had put forth the need for an organic act. No one knew more about American forests than Pinchot did, and he seemed the only logical choice to head the Department of Agriculture's Forestry Division when the position of director fell vacant in May 1898.

On the face of it, Pinchot's new post was less than prestigious. The Forestry Division was housed in two rooms of the old red-brick Agriculture Building on the south side of the Mall in Washington, D.C. It enjoyed a total of eleven employees and an annual appropriation of $28,500. And since the forest reserves remained under the jurisdiction of the Interior Department, the Forestry Division had little to do beyond advising private landowners on the proper management of their wood lots and forests. This was anathema to an activist like Pinchot, and he was soon honing the skills that would make him one of the most persistent and effective lobbyists who ever prowled the cloakrooms and cubbyholes of Congress.

His ambition was not a small one: He wanted nothing less than to get the forest reserves transferred to Agriculture and placed under his care in the Forestry Division and then to build the division into the first effective agency for the management and conservation of public lands in the history of the nation. It did not hurt his chances when he became intimate with another early American conservationist—Theodore Roosevelt. . . .

The two men combined almost immediately in an effort to get the forest reserves into Pinchot's care. The public lands committees of both the House and Senate, however, were dominated by Westerners, many of whom had vested interests in the status quo, and it took more than three years of public campaigning and artful cajolery, Roosevelt himself bringing the full weight of the Presidency to bear

A solitary pine tree adorns the original badge of the U.S. Forest Service, which was founded by Gifford Pinchot at the beginning of the century.

on the point, before Pinchot was given his heart's desire: passage of the Forest Transfer Act, on February 1, 1905. In addition to bringing over the forests—which now totaled more than sixty-three million acres—the new law provided for the charging of fees for cutting timber and grazing cattle and sheep, and this was followed by the Agricultural Appropriation Act of March 3, a section of which gave federal foresters "authority to make arrests for the violation of laws and regulations relating to the forest reserves. . . ."

The government was now in the tree business with a vengeance. Shortly the name of the reserves was changed to that of national forests, the Forestry Division to that of the U.S. Forest Service, and Gifford Pinchot was solidly in place as the nation's first chief forester, a position he would hold officially only until his resignation in 1910 but would hold in his heart for the rest of his life.

With his President's blessing, Pinchot crafted the young agency into a public body whose dedication to the ideal of service to the public was nearly unique for its time (or our own, for that matter). It came directly out of Pinchot's own convictions. "It is the first duty of a public officer to obey the law," he wrote in *The Fight for Conservation,* in 1910. "But it is his second duty, and a close second, to do everything the law will let him do for the public good. . . ."

It was an elite corps that Pinchot created, built on merit and merit alone, one in which both competence and stupidity were swiftly rewarded—and little went unnoticed by the chief forester ("I found him all tangled up," Pinchot wrote to a lieutenant about one hapless employee, "and generally making an Ass of himself, with splendid success"). William R. Greeley, one of the twenty-five hundred foresters who served under Pinchot (and who later became chief forester himself), caught the spirit of Pinchot's influence precisely: "He made us . . . feel like soldiers in a patriotic cause."

The system this exemplary body of men administered was carefully structured by the chief forester. Individual forests were divided up into management units, each with its own ranger or ranger force, and administrative headquarters were established in the six districts across the West where most of the forests were grouped, from Missoula, Montana, to Portland, Oregon. Pinchot gave his district supervisors a great deal of autonomy and encouraged them to give their rangers similarly loose reins in the field—whether selecting stands of harvestable trees, supervising a timber sale, regulating the number of cows or sheep that might be allowed on a piece of grazing land, or fighting fires. . . .

. . . By the time Roosevelt left office in March 1909, the national forest system had been enlarged to 148 million acres, and the Forest Service had become one of the most respected government services in the nation—reason enough for the historian M. Nelson McGeary's encomium of 1960: "Had there been no Pinchot to build the U.S. Forest Service into an exceptionally effective agency, it would hardly have been possible to report in 1957 that 'most' of the big lumber operators had adopted forestry as a policy; or that the growth of saw timber has almost caught up with the rate of drain on forest resources from cutting, fire, and natural losses. . . ."

Nor, it is safe to say, would there have been much left of the forests themselves. The principles Pinchot put to work would inform the management of the public lands throughout most of the twentieth century and become one of the roots of the sensibility we call environmentalism. It was called conservation then, and Pinchot always claimed that he was the first to put that use upon the word. "Conservation," he wrote, "means the wise use of the earth and its resources for the lasting good of men. Conservation is the foresighted utilization, preservation, and/or renewal of forests, waters, lands, and minerals, for the greatest good of the greatest number for the longest time."

Wise use was the cornerstone, and Pinchot and his followers had little patience with the still-embryonic notion that the natural world deserved preservation quite as much for its own sake as for the sake of the men and women who used it. John Muir, a hairy wood sprite of a naturalist whom Pinchot had met and befriended as early as 1896, personified this more idealistic instinct, tracing the roots of his own inspiration back to Henry David Thoreau's declaration that "in Wildness is the preservation of the World." For a time, the two men were allies in spite of their differences, but the friendship disintegrated after 1905, when Pinchot lent his support to the efforts of the city of San Francisco to dam the Hetch Hetchy Valley in Yosemite National Park for a public water-and-power project in order to free the city from a private power monopoly.

Muir, whose writings about Yosemite had brought him a measure of fame, had founded the Sierra Club in 1892 largely as a tool to protect the glorious trench of the Yosemite Valley and other pristine areas in the Sierra Nevada. Among these was the Hetch Hetchy Valley, which these early preservationists maintained was the equal of Yosemite itself in beauty. The reservoir that would fill up behind the proposed dam on the Tuolumne River would obliterate that beauty. But this was exactly the sort of public power-and-water project that spoke most eloquently to the deepest pragmatic instincts of Pinchot and his kind, who argued that every measure of conservation as they understood it would be fulfilled by approval of the project. "Whoever dominates power," Pinchot wrote, "dominates all industry. . . ."

Pinchot's devotion to the principles of conservation went beyond the immediate question of use versus preservation. Monopoly was evil personified, and monopoly, he believed, stemmed directly from the control of the natural world. "Monopoly of resources," he wrote in *Breaking New Ground,* "which prevents, limits, or destroys equality of opportunity is one of the most effective of all ways to control and limit human rights, especially the right of self-government." With this conviction to guide him, it did not take him long to find his way from the world of conservation to the world of politics, where, like thousands of his class, he found his imagination seized by Progressive Republicanism.

The movement had been distilled from more than forty years of what the historian Howard Mumford Jones called "exuberance and wrath" following the Civil War. Its followers saw themselves and their values caught in a vise: threatened on one side by an increasingly violent and potentially revolutionary uprising on the part of the great unwashed—largely represented by the Democratic party—and on the other by a cynical plutocratic brotherhood—largely represented by the regular Republican party—which brutally twisted and subverted American institutions for purposes of personal greed and power.

Imperfectly but noisily, Theodore Roosevelt had given these people in the middle a voice and a symbol to call their own, and when he chose not to run for a third term in 1908, they felt abandoned. Prominent among them was Gifford Pinchot, and there is some evidence to suggest that he engineered his own dismissal as chief forester by President William Howard Taft, whom Roosevelt had groomed as his own chosen successor. The opportunity came in 1909, when Pinchot learned that Taft's Secretary of the Interior, Richard Ballinger, was determined to honor a number of coal-mining claims on lands in Alaska that Roosevelt had earlier withdrawn from such uses.

When Taft backed his Interior Secretary, Pinchot chose to see it as the beginning of a wholesale repudiation of all that Roosevelt had done to champion the public interest. He made no secret of his conclusions, and Taft was certain that more than bureaucratic integrity was behind Pinchot's loudly voiced concerns. . . .

Taft resisted as long as he reasonably could, but when Pinchot violated the President's direct orders to maintain silence by writing an open letter to a Senate committee investigating the Ballinger matter, he decided he had no choice. Calling the letter an example of insubordination "almost unparalleled in the history of the government," Taft fired the chief forester of the United States on January 7, 1910. . . .

But the essential legacy of this committed, driven man, this public servant, this prince of rectitude, is the national forests themselves. There are 191 million acres of them now, spreading over the mountain slopes and river valleys of the West like a great dark blanket, still the center of controversy, still threatened and mismanaged and nurtured and loved as they were when the son of a dry goods merchant first walked in an American wood and wondered what could be done to save it for the future.

4

America in World Affairs

A mushroom cloud hovers over Nagasaki after the United States dropped an atomic bomb on the city, August 9, 1945.

The Needless War with Spain

William E. Leuchtenburg

Seldom have events so pregnant with future significance occurred in an atmosphere so devoid of an understanding of their significance as in 1898 when the United States went to war with Spain. It is perhaps not quite accurate to say that the United States emerged from that war as a world power. In retrospect, the nation was a world power well before the war began. But the war made Americans aware that the United States was a world power, and from that awareness flowed American imperialism, American participation in World War I, and much that followed.

As William E. Leuchtenburg explains in this essay, there was no shortage of "aggressive, expansionistic, and jingoistic" feeling in America during the early 1890s. But the conflict with Spain derived chiefly from the desire of Americans to help the beleaguered Cubans with their independence from Spain. Americans wanted the war (which could well have been avoided), but they had little understanding of what the results of that war would be.

Mr. Leuchtenburg, William Rand Kenan professor of history at the University of North Carolina, is the author of *Franklin D. Roosevelt and the New Deal, 1932–1940,* which won a Francis Parkman Prize, awarded each year to the book in American history that best combines sound scholarship and literary distinction. This essay also combines these two qualities.

■ ■ ■ ■ ■ ■ ■

The United States in the 1890's became more aggressive, expansionistic, and jingoistic than it had been since the 1850's. In less than five years, we came to the brink of war with Italy, Chile, and Great Britain over three minor incidents in which no American national interest of major importance was involved. In each of these incidents, our secretary of state was highly aggressive, and the American people applauded. During these years, we completely overhauled our decrepit Navy, building fine new warships like the *Maine.* The martial virtues of Napoleon, the imperial doctrines of Rudyard Kipling, and the naval theories of Captain Alfred T. Mahan all enjoyed a considerable vogue.

There was an apparently insatiable hunger for foreign conquest. Senator Shelby M. Cullom declared in 1895: "It is time that some one woke up and realized the necessity of annexing some property. We want all this northern hemisphere, and when we begin to reach out to secure these advantages we will begin to have a nation and our lawmakers will rise above the grade of politicians and become true statesmen." When, in 1895, the United States almost became involved in a war with Great Britain over the Venezuelan boundary, Theodore Roosevelt noted: "The antics of the bankers, brokers and anglo-maniacs generally are humiliating to a degree. . . . Personally I rather hope the fight will come soon. The clamor of the peace faction has convinced me that this country needs a war." The Washington *Post* concluded: "The taste of Empire is in the mouth of the people. . . ."

In the early nineteenth century, under the leadership of men like Simon Bolivar, Spain's colonies in the New World had launched a series of successful revolutions; of the great Spanish empire that Cortes and Pizarro had built, the island of Cuba, "the Ever Faithful Isle," was the only important Spanish possession to stay loyal to the Crown. Spain exploited the economy of the island mercilessly, forcing Cubans to buy Spanish goods at prices far above the world market, and Madrid sent to Cuba as colonial officials younger sons who had no interest in the island other than making a quick killing and returning to Spain. High taxes to support Spanish officialdom crippled the island; arbitrary arrests and arbitrary trials made a mockery of justice; and every attempt at public education was stifled.

The island of Cuba had been in a state of political turbulence for years when in 1894 the American Wilson-Gorman Tariff placed duties on Cuban sugar which, coupled with a world-wide depression, brought ruin to the economy of the island. The terrible hardship of the winter was the signal for revolution; on February 24, 1895, under the leadership of a junta in New York City headed by José Martí, rebels once more took the field against Spain. At first, the American people were too absorbed with the Venezuelan crisis to pay much attention to another revolt in Cuba. Then, in September, 1895, came the event which changed the course of the Cuban rebellion: William Randolph Hearst, a young man of 32 who had been operating the San Franciso *Examiner* in a sensational fashion, purchased the New York *Morning Journal,* and immediately locked horns with Joseph Pulitzer and the *World* in a circulation war that was to make newspaper history.

Hearst capitalized on the fact that the American people had only the most romantic notions of the nature of the Cuban conflict. The rebels under General Máximo Gómez, a tough Santo Domingan guerrilla fighter, embarked on a program of burning the cane fields in the hope not only of depriving the government of revenue but also of so disrupting the life of the island that the government would be forced to submit. Although there were some noble spirits in the group, much of the rebellion had an unsavory odor; one of the main financial supports for the uprising came from American property owners who feared that their sugar fields would be burned unless protection money was paid.

While Gómez was putting Cuba to the torch, American newsmen were filing reports describing the war in terms of nonexistent pitched battles between the liberty-loving Cubans and the cruel Spaniards. The war was presented, in short, as a Byronic conflict between the forces of freedom and the forces of tyranny, and the American people ate it up. When Hearst bought the *Journal* in late 1895, it had a circulation of 30,000; by 1897 it had bounded to over 400,000 daily, and during the Spanish-American War it was to go well over a million.

The sensational newspapers had influence, yet they represented no more than a minority of the press of the country; and in the South and the Middle West, where anti-Spanish feeling became most intense, the representative newspaper was much more conservative. Certainly the yellow press played a tremendous part in whipping up sentiment for intervention in Cuba, but these feelings could not be carried into action unless American political leaders of both parties were willing to assume the terrible responsibility of war.

By the beginning of 1896 the rebels had achieved such success in their guerrilla tactics that Madrid decided on firmer steps and sent General Don Valeriano Weyler y Nicolau to Cuba. When Weyler arrived in February, he found the sugar industry severely disrupted and the military at a loss to meet the rebel tactic of setting fire to the cane fields. Weyler declared martial law and announced that men guilty of incendiarism would be dealt with summarily; he was promptly dubbed "The Butcher" by American newspapermen.

By late 1896 Weyler still had not succeeded in crushing the insurrection, and his measures became more severe. On October 21 he issued his famous *reconcentrado* order, directing the "reconcentration" of the people of Pinar del Río in the garrison towns, and forbidding the export of supplies from the towns to the countryside. Reasoning that he could never suppress the rebellion so long as the rebels could draw secret assistance from people in the fields, Weyler moved the people from the estates into the towns and stripped the countryside of supplies to starve out the rebellion. Since many of the people had already fled to the towns, the *reconcentrado* policy was not as drastic as it appeared; yet the suffering produced by the policy was undeniable. Lacking proper hygienic care, thousands of Cubans, especially women and children, died like flies.

When William McKinley entered the White House in 1897, he had no intention of joining the War Hawks. "If I can only go out of office . . . with the knowledge that I have done what lay in my power to avert this terribly calamity," McKinley told Grover Cleveland on the eve of his inauguration, "I shall be the happiest man in the world." McKinley came to power as the "advance agent of prosperity," and business interests were almost unanimous in opposing any agitation of the Cuban question that might lead to war. Contrary to the assumptions of Leninist historians, it was Wall Street which, first and last, resisted a war which was to bring America its overseas empire.

The country had been gripped since 1893 by the deepest industrial depression in its history, a depression that was to persist until the beginning of 1897. Each time it appeared recovery might be on its way, a national crisis had cut it off: first the Venezuelan boundary war scare of December, 1895, then the bitter free silver campaign of 1896. What business groups feared more than anything else was a new crisis. As Julius Pratt writes: "To this fair prospect of a great business revival the threat of war was like a specter at the feast."

McKinley was not a strong President, and he had no intention of being one. Of all the political figures of his day, he was the man most responsive to the popular will. It was his great virtue and, his critics declared, his great weakness. Uncle Joe Cannon once remarked: "McKinley keeps his ear to the ground so close that he gets it full of grasshoppers much of the time." If McKinley was not one of our greatest Presidents, he was certainly the most representative and the most responsive. Anyone who knew the man knew that, although he was strongly opposed to war, he would not hold out against war if the popular demand for war became unmistakable. "Let the voice of the people rule"—this was McKinley's credo, and he meant it.

The threat to peace came from a new quarter, from the South and West, the strongholds of Democracy and free silver. Many Bryanite leaders were convinced that a war would create such a strain on the currency system that the opposition to free silver would collapse. Moreover, with the opposition to war strongest in Wall Street, they found it easy to believe that Administration policy was the product of a conspiracy of bankers who would deny silver to the American people, who would deny liberty to the people of Cuba, who were concerned only with the morality of the countinghouse. Moreover, Bryan was the spokesman for rural Protestantism, which was already speaking in terms of a righteous war against Spain to free the Cubans from bondage. These were forces too powerful for McKinley to ignore. McKinley desired peace, but he was above all, a Republican partisan, and he had no intention of handing the Democrats in 1900 the campaign cry of Free Cuba and Free Silver.

While McKinley attempted to search out a policy that would preserve peace without bringing disaster to the Republican party, the yellow press made his job all the more difficult by whipping up popular anger against Spain. On February 12 the *Journal* published a dispatch from Richard Harding Davis, reporting that as the American steamship *Olivette* was about to leave Havana Harbor for the United States, it was boarded by Spanish police officers who searched three young Cuban women, one of whom was suspected of carrying messages from the rebels. The *Journal* ran the story under the headline, "Does Our Flag Protect Women?" with a vivid drawing by Frederic Remington across one half a page showing Spanish plainclothes men searching a wholly nude woman. War, declared the *Journal,* "is a dreadful thing, but there are things more dreadful than even war, and one of them is dishonor." It shocked the country, and Congressman Amos Cummings immediately resolved to launch a congressional inquiry into the *Olivette* outrage. Before any steps could be taken, the true story was revealed. The *World* produced one of the young women who indignantly protested the *Journal*'s version of the incident. Pressured by the *World,* the *Journal* was forced to print a letter from Davis explaining that his article had not said that male policemen had searched the women and that, in fact, the search had been conducted quite properly by a police matron with no men present.

The *Olivette* incident was manufactured by Hearst, but by the spring of 1897 the American press had a new horror to report which was all too true. Famine was stalking the island. Cuba had been in a serious economic state when the rebellion broke out in 1895; two years of war would, under any circumstances, have been disastrous, but the deliberate policies pursued both by the insurgents and by the government forces made the situation desperate. It was a simple matter for Hearst and Pulitzer reporters to pin the full responsibility on Weyler.

By the middle of July, McKinley had formulated a policy which he set down in a letter of instructions to our new American minister to Spain, General Stewart L. Woodford. The letter emphasized the need of bringing the Cuban war to an end and said that this could be done to the mutual advantage of both Spain and the Cubans by granting some kind of autonomy to Cuba. If Spain did not make an offer to the rebels and if the "measures of unparalleled severity" were not ended, the United States threatened to intervene.

On August 8 an Italian anarchist assassinated the Spanish premier; and when Woodford reached Madrid in September, a new government was about to take over headed by Señor Sagasta and the Liberals, who had repeatedly denounced the "barbarity" of the previous government's policy in Cuba. Sagasta immediately removed General Weyler, and the prospects for an agreement between the United States and Spain took a decided turn for the better.

While Woodford was carrying on skillful diplomatic negotiations for peace in Madrid, the Hearst press was creating a new sensation in this country with the Cisneros affair. Evangelina Cisneros was a young Cuban woman who had been arrested and imprisoned in the Rocojidas in Havana, guilty, according to the American press, of no other crime than protecting her virtue from an unscrupulous Spanish colonel, an aide to Butcher Weyler. The Rocojidas, Hearst's reporter told American readers, was a cage where the innocent beauty was herded with women criminals of every type, subject to the taunts and vile invitations of men who gathered outside.

When it was reported that Señorita Cisneros, whose father was a rebel leader, was to be sent for a long term to a Spanish penal colony in Africa or in the Canaries, the *Journal* launched one of the most fabulous campaigns in newspaper history. "Enlist the women of America!" was the Hearst war cry, and the women of America proved willing recruits. Mrs. Julia Ward Howe signed an appeal to Pope Leo XIII, and Mrs. Jefferson Davis, the widow of the president of the Confederacy, appealed to the queen regent of Spain to "give Evangelina Cisneros to the women of America to save her from a fate worse than death." When the *Journal* prepared a petition on behalf of Señorita Cisneros, it obtained the names of Mrs. Nancy McKinley, the mother of the President, and Mrs. John Sherman, the wife of the secretary of state, as well as such other prominent ladies as Julia Dent Grant and Mrs. Mark Hanna.

It was a startling coup for Mr. Hearst, but he had not yet even begun to display his ingenuity. On October 10, 1897, the *Journal* erupted across its front page with the banner headline: "An American Newspaper Accomplishes at a Single Stroke What the Best Efforts of Diplomacy Failed Utterly to Bring About in Many Months." Hearst had sent Karl Decker, one of his most reliable correspondents, to Havana in late August with orders to rescue the Cuban Girl Martyr "at any hazard"; and Decker had climbed to the roof of a house near the prison, broken the bar of a window of the jail, lifted Evangelina out, and, after hiding her for a few days in Havana, smuggled her onto an American steamer. Decker, signing his dispatch to the *Journal* "Charles Duval," wrote: "I have broken the bars of Rocojidas and have set free the beautiful captive of monster Weyler. Weyler could blind the Queen to the real character of Evangelina, but he could not build a jail that would hold against *Journal* enterprise when properly set to work." The Cuban Girl Martyr was met at the pier by a great throng, led up Broadway in a triumphal procession, taken to a reception at Delmonico's where 120,000 people milled about the streets surrounding the restaurant, and hailed at a monster reception in Madison Square Garden. The Bishop of London cabled his congratulations to the *Journal*, while Governor Stephens of Missouri proposed that the *Journal* send down 500 of its reporters to free the entire island.

On October 23 Sagasta announced a "total change of immense scope" in Spanish policy in Cuba. He promised to grant local autonomy to the Cubans immediately, reserving justice, the armed forces, and foreign relations to Spain. On November 13 Weyler's successor, Captain-General Blanco, issued a decree modifying considerably the *reconcentrado* policy, and on November 25 the queen regent signed the edicts creating an autonomous government for the island. In essence, Madrid had acceded to the American demands.

While Woodford was conducting negotiations with a conciliatory Liberal government in Madrid and while there was still hope for peace, the fatal incident occurred which made war virtually inevitable. On January 12, 1898, a riot broke out in Havana, and Spanish officers attacked newspaper offices. The nature of the riot is still not clear; it was over in an hour, and it had no anti-American aspects. If the United States now sent a naval vessel to Havana, it might be buying trouble with Spain. Yet if a riot did break out and Americans were killed, the Administration would be stoned for not having a ship there to protect them. For several days McKinley wavered; then he ordered the *Maine* to Havana, but with the explanation that this was a courtesy visit demonstrating that so nonsensical were the rumors of danger to American citizens that our ships could again resume their visits to the island.

As the *Maine* lay at anchor in Havana Harbor, the rebels, with a perfect sense of timing, released a new propaganda bombshell. In December, 1897, in a private letter, Señor Enrique Dupuy De Lôme, the Spanish minister at Washington, had set down his opinions of President McKinley's annual message to Congress: "Besides the ingrained and inevitable bluntness (*grosería*) with which it repeated all that the press and public opinion in Spain have said about Weyler," De Lôme wrote, "it once more shows what McKinley is, weak and a bidder for the admiration of the crowd, besides being a would-be politician (*politicastro*) who tries to leave a door open behind himself while keeping on good terms with the jingoes of his party." De Lôme added: "It would be very advantageous to take up, even if only for effect, the question of commercial relations, and to have a man of some prominence sent here in order that I may make use of him to carry on a propaganda among the Senators and others in opposition to the junta."

De Lôme had, to be sure, written all this in a private letter (which was stolen by an insurgent spy in the Havana post office), not in his official capacity, and his characterization of McKinley was not wholly without merit, but it was a blunder of the highest magnitude. Not only had De Lôme attacked the President, but he had gone on to suggest that the negotiations then going on over a commercial treaty were not being conducted in good faith. Throughout the letter ran precisely the tone which Hearst had been arguing expressed the Spanish temper—a cold, arrogant contempt for democratic institutions. The State Department immediately cabled Woodford to demand the recall of the Spanish minister, but Madrid had the good fortune of being able to tell Woodford that De Lôme, informed of the disaster the night before, had already resigned.

A week after the publication of the De Lôme indiscretion, at 9:40 on the night of February 15, 1898, came the terrible blow which ended all real hope for peace. In the harbor of Havana, the *Maine* was blown up by an explosion of unknown origin. In an instant, the ship was filled with the sounds of shrieking men and rushing water. The blast occurred in the forward part of the ship where, a half hour before, most of the men had turned in for the night; they were killed in their hammocks. Of the 350 officers and men on board, 260 were killed. By morning the proud *Maine* had sunk into the mud of Havana Harbor.

"Public opinion should be suspended until further report," Captain Sigsbee cabled to Washington, but even Sigsbee could not down his suspicions. The *Maine* had gone to a Spanish possession on a courtesy call, and the *Maine* now lay at the bottom of Havana Harbor. What could it mean but war? "I would give anything if President McKinley would order the fleet to Havana tomorrow," wrote Theodore Roosevelt. "The *Maine* was sunk by an act of dirty treachery on the part of the Spaniards." Volunteers lined up for war service, even though there was no one to enlist them; in New York 500 sharpshooting Westchester businessmen volunteered as a unit for the colors. The *Journal* reported: "The Whole Country Thrills With War Fever."

The cause of the explosion of the *Maine* has never been finally established. That Spain deliberately decided to blow up the *Maine* is inconceivable, although it is possible that it might have been the work of unauthorized Spanish extremists. The one group which had everything to gain from such an episode was the rebels; yet it seems unlikely that either they or Spanish hotheads could have carried out such an act and remained undetected. The most likely explanation is that it was caused by an explosion of internal origin; yet the evidence for this is not conclusive. In any event, this was the explanation that the Navy in 1898 was least willing to con-

Headlines such as this one from the New York World *left little doubt among readers that Spain had sunk the* Maine.

sider since it would reflect seriously on the care with which the Navy was operating the *Maine*.

The move toward war seemed relentless. On March 9 Congress unanimously voted $50,000,000 for war preparations. Yet the days went by and there was no war, in part because important sectors of American opinion viewed Hearst's stories of the atrocious conditions on the island with profound skepticism. Senator Redfield Proctor of Vermont decided to launch his own investigation into conditions on the island. On March 17, after a tour of Cuba, Proctor made one of the most influential speeches in the history of the United States Senate.

Proctor, who Roosevelt reported was "very ardent for the war," had not generally been regarded as a jingo, and no man in the Senate commanded greater respect for personal integrity. Proctor declared that he had gone to Cuba skeptical of reports of suffering there, and he had come back convinced. "Torn from their homes, with foul earth, foul air, foul water, and foul food or none, what wonder that one-half have died and that one-quarter of the living are so diseased that they can not be saved?" Proctor asked. "Little children are still walking about with arms and chest terribly emaciated, eyes swollen, and abdomen bloated to three times the natural size. . . . I was told by one of our consuls that they have been found dead about the markets in the morning, where they had crawled, hoping to get some stray bits of food from the early hucksters."

The question of peace or war now lay with McKinley. The Spaniards, Woodford had conceded, had gone about as far as they could go; but with the *Maine* in the mud of Havana Harbor, with the country, following Proctor's speech, crying for war, how much longer could McKinley hold out? The jingoes were treating his attempt to preserve peace with outright contempt; McKinley, Roosevelt told his friends, "has no more backbone than a chocolate éclair."

"We will have this war for the freedom of Cuba," Roosevelt shouted at a Gridiron Dinner on March 26, shaking his fist at Senator Hanna, "in spite of the timidity of the commercial interests." Nor was McKinley permitted to forget the political consequences. The Chicago *Times-Herald* warned: "Intervention in Cuba, peacefully if we can, forcibly if we must, is immediately inevitable. Our own internal political conditions will not permit its postponement. . . . Let President McKinley hesitate to rise to the just expectations of the American people, and who can doubt that 'war for Cuban liberty' will be the crown of thorns the free silver Democrats and Populists will adopt at the elections this fall?"

On March 28 the President released the report of the naval court of inquiry on the *Maine* disaster. "In the opinion of the court the *Maine* was destroyed by the explosion of a submarine mine, which caused the partial explosion of two or more of the forward magazines," the report concluded. Although no one was singled out for blame, the conclusion was inescapable that if Spain had not willfully done it, Spain had failed to provide proper protection to a friendly vessel on a courtesy visit in its waters. Overnight a slogan with the ring of a child's street chant caught the fancy of the country:

Remember the Maine!
To hell with Spain!

"I have no more doubt than that I am now standing in the Senate of the United States," declared Henry Cabot Lodge, "that that ship was blown up by a government mine, fired by, or with the connivance of, Spanish officials."

Desiring peace yet afraid of its consequences, McKinley embarked on a policy of attempting to gain the fruits of war without fighting. On March 29 Woodford demanded that Spain agree to an immediate armistice, revoke the reconcentration order, and co-operate with the United States to provide relief; Spain was given 48 hours to reply. On March 31 Spain replied that it had finally revoked the reconcentration orders in the western provinces; that it had made available a credit of three million pesetas to resettle the natives; that it was willing to submit the *Maine* controversy to arbitration; and that it would grant a truce if the insurgents would ask for it. In short, Spain would yield everything we demanded, except that it would not concede defeat; the appeal for a truce would have to come from the rebels. Since the rebels would not make such an appeal, since they were confident of ultimate American intervention, the situation was hopeless; yet Spain had come a long way. Woodford cabled to Washington: "The ministry have gone as far as they dare go to-day. . . . No Spanish ministry would have dared to do one month ago what this ministry has proposed to-day."

For a week the Spaniards attempted to cling to their last shreds of dignity. On Saturday, April 9, Madrid surrendered. Driven to the wall by the American demands, the Spanish foreign minister informed Woodford that the government had decided to grant an armistice in Cuba immediately. Gratified at achieving the final concession, Woodford cabled McKinley: "I hope that nothing will now be done to humiliate Spain, as I am satisfied that the present Government is going, and is loyally ready to go, as fast and as far as it can."

It was too late. McKinley had decided on war. Spain had conceded everything, but Spain had waited too long. Up until the very last moment, Spanish officials had feared that if they yielded to American demands in Cuba, it might mean the overturn of the dynasty, and they preferred even a disastrous war to that. Proud but helpless in the face of American might, many Spanish officials appeared to prefer the dignity of being driven from the island in a heroic defensive war to meek surrender to an American ultimatum. In the end they surrendered and promised reforms. But they had promised reforms before—after the Ten Years' War which ended in 1878—and they had not kept these promises. Throughout the nineteenth century, constitutions had been made and remade, but nothing had changed. Even in the last hours of negotiations with the American minister, they had told Woodford that the President had asked the Pope to intervene, when the President had done nothing of the sort. Even if their intentions were of the best, could they carry them out? Spain had had three full years to end the war in Cuba and, with vastly superior numbers of troops, had not been able to do it. And the insurgents would accept nothing from Madrid, not even peace.

On Monday, April 11, McKinley sent his message to Congress, declaring that "the forcible intervention of the United States as a neutral to stop the war, according to the large dictates of humanity and following many historical precedents" was "justifiable on rational grounds." The fact that Spain had met everything we had asked was buried in two paragraphs of a long plea for war. It took Congress a full week to act. On Monday night, April 18, while the resolution shuttled back and forth between the two chambers and the conference room, congressmen sang "The Battle Hymn of the Republic" and "Dixie" and shook the chamber with the refrain of "Hang General Weyler to a Sour Apple Tree." At three o'clock the next morning the two houses reached an agreement—the United States recognized the independence of Cuba, asserted that we would not acquire Cuba for ourselves, and issued an ultimatum to Spain to withdraw within three days. On April 20 President McKinley signed the resolution. War had come at last. But not quite. Although hostilities had begun, not until four days later did Congress declare war. When it did declare war, it dated it from McKinley's action in establishing a blockade four days before. To the very end, we protested our peaceful intentions as we stumbled headlong into war.

We entered a war in which no vital American interest was involved, and without any concept of its consequences. Although McKinley declared that to enter such a war for high purposes, and then annex territory, would be "criminal aggression," we acquired as a result of the war the Philippines and other parts of an overseas empire we had not intended to get and had no idea how to defend. Although we roundly attacked Spain for not recognizing the rebel government, we, in our turn, refused to recognize the rebels. Although we were shocked by Weyler's policies in Cuba, we were soon in the unhappy position of using savage methods to put down a rebel uprising in the Philippines, employing violence in a measure that easily matched what Weyler had done.

It would be easy to condemn McKinley for not holding out against war, but McKinley showed considerable courage in bucking the tide. McKinley's personal sympathy for the Cubans was sincere; only after his death was it revealed that he had contributed $5,000 anonymously for Cuban relief. It would be even easier to blame it all on Hearst; yet no newspaper can arouse a people that is not willing to be aroused. At root lay the American gullibility about foreign affairs, with the penchant for viewing politics in terms of a simple morality play; equally important were the contempt of the American people for Spain as a cruel but weak Latin nation and the desire for war and expansion which permeated the decade. The American people were not led into war; they got the war they wanted. "I think," observed Senator J. C. Spooner, "possibly the President could have worked out the business without war, but the current was too strong, the demagogues too numerous, the fall elections too near."

■ ■ ■ ■ ■ ▫

The Enemies of Empire

Harold A. Larrabee

When the war with Spain ended, the United States found itself in control of Spain's Pacific and Caribbean colonies; what to do with them was the first problem the new proprietor had to confront. The controversy that developed over this issue in America was relatively brief—by 1900 it appeared to have been settled in favor of those who wanted to create an American empire. However, the basic issues raised in this debate have never been settled; the history of American foreign policy in the twentieth century is full of the repercussions and elaborations of the arguments of 1898–1900. To what extent, if any, should questions of national interest and honor take precedence over those of morality and the national interests of other peoples? What is "national honor"? Is colonialism always evil, no matter how it is administered or for what end?

Professor Harold A. Larrabee of Union College, author of *Decision at the Chesapeake,* describes the argument as it first developed between imperialists and anti-imperialists after the Spanish-American War. He takes a strong anti-imperialist position, and few today would disagree. That he is probably too favorable in his estimate of the anti-imperialists of that day—many of them, for example, opposed annexing colonies because they disliked bringing nonwhites under the American flag—detracts little from the value of his essay as a graphic recreation of the mood of the times. Larrabee provides fascinating glimpses into the minds of the anti-imperialists, the defenders of expansionism, and those many sincere but somewhat befuddled citizens who, like President McKinley, had great trouble deciding between these two positions.

■ ■ ■ ■ ■ ■ ■

We know, to the hour and minute, when this country reached the point of no return on its way to becoming a world power. It was at exactly 5:39 A.M., Manila time, on Sunday, May 1, 1898, when Commodore George Dewey, U.S.N., commanding the Asiatic Squadron of four small cruisers and two gunboats, coolly turned from his position on the bridge of his flagship *Olympia,* and said to its captain in words that were to echo across distant America: "You may fire when you are ready, Gridley." The command loosed salvos of shells that swiftly crushed the decrepit fleet of the Spanish Admiral Montojo (two cruisers and seven small gunboats of an antiquated type), which had been huddling under the defenses of Manila. The battle was, in the words of the English historian Herbert W. Wilson, "a military execution rather than a real contest."

Its effects on American foreign policy, however, were incalculable, and the end is not yet. Hawaii was swiftly annexed as a territory on July 7, 1898; and by the ratification of the Treaty of Paris ending the war on February 6, 1899, we found ourselves the sovereign rulers of all the Spanish colonial possessions in the Philippines, there to remain for the next forty-seven years. The Pacific Ocean was thenceforth to be regarded as "an American lake." What we now often forget, however, is how many Americans were in those early days opposed to the idea of an American Empire. Sixty years ago imperialism, then defined as the raising of the flag by force over noncontiguous territory, and called by its friends "expansionism," was the burning issue of the day. It was bitterly contested, largely on abstract moral grounds as a gross betrayal of American principles, by a small but tenacious band of New England reformers.

The hard core of the anti-imperialist movement, both at the start and at the finish, was composed of conservative Boston lawyers and bankers, many of them lineal descendants of the Pilgrims. They soon gathered about them a remarkable nationwide galaxy of literary lights, college presidents, leaders of industry and labor, editors, and politicians, constituting what has been called "the first great national propaganda organization of the twentieth century." Their achievements were greater in the vigorous expression of their views than in practical politics. Yet they lost one of their major battles in the Senate by only one vote; for a time they threatened to endanger McKinley's re-election in 1900; and there can be no doubt that their tireless needling of the American conscience about colonialism, which continued until 1920, hastened the eventual independence of the Philippines.

Crusades being somewhat out of fashion nowadays, it may be difficult to recover the fervor of these heirs of Wendell Phillips and Charles Sumner as they denounced the extension of American rule by force in the Philippines, not because of what it might do to the Filipinos, but because of what they were convinced it was bound to do to American democratic ideals. They saw in the American seizure and retention of the Islands "the infamy of the doctrine that a people may be governed without their consent." At least some of the Filipinos, under Emilio Aguinaldo, were not "consenting" to their "pacification" by our troops. A spineless administration in Washington, too much influenced by a group of jingoes in high places and by the yellow press, had liberated the Islanders from Spain only to try to enslave them again. This was rank apostasy from our professed principles in the Declaration of Independence and the Gettysburg Address. Could it be that Aguinaldo was fighting for *our* principles, while we had succumbed to the evil colonial policy of defeated Spain?

The expansionists' reply to this plea for democracy was the twin slogan: duty and destiny. It was, they said, the moral and religious duty of a civilized nation to accept the white man's burden, imposed upon us, in this instance, by our own idealistic crusade to free the Spanish possessions from centuries of misrule. As a moral aristocrat among nations, blessed with so many special advantages, America must, as a matter of *noblesse oblige,* undertake a self-sacrificing mission of political education in a world of backward peoples. In the words of the archexpansionist Theodore Roosevelt: "Peace cannot be had until the civilized nations have expanded in some shape over the barbarous nations." And besides, such expansion was inevitable. What John Hay called "cosmic tendency" and others invoked as Manifest Destiny (now enlarged to a global scale) was irresistibly impelling the onward march of the white men who spoke what Sir Cecil Spring-Rice called "God's language." Richard Croker, the boss of Tammany, remarked that "My idea of anti-imperialism is opposition to the fashion of shooting everybody who doesn't speak English."

What intensified and prolonged the conflict was the fact that both sides professed to want liberty for the Filipinos: the anti-imperialists believed that for us, as democrats, to deny them *immediate* liberty was to stultify our own ideals; while the expansionists maintained that the hopelessly backward Islanders were to be granted *eventual* liberty after a sufficient but indefinite period of Yankee tutelage. On both sides, then, there was an appeal to conscience by sincere but profoundly ignorant American patriots who found themselves enmeshed in the toils and tangles of historical circumstances, including domestic party politics. Since a moral issue was involved, the other side was not only wrong, but wicked, and words like "blood lust" and "murderer" were hurled at the imperialists, while the antis were denounced as "cowards" and "traitors." Nothing stirs the American people so deeply as a controversy in which both parties claim to be morally right: witness the battles over slavery, woman suffrage, and prohibition. In our day, "imperialism" has become a term battered almost beyond recognition in the cold war. But the central issue of 1898–1902—what constitutes the consent of the governed, and who is qualified to give it—has never been more alive than today, as one former colonial possession after another struggles toward a precariously independent nationhood.

"You have a wolf by the ears in the Philippines. You cannot let go of him with either dignity or safety, and he will not be easy to tame," said an anonymous American diplomat to one of our peace commissioners who was leaving for Paris in the fall of 1898. Even some of the expansionists themselves deplored our grip on the wolf in the first place, but were nevertheless extremely reluctant to let go. This was at once the strength and the weakness of the anti-imperialists' case. The imperialists had to admit, in the words of one of their leaders, Ambassador Whitelaw Reid, that "it was perfectly true that the American people did not wish for more territory, and never dreamed of distant colonies." Yet the grip on the wolf was an accomplished fact, and the practical difficulty of letting go with dignity and safety was the fatal flaw in the position into which the anti-imperialists found themselves maneuvered.

The clinching argument of the imperialists was "where once the flag goes up, it must never come down." The crucial decisions that sent Dewey to Manila in the first place, and ordered troops to his support as early as May 4, even before the news of his victory had reached Washington, were the work of a small elite group in the Republican administration who had managed to convert a pliable President. In 1897, McKinley had told Carl Schurz, "Ah, you may be sure there will be no jingo nonsense under my administration." But there was some truth in the popular conundrum: "Why is McKinley's mind like an unmade bed? Answer: Because it has to be made up for him every time he wants to use it." Theodore Roosevelt's friend Henry Adams spoke of his "alarm and horror of seeing poor weak McKinley, in gaiety . . . plunge into an inevitable war to conquer the Philippines contrary to every profession or so-called principle of our lives and history."

The ringleaders in the open conspiracy to move into the Orient via Hawaii and an isthmian canal, without ever consulting the American people, were two ardent disciples of Captain Alfred Thayer Mahan, U.S.N., the author of *The Influence of Sea Power Upon History, 1660–1783,* namely—Senator Henry Cabot Lodge of Massachusetts and the young and aggressive Assistant Secretary of the Navy, Theodore Roosevelt. It is one of the ironies of history that Captain Mahan himself was an anti-imperialist until the year 1885, and for precisely the reason most often advanced against his later followers: empire "would destroy free government." By 1890, however, a study of British sea power had converted him to the belief that the United States could take "a larger part in external affairs without risk to their institutions and with benefit to the world at large." Theodore Roosevelt, then a civil service commissioner, devoured Mahan's book, and reviewed it with enthusiasm in the *Atlantic Monthly,* later proclaiming Mahan "the only great naval expert who also possessed in international matters the mind of a stateman of the first rank."

Mahan's advice to Roosevelt in May, 1897, was: "Do nothing unrighteous; but take the [Hawaiian] islands first, and solve afterwards." The Roosevelt of 1898, described by William James as "still mentally in the *Sturm und Drang* period of early adolescence," needed little urging. He had been frustrated by President Cleveland's blocking of the annexation of Hawaii, but with the advent of a Republican administration his hopes were high. He was, however, soon indignant over the hesitancy of President McKinley, who, he said, "has no more backbone than a chocolate éclair." Behind McKinley stirred the powerful boss Mark Hanna, senator from Ohio, who flatly opposed the coming Spanish war at a Gridiron dinner on March 26, 1898, less than three weeks before it was declared. Introduced by the toastmaster at the same dinner as "At least one man connected with this administration who is not afraid to fight," Theodore Roosevelt, by that time in the Navy Department, declared: "We will have this war for the freedom of Cuba, Senator Hanna, in spite of the timidity of commercial interests." As William James put it, "Roosevelt gushes over war as the ideal condition of human society, for the manly strenuousness which it involves, and treats peace as a condition of blubberlike and swollen ignobility, fit only for huckstering weaklings, dwelling in gray twilight and heedless of the higher life. . . . One foe is as good as another, for aught he tells us."

Roosevelt's superior, Secretary John D. Long, seems to have had few inklings of what was to come, and "every time his back was turned," says David S. Barry, "Roosevelt would issue some kind of order in the line of military preparedness. . . ." On February 25, 1898, Long went home early, and as Acting Secretary of the Navy for a few hours, Roosevelt proceeded to send his momentous cable to Dewey in Hong Kong specifying "offensive operations in the Philipine [*sic*] islands." Next morning Long found that "in his precipitate way," his assistant had "come very near causing more of an explosion than happened to the *Maine*. . . . He has gone at things like a bull in a china shop." Roosevelt was never again left in charge of the Navy Department for even part of a day, but his order to Dewey was not rescinded. Long seems to have thought he was dealing merely with a young subordinate who was unduly impetuous, rather than with the representative of a coterie with an elaborate imperialist philosophy and the determination to do something about it. Roosevelt was showing what a man of daring with a plan, influential associates, amenable superiors, and a little brief authority could do in the making of American foreign policy.

That the American people were unprepared for the new possessions supposedly "flung into their arms by Dewey's guns" is a gross understatement of the facts. McKinley freely confessed that, before consulting a globe, he could not have told "within two thousand miles" where the Philippines were. Incredible as it may seem to us, Dewey's staff did not include a public relations officer, and the presence of two newspapermen on board the revenue cutter *McCulloch* was a pure accident.

The public's state of bewilderment, after the first delirious celebrations of Dewey's bloodless victory had subsided, was best expressed by Finley Peter Dunne, editor of the Chicago *Journal,* whose Mr. Dooley conversed with his friend Mr. Hennessy "On the Philippines."

> "I know what I'd do if I was Mack," said Mr. Hennessy, "I'd hist a flag over th' Ph'lipeens, an' I'd take in th' whole lot iv thim."
>
> "An' yet," said Mr. Dooley, "'tis not more thin two months since ye larned whether they were islands or canned goods. . . . If yer son Packy was to ask ye where th' Ph'lipeens is, cud ye give him anny good idea whether they was in Rooshia or jus' west iv th' thracks?"
>
> "Mebbe I cudden't," said Mr. Hennessy, haughtily, "but I'm f'r taking thim in, annyhow."

Not everyone in the country, however, went along with the bulk of the press and the expansionist-led administration. One month and one day after Dewey's triumph, the first recorded protest was made against "the insane and wicked ambition which is driving this country to ruin . . . and a slavery worse for Massachusetts, at least, than that of the Negro." It came in the form, classically correct for a proper Bostonian, of a letter to the editor of the *Evening Transcript* of June 2, 1898, entitled "A Cry for Help." It was written by Gamaliel Bradford, father of the well-known biographer. He was a seventh-generation descendant of Governor William Bradford of Plymouth, a retired banker, a Republican mugwump (he had deserted Blaine for Cleveland in 1884), and the author of several thousand letters to the newspapers in behalf of various reforms. His offer to join with any others who would help him in securing Boston's traditional Cradle of Liberty, Faneuil Hall, resulted in the first public meeting "to protest against the adoption of a so-called imperial policy by the United States."

Bradford was soon joined by another Pilgrim descendant, Erving Winslow, who was to prove the most undiscourageable of all the anti-imperialists, and by the able Boston lawyer Moorfield Storey, who was to become the acknowledged long-time champion of the movement. Presiding at the June 15 meeting that he had convened, Bradford took good care to say that its purpose was not to oppose "the vigorous prosecution of the war," but rather to check "the rush of reckless and unbridled ambition for dominion" evident in "a certain faction in Congress," which might turn "a war of liberation into a war of conquest." Storey laid down what was to be the most enduring plank in the anti-imperialist platform when he declared: "When Rome began her career of conquest, the Roman Republic began to decline. . . . Let us once govern any considerable body of men without their consent, and it is a question of time how soon this republic shares the fate of Rome." The *Evening Transcript* spoke of the meeting as "a solemn warning against surrendering to the madness of the hour"; but Lodge depicted it to Roosevelt (en route to Cuba with his Rough Riders) as "a very comic incident."

The strange mixture of popular war hysteria, whipped up for their own purposes by Joseph Pulitzer of the *World* and William Randolph Hearst of the *Journal,* and the as-yet-unshaken confidence of many intellectuals in the pacific intentions of McKinley was vividly portrayed and analyzed by the philosopher William James in a letter written to his French friend François Pillon, just before James left his house in Cambridge to attend the Faneuil Hall meeting:

> A curious episode of history, showing how a nation's ideals can be changed in the twinkling of an eye, by a succession of outward events partly accidental. It is quite possible that, without the explosion of the *Maine,* we should still be at peace. . . . The actual declaration of war by Congress, however, was a case of *psychologie des foules,* a genuine hysteric stampede at the last moment. . . . Our Executive has behaved very well. The European nations of the Continent cannot believe that our pretense of humanity, and our disclaiming of all ideas of conquest, is sincere. It has been *absolutely* sincere! The self-conscious feeling of our people has been entirely based in a sense of philanthropic duty. . . . But here comes in the psychologic factor: once the excitement of action gets loose, the taxes levied, the victories achieved, etc., the old human instincts will get into play with all their old strength, and the ambition and sense of mastery which our nation has will set up new demands. We shall never take Cuba. . . . But Porto Rico, and even the Philippines, are not so sure. We had supposed ourselves (with all our crudity and barbarity in certain ways) a better nation morally than the rest, safe at home, and without the old savage ambition, destined to exert great international influence by throwing in our "moral weight," etc. Dreams! Human Nature is everywhere the same, and at the least temptation all the old military passions rise, and sweep everything before them. . . . It all shows by what short steps progress is made. . . .

It soon became evident that William James had not overestimated the immense task facing the small band of anti-imperialists: no less than the complete reversal of public opinion in the face of easy victories, promised spoils, and a flag-waving press. For one thing, during the summer of 1898, history was being made at a furious pace. Whether one accepts the John Hay version, "a splendid little war," or "a jolly war," or the London *Saturday Review*'s estimate, "never a more shabby war," it was decidedly a short one. In less than four months it was all over but the disposition of "the waifs of the world deposited on our doorsteps." At a foreign policy conference at Saratoga Springs, New York, on August 18, 1898, just five days after the armistice, Carl Schurz, who had embarked upon a one-man crusade to impress McKinley, delivered a vigorous anti-imperialist address in which, ironically, he used against Senator Lodge and his fellow expansionists "the very principles which Lodge was to exalt so extravagantly twenty years later in the fight against the Covenant of the League of Nations." A delegation from the Saratoga conference, with Samuel Gompers as one of its members, waited upon McKinley but was received only with suave hospitality.

To the public in the fall of 1898 the President offered the image of a sorely tried pacifist in doubt about the propriety of retaining the Philippines, even speculating that "if old Dewey had just sailed away after he had smashed the Spanish fleet, what a lot of trouble he would have saved us." But his every action was in line with what Lodge called "our large policy" of complete possession. McKinley packed the peace commission virtually four-to-one in favor of expansionism (three of them senators who would later have to vote on their own work), and gave them ever more sweeping instructions about what was to be demanded of the Spaniards, even though his Cabinet was divided on the issue. How he arrived at his final decision to tell the peace commission to demand "the whole archipelago or none" was told by the President himself on November 21, 1899, to a committee representing the General Missionary Committee of the Methodist Episcopal Church, then in session in Washington. Surely it is one of the most amazing descriptions of the workings of a Chief Executive's conscience in the field of foreign policy that has ever been recorded.

The delegation was about to leave the White House, when McKinley turned to them, and said earnestly:

> Hold a moment longer! Not quite yet, gentlemen! Before you go I would like to say just a word about the Philippine business. I have been criticized a good deal about the Philippines, but don't deserve it. The truth is I didn't want the Philippines, and when they came to us, as a gift from the gods, I did not know what to do with them. . . . I sought counsel from all sides—Democrats as well as Republicans—but got little help. I thought first we would take only Manila; then Luzon; then other islands, perhaps, also. I walked the floor of the White House night after night until midnight; and I am not ashamed to tell you, gentlemen, that I went down on my

In this cartoon from Frank Leslie's Official History of the Spanish-American War, *captioned "Better rags with honor than patches with dishonor," Uncle Sam peers angrily over his shoulder at patches showing the* Maine *exploding and Spanish soldiers blowing off the heads of members of the* Virginius's *crew.*

knees and prayed Almighty God for light and guidance more than one night. And one night late it came to me this way—I don't know how it was, but it came: (1) That we could not give them back to Spain—that would be cowardly and dishonorable; (2) that we could not turn them over to France or Germany—our commercial rivals in the Orient—that would be bad business and discreditable; (3) that we could not leave them to themselves—they were unfit for self-government—and they would soon have anarchy and misrule over there worse than Spain's was; and (4) that there was nothing left for us to do but take them all, and to educate the Filipinos, and uplift and civilize and Christianize them, and by God's grace do the very best we could by them, as our fellow men for whom Christ also died. And then I went to bed, and went to sleep, and slept soundly, and the next morning I sent for the chief engineer of the War Department (our map-maker), and I told him to put the Philippines on the map of the United States [pointing to a large map on the wall of his office], and there they are, and there they will stay while I am President!

The anti-imperialists' first battle, for the mind of the President as the chief architect of the nation's foreign policy, was thus lost to higher authority before it had hardly begun. But the country might still be persuaded to reject McKinley's Philippine policy. On November 19, 1898, in the Boston office of Edward Atkinson, retired textile manufacturer—later to become notorious because of the Postmaster General's closing of the mails to his publications—the Anti-Imperialist League was organized. Its object was: "to oppose, by every legitimate means, the acquisition of the Philippine Islands, or of any colonies away from our shores, by the United States."

The only thing more remarkable than the high quality of the League's adherents was their extreme diversity. As its perpetual secretary, Erving Winslow, remarked: "We must in our organization stand shoulder to shoulder: Republican, Democrat, Socialist, Populist, Gold-Man, Silver-Man, and Mugwump, for the one momentous, vital, paramount issue, Anti-Imperialism and the preservation of the Republic." Such advice, however, was not always easy to follow, since the anti-imperialist leader in the Senate, George F. Hoar, regular Republican, had once called the Mugwumps "the vilest set of political assassins that ever disgraced this or any other country."

Besides every shade in the country's political spectrum, the League's ever-lengthening list of vice presidents, many of whom lent only their names to the movement, included every variety of American reformer: municipal, civil service, social welfare, single-taxer, freetrader, pacifist, and prohibitionist. Education furnished a long list of college presidents: Eliot, Jordan, Rogers, Alderman, Stanley Hall, Schurman, King, and Faunce, with such distinguished teachers as Charles Eliot Norton, George Herbert Palmer, William Graham Sumner, Felix Adler, William James, John Dewey, and Franklin H. Giddings. From industry and finance came the extremely active donor Andrew Carnegie, and Richard T. Crane and George Foster Peabody. The contribution of "interest" groups (beet sugar and tobacco), which wanted no Philippine competition, was remarkably small.

At the peak of the League's activities in 1899, it claimed thirty thousand members and "half a million contributors" in branches located in a dozen large cities from Boston to Portland, Oregon. One of its conferences, in Chicago on October

17–18, 1899, attracted ten thousand delegates; and by 1900 the League claimed to have distributed four hundred thousand pieces of literature. This spreading of its work enhanced its prestige, no doubt, but it proved to be a handicap in exerting political influence. For what leader could be found who could win and keep the confidence of quite so many kinds of followers?

The first political battle fought by the anti-imperialists was the one in which they came the closest to victory: the heated conflict over the ratification of the treaty of peace with Spain in January and February, 1899. The only controversial section in the document was the article providing for the cession of the whole Philippine archipelago to the United States. As Peace Commissioner Whitelaw Reid put it: he and his associates were accused of "overdoing the business, looking after the interests of the country too thoroughly. . . ." Since a two-thirds vote was required for ratification in a Senate composed of forty-six Republicans, thirty-four Democrats, and ten members of minor parties, it was evident that a substantial number of Democratic senators would have to be won over.

Fresh from his discharge from the Army, William Jennings Bryan announced in an interview at Savannah, Georgia, on December 13, 1898, that although he was firmly anti-imperialist, he believed that the treaty should be ratified and the issue of imperialism settled by resolution at a later date. The less politically minded anti-imperialists (Carnegie, Schurz, and Storey) regarded this as a sacrifice of principle in order to secure a campaign issue to go along with free silver (which they detested) in the election of 1900. Ten Democratic senators helped to ratify the treaty by only one vote more than the necessary two thirds, and although two or three of them may have been swayed by the outbreak of fighting, two days earlier, between Filipino and American soldiers, Bryan has generally been credited with influencing the key votes. Many senators were undoubtedly influenced by Lodge's argument that failure to ratify would be a repudiation of McKinley and a continuation of the war. If there could have been a clear-cut decision regarding the retention of the Philippines, "the imperialists," says the diplomatic historian Thomas A. Bailey, "would almost certainly have failed to obtain a two-thirds majority." A few days later the Bacon amendment, pledging ultimate independence to the Filipinos, resulted in a tie vote, decided in the negative by the vote of Vice President Garret A. Hobart.

Despite this setback, the movement grew, rather than declined, as the 1900 election approached, although Bryan had created an amount of distrust in the minds of the "true" anti-imperialists, which led to talk of a third-party ticket designed to split the McKinley vote. Bryan agreed to make anti-imperialism "the paramount issue" of his campaign, and was finally endorsed by the League's Liberty Congress in Indianapolis in August, 1900. But many of the anti-imperialists refused to stomach Bryan's continued insistence upon free silver, and either voted for McKinley or held aloof from both candidates. Bryan secured fewer votes in 1900 than in 1896, and his defeat "marked the end of anti-imperialism as an important factor in American politics."

Political failure did not prevent literary success for the cause, although most of the blows struck by the pen came too late to turn the tide of public opinion. The one man whose emotional response to imperialism became enduring literature was the poet William Vaughn Moody. He risked his position as teacher of English at the

University of Chicago by publishing several anti-imperialist poems in the *Atlantic Monthly*. In contrast to its noble sacrifices in the Civil War, Moody saw his country engaged in "ignoble battle," but protested:

> *We have not sold our loftiest heritage*
> *The proud republic hath not stooped to cheat and scramble in the market place of war . . .*
> *That so our hand with better ease*
> *May wield the driver's whip and grasp the jailer's keys.*

Warning the country's leaders to "tempt not our weakness, our cupidity," the poet declares that "save we let the island men go free," our soldiers will have died in vain. In a shorter poem entitled "On a Soldier Fallen in the Philippines," (*Atlantic Monthly*, February, 1901), Moody makes use of the poignant contradiction between the honor due to the fallen and the dishonor of his cause:

> *Toll! Let him never guess*
> *What work we set him to . . .*
> *Let him never dream that his bullet's scream went wide of its island mark,*
> *Home to the heart of his darling land where she stumbled and sinned in the dark.*

Moody's language was mild and temperate compared with that of his fellow Chicagoan, the novelist Henry Blake Fuller, who became convinced that McKinley's policies were not only ignorant and stupid but actually vicious. Fuller addressed the President:

> *Thou sweating chattel slave to swine!*
> *Who dost befoul the holy shrine*
> *Of liberty with murder! . . .*

A much saner poetic approach was that of Ernest Crosby, president of the New York branch of the movement, whose Whitmanesque lines ran:

> *There is only one possession worth the capturing, and that is the hearts of men;*
> *And these hearts can never be won by a nation of slaves.*
> *Be free, and all mankind will flock to your standard.*

Mark Twain was one literary figure who was won over from the opposition, in part by the urging of his friend William Dean Howells. "I left these shores at Vancouver [on his way to Vienna]," he wrote, "a red-hot imperialist. I wanted the American eagle to go screaming into the Pacific. It seemed tiresome and tame for it to content itself with the Rockies. Why not spread its wings over the Philippines, I asked myself? And I thought it would be a real good thing to do." But gradually Twain began to see the Philippines in a different light, for early in 1900 he wrote to Joseph Twichell: "Apparently we are not proposing to set the Filipinos free and give their islands to them. . . . If these things are so, the war out there has no interest for me." From the day of Twain's triumphant return to this country in October, 1900, he joined forces with Howells in a steady barrage of articles, interviews, petitions, and pamphlets in behalf of anti-imperialism. The League made extensive use on cards of his "salutation-speech from the Nineteenth Century to the Twentieth," in which he said:

> I bring you the stately matron named Christendom, returning bedraggled, be-smirched, and dishonored from pirate-raids in Kiao-Chou, Manchuria, South Africa, & the Philippines, with her soul full of meanness, her pocket full of boodle and her mouth full of pious hypocrisies. Give her soap and a towel, but hide the looking glass.

At a welcoming dinner for the young English war correspondent Winston Spencer Churchill in the Waldorf-Astoria Hotel on December 13, 1900, Mark Twain introduced the half-English, half-American speaker with these words: "I think that England sinned when she got herself into a war in South Africa which she could have avoided, just as we have sinned in getting into a similar war in the Philippines . . . yes, we are kin. And now that we are also kin in sin, there is nothing more to be desired. The harmony is complete, the blend is perfect—like Mr. Churchill himself, whom I now have the honor to present to you."

One of the most effective presentations of the case for anti-imperialism was made by the peppery Yale sociologist William Graham Sumner under the striking title, "The Conquest of the United States by Spain," but it was buried in the *Yale Law Journal* for January, 1899. Logic in terms of political theory, however, proved a poor match for the logic of events. Professor Richard Hofstadter has acutely observed that the Spanish-American War was fought because the American people wanted "not so much the freedom of Cuba as a *war* for the freedom of Cuba." Once war was under way, in the opinion of the late Vice President Charles G. Dawes, who was a close McKinley associate, "the retention of the Philippines was inevitable. . . . No man, or no party, could have prevented it." Yet in the sober judgement of Samuel Flagg Bemis, "looking back on those years of adolescent irresponsibility, we can now see the acquisition of the Philippines, the climax of American expansion, as a great national aberration."

But it was in vain that the anti-imperialists of that era cited the words of Abraham Lincoln: "No man is good enough to govern another without that other's consent." The missing premise in the arguments of both sides was the lack of adequate knowledge of the Filipinos and their capacity for solving their immediate political problems. The anti-imperialists saw them as ready and able to govern themselves democratically; the imperialists were just as convinced that they were mostly untutored barbarians. Neither side had enough facts, and as a result both substituted passion for logic.

The anti-imperialists saw the whole problem as a simple matter of political morality, which could never be settled until settled "right." By their indefatigable agitating they administered such a shock to sensitive American consciences that the burden of guilt could not be lifted. In time it came to be assumed that the pledge of Philippine independence defeated by a single vote in 1899 had, morally speaking, been given.

What the imperialists, notably Theodore Roosevelt, could never grasp was the Filipinos' yearning for *self*-government. Both sides entertained illusions: the imperialists saw a mirage of untold wealth in trade with the Orient, which did not materialize; the anti-imperialists foresaw "tyranny at home" as the sure result of "tyranny abroad." The latter were also incorrect in their belief that their opponents would never "let go" of the archipelago, although it was not until 1935 that the Commonwealth was established, with complete independence promised in 1946. The promise was kept, and the Philippines became "the first colony ever to be surrendered voluntarily."

The annual reports of the Anti-Imperialist League, which continued until its nineteenth and last meeting in 1917, make melancholy reading as the necrology lengthened and the budgets shrank. Treasurer Greene declared doggedly: "Anti-Imperialists are not quitters"; but when Erving Winslow died in 1923, Moorfield Storey wrote: "Almost everybody who belonged to the League is dead, and the young men do not take up the work. I am still its representative, but I have no followers."

One of the striking characteristics of the League in its heyday was the lack of contact between its zealous leaders in America and the Filipinos in whose behalf they were enduring a steady rain of epithets: little Americans, seditionists, cowards, and traitors. But the Filipinos had subtle ways of showing their appreciation. Long before they were allowed the privilege of self-government, they named the square directly in front of the Malacañang Palace in Manila, the official residence of the American Governor General, *La Liga Anti-Imperialistica.*

■ ■ ■ ■ ■ ■ ■

Pearl Harbor: The "Day of Infamy"

Richard Ketchum

The "you are there" technique for describing dramatic events perfectly suits the problem of describing how the United States government responded to the shocking news that the Japanese had attacked the great American naval base at Pearl Harbor in the Hawaiian Islands. As used here by Richard Ketchum, a former editor of *American Heritage* and the author of *The Borrowed Years: American on the Way to War,* it demonstrates conclusively that President Roosevelt did not "trick" the Japanese into striking the first blow; it also shows how he and the top members of his administration responded to the emergency. Ketchum has captured the shock and confusion of the moment as well as the anger and determination with which all the leading actors in the drama reacted. His account takes the reader inside the White House, across the Atlantic to London, and across the Pacific to Tokyo. Generals, admirals, foreign potentates like Winston Churchill, and famous reporters speak. But so do lesser bureaucrats and secretaries unknown to the public.

■ ■ ■ ■ ■ ■ ■

For most Americans Sunday began quietly, with nothing to suggest that this was the last morning for almost four years when the nation would be at peace. It was cold and crisp, a glorious day across the eastern half of the country. The Roosevelts had company for the weekend—all old friends. The President's cousin Ellen Delano Adams and her husband, with their son and daughter-in-law, were there, as was Mrs. Charles Hamlin, known as Bertie, whom Franklin had met years before in Albany, New York, at his uncle Ted's inauguration as governor. The White House was silent when Bertie Hamlin awoke, and she dressed quietly, walked down the long hallway past the closed doors leading to the President's bedroom and study, went downstairs, and crossed Pennsylvania Avenue to St. John's Church on Lafayette Square, where the bells were pealing for morning worship. By the time she returned, a number of people were climbing the stairs from the East Entrance. The luncheon guests had arrived—some thirty-one of them, and a mixed bag they were, friends, relatives, minor officials, Army Medical Corps officers—prompting someone to observe that the First Lady's secretary was cleaning up around the edges of the invitation list.

Although they may have hoped to see the President, none of the guests much expected him to put in an appearance; he was understandably preoccupied with the tense situation in the Far East, and on top of that, Mrs. Roosevelt explained, his sinuses were acting up. He was having a relaxed lunch in his upstairs study with his friend and adviser Harry Hopkins, who recalled that they were talking about "things far removed from war." Saturday, while the White House staff took half a day off for Christmas shopping, the President had worked late, and now, after finishing the lunch on his tray, he was enjoying the undemanding company of his old friend and his Scottie dog, Fala, while he paid a little overdue attention to his stamp collection.

At the Navy communication station the clocks read 1348 when Chief Frank Ackerson was called to the Washington–Honolulu operator's message AIR RAID ON PEARL HARBOR THIS IS NOT DRILL.

While the President and Hopkins talked, the telephone rang, and it was Frank Knox calling Roosevelt—a stunned, stricken Secretary of the Navy, reporting the staggering news from Pearl Harbor. Hopkins, hearing that Japanese planes were still attacking thought there must be some mistake—surely Japan would not attack Hawaii—but the President thought the report was probably true. It was just the sort of surprise the Japanese *would* spring on us, he said, talking peace in the Pacific while plotting to overthrow it.

That morning the corridors of the old State, War and Navy Building had been deserted when Secretary of State Cordell Hull arrived at ten-fifteen for a meeting with Knox and Secretary of War Henry Stimson. By two o'clock they were ready to call it quits and go to the Mayflower Hotel for lunch, and they were just leaving when the Japanese envoys Kichisaburo Nomura and Saburo Kurusu arrived outside Hull's office. They had a cable for the Secretary of State, a long and insulting reply to the imperious "Ten Point Plan" that Hull had submitted to them on November 27, which demanded that the Japanese withdraw from China and Indochina.

Hull already knew the contents of the document; American cryptanalysts had broken the Japanese code in 1940, and in this particular case they had translated Japan's reply before the Japanese embassy could. In fact, the ambassadors had been so hard pressed that they were an hour late getting their translation to Hull.

When they arrived at his office, the Secretary of State was busy on the telephone. His visitors could not know it, but the President was calling to inform him of the report from Pearl Harbor, advising him to receive the ambassadors formally but under no circumstances to inform them of the attack. He was to accept the reply to his note "coolly and bow them out."

Hull let the agitated Japanese sit outside for fifteen minutes—a tense quarter of an hour that marked an end to innocence and the beginning of a new and different era in American history. When the two men were finally admitted to his office, he greeted them coldly and kept them standing, and when Nomura handed him the note, explaining that he had been instructed to deliver it at one o'clock, Hull asked why. Nomura said he did not know, but those were his instructions; the Secretary retorted sharply that he was receiving the message at two o'clock. Hull glanced perfunctorily through the document and then, according to the subsequent State Department press release, said indignantly, "In all my conversations with you during the last nine months, I have never uttered one word of untruth. This is borne out absolutely by the record.

"In all my fifty years of public service I have never seen a document that was more crowded with infamous falsehoods and distortions—infamous falsehoods and distortions on a scale so huge that I never imagined until today that any government on this planet was capable of uttering them."

If the Japanese wondered how a man could know so much about a document he had barely skimmed, they did not say, but Nomura was about to speak when

Hull cut him short with a motion of his hand and gestured toward the door. The two ambassadors left without a word.

Thus the authorized version. But when Dean Acheson arrived at the department several hours later—having rushed in from his Maryland farm as soon as he heard the news on the radio—little groups of people stood in the corridor, talking in whispers, while the Secretary, still in a towering rage, remained closeted with several intimates, and the word Acheson got from those who had overheard Mr. Hull ridding himself of the two Japanese was that he had done so in "native Tennesseean," calling them "scoundrels" and "pissants" in his fury.

Secretary of War Henry Stimson was weary, and he was feeling his seventy-four years. He had hoped to get away to his Long Island place for a rest, but the news that morning got progressively worse, convincing him that something bad was going to happen, so he stayed in Washington. He was eating lunch at Woodley, his handsome Southern colonial home overlooking Rock Creek Park, when the President called and asked, in an excited voice, "Have you heard the news?"

"Well," Stimson replied, "I have heard the telegrams which have been coming in about the Japanese advances in the Gulf of Siam."

"Oh, no," Roosevelt said, "I don't mean that. They have attacked Hawaii. They are now bombing Hawaii."

That was an excitement indeed, Stimson thought, and as he prepared to leave for the White House it occurred to him that American forces in Hawaii might have won a major victory; the defense forces in the islands had been alerted and were capable of inflicting severe damage on the attackers.

At 2:28 P.M. Adm. Harold Stark, Roosevelt's chief of naval operations, phoned the White House and informed the President that the first report was true, that the attack had caused some damage to the fleet and some loss of life—no one could yet say how much. Throughout the afternoon and evening the phone at the President's side continued to ring, each time bringing an even more distressing bulletin about the extent of the devastation. Roosevelt listened calmly to each report, usually without comment, and then returned to the business at hand.

About the time of Stark's first call, Mrs. Roosevelt was bidding good-bye to her departing luncheon guests when one of the ushers told her the news. The report was so stunning, she said, that there was complete quiet, and after she had seen her guests to the door she waited until Franklin was alone, hoping to slip into his study. It took only a quick glance to make her realize that he was concentrating on what had to be done and wouldn't talk of what had happened until the first strain was over, so she went back to work—work, at that moment, consisting of going through her mail and writing letters, with one ear cocked to the voices of people going in and out of the President's study, and finding the time and strength of character to concentrate on what she would say in her weekly radio broadcast that afternoon.

Roosevelt's first move, after Stark confirmed the report, was to summon his press secretary, Stephen T. Early, and dictate a statement for immediate release, and at two-thirty Louise Hachmeister, who supervised the White House switchboard, called the three wire services, put them on a conference hookup, and asked, "All on? AP? UP? INS? Here's Mr. Early."

"This is Steve Early at the White House," the press secretary said. "At 7:55 A.M., Hawaiian time, the Japanese bombed Pearl Harbor. The attacks are continuing and . . . no I don't know how many are dead." Almost instantaneously alarm bells on teletype machines in every city across the country began to ring.

In London the CBS correspondent Robert Trout was sitting in the BBC's Studio B-2, two stories underground. He had been stationed there since early November, temporarily replacing Edward R. Murrow, who had returned to the United States with his wife, Janet, for some rest and recreation, and as Trout looked at the wall of the studio, he found himself thinking that there was a huge bomb crater on the other side and that all that stood between him and the hole was a single course of bricks.

For these nightly broadcasts, CBS leased a transatlantic telephone line for ten minutes. Even though the transmission might last for only a fraction of that, ten minutes was the minimum rental, with the result that some of the time was used in preparing for the broadcast and testing voice levels, with engineers, announcers, and others in studios on opposite sides of the ocean conversing. Trout was waiting for his cue from the CBS news department chief, Paul White, to go on the air, while next to him, as always, sat a British censor.

The procedure called for the censor to read the script that the reporter had prepared in advance, approving it or asking him to delete or alter something, but both parties knew that the censor had his hand on the control by which he could cut off Trout if he extemporized and said something that was not permitted. The regulars like Murrow and Trout had a good working relationship with the censors. It was all very informal and friendly, and in addition to his official duties the censor actually served as a technician, by cutting Trout in and out.

Trout was wearing earphones, listening to a British engineer and an American in Riverhead, Long Island, discuss the transmission. He recognized other voices from the CBS studio in New York—none of them on the air, of course, just desultory conversation between people waiting for the broadcast to begin. Paul White loved to sit in front of the complex instrument panel, surrounded by gadgets, and he would either push a lever and tell Trout to start talking or simply let his man in London listen to the broadcast and wait for the announcer to say, "And now we bring you Robert Trout in London—come in, Bob Trout."

But tonight Trout realized that his cue was being delayed for some reason, and he didn't hear White's voice. He was also aware that the door to the studio in New York had opened because he could hear the clatter of teletype machines in the hall outside, then a babble of voices, and someone saying, "Of course it means war . . . but why Pearl Harbor?," which is how he became aware of what had occurred.

Then White came on, to say he would have to tell Trout what they had just seen on the wire. "I already know," Trout told him. White didn't ask how he knew (he died before Trout ever had a chance to tell him); instead he said, "Okay then, I'm cutting you in. Give us the reaction from London."

For a horrified moment Trout couldn't believe his ears. He turned to the censor, who realized immediately the spot he was in, thought for a moment, and then nodded his approval—meaning that Trout could go ahead with the "reaction" as best he could.

"I have no idea what I said," Bob Trout recalled, "but somehow I put some words together and delivered a two-minute talk. Then I was off the air—though only for a while. I was on again any number of times that night."

A few minutes later Trout had a telephone call from Ambassador John G. Winant, who was visiting the British prime minister at Chequers and was furious. Why hadn't Trout called the embassy and told them we were at war before he began his broadcast? What did he think I should do, Trout wondered, call the American embassy and announce, "We are at war"? Until Winant asked the question, Trout hadn't realized that he had been the first person in Great Britain to learn that hostilities had begun between the United States and Japan.

Ambassador Winant had had a busy weekend. He was supposed to have gone to Anthony Eden's country house on Friday evening, to discuss the foreign secretary's forthcoming conversations with Joseph Stalin in Moscow (Eden was leaving for Russia on Sunday), but the news from the Far East intruded on the U.S. ambassador's plans. What with one thing and another, he didn't arrive at Eden's place until after midnight on Saturday, but his obliging host "found me some supper and we stayed up until the early hours of the morning discussing his mission." When Eden departed at ten o'clock, Winant left for Chequers, a hundred miles away, to see the prime minister, whom he found pacing back and forth outside the front door, the other guests having gone inside to lunch.

Churchill at once asked Winant if he thought war with Japan was imminent. When the ambassador replied yes, Churchill stated with some vehemence, "If they declare war on you, we shall declare war on them within the hour."

After lunch most of the guests departed, leaving the prime minister to work and to rest, since he had been up most of the previous night, while Winant spent a quiet afternoon with Averell Harriman, who was in England coordinating the Lend-Lease program, and his daughter. A few minutes before nine o'clock they assembled in the dining room and found Churchill sitting alone, grim and silent; as soon as they took their places, he called out to Sawyers, the butler, asking him to put a portable radio on the table so he could hear the news. Churchill switched it on, and as the sound of music faded away, it was replaced by a voice announcing that the Japanese had attacked the U.S. fleet at Pearl Harbor. As the diners looked at each other incredulously, Sawyers came back into the room to assure them, "It's quite true. We heard it ourselves outside. The Japanese have attacked the Americans."

Churchill bounded to his feet and headed for the door, exclaiming, "We shall declare war on Japan."

Winant got up and hurried after him, saying, "Good God! You can't declare war on a radio announcement! Don't you think you'd better get confirmation first?"

Churchill walked through the hall to the office, which was manned twenty-four hours a day, and told his staff to put through a call to the White House.

"Mr. President, what's this about Japan?" Churchill asked when the connection was made.

"It's quite true. They have attacked us at Pearl Harbor," Roosevelt replied. "We are all in the same boat now."

After the two leaders talked briefly (no mention was made of the serious losses that had been suffered), the prime minister and his guests returned to the table and, as Churchill said, "tried to adjust our thoughts to the supreme world event which had occurred." To the man who represented Britain's last chance, the indomitable leader whose courage and conviction had rallied his countrymen when the nation seemed doomed, the news that America would be in the war—"up to the neck and in to the death"—was a gift from the gods. "So we had won after all!" he exulted, confident now that "England would live; Britain would live; the Commonwealth of Nations and the Empire would live." After the long succession of defeats, the trials that were enough to scar men's souls—Dunkirk, the fall of France, the threat of invasion, the blitz, the U-boat war—he knew at last that there was "no more doubt about the end."

From New York, Ed and Janet Murrow had come to Washington, where they were to have dinner at the White House on Sunday, December 7. That afternoon Murrow was playing golf at the Burning Tree club when a man rushed out of the clubhouse shouting that Pearl Harbor had just been bombed. Murrow went at once to the CBS office to confirm the report and phoned Paul White in New York. Earlier in the day a friend had driven Janet Murrow to an Army airfield near Washington so that she could see the planes awaiting shipment to England. She was amazed. The field was jammed with aircraft, and until then she had had no idea that Lend-Lease was producing aid on such a scale for Britain. In the afternoon she was with their hosts, listening to the New York Philharmonic, and when the program was interrupted with a bulletin about the attack, she assumed at once that their dinner engagement would be canceled. To her surprise, when she phoned the White House, Mrs. Roosevelt told her that they were still expected.

At three o'clock the President met with the War Council—Hull, Stimson, Knox—plus the two military chiefs, Gen. George Marshall and Adm. Harold Stark, and despite the gravity of the circumstances, Harry Hopkins remarked the absence of tension. These men, for whom the imminence of war had been a constant presence, reacted as Churchill did when he heard of the attack. They had concluded long since that the ultimate enemy was Hitler; they knew the Germans could never be defeated without the force of arms; sooner or later, moreover, the United States was bound to be in the war, so it was an unexpected boon that "the crisis had come in a way which would unite all our people," as Stimson remarked.

Harry Hopkins saw things in an even more positive light. "Japan had given us an opportunity," he felt. Others looked on the day's bloody events not as opportunity but as unmitigated disaster, and Assistant Secretary of State Breckinridge Long expressed that point of view in the diary he kept for most of his life. "Sick at heart," he wrote. "I am so damned mad at the Navy for being asleep at the switch at Honolulu. It is the worst day in American history. They spent their lives in preparation for a supreme moment—and then were asleep when it came."

That state of mind was hardly unique to Long. It was the kind of reaction that was bound to surface publicly after the first shock wore off, and with the idea of controlling the damage promptly, Hopkins suggested to the President that he schedule two conferences that evening—one with the full cabinet, the other with legislative leaders. Roosevelt agreed on both counts; the cabinet would meet at eight-thirty, the congressional delegation an hour later.

Grace Tully, one of the President's private secretaries, had been resting at home that afternoon, after the grueling demands of the past few weeks, when the telephone rang. It was Louise Hachmeister, and, with a long list of people to call, she wasted no words: "The President wants you right away. There's a car on the way to pick you up. The Japs just bombed Pearl Harbor!" Twenty minutes later Tully pulled into the White House driveway, which was swarming with extra police and Secret Service men, reporters, and military brass.

In the second-floor study she found Knox, Stimson, and Hopkins, who were joined a few moments later by Marshall and Hull, whose face looked as white as his hair. Since most of the news from Pearl Harbor was coming in to Admiral Stark at the Navy Department, it was her job to answer calls from him, take down the "fragmentary and shocking reports . . . by shorthand, type them up and relay them to the Boss." At first she used a telephone in the second-floor hall, but the noise and confusion were such that she moved into the President's bedroom. Each time she put down the phone and rushed to the typewriter to transcribe her notes, a quartet of White House aides—Gen. Edwin M. Watson, Adm. Ross T. McIntire, Capt. John R. Beardall, and Marvin H. McIntyre—followed and crowded in behind her to peer over her shoulder as she typed. To all of them the news was shattering. Each time Stark called she heard the shocked disbelief in his voice; the men around the President were first incredulous, then angry; and while "the Boss maintained greater outward calm than anybody else . . . there was rage in his very calmness. With each new message he shook his head grimly and he tightened the expression of his mouth."

After talking to Churchill, the President had a long conversation with General Marshall about the disposition of troops and the Air Force, and it was evident that Marshall was increasingly edgy, impatient to get back to the War Department, where he could be in touch with commanders in the field (he had already warned Lt. Gen. Douglas MacArthur, commander of U.S. Army forces in the Far East, to take every precaution). Roosevelt impressed on Hull the necessity of keeping all the South American republics informed; he ordered protection for the Japanese embassy and consulates and had the Justice Department put Japanese citizens under surveillance; Stimson and Knox were to see to the protection of U.S. arsenals, private munitions factories, and bridges (though under no circumstances was there to be a military guard at the White House). Then the discussion turned to Roosevelt's message to Congress, which he had already decided to deliver the following day. The President dug in his heels when Hull recommended a review of the entire history of relations with Japan; no, he said, it would be a short, precise message.

For an immensely energetic man whose infirmity bound him to a chair, all this activity was a relief and a release, a means of channeling that inner rage and putting it to work, and Eleanor Roosevelt could see that at that moment "in spite of his anxiety Franklin was in a way more serene than he had appeared in a long time." Despite the confusion whirling around him, it occurred to some witnesses that the White House was the calmest place in town, with the President in his study the center of the hurricane's eye. The Under Secretary of State Sumner Welles was close by during those hectic hours and thought that of all the times he had seen the President in action he had never had such reason to admire him. Sitting calmly at his desk, receiving a continuous flow of reports on a national disaster, "he demonstrated that ultimate capacity to dominate and to control a supreme emergency which is perhaps the rarest and most valuable characteristic of any statesman." With his talent for grasping the significance of each development, by the end of the evening Roosevelt had personally handled every detail of the situation laid before him by his military advisers, had written the text of a message to Congress, and had overseen the text of the declaration of war to be submitted to that body. All the uncertainty of the recent past was over, and however daunting the future might be, it was calming to know what must be done.

The White House switchboard had an open circuit now to Gov. Joseph Poindexter in Hawaii, who confirmed the news, or as much of it as he knew. As he and the President spoke, the governor suddenly shouted into the phone, and Roosevelt turned to the group in the room to say, "My God, there's another wave of Jap planes over Hawaii right this minute!"

Reports continued to come in to what was now the nation's command headquarters, and in the meantime those present were passing on to the others their fragmentary knowledge of events. Hull, still bitterly angry, repeated "in a tone as cold as ice" his remarks to the Japanese envoys, but as Grace Tully noted, "there was nothing cold or diplomatic in the words he used." Knox and Stimson were interrogated by the President on the situation in Hawaii, on why they believed this could have happened, on what might happen next, on what could be done to repair the damage, but as the bad news continued to pour in, it became evident that the Pacific fleet had been severely crippled, that the Army and air units there were in no condition to fight off an invasion of Hawaii, and that the West Coast of the United States might even be an invasion target.

Meantime, bulletin by bulletin, a smattering of information at a time, the public at large was learning the news, struggling to comprehend and digest it and figure out how to react. Sunday afternoon still had a particular niche in the average American home; with morning church attendance behind them and the big midday dinner cooked, consumed, and cleaned up, members of the family could settle down to a few hours of quiet and rest—napping, listening to the radio, reading the Sunday paper, going for a leisurely walk. Professional football was beginning to make inroads into this domestic tranquillity, and at Washington's dingy Griffith Stadium the crowd was watching the Redskins play their last game of the season against the Philadelphia Eagles when the first bulletin hit the press box. Nearby spectators heard the news from sportswriters, the word spread from seat to seat and section to section, and soon the loudspeaker announcer began paging high-ranking Army and Navy officers, telling them to get in touch with their offices immediately; this was interspersed with summonses to editors and reporters, foreign ambassadors, and others, until individuals in every section of the grandstand seats were hurriedly leaving and running for their cars.

At the Polo Grounds in New York City, no one expected the Brooklyn Dodgers football team to be leading the Eastern champion Giants, but that was exactly what was happening, and the radio audience was as intent on the play-by-play account as

Wall Street crowds listen to FDR call for war.

those in the stands were on the game they were watching. "It's a long one down to the three-yard line," the announcer shouted; the ball was intercepted by Ward Cuff, who picked up a nice block by Alphonse Leemans before he was hit hard around the twenty-seven-yard line—at which moment another voice broke in to say, "We interrupt this broadcast to bring this important bulletin from United Press: Flash! The White House announces Japanese attack on Pearl Harbor!" Predictably, the Mutual Broadcasting System was suddenly deluged with calls from furious fans, wanting to know what was happening in the game. Mutual put the Pearl Harbor story on the air immediately; astonishingly, NBC and CBS decided not to interrupt scheduled music programs but waited until their two-thirty news broadcasts to announce the news.

At Fort Sam Houston in San Antonio, Texas, an Army officer whose exceptional performance in the Louisiana maneuvers a few months before had won him a brigadier general's star was taking a nap after lunch, having told his aide that he was tired and didn't want to be awakened under any circumstances. Under these particular circumstances, however, the aide decided that disobedience was warranted, and he called General Eisenhower. From another room, Mamie Eisenhower heard her husband saying, "Yes? When? I'll be right down," and as he ran for

Air-raid wardens take their posts atop the Nassau County courthouse in Mineola, Long Island, New York, the day after the raid.

the door, pulling on his uniform jacket, he told her he would be at headquarters and didn't know when he would be back.

Paul Tibbets was flying a Douglas A-20 bomber from Fort Bragg, North Carolina, to Savannah, Georgia, navigating by tuning in to a Savannah station and steering by radio compass. He was listening to a Glenn Miller recording and was about twenty miles from his destination when someone interrupted the music to announce the bombing of Pearl Harbor. For Tibbets, that was the first news of the war whose end he would help bring about less than four years later, piloting a B-29 Superfortress called the *Enola Gay* over Hiroshima, Japan. (By some extraordinary turn of fate and timing, a few minutes after the atomic bomb dropped from the *Enola Gay,* Mitsuo Fuchida flew into the area. This was the same Mitsuo Fuchida who led the Japanese planes from their carriers to Pearl Harbor on December 7, 1941, bringing war to America, and as he flew past Hiroshima, he wondered what had caused the curious mushroom-shaped cloud he saw rising above the city. So the man who was present at the beginning was there at the end as well.) . . .

A few minutes before five o'clock, President Roosevelt asked Grace Tully to come to his study, and she found him alone, with two or three neat piles of notes before him on his desk containing the information he had received in the last two hours. As she came in with her notebook, he lit a cigarette, took a deep drag, and said, "Sit down, Grace. I'm going before Congress tomorrow. I'd like to dictate my message. It will be short."

With that he took another long pull on the cigarette and began to speak in a calm tone as if he were dictating a letter, but she noticed that his diction was unusually incisive and slow and that he specified each punctuation mark.

"Yesterday comma December seventh comma 1941 dash a day which will live in infamy dash the United States of America was suddenly and deliberately attacked by naval and air forces of the Empire of Japan period paragraph."

In fewer than five hundred words, spoken without hesitation or second thought, Roosevelt dictated the speech intended to lay America's case before Congress and the world. The message had none of Churchill's soaring prose, no patriotic summons, no bugle calls to action—only a simple, direct recitation of the facts, as in the conclusion: "I ask that the Congress declare that since the unprovoked

FDR signs the joint congressional resolution declaring war on Japan.

and dastardly attack by Japan on Sunday comma December seventh comma a state of war has existed between the United States and the Japanese Empire period end."

When Grace Tully had transcribed her notes, the President called Hull back to the White House to go over the draft. As he anticipated, the Secretary of State had in hand a much longer message relating in explicit detail the long train of circumstances leading to war; again, Roosevelt was ready for him and would have none of it. He must have known that his wish in this grave instance was the wish of the whole American people, for he sensed that they wanted no oratory, no lawyer's brief, only the briefest summary of the facts, set forth by him in what might be described as controlled rage, so that the nation could get on with what needed to be done as quickly as possible. Except for a few minor changes of words, the only real addition he permitted was volunteered by Harry Hopkins, who suggested what appeared as the next-to-last sentence of the message: "With confidence in our armed forces—with the unbounded determination of our people—we will gain the inevitable triumph—so help us God."

Eleanor Roosevelt was carrying on gallantly downstairs, on the theory that her dinner guests had to eat somewhere and it might as well be there, but it was not a relaxed occasion for the visitors, who were acutely aware of the empty chair at the head of the table and the stream of worried-looking men scurrying through the hall to or from the study that was the focus of the nation's attention. Ed and Janet Murrow were with Mrs. Roosevelt, as were her young friends Joe Lash and Trude

Pratt, and during dinner the President sent word that Murrow was to wait, that he wanted to see him.

After the meal Janet departed to attend another party, at which the Murrows were to have been the guests of honor, while Ed went upstairs to sit on a bench outside the President's study. As he waited to be summoned, he observed the continuing procession of VIPs and overheard snatches of conversation as they passed, including a snarled rebuke to Frank Knox—"God-damnit, sir, you ought not to be in charge of a rowboat, let alone the United States Navy!" Some years later, commenting on the charges that Roosevelt and his top advisers possessed advance knowledge of the attack on Pearl Harbor, Murrow recalled the opportunity he had had that night to observe these men off guard and said, "If they were *not* surprised by the news from Pearl Harbor, then that group of elderly men were putting on a performance which would have excited the admiration of any experienced actor." . . .

By evening people were standing five and six deep on the sidewalk beyond the tall iron fence around the White House grounds, peering at the lighted windows in hopes of spotting movement inside, watching intently the arrival of each automobile to see if they could identify passengers, and by the time Secretary of the Interior Harold Ickes appeared for the cabinet meeting the moon was up, misty and indistinct. He noticed especially how quiet and serious the crowds were, and he decided their presence was an example of the human instinct to get close to the scene of action even if one could see or hear nothing. Some cabinet officers had been trying all afternoon to get back to Washington, and Ickes was pleased to see that everyone had made it. Postmaster General Frank Walker and Frances Perkins, Secretary of Labor, had flown from New York in a special plane; so had the Treasury Secretary, Henry Morgenthau.

Promptly at eight-thirty the full cabinet met, with the members forming a ring completely around the President's desk. Ickes noticed at once how solemn Roo-

The lights in the White House burned all night, and crowds waited quietly outside.

sevelt was: no wisecracks or jokes this evening, not even a smile, and the calmness he had displayed earlier in the afternoon was largely gone, replaced by tension and signs of enormous fatigue. The President began by telling them that this was probably the gravest crisis to confront a cabinet since 1861; then he filled them in on everything he had heard from Hawaii, making clear that what they had on their hands was the worst naval defeat in American history. Not only that: Guam had probably been captured, and it was likely that Wake was gone, while the Japanese were advancing on Manila, Singapore, Hong Kong, and other locations in the Malay States. For all anyone knew, an attack might be taking place in Hawaii at that very moment.

Even though they had heard some of this news before they arrived, the detailed catalogue of catastrophe shocked the cabinet members—that and the manner in which Roosevelt described the disaster. Frances Perkins said he actually had "physical difficulty in getting out the words that put him on record as knowing that the navy was caught unawares." It was obvious to her that he was "having a dreadful time just accepting the idea." Yet she knew him well, and she detected an evasive look, revealing the wave of relief he was reluctant to acknowledge—relief that the long period of tension, of not knowing what the Japanese would do and when they would do it, was over. The men in Tokyo, after all, had taken the decision for war or peace from the President's hands.

Throughout the meeting, according to Ickes, Hull behaved more than ever like a Christian martyr—indignant that he was the one to have been duped by the Japanese diplomats while their army and navy were plotting against us, since it was obvious that the expedition against Pearl Harbor had been in the works for months. Despite FDR's annoyance, moreover, Hull was still plumping for a long presidential message to Congress, but when Roosevelt read his own draft aloud, all but the Secretary of State agreed that he had struck exactly the right note.

Shortly after nine-thirty the congressional leaders were ushered into the study, and the cabinet members moved back to let them have the chairs surrounding the President's desk. The President reviewed the situation with them in much the same words he had used with the cabinet, informing them that "the casualties, I am sorry to say, were extremely heavy" and that "we have lost the majority of the battleships there."

Following his summary of the attack, there was dead silence until the man most visibly outraged said what most of the others were thinking. Tom Connolly of Texas, chairman of the Senate Foreign Relations Committee, asked, "How did it happen that our warships were caught like tame ducks in Pearl Harbor? I am amazed at the attack by Japan, but I am still more astounded at what happened to our navy. They were all asleep!" he exploded. "Where were our patrols? They knew these negotiations were going on." Knox was obviously deeply embarrassed by these and other questions but made no attempt to reply.

Finally, at twelve-thirty, it was Ed Murrow's turn in the study, and the President ordered beer and sandwiches. Joining them was Col. William Donovan, who was then engaged in setting up an intelligence organization that would be known as the Office of Strategic Services (OSS). Mr. Roosevelt, dead tired, his face ashen, asked Murrow a few questions about the bombing of London and the morale of the

British and then informed his visitors in detail about the losses at Pearl Harbor—the loss of life, how ships had been sunk at their moorings and planes destroyed on the airstrips—and he pounded his fist on the table and groaned, "On the ground, by God, on the ground!"

For a reporter on this night of nights, it was the chance of a lifetime, since the details that Roosevelt gave them—with no indication that what he said should be off the record—would not be made public for hours—in some cases, for months. The President mentioned that he had talked with Churchill, who told him of attacks on British bases, and he asked Donovan if he thought this might be part of an overall Axis plan. The latter had no evidence to offer but said it was certainly a reasonable assumption. Then Roosevelt asked a rather curious question, hinting at the isolationists' powerful influence on his thinking and his intense concern about public unity: Did they believe the nation would now support a declaration of war? Both men assured him that it would.

As Murrow was taking his leave after more than half an hour's conversation, the President inquired, "Did this surprise you?"

"Yes, Mr. President," he replied.

"Maybe you think it didn't surprise us!" Roosevelt responded.

In the early hours of the morning Murrow returned to the hotel and for hours paced the floor, smoking continuously, debating whether or not he could reveal the information he had heard from the President. "The biggest story of my life," he kept telling his wife, "and I can't make up my mind whether it's my duty to tell it or forget it." In the end he decided it had been told him in confidence and he should not report what Roosevelt had said.

The telephone awakened Ambassador Joseph Grew in Tokyo at 7:00 A.M. on December 8. The call was urgent, requesting that he come as quickly as possible to see Foreign Minister Shigenori Togo, and, without taking time even to shave, he threw on some clothes. When he arrived at 7:30, he found Togo grim, formal, and—as always—imperturbable. The Japanese official made a brief statement and slapped down on the table the thirteen-page memorandum that Nomura had delivered to Hull. Then he made a pretty little speech thanking Grew for his cooperation during the long negotiations and walked downstairs to see him to the door. Not a word was spoken about Pearl Harbor. Indeed, not until after he had shaved and breakfasted did Grew learn that the two countries were at war, and this was not confirmed until late morning, when a functionary appeared at the embassy and, hands trembling, read the official announcement.

Shortly thereafter the embassy gates were closed and the ambassador was told that no one could enter or leave, that no cipher messages could be sent, and that all telegrams must be submitted to the Foreign Office for approval. The British ambassador and several others from the diplomatic colony managed to get past the police outside the gates and bid farewell to the Americans, and they were followed by a group of extremely polite Japanese, who apologized profusely before confiscating all the short-wave radios in the embassy. None of the Americans knew, of course, how long it would be before they might be exchanged for Japan's diplomats in Washington, and about sixty members of the staff assembled for cocktails that evening, livened by a few brave speeches. Arrangements were made for those who

FDR's press secretary, Steve Early, briefs reporters.

lived outside the compound to move into the embassy, sharing apartments, bunking down on mattresses on the floor.

Reflecting on the way Tokyo had borrowed blitzkrieg tactics from its allies in Berlin, Grew concluded that "if the Japanese had confined themselves to the Far East and had attacked only the Philippines, there would have been pacifists and isolationists at home who would have said that we have no business in the Far East anyway, but once they attacked Hawaii it was certain that the American people would rise up in a solid unit of fury." The task ahead would not be easy, he knew, but Japan's defeat was absolutely certain, and he permitted himself a smile of satisfaction as he recalled how he had warned Washington to be ready for a step of "dangerous and dramatic suddenness"—exactly what had occurred.

Grew might be right that victory over Japan was certain, but what good was that if Britain and Russia should fall, if Hitler should triumph in Europe? Despite pressure from Stimson, in particular, who argued that Germany had pushed Japan to attack, President Roosevelt resisted the temptation to declare war on Germany and Italy, hoping that Hitler would relieve him of the necessity to act. He detected "a lingering distinction in some quarters of the public between war with Japan and war with Germany," he told the British ambassador, and although Berlin was ominously silent, he decided to wait it out to see if the Führer would resolve his dilemma.

Hitler had his hands full. Winter had closed in on Russia, and his dream of conquering that nation in a single summer campaign ended as the days grew shorter and brutal cold and blizzards descended on the land. On December 6, to the utter surprise of the German high command, the Russians seized the initiative when the temperature was thirty-five degrees below zero, launched a major assault with one hundred fresh divisions, and threw back the Wehrmacht within twelve miles of the center of Moscow. Simultaneously, Gen. Erwin Rommel's Afrika Corps began to retreat in the desert, and Hitler assumed control of all military operations. Curiously, despite the many warning signs from the Far East, the Japanese attack took him by surprise. In the spring he had urged his allies in Tokyo to move against Singapore, saying that one of the benefits would be to deter the United States from entering the war, but he had not contemplated hostilities between Japan and America. As the German foreign minister Joachim von Ribbentrop perceived, the Japanese attack "brought about what we had wanted to avoid at all costs, war between Germany and America," but Hitler himself was jubilant. Rejoicing in the news—"The turning point!" he proclaimed when he heard it—he dismissed the advice of those around him and made another monumental miscalculation: He would declare war on the United States.

Knowing virtually nothing about the United States, viewing it merely as a decadent bourgeois democracy incapable of waging or sustaining a prolonged war, he disastrously underestimated its strength (an opinion bolstered by the apparent ease of the Japanese triumph), and despite the lack of the most elementary preparations (one of his headquarters officers admitted that "we have never even considered a war against the United States") and the certainty of U.S. intervention in the European war, he left his Wolf's Lair bunker on the evening of December 8, returned to Berlin, and began to prepare a speech to the Reichstag. On December 11, after denouncing Roosevelt as "the main culprit of this war" and a creature of the Jews, he announced to deafening applause that he had arranged for the American chargé d'affaires to be handed his passport. Now the fire he had ignited with the invasion of Poland on September 1, 1939, would rage around the world.

■ ■ ■ ■ ■ ■ ■

Why We Had to Drop the Atomic Bomb

Robert James Maddox

That the American decision to use the atom bomb against Japan ended World War II is beyond dispute. But whether the atomic bomb was the best way to accomplish that objective is still a subject of controversy among historians who have studied the question carefully.

No one argues that Japan could have escaped defeat if Hiroshima and Nagasaki had not been leveled. But at what cost in human lives, Japanese and Allied alike? In this essay, Professor Robert James Maddox discusses whether or not the killing of so many thousands of Japanese civilians was morally justified. He makes a powerful case that it was. As editor, I agree. But many readers may not. Like so many crucial events, the truth is a matter of opinion, a fact which makes history endlessly fascinating.

■ ■ ■ ■ ■ ■ ■

On the morning of August 6, 1945, the American B-29 *Enola Gay* dropped an atomic bomb on the Japanese city of Hiroshima. Three days later another B-29, *Bock's Car*, released one over Nagasaki. Both caused enormous casualties and physical destruction. These two cataclysmic events have preyed upon the American consciousness ever since. . . . Harry S Truman and other officials claimed that the bombs caused Japan to surrender, thereby avoiding a bloody invasion. Critics have accused them of at best failing to explore alternatives, at worst of using the bombs to make the Soviet Union "more manageable" rather than to defeat a Japan that they already knew was on the verge of capitulation.

By any rational calculation Japan was a beaten nation by the summer of 1945. Conventional bombing had reduced many of its cities to rubble, blockade had strangled its importation of vitally needed materials, and its navy had sustained such heavy losses as to be powerless to interfere with the invasion everyone knew was coming. By late June advancing American forces had completed the conquest of Okinawa, which lay only 350 miles from the southernmost Japanese home island of Kyushu. They now stood poised for the final onslaught.

Rational calculations did not determine Japan's position. Although a peace faction within the government wished to end the war—provided certain conditions were met—militants were prepared to fight on regardless of consequences. They claimed to welcome an invasion of the home islands, promising to inflict such hideous casualties that the United States would retreat from its announced policy of unconditional surrender. The militarists held effective power over the government and were capable of defying the emperor, as they had in the past, on the ground that his civilian advisors were misleading him.

Okinawa provided a preview of what invasion of the home islands would entail. Since April 1 the Japanese had fought with a ferocity that mocked any notion that their will to resist was eroding. They had inflicted nearly 50,000 casualties on the invaders, many resulting from the first large-scale use of kamikazes. They also had dispatched the superbattleship *Yamato* on a suicide mission to Okinawa where, after attacking American ships offshore, it was to plunge ashore to become a huge, doomed fortress. *Yamato* was sunk shortly after leaving port, but its mission symbolized Japan's willingness to sacrifice everything in an apparently hopeless cause.

The Japanese could be expected to defend their sacred homeland with even greater fervor, and kamikazes flying at short range promised to be even more devastating than at Okinawa. The Japanese had more than 2,000,000 troops in the home islands, were training millions of irregulars, and for some time had been conserving aircraft that might have been used to protect Japanese cities against American bombers. Reports from Tokyo indicated that Japan meant to fight the war to a finish. On June 8 an imperial conference adopted "The Fundamental Policy to Be Followed Henceforth in the Conduct of the War," which pledged to "prosecute the war to the bitter end in order to uphold the national polity, protect the imperial land, and accomplish the objectives for which we went to war." Truman had no reason to believe that the proclamation meant anything other than what it said.

Against this background, while fighting on Okinawa still continued, the President had his naval chief of staff, Adm. William D. Leahy, notify the Joint Chiefs of Staff (JCS) and the Secretaries of War and Navy that a meeting would be held at the White House on June 18. The night before the conference Truman wrote in his diary that "I have to decide Japanese strategy - shall we invade Japan proper or shall we bomb and blockade? That is my hardest decision to date. But I'll make it when I have all the facts."

Truman met with the chiefs at three-thirty in the afternoon. Present were Army Chief of Staff Gen. George C. Marshall, Army Air Force's Gen. Ira C. Eaker (sitting in for the Army Air Force's chief of staff, Henry H. Arnold, who was on an inspection tour of installations in the Pacific), Navy Chief of Staff Adm. Ernest J. King, Leahy (also a member of the JCS), Secretary of the Navy James Forrestal, Secretary of War Henry L. Stimson, and Assistant Secretary of War John J. McCloy. Truman opened the meeting, then asked Marshall for his views. Marshall was the dominant figure on the JCS. He was Truman's most trusted military adviser, as he had been Roosevelt's.

Marshall reported that the chiefs, supported by the Pacific commanders Gen. Douglas MacArthur and Adm. Chester W. Nimitz, agreed that an invasion of Kyushu "appears to be the least costly worthwhile operation following Okinawa." Lodgment in Kyushu, he said, was necessary to make blockade and bombardment more effective and to serve as a staging area for the invasion of Japan's main island of Honshu. The chiefs recommended a target date of November 1 for the first phase, code name Olympic, because delay would give the Japanese more time to prepare and because bad weather might postpone the invasion "and hence the end of the war" for up to six months. Marshall said that in his opinion, Olympic was "the only course to pursue." The chiefs also proposed that Operation Cornet be launched against Honshu on March 4, 1946.

Leahy's memorandum calling the meeting had asked for the casualty projections which that invasion might produce. Marshall stated that campaigns in the Pacific had been so diverse "it is considered wrong" to make total estimates. All he would say was that casualties during the first thirty days on Kyushu should not exceed those sustained in taking Luzon in the Philippines—31,000 men killed, wounded, or missing in action. "It is a grim fact," Marshall said, "that there is not an easy, bloodless way to victory in war." Leahy estimated a higher casualty rate similar to Okinawa, and King guessed somewhere in between.

King and Eaker, speaking for the Navy and the Army Air Forces respectively, endorsed Marshall's proposals. King said that he had become convinced that Kyushu was "the key to the success of any siege operations." He recommended that "we should do Kyushu now" and begin preparations for invading Honshu. Eaker "agreed completely" with Marshall. He said he had just received a message from Arnold also expressing "complete agreement." Air Force plans called for the use of forty groups of heavy bombers, which could not be deployed without the use of airfields on Kyushu. Stimson and Forrestal concurred.

Truman summed up. He considered "the Kyushu plan all right from the military standpoint" and directed the chiefs to "go ahead with it." He said he "had hoped that there was a possibility of preventing an Okinawa from one end of Japan to the other," but "he was clear on the situation now" and was "quite sure" the chiefs should proceed with the plan. Just before the meeting adjourned, McCloy raised the possibility of avoiding an invasion by warning the Japanese that the United States would employ atomic weapons if there were no surrender. The ensuing discussion was inconclusive because the first test was a month away and no one could be sure the weapons would work.

In his memoirs Truman claimed that using atomic bombs prevented an invasion that would have cost 500,000 American lives. Other officials mentioned the same or even higher figures. Critics have assailed such statements as gross exaggerations designed to forestall scrutiny of Truman's real motives. They have given wide publicity to a report prepared by the Joint War Plans Committee (JWPC) for the chiefs' meeting with Truman. The committee estimated that the invasion of Kyushu, followed by that of Honshu, as the chiefs proposed, would cost approximately 40,000 dead, 150,000 wounded, and 3,500 missing in action for a total of 193,500 casualties.

That those responsible for a decision should exaggerate the consequences is commonplace. Some who cite the JWPC report profess to see more sinister motives, insisting that such "low" casualty projections call into question the very idea that atomic bombs were used to avoid heavy losses. By discrediting that justification as a cover-up, they seek to bolster their contention that the bombs were really used to permit the employment of "atomic diplomacy" against the Soviet Union.

The notion that 193,500 anticipated casualties were too insignificant to have caused Truman to resort to atomic bombs might seem bizarre to anyone other than an academic, but let it pass. Those who have cited the JWCP report in countless op-ed pieces in newspapers and in magazine articles have created a myth by omitting key considerations: First, the report itself is studded with qualifications that casualties "are not subject to accurate estimate" and that the projection "is admittedly only an educated guess." Second, the figures never were conveyed to Truman. They were excised at high military echelons, which is why Marshall cited only estimates for the first thirty days on Kyushu. And indeed, subsequent Japanese troop buildups on Kyushu rendered the JWPC estimates totally irrelevant by the time the first atomic bomb was dropped.

Another myth that has attained wide attention is that at least several of Truman's top military advisers later informed him that using atomic bombs against Japan would be militarily unnecessary or immoral, or both. There is no persuasive evidence that any of them did so. None of the Joint Chiefs ever made such a claim, although one inventive author has tried to make it appear that Leahy did by braiding together several unrelated passages from the admiral's memoirs. Actually, two days after Hiroshima, Truman told aides that Leahy had "said up to the last that it wouldn't go off."

Neither MacArthur nor Nimitz ever communicated to Truman any change of mind about the need for invasion or expressed reservations about using the bombs. When first informed about their imminent use only days before Hiroshima, MacArthur responded with a lecture on the future of atomic warfare and even after Hiroshima strongly recommended that the invasion go forward. Nimitz, from whose jurisdiction the atomic strikes would be launched, was notified in early 1945. "This sounds fine," he told the courier, "but this is only February. Can't we get one earlier?" Nimitz later would join Air Force generals Carl D. Spaatz, Nathan Twining, and Curtis LeMay in recommending that a third bomb be dropped on Tokyo.

Only Dwight D. Eisenhower later claimed to have remonstrated against the use of the bomb. In his *Crusade in Europe,* published in 1948, he wrote that when Secretary Stimson informed him during the Potsdam Conference of plans to use the bomb, he replied that he hoped "we would never have to use such a thing against any enemy," because he did not want the United States to be the first to use such a weapon. He added, "My views were merely personal and immediate reactions; they were not based on any analysis of the subject."

Eisenhower's recollections grew more colorful as the years went on. A later account with Stimson had it taking place at Ike's headquarters in Frankfurt on the very day news arrived of the successful test in New Mexico. "We'd had a nice evening at headquarters in Germany," he remembered. Then, after dinner, "Stimson got this cable saying that the bomb had been perfected and and was ready to be dropped. The cable was in code . . . 'the lamb is born' or some damn thing like that." In this version Eisenhower claimed to have protested vehemently that "the Japanese were ready to surrender and it wasn't necessary to hit them with that awful thing." "Well," Eisenhower concluded, "the old gentleman got furious."

This 1984 display in an Osaka department store recalls the destruction wrought by the atomic bombs dropped on Japan in 1945.

The best that can be said about Eisenhower's memory is that it had become flawed by the passage of time. Stimson was in Potsdam and Eisenhower in Frankfurt on July 16, when word came of the successful test. Aside from a brief conversation at a flag-raising ceremony in Berlin on July 20, the only other time they met was at Ike's headquarters on July 27. By then orders already had been sent to the Pacific to use the bombs if Japan had not yet surrendered. Notes made by one of Stimson's aides indicate that there was a discussion of atomic bombs, but there is no mention of any protest on Eisenhower's part. Even if there had been, two factors must be kept in mind. Eisenhower had commanded Allied forces in Europe, and his opinion on how close Japan was to surrender would have carried no special weight. More important, Stimson left for home immediately after the meeting and could not have personally conveyed Ike's sentiments to the President, who did not return to Washington until after Hiroshima.

On July 8 the Combined Intelligence Committee submitted to the American and British Combined Chiefs of Staff a report entitled "Estimate of the Enemy Situation." The committee predicted that as Japan's position continued to deteriorate, it might "make a serious effort to use the USSR [then a neutral] as a mediator in ending the war." Tokyo also would put out "intermittent peace feelers" to "weaken the determination of the United Nations to fight to the bitter end, or to create inter-allied dissension." While the Japanese people would be willing to make large concessions to end the war, "For a surrender to be acceptable to the Japanese army, it would be necessary for the military leaders to believe that it would not entail discrediting warrior tradition and that it would permit the ultimate resurgence of a military Japan."

Small wonder that American officials remained unimpressed when Japan proceeded to do exactly what the committee predicted. On July 12 Japanese Foreign Minister Shigenori Togo instructed Ambassador Naotaki Sato in Moscow to inform the Soviets that the emperor wished to send a personal envoy, Prince Fuminaro Konoye, in an attempt "to restore peace with all possible speed." Although he realized Konoye could not reach Moscow before the Soviet leader Joseph Stalin and Foreign Minister V. M. Molotov left to attend a Big Three meeting scheduled to begin in Potsdam on the fifteenth, Togo sought to have negotiations begin as soon as they returned.

American officials had long since been able to read Japanese diplomatic traffic through a process known as the MAGIC intercepts. Army intelligence (G-2) prepared for General Marshall its interpretation of Togo's message the next day. The report listed several possible constructions, the most probable being that the Japanese "governing clique" was making a coordinated effort to "stave off defeat" through Soviet intervention and an "appeal to war weariness in the United States." The report added that Undersecretary of State Joseph C. Crew, who had spent ten years in Japan as ambassador, "agrees with these conclusions."

Some have claimed that Togo's overture to the Soviet Union, together with attempts by some minor Japanese officials in Switzerland and other neutral countries to get peace talks started through the Office of Strategic Services (OSS), constituted clear evidence that the Japanese were near surrender. Their sole prerequisite was retention of their sacred emperor, whose unique cultural/religious status within the Japanese polity they would not compromise. If only the United States had extended assurances about the emperor, according to this view, much bloodshed and the atomic bombs would have been unnecessary.

A careful reading of the MAGIC intercepts of subsequent exchanges between Togo and Sato provides no evidence that retention of the emperor was the sole obstacle to peace. What they show instead is that the Japanese Foreign Office was trying to cut a deal through the Soviet Union that would have permitted Japan to retain its political system and its prewar empire intact. Even the most lenient of American officials could not have countenanced such a settlement.

Togo on July 17 informed Sato that "we are not asking the Russians' mediation in *anything like unconditional surrender* [emphasis added]." During the following weeks Sato pleaded with his superiors to abandon hope of Soviet intercession and to approach the United States directly to find out what peace terms would be offered. "There is . . . no alternative but immediate unconditional surrender," he cabled on July 31, and he bluntly informed Togo that "your way of looking at things and the actual situation in the Eastern area may be seen to be absolutely contradictory." The Foreign Ministry ignored his pleas and continued to seek Soviet help even after Hiroshima.

"Peace feelers" by Japanese officials abroad seemed no more promising from the American point of view. Although several of the consular personnel and military attachés engaged in these activities claimed important connections at home, none produced verification. Had the Japanese government sought only an assurance about the emperor, all it had to do was grant one of these men authority to begin talks through the OSS. Its failure to do so led American officials to assume that those involved were either well-meaning individuals acting alone or that they were being orchestrated by Tokyo. Grew characterized such "peace feelers" as "familiar weapons of psychological warfare" designed to "divide the Allies."

Some American officials, such as Stimson and Grew, nonetheless wanted to signal to the Japanese that they might retain the emperorship in the form of a constitutional monarchy. Such an assurance might remove the last stumbling block to surrender, if not when it was issued, then later. Only an imperial rescript would bring about an orderly surrender, they argued, without which Japanese forces would fight to the last man regardless of what the government in Tokyo did. Besides, the emperor could serve as a stabilizing factor during the transition to peacetime.

There were many arguments against an American initiative. Some opposed retaining such an undemocratic institution on principle and because they feared it might later serve as a rallying point for future militarism. Should that happen, as one assistant Secretary of State put it, "those lives already spent will have been sacrificed in vain, and lives will be lost again in the future." Japanese hard-liners were certain to exploit an overture as evidence that losses sustained at Okinawa had weakened American resolve and to argue that continued resistance would bring further concessions. Stalin, who earlier had told an American envoy that he favored abolishing the emperorship because the ineffectual Hirohito might be succeeded by "an energetic and vigorous figure who could cause trouble," was just as certain to interpret it as a treacherous effort to end the war before the Soviets could share in the spoils.

There were domestic considerations as well. Roosevelt had announced the unconditional surrender policy in early 1943, and it since had become a slogan of the war. He also had advocated that peoples everywhere should have the right to choose their own form of government, and Truman had publicly pledged to carry out his predecessor's legacies. For him to have formally guaranteed continuance of the emperorship, as opposed to merely accepting it on American terms pending free elections, as he later did, would have constituted a blatant repudiation of his own promises.

Nor was that all. Regardless of the emperor's actual role in Japanese aggression, which is still debated, much wartime propaganda had encouraged Americans to regard Hirohito as no less a war criminal than Adolf Hitler or Benito Mussolini. Although Truman said on several occasions that he had no objection to retaining the emperor, he understandably refused to make the first move. The ultimatum he issued from Potsdam on July 26 did not refer specifically to the emperorship. All it said was that occupation forces would be removed after a "peaceful and responsible" government had been established according to the "freely expressed will of the Japanese people." When the Japanese rejected the ultimatum rather than at last inquire whether they might retain the emperor, Truman permitted the plans for using the bombs to go forward.

Reliance on MAGIC intercepts and the "peace feelers" to gauge how near Japan was to surrender is misleading in any case. The army, not the Foreign Office, controlled the situation. Intercepts of Japanese military communications, designated ULTRA, provided no reason to believe the army was even considering surrender. Japanese Imperial Headquarters had correctly guessed that the next operation after Okinawa would be Kyushu and was making every effort to bolster its defenses there.

General Marshall reported on July 24 that there were "approximately 500,000 troops in Kyushu" and that more were on their way. ULTRA identified new units arriving almost daily. MacArthur's G-2 reported on July 29 that "this threatening development, if not checked, may grow to a point where we attack on a ratio of one (1) to one (1) which is not the recipe for victory." By the time the first atomic bomb fell, ULTRA indicated there were 560,000 troops in southern Kyushu (the actual figure was closer to 900,000), and projections for November 1 placed the number at 680,000. A report, for medical purposes, of July 31 estimated that total battle and non-battle casualties might run as high as 394,859 *for the Kyushu operation alone.* This figure did not include those men expected to be killed outright, for obviously they would need no medical attention. Marshall regarded Japanese defenses as so formidable that even after Hiroshima he asked MacArthur to consider alternate landing sites and began contemplating the use of atomic bombs as tactical weapons to support the invasion.

The thirty-day casualty projection of 31,000 Marshall had given Truman at the June 18 strategy meeting had become meaningless. It had been based in the assumption that the Japanese had about 350,000 defenders in Kyushu and that naval and air interdiction would provide reinforcement. But the Japanese buildup since that time meant that the defenders would have nearly twice the number of troops available by "X-day" than earlier assumed. The assertion that apprehensions about casualties are insufficient to explain Truman's use of the bombs, therefore, cannot be taken seriously. On the contrary, as Winston Churchill wrote after a conversation with him at Potsdam, Truman was tormented by "the terrible responsibilities that rested upon him in regard to the unlimited effusions of American blood."

Some historians have argued that while the first bomb might have been required to achieve Japanese surrender, dropping the second constituted a needless barbarism. The record shows otherwise. American officials believed more than one bomb would be necessary because they assumed Japanese hard-liners would minimize the first explosion or attempt to explain it away as some sort of natural catastrophe, precisely what they did. The Japanese minister of war, for instance, at first refused to admit that the Hiroshima bomb was atomic. A few hours after Nagasaki he told the cabinet that "the Americans appeared to have one hundred atomic bombs . . . they could drop three per day. The next target might well be Tokyo."

Even after both bombs had fallen and Russia entered the war, Japanese militants insisted on such lenient peace terms that moderates knew there was no sense even transmitting them to the United States. Hirohito had to intervene personally on two occasions during the next few days to induce hard-liners to abandon their conditions and to accept the American stipulation that the emperor's authority "shall be subject to the Supreme Commander of the Allied Powers." That the militarists would have accepted such a settlement before the bombs is farfetched, to say the least.

Some writers have argued that the cumulative effects of battlefield defeats, conventional bombing, and naval blockade already had defeated Japan. Even without extending assurances about the emperor, all the United States had to do was wait. The most frequently cited basis for this contention is the *United States Strategic Bombing Survey*, published in 1946, which stated that Japan would have surrendered by November 1 "even if the atomic bombs had not been dropped, even if Russia had not entered the war, and even if no invasion had been planned or contemplated." Recent scholarship by the historian Robert P. Newman and others has demonstrated that the survey was "cooked" by those who prepared it to arrive at such a conclusion. No matter. This or any other document based on information available only after the war ended is irrelevant with regard to what Truman could have known at the time.

What often goes unremarked is that when the bombs were dropped, fighting was still going on in the Philippines, China, and elsewhere. Every day that the war continued thousands of prisoners of war had to live in abysmal conditions, and there were rumors that the Japanese intended to slaughter them if the homeland was invaded. Truman was Commander in Chief of the American armed forces, and he had a duty to the men under his command not shared by those sitting in moral judgment decades later. Available evidence points to the conclusion that he acted for the reason he said he did: to end the bloody war that would have been far bloodier had invasion proved necessary. One can only imagine what would have happened if tens of thousands of American boys had died or been wounded on Japanese soil and then it had become known that Truman had chosen not to use weapons that could have ended the war months sooner.

■　■　■　■　■　■　■

5

The Great Depression and the New Deal

This photograph by Dorothea Lange captures the despair of a typical migrant California family during the Great Depression.

The Causes of the Great Crash

John Kenneth Galbraith

The following essay is an example of analytical history at its best. Without relying on narrative techniques, Harvard economist John Kenneth Galbraith takes apart the economy of the 1920s and shows us how its weaknesses led to the Great Depression of the 1930s. In the course of doing so, he also "takes apart," in the colloquial sense of that expression, the presidents of the 1920s and a number of their leading advisers.

The effectiveness and power of the essay depend on a number of factors. One is Galbraith's mastery both of the facts he deals with and of the economic mechanisms of the society; he discusses few events that are not thoroughly familiar to students of the subject, but he has an unfailing eye for what is significant. Another is his gift for anecdote and the pithy phrase. As he says, the epigram that Elbert H. Gary of U.S. Steel "never saw a blast furnace until his death" is well known; but not everyone who writes about Gary knows enough to use it. Still a third is Galbraith's ability to state his own opinions without qualification and at the same time without passion, to make the kind of calm, reasoned judgments that are characteristic of a convinced but unprejudiced and intelligent mind. All these qualities explain why his books, such as *American Capitalism, The Affluent Society,* and *The Great Crash, 1929* (a fuller treatment of the subject of this essay), have been both popular and critical successes.

■ ■ ■ ■ ■ ■ ■

The decade of the twenties, or more exactly the eight years between the postwar depression of 1920–21 and the sudden collapse of the stock market in October, 1929, were prosperous ones in the United States. The total output of the economy increased by more than 50 per cent. The preceding decades had brought the automobile; now came many more and also roads on which they could be driven with reasonable reliability and comfort. There was much building. The downtown section of the mid-continent city—Des Moines, Omaha, Minneapolis—dates from these years. It was then, more likely than not, that what is still the leading hotel, the tallest office building, and the biggest department store went up. Radio arrived, as of course did gin and jazz.

These years were also remarkable in another respect, for as time passed it became increasingly evident that the prosperity could not last. Contained within it were the seeds of its own destruction. The country was heading into the gravest kind of trouble. Herein lies the peculiar fascination of the period for a study in the problem of leadership. For almost no steps were taken during these years to arrest the tendencies which were obviously leading, and did lead, to disaster.

At least four things were seriously wrong, and they worsened as the decade passed. And knowledge of them does not depend on the always brilliant assistance of hindsight. At least three of these flaws were highly visible and widely discussed. In ascending order, not of importance but of visibility, they were as follows:

First, income in these prosperous years was being distributed with marked inequality. Although output per worker rose steadily during the period, wages were fairly stable, as also were prices. As a result, business profits increased rapidly and so did incomes of the wealthy and the well-to-do. This tendency was nurtured by assiduous and successful efforts of Secretary of the Treasury Andrew W. Mellon to reduce income taxes with special attention to the higher brackets. In 1929 the 5 per cent of the people with the highest incomes received perhaps a quarter of all personal income. Between 1919 and 1929 the share of the one per cent who received the highest incomes increased by approximately one seventh. This meant that the economy was heavily and increasingly dependent on the luxury consumption of the well-to-do and their willingness to reinvest what they did not or could not spend on themselves. Anything that shocked the confidence of the rich either in their personal or in their business future would have a bad effect on total spending and hence on the behavior of the economy.

This was the least visible flaw. To be sure, farmers, who were not participating in the general advance, were making themselves heard; and twice during the period the Congress passed far-reaching relief legislation which was vetoed by Coolidge. But other groups were much less vocal. Income distribution in the United States had long been unequal. The inequality of these years did not seem exceptional. The trade-union movement was also far from strong. In the early twenties the steel industry was still working a twelve-hour day and, in some jobs, a seven-day week. (Every two weeks when the shift changed a man worked twice around the clock.) Workers lacked the organization or the power to deal with conditions like this; the twelve-hour day was, in fact, ended as the result of personal pressure by President Harding on the steel companies, particularly on Judge Elbert H. Gary, head of the United States Steel Corporation. Judge Gary's personal acquaintance with these working conditions was thought to be slight, and this gave rise to Benjamin Stolberg's now classic observation that the Judge "never saw a blast furnace until his death." In all these circumstances the increasingly lopsided income distribution did not excite much comment or alarm. Perhaps it would have been surprising if it had.

But the other three flaws in the economy were far less subtle. During World War I the United States ceased to be the world's greatest debtor country and became its greatest creditor. The consequences of this change have so often been described that they have the standing of a cliché. A debtor country could export a greater value of goods than it imported and use the difference for interest and debt repayment. This was what we did before the war. But a creditor must import a greater value than it exports if those who owe it money are to have the wherewithal to pay interest and principal. Otherwise the creditor must either forgive the debts or make new loans to pay off the old.

During the twenties the balance was maintained by making new foreign loans. Their promotion was profitable to domestic investment houses. And when the supply of honest and competent foreign borrowers ran out, dishonest, incompetent, or fanciful borrowers were invited to borrow and, on occasion, bribed to do so. In

1927 Juan Leguia, the son of the then dictator of Peru, was paid $450,000 by the National City Company and J. & W. Seligman for his services in promoting a $50,000,000 loan to Peru which these houses marketed. Americans lost and the Peruvians didn't gain appreciably. Other Latin American republics got equally dubious loans by equally dubious devices. And, for reasons that now tax the imagination, so did a large number of German cities and municipalities. Obviously, once investors awoke to the character of these loans or there was any other shock to confidence, they would no longer be made. There would be nothing with which to pay the old loans. Given this arithmetic, there would be either a sharp reduction in exports or a wholesale default on the outstanding loans, or more likely both. Wheat and cotton farmers and others who depended on exports would suffer. So would those who owned the bonds. The buying power of both would be reduced. These consequences were freely predicted at the time.

The second weakness of the economy was the large-scale corporate thimblerigging that was going on. This took a variety of forms, of which by far the most common was the organization of corporations to hold stock in yet other corporations, which in turn held stock in yet other corporations. In the case of the railroads and the utilities, the purpose of this pyramid of holding companies was to obtain control of a very large number of operating companies with a very small investment in the ultimate holding company. A $100,000,000 electric utility, of which the capitalization was represented half by bonds and half by common stock, could be controlled with an investment of a little over $25,000,000—the value of just over half the common stock. Were a company then formed with the same capital structure to hold *this* $25,000,000 worth of common stock, it could be controlled with an investment of $6,250,000. On the next round the amount required would be less than $2,000,000. That $2,000,000 would still control the entire $100,000,000 edifice. By the end of the twenties, holding-company structures six or eight tiers high were commonplace. Some of them—the utility pyramids of Insull and Associated Gas & Electric, and the railroad pyramid of the Van Sweringens—were marvelously complex. It is unlikely that anyone fully understood them or could.

In other cases companies were organized to hold securities in other companies in order to manufacture more securities to sell to the public. This was true of the great investment trusts. During 1929 one investment house, Goldman, Sachs & Company, organized and sold nearly a billion dollars' worth of securities in three interconnected investment trusts—Goldman Sachs Trading Corporation; Shenandoah Corporation; and Blue Ridge Corporation. All eventually depreciated virtually to nothing.

This corporate insanity was also highly visible. So was the damage. The pyramids would last only so long as earnings of the company at the bottom were secure. If anything happened to the dividends of the underlying company, there would be trouble, for upstream companies had issued bonds (or in practice sometimes preferred stock) against the dividends on the stock of the downstream companies. Once the earnings stopped, the bonds would go into default or the preferred stock would take over and the pyramid would collapse. Such a collapse would have a bad effect not only on the orderly prosecution of business and investment by the operating companies but also on confidence, investment, and spending by the community at large. The likelihood was increased because in any number of cities—Cleveland, Detroit, and Chicago were notable examples—the banks were deeply committed to these pyramids or had fallen under the control of the pyramiders.

Finally, and most evident of all, there was the stock market boom. Month after month and year after year the great bull market of the twenties roared on. Sometimes there were setbacks, but more often there were fantastic forward surges. In May of 1924 the New York *Times* industrials stood at 106; by the end of the year they were 134; by the end of 1925 they were up to 181. In 1927 the advance began in earnest—to 245 by the end of that year and on to 331 by the end of 1928. There were some setbacks in early 1929, but then came the fantastic summer explosion when in a matter of three months the averages went up another 110 points. This was the most frantic summer in our financial history. By its end, stock prices had nearly quadrupled as compared with four years earlier. Transactions on the New York Stock Exchange regularly ran to 5,000,000 or more shares a day. Radio Corporation of America went to 573 $^3/_4$ (adjusted) without ever having paid a dividend. Only the hopelessly eccentric, so it seemed, held securities for their income. What counted was the increase in capital values.

And since capital gains were what counted, one could vastly increase his opportunities by extending his holdings with borrowed funds—by buying on margin. Margin accounts expanded enormously, and from all over the country—indeed from all over the world—money poured into New York to finance these transactions. During the summer, brokers' loans increased at the rate of $400,000,000 a month. By September they totaled more than $7,000,000,000. The rate of interest on these loans varied from 7 to 12 per cent and went as high as 15.

This boom was also inherently self-liquidating. It could last only so long as new people, or at least new money, were swarming into the market in pursuit of the capital gains. This new demand bid up the stocks and made the capital gains. Once the supply of new customers began to falter, the market would cease to rise. Once the market stopped rising, some, and perhaps a good many, would start to cash in. If you are concerned with capital gains, you must get them while the getting is good. But the getting may start the market down, and this will one day be the signal for much more selling—both by those who are trying to get out and those who are being forced to sell securities that are no longer safely margined. Thus it was certain that the market would one day go down, and far more rapidly than it went up. Down it went with a thunderous crash in October of 1929. In a series of terrible days, of which Thursday, October 24, and Tuesday, October 29, were the most terrifying, billions in values were lost, and thousands of speculators—they had been called investors—were utterly and totally ruined.

This too had far-reaching effects. Economists have always deprecated the tendency to attribute too much to the great stock market collapse of 1929: this was the drama; the causes of the subsequent depression really lay deeper. In fact, the stock market crash was very important. It exposed the other weakness of the economy. The overseas loans on which the payments balance depended came to an end. The jerry-built holding-company structures came tumbling down. The investment-trust stocks collapsed. The crash put a marked crimp on borrowing for investment and therewith on business spending. It also removed from the economy some billions

Cartoonist Forbell titled this 1929 drawing "Club Life in America—
The Stock Brokers."

of consumer spending that was either based on, sanctioned by, or encouraged by the fact that the spenders had stock market gains. The crash was an intensely damaging thing.

And this damage, too, was not only foreseeable but foreseen. For months the speculative frenzy had all but dominated American life. Many times before in history—the South Sea Bubble, John Law's speculations, the recurrent real-estate booms of the last century, the great Florida land boom earlier in the same decade—there had been similar frenzy. And the end had always come, not with a whimper but a bang. Many men, including in 1929 the President of the United States, knew it would again be so.

The increasingly perilous trade balance, the corporate buccaneering, and the Wall Street boom—along with the less visible tendencies in income distribution—

were all allowed to proceed to the ultimate disaster without effective hindrance. How much blame attaches to the men who occupied the presidency?

Warren G. Harding died on August 2, 1923. This, as only death can do, exonerates him. The disorders that led eventually to such trouble had only started when the fatal blood clot destroyed this now sad and deeply disillusioned man. Some would argue that his legacy was bad. Harding had but a vague perception of the economic processes over which he presided. He died owing his broker $180,000 in a blind account—he had been speculating disastrously while he was President, and no one so inclined would have been a good bet to curb the coming boom. Two of Harding's Cabinet officers, his secretary of the interior and his attorney general, were to plead the Fifth Amendment when faced with questions concerning their official acts, and the first of these went to jail. Harding brought his fellow townsman Daniel R. Crissinger to be his comptroller of the currency, although he was qualified for this task, as Samuel Hopkins Adams has suggested, only by the fact that he and the young Harding had stolen watermelons together. When Crissinger had had an ample opportunity to demonstrate his incompetence in his first post, he was made head of the Federal Reserve System. Here he had the central responsibility for action on the ensuing boom. Jack Dempsey, Paul Whiteman, or F. Scott Fitzgerald would have been at least equally qualified.

Yet it remains that Harding was dead before the real trouble started. And while he left in office some very poor men, he also left some very competent ones. Charles Evans Hughes, his secretary of state; Herbert Hoover, his secretary of commerce; and Henry C. Wallace, his secretary of agriculture, were public servants of vigor and judgment.

The problem of Herbert Hoover's responsibility is more complicated. He became President on March 4, 1929. At first glance this seems far too late for effective action. By then the damage had been done, and while the crash might come a little sooner or a little later, it was now inevitable. Yet Hoover's involvement was deeper than this—and certainly much deeper than Harding's. This he tacitly concedes in his memoirs, for he is at great pains to explain and, in some degree, to excuse himself.

For one thing, Hoover was no newcomer to Washington. He had been secretary of commerce under Harding and Coolidge. He had also been the strongest figure (not entirely excluding the President) in both Administration and party for almost eight years. He had a clear view of what was going on. As early as 1922, in a letter to Hughes, he expressed grave concern over the quality of the foreign loans that were being floated in New York. He returned several times to the subject. He knew about the corporate excesses. In the latter twenties he wrote to his colleagues and fellow officials (including Crissinger) expressing his grave concern over the Wall Street orgy. Yet he was content to express himself—to write letters and memoranda, or at most, as in the case of the foreign loans, to make an occasional speech. He could with propriety have presented his views of the stock market more strongly to the Congress and the public. He could also have maintained a more vigorous and persistent agitation within the Administration. He did neither. His views of the market were so little known that it celebrated his election and inauguration with a great upsurge. Hoover was in the boat and, as he himself tells, he knew where it was headed. But, having warned the man at the tiller, he rode along into the reef.

And even though trouble was inevitable, by March, 1929, a truly committed leader would still have wanted to do something. Nothing else was so important. The resources of the Executive, one might expect, would have been mobilized in a search for some formula to mitigate the current frenzy and to temper the coming crash. The assistance of the bankers, congressional leaders, and the Exchange authorities would have been sought. Nothing of the sort was done. As secretary of commerce, as he subsequently explained, he had thought himself frustrated by Mellon. But he continued Mellon in office. Henry M. Robinson, a sympathetic Los Angeles banker, was commissioned to go to New York to see his colleagues there and report. He returned to say that the New York bankers regarded things as sound. Richard Whitney, the vice-president of the Stock Exchange, was summoned to the White House for a conference on how to curb speculation. Nothing came of this either. Whitney also thought things were sound.

Both Mr. Hoover and his official biographers carefully explained that the primary responsibility for the goings on in New York City rested not with Washington but with the governor of New York State. That was Franklin D. Roosevelt. It was he who failed to rise to his responsibilities. The explanation is far too formal. The future of the whole country was involved. Mr. Hoover was the President of the whole country. If he lacked authority commensurate with this responsibility, he could have requested it. This, at a later date, President Roosevelt did not hesitate to do.

Finally, while by March of 1929 the stock market collapse was inevitable, something could still be done about the other accumulating disorders. The balance of payments is an obvious case. In 1931 Mr. Hoover did request a one-year moratorium on the inter-Allied (war) debts. This was a courageous and constructive step which came directly to grips with the problem. But the year before, Mr. Hoover, though not without reluctance, had signed the Hawley-Smoot tariff. "I shall approve the Tariff Bill. . . . It was undertaken as the result of pledges given by the Republican Party at Kansas City. . . . Platform promises must not be empty gestures." Hundreds of people—from Albert H. Wiggin, the head of the Chase National Bank, to Oswald Garrison Villard, the editor of the *Nation*—felt that no step could have been more directly designed to make things worse. Countries would have even more trouble earning the dollars of which they were so desperately short. But Mr. Hoover signed the bill.

Anyone familiar with this particular race of men knows that a dour, flinty, inscrutable visage such as that of Calvin Coolidge can be the mask for a calm and acutely perceptive intellect. And he knows equally that it can conceal a mind of singular aridity. The difficulty, given the inscrutability, is in knowing which. However, in the case of Coolidge the evidence is in favor of the second. In some sense, he certainly knew what was going on. He would not have been unaware of what was called the Coolidge market. But he connected developments neither with the well-being of the country nor with his own responsibilities. In his memoirs Hoover goes to great lengths to show how closely he was in touch with events and how clearly he foresaw their consequences. In his *Autobiography,* a notably barren document, Coolidge did not refer to the accumulating troubles. He confines himself to such unequivocal truths as "Every day of Presidential life is crowded with activities" (which in his case, indeed, was not true); and "The Congress makes the laws, but it is the President who causes them to be executed."

At various times during his years in office, men called on Coolidge to warn him of the impending trouble. And in 1927, at the instigation of a former White House aide, he sent for William Z. Ripley of Harvard, the most articulate critic of the corporate machinations of the period. The President became so interested that he invited him to stay for lunch, and listened carefully while his guest outlined (as Ripley later related) the "prestidigitation, double-shuffling, honey-fugling, hornswoggling, and skulduggery" that characterized the current Wall Street scene. But Ripley made the mistake of telling Coolidge that regulation was the responsibility of the states (as was then the case). At this intelligence Coolidge's face lit up and he dismissed the entire matter from his mind. Others who warned of the impending disaster got even less far.

And on some occasions Coolidge added fuel to the fire. If the market seemed to be faltering, a timely statement from the White House—or possibly from Secretary Mellon—would often brace it up. William Allen White, by no means an unfriendly observer, noted that after one such comment the market staged a 26-point rise. He went on to say that a careful search "during these halcyon years . . . discloses this fact: Whenever the stock market showed signs of weakness, the President or the Secretary of the Treasury or some important dignitary of the administration . . . issued a statement. The statement invariably declared that business was 'fundamentally sound,' that continued prosperity had arrived, and that the slump of the moment was 'seasonal.'"

Such was the Coolidge role. Coolidge was fond of observing that "if you see ten troubles coming down the road, you can be sure that nine will run into the ditch before they reach you and you have to battle with only one of them." A critic noted that "the trouble with this philosophy was that when the tenth trouble reached him he was wholly unprepared. . . . The outstanding instance was the rising boom and orgy of mad speculation which began in 1927." The critic was Herbert Hoover.

Plainly; in these years, leadership failed. Events whose tragic culmination could be foreseen—and was foreseen—were allowed to work themselves out to the final disaster. The country and the world paid. For a time, indeed, the very reputation of capitalism itself was in the balance. It survived in the years following perhaps less because of its own power or the esteem in which it was held, than because of the absence of an organized and plausible alternative. Yet one important question remains. Would it have been possible even for a strong President to arrest the plunge? Were not the opposing forces too strong? Isn't one asking the impossible?

No one can say for sure. But the answer depends at least partly on the political context in which the Presidency was cast. That of Coolidge and Hoover may well have made decisive leadership impossible. These were conservative Administrations in which, in addition, the influence of the businessman was strong. At the core of the business faith was an intuitive belief in *laissez faire*—the benign tendency of things that are left alone. The man who wanted to intervene was a meddler. Perhaps, indeed, he was a planner. In any case, he was to be regarded with mistrust. And, on the businessman's side, it must be borne in mind that high government office often nurtures a spurious sense of urgency. There is no more important public function than the suppression of proposals for unneeded action. But these should have been distinguished from action necessary to economic survival.

A bitterly criticized figure of the Harding-Coolidge-Hoover era was Secretary of the Treasury Andrew W. Mellon. He opposed all action to curb the boom, although once in 1929 he was persuaded to say that bonds (as distinct from stocks) were a good buy. And when the depression came, he was against doing anything about that. Even Mr. Hoover was shocked by his insistence that the only remedy was (as Mr. Hoover characterized it) to "liquidate labor, liquidate stocks, liquidate the farmers, liquidate real estate." Yet Mellon reflected only in extreme form the conviction that things would work out, that the real enemies were those who interfered.

Outside of Washington in the twenties, the business and banking community, or at least the articulate part of it, was overwhelmingly opposed to any public intervention. The tentative and ineffective steps which the Federal Reserve did take were strongly criticized. In the spring of 1929 when the Reserve system seemed to be on the verge of taking more decisive action, there was an anticipatory tightening of money rates and a sharp drop in the market. On his own initiative Charles E. Mitchell, the head of the National City Bank, poured in new funds. He had an obligation, he said, that was "paramount to any Federal Reserve warning, or anything else" to avert a crisis in the money market. In brief, he was determined, whatever the government thought, to keep the boom going. In that same spring Paul M. Warburg, a distinguished and respected Wall Street leader, warned of the dangers of the boom and called for action to restrain it. He was deluged with criticism and even abuse and later said that the subsequent days were the most difficult of his life. There were some businessmen and bankers—like Mitchell and Albert Wiggin of the Chase National Bank—who may have vaguely sensed that the end of the boom would mean their own business demise. Many more had persuaded themselves that the dream would last. But we should not complicate things. Many others were making money and took a short-run view—or no view—either of their own survival or of the system of which they were a part. They merely wanted to be left alone to get a few more dollars.

And the opposition to government intervention would have been nonpartisan. In 1929 one of the very largest of the Wall Street operators was John J. Raskob. Raskob was also chairman of the Democratic National Committee. So far from calling for preventive measures, Raskob in 1929 was explaining how, through stock market speculation, literally anyone could be a millionaire. Nor would the press have been enthusiastic about, say, legislation to control holding companies and investment trusts or to give authority to regulate margin trading. The financial pages of many of the papers were riding the boom. And from the speculating public, which was dreaming dreams of riches and had yet to learn that it had been fleeced, there would have been no thanks. Perhaps a President of phenomenal power and determination might have overcome the Coolidge-Hoover environment. But it is easier to argue that this context made inaction inevitable for almost any President. There were too many people who, given a choice between disaster and the measures that would have prevented it, opted for disaster without either a second or even a first thought.

On the other hand, in a different context a strong President might have taken effective preventive action. Congress in these years was becoming increasingly critical of the Wall Street speculation and corporate piggery-pokery. The liberal Republicans—the men whom Senator George H. Moses called the Sons of the Wild Jackass—were especially vehement. But conservatives like Carter Glass were also critical. These men correctly sensed that things were going wrong. A President such as Wilson or either of the Roosevelts (the case of Theodore is perhaps less certain than that of Franklin) who was surrounded in his Cabinet by such men would have been sensitive to this criticism. As a leader he could both have reinforced and drawn strength from the contemporary criticism. Thus he might have been able to arrest the destructive madness as it became recognizable. The American government works far better—perhaps it only works—when the Executive, the business power, and the press are in some degree at odds. Only then can we be sure that abuse or neglect, either private or public, will be given the notoriety that is needed.

Perhaps it is too much to hope that by effective and timely criticism and action the Great Depression might have been avoided. A lot was required in those days to make the United States in any degree depression-proof. But perhaps by preventive action the ensuing depression might have been made less severe. And certainly in the ensuing years the travail of bankers and businessmen before congressional committees, in the courts, and before the bar of public opinion would have been less severe. Here is the paradox. In the full perspective of history, American businessmen never had enemies as damaging as the men who grouped themselves around Calvin Coolidge and supported and applauded him in what William Allen White called "that masterly inactivity for which he was so splendidly equipped."

■ ■ ■ ■ ■ ■ ■

The Big Picture of the Great Depression

John A. Garraty

The Great Depression of the 1930s was such a cataclysmic event and it produced such extraordinary changes in the political, economic, and social structure of the United States that it is understandable that American historians have tended to emphasize its uniqueness. The country has experienced other "panics" and periods of "bad times," but none, before or for that matter since, compare with it in severity or in length. To cite a single statistic, during the entire decade the unemployment rate never fell below 10 percent.

But the Great Depression was not unique to the United States. It ravaged the industrial nations of Europe and every region of the world where coal or copper or other mineral was mined or where wheat or cotton or tea or coffee or any other agricultural product was produced for export. Furthermore, the reactions of governments everywhere were quite similar. The many New Deal reform programs were "new" in the sense that they had not been tried before in America, but as I have tried to show in this article, which is based on my more detailed work, The Great Depression, the same kinds of policies were being applied all over the world.

■ ■ ■ ■ ■ ■ ■

Back in 1955 John Kenneth Galbraith called the Great Depression of the 1930s "the most momentous economic occurrence in the history of the United States," and thirty-odd years later that judgment, recorded in Galbraith's best seller, *The Great Crash,* still holds. Since then there have been more recessions, some quite severe, but nothing like what happened in the thirties. As dozens of economists and historians have shown, we now know, in theory, how to deal with violent cyclical downturns. We have learned what we should do to manipulate what Lester V. Chandler of Atlanta University has called "the determinants that influence the behavior of employment, output, and prices."

Yet fears of another terrible collapse persist, even among the experts. And the higher the stock market soars, the greater the underlying fear. In *The Great Crash* Galbraith spoke of "fissures" that "might open at . . . unexpected places," and Chandler warned of some sort of "political deadlock" that might prevent the government from doing the things that would revive a faltering economy.

These fears are not without foundation. The American economy is complex and influenced by forces beyond the control of economists or politicians. More and more, economists are becoming aware of what historians have always known: that they can do a good job of explaining why the economy is the way it is and how it got to be that way, but that knowing exactly what to do to make it behave in any particular way in the future is another matter entirely.

The Great Depression of the 1930s was a worldwide phenomenon, great not only in the sense of "severe," but also in the sense of "scope." While there were differences in its impact and in the way it was dealt with from one country to another, the course of events nearly everywhere ran something like this: By 1925 most countries had recovered from the economic disruptions caused by the Great War of 1914–18. There followed a few years of rapid growth, but in 1929 and 1930 the prosperity ended. Then came a precipitous plunge that lasted until early 1933. This dark period was followed by a gradual, if spotty, recovery. The revival, however, was aborted by the steep recession of 1937–38. It took a still more cataclysmic event, the outbreak of World War II, to end the Great Depression. All this is well known.

The effects of the Great Depression on the economy of the United States, and the attitudes of Americans toward both the Depression and the politics of their government, did not differ in fundamental ways from the situation elsewhere. This, too, scarcely needs saying.

However, there has been a tendency among historians of the Depression, except when dealing with specific international events, such as the London Economic Conference, and with foreign relations generally, to concentrate their attentions on developments in a single country or region. The result has been to make the policies of particular nations and particular interest groups seem both more unique and, for good or ill, more effective than they were.

The Depression was not limited to the United States. This photograph of a soup kitchen was taken in the mid-1930s in Vienna, Austria.

It is true, to begin with, that neither President Calvin Coolidge nor President Herbert Hoover anticipated the Depression. In campaigning for the Presidency in 1928, Hoover stressed the good times, which, he assured the voters, would continue if he was handling the reins of government. After the election, in his last annual message to Congress, Coolidge remarked that "the country can regard the present with satisfaction and anticipate the future with optimism." When the bottom fell out of the American economy some months later, statements such as these came back to haunt Hoover and his party, and many historians have chortled over his discomfiture.

However, the leaders of virtually all the industrial nations were as far off the mark in their prognostications as Hoover and Coolidge were. When the German Social Democrats rode a "wave of prosperity" to power in June 1928, Hermann Müller, the new chancellor, assured the Reichstag that the Fatherland was in a "firm and unshakable" condition.

Great Britain had been plagued by high unemployment and lagging economic growth in the late 1920s, but in July 1929 Prime Minister Ramsay MacDonald scoffed at the possibility of a slump. And as late as December 1929, the French Premier, André Tardieu, announced what he described as a "politics of prosperity." Fewer than a thousand people were out of work in France, and the Treasury was full to overflowing. The government planned to spend five billion francs over the next five years on a "national retooling" of agriculture, industry, commerce, health care, and education. Statesmen of many other nations made similar comments in 1928 and 1929.

Hoover has been subject to much criticism for the way in which he tried to put the blame for the Depression on the shoulders of others. In his memoirs he offered an elaborate explanation, complete with footnote references to the work of many economists and other experts. "The Depression was not started in the United States," he insisted. The "primary cause" was the World War. In four-fifths of what he called the "economically sensitive" nations of the world, including such remote areas as Bolivia, Bulgaria, and Australia, the downturn was noticeable long before 1929, a time when the United States was enjoying a period of great prosperity.

Hoover blamed America's post-1929 troubles on an "orgy of stock speculation" resulting from the cheap-money policies adopted by the "mediocrities" who made up the majority of the Federal Reserve Board in a futile effort to support the value of the British pound and other European currencies. Hoover called Benjamin Strong, the governor of the Federal Reserve Bank of New York, a "mental annex of Europe," because the Fed had kept American interest rates low to discourage foreign investors.

According to Hoover, he had warned of the danger, but neither the Fed nor his predecessor, Calvin Coolidge (whom he detested), had taken his advice. Coolidge's announcement at the end of his term that stocks were "cheap at current prices" was, Hoover believed, particularly unfortunate, since it undermined his efforts to check the speculative mania on Wall Street after his inauguration.

But Hoover could not use this argument to explain the decline that occurred in the United States in 1930, 1931, and 1932, when he was running the country. Instead he blamed the decline on foreign countries. European statesmen "did not have the courage to meet the real issues." Their rivalries and their heavy spending on arms and "frantic public works programs to meet unemployment" led to unbalanced budgets and inflation that "tore their systems asunder." These unsound policies led to the collapse of the German banking system in 1931, which transformed what would have been no more than a minor economic downturn into the Great Depression. "The hurricane that swept our shores," wrote Hoover, was of European origin.

These squirmings to avoid taking any responsibility for the Depression do Hoover no credit. But he was certainly not alone among statesmen of the time in doing so. Prime Minister MacDonald, a socialist, blamed capitalism for the debacle. "We are not on trial," he said in 1930, "it is the system under which we live. It has broken down, not only on this little island . . . it has broken down everywhere as it was bound to break down." The Germans argued that the Depression was political in origin. The harsh terms imposed on them by the Versailles Treaty, and especially the reparations payments that, they claimed, sapped the economic vitality of their country, had caused it. One conservative German economist blamed the World War naval blockade for his country's troubles in the 1930s. In the nineteenth century "the English merchant fleet helped build up the world economy," he said. During the war "the British navy helped to destroy it."

When in its early stages the Depression appeared to be sparing France, French leaders took full credit for this happy circumstance. "France is a garden," they explained. But when the slump became serious in 1932, they accused Great Britain of causing it by going off the gold standard and adopting other irresponsible monetary policies, and the United States of "exporting unemployment" by substituting machines for workers. "Mechanization," a French economist explained in 1932, "is an essential element in the worsening of the depression."

Commentators in most countries, including the United States, tended to see the Wall Street crash of October 1929 as the cause of the Depression, placing a rather large burden of explanation on a single, local event. But in a sense the Depression was like syphilis, which before its nature was understood was referred to in England as the French pox, as the Spanish disease in France, the Italian sickness in Spain, and so on.

When the nations began to suffer the effects of the Depression, most of the steps they took in trying to deal with it were either inadequate or counterproductive. Hoover's signing of the Hawley-Smoot protective tariff further shriveled an already shrinking international trade. The measure has been universally deplored by historians, who point with evident relish to the fact that more than a thousand economists had urged the President to veto the bill. The measure was no doubt a mistake because it caused a further shrinking of economic activity, but blaming Hoover for the result ignores the policies of other countries, to say nothing of the uselessness of much of what the leading economists of the day were suggesting about how to end the Depression. Even Great Britain, a nation particularly dependent on international trade, adopted the protective imperial preference system, worked out with the dominions at Ottawa in 1932. Many Latin American countries, desperately short of foreign exchange because of the slumping prices of the raw materials they exported, tried to make do with home manufactures and protected these fledgling industries with tariffs. In Europe, country after country passed laws aimed at reducing their imports of wheat and other foreign food products.

And while the Hawley-Smoot tariff was unfortunate, if Hoover had followed all the advice of the experts who had urged him to veto it, he would surely have been pushing the American economy from the frying pan into the fire, because most of their recommendations are now seen to have been wrongheaded. Opposition to protective tariffs, almost universal among conservative economists since the time of Adam Smith and Ricardo, was no sign of prescience, then as now. In their *Monetary History of the United States,* Milton Friedman and Anna Jacobson Schwartz characterize the financial proposals of the economists of the 1930s as "hardly distinguished by the correctness or profundity of understanding of the economic forces at work." A leading French economic historian, Alfred Sauvy, compares the typical French economist of the period to a "doctor, stuffed with theories, who has never seen a sick person." An Australian historian characterizes the policies of that country as "deeply influenced by shibboleths."

The most nearly universal example of a wrongheaded policy during the Depression was the effort that nations made to balance their annual budgets. Hoover was no exception; Albert Romasco has counted no fewer than twenty-one public statements stressing the need to balance the federal budget that the President made in a four-month period. As late as February 1933, after his defeat in the 1932 election, Hoover sent a desperate handwritten letter to President-elect Roosevelt pleading with him to announce that "there will be no tampering or inflation of the currency [and] that the budget will be unquestionably balanced even if further taxation is necessary."

But Hoover had plenty of company in urging fiscal restraint. Roosevelt was unmoved by Hoover's letter, but his feelings about budget balancing were not very different. In 1928 William Trufant Foster and Waddill Catchings published a book, *The Road to Plenty,* which attracted considerable attention. Roosevelt read it. After coming across the sentence "When business begins to look rotten, more public spending," he wrote in the margin: "Too good to be true—you can't get something for nothing." One of Roosevelt's first actions as President was to call for a tax increase. According to his biographer Frank Freidel, fiscal conservatism was a "first priority" in Roosevelt's early efforts to end the Depression.

Budget balancing was an obsession with a great majority of the political leaders of the thirties, regardless of country, party, or social philosophy. In 1930 Ramsay MacDonald's new socialist government was under pressure to undertake an expensive public works program aimed at reducing Great Britain's chronic unemployment. Instead the government raised taxes by £47 million in an effort to balance the budget. The conservative Heinrich Brüning recalled in his memoirs that when he became chancellor of Germany in 1932, he promised President Hindenburg "that as long as I had his trust, I would at any price make the government finances safe."

France had fewer financial worries in the early stages of the Depression than most nations. Its 1930 budget was designed to show a small surplus. But revenues did not live up to expectations, and a deficit resulted. The same thing happened in 1931 and again in 1932, but French leaders from every point on the political spectrum remained devoted to "sound" government finance. "I love the working class,"

Premier Pierre Laval told the National Assembly during the debate on the 1932 budget. Hoots from the left benches greeted this remark, but Laval went on: "I have seen the ravages of unemployment. . . . The government will never refuse to go as far as the resources of the country will permit [to help]. But do not ask it to commit acts that risk to compromise the balance of the budget." In 1933, when France began to feel the full effects of the Depression, Premier Joseph Paul-Boncour, who described himself as a socialist though he did not belong to the Socialist party, called for rigid economies and a tax increase. "What good is it to talk, what good to draw up plans," he said, "if one ends with a budget deficit?"

Leaders in countries large and small, in Asia, the Americas, and Europe, echoed these sentiments. A Japanese finance minister warned in 1930 that "increased government spending" would "weaken the financial soundness of the government." Prime Minister William Lyon Mackenzie King of Canada, a man who was so parsimonious that he cut new pencils into three pieces and used them until they were tiny stubs, believed that "governments should live within their means." When King's successor, R. B. Bennett, took office in 1931, he urged spending cuts and higher taxes in order to get rid of a budget deficit of more than eighty million dollars. "When it came to . . . 'unbalancing' the budget," Bennett's biographer explains, "he was as the rock of Gibraltar."

The Brazilian dictator Getúlio Vargas is reported to have had a "high respect for a balanced budget." When a journalist asked Jaime Carner, one of a succession of like-minded Spanish finance ministers in the early 1930s, to describe his priorities, Carner replied that he had three: "a balanced budget, a balanced budget, and a balanced budget." A recent historian of Czechoslovakia reports that the statesmen of the Depression era in that country displayed an "irrational fear of the inflationary nature of a budget deficit."

These examples could be extended almost without limit. The point is not that Hoover was correct in his views of proper government finance; obviously he was not. But describing his position without considering its context distorts its significance. Furthermore, the intentions of the politicians rarely corresponded to what actually happened. Deficits were the rule through the Depression years because government revenues continually fell below expectations and unavoidable expenditures rose. Even if most budgets had been in balance, the additional sums extracted from the public probably would not have had a decisive effect on any country's economy. Government spending did not have the impact on economic activity that has been the case since World War II. The historian Mark Leff has recently reminded us, for example, that the payroll tax enacted to finance the new American Social Security system in 1935 "yielded as much each month as the notorious income tax provisions of Roosevelt's 1935 Wealth Tax did in a year."

It is equally revealing to look at other aspects of the New Deal from a broad perspective. Franklin Roosevelt's Brain Trust was novel only in that so many of these advisers were academic types. Many earlier Presidents made use of informal groups of advisers—Theodore Roosevelt's Tennis Cabinet and Andrew Jackson's Kitchen Cabinet come to mind. There is no doubt that political leaders in many nations were made acutely aware of their ignorance by the Depression, and in their bafflement they found that turning to experts was both psychologically and politically beneficial. Sometimes the experts' advice actually did some good. Sweden was blessed during the interwar era with a number of articulate, first-rate economists. The Swedish government, a recent scholar writes, was "ready to listen to the advice of [these] economists," with the result that by 1935 Sweden was deliberately practicing deficit spending, and unemployment was down nearly to pre-Depression levels.

Throughout the period British prime ministers made frequent calls on the expertise of economists such as Ralph Hawtrey, A. C. Pigou, and, of course, John Maynard Keynes. In 1930 Ramsay MacDonald, who was particularly fond of using experts to do his thinking for him, appointed a committee of five top-flight economists to investigate the causes of the Depression and "indicate the conditions of recovery." (The group came up with a number of attractive suggestions, but avoided the touchy subject of how to finance them.) The next year MacDonald charged another committee with the task of suggesting "all possible reductions of national Expenditure" in a futile effort to avoid going off the gold standard. Even in France, where political leaders tended to deny that the world depression was affecting their nation's economy and where most economists still adhered to laissez-faire principles, French premiers called from time to time on experts "to search," Sauvy explains, "for the causes of the financial difficulties of the country and propose remedies."

Many specific New Deal policies were new only in America. In 1933 the United States was far behind most industrial nations in social welfare. Unemployment insurance, a major New Deal reform when enacted in 1935, was established in Great Britain in 1911 and in Germany shortly after World War I, well before the Depression struck. The creation of the New Deal Civilian Conservation Corps and the Civil Works Administration in 1933, and later of the Works Progress Administration and Public Works Administration, only made up for the absence of a national public welfare system before 1936.

The New Deal National Recovery Administration also paralleled earlier developments. The relation of its industrywide codes of "fair" business practices to the American trade-association movement of the 1920s and to such early Depression proposals as the plan advanced by Gerard Swope of General Electric in 1931 are well known. (The Swope Plan provided that in each industry "production and consumption should be coordinated . . . preferably by the joint participation and joint administration of management and employees" under the general supervision of the Federal Trade Commission, a system quite similar to NRA, as Roosevelt himself admitted.)

That capital and labor should join together to promote efficiency and harmony, and that companies making the same products should consult in order to fix prices and allocate output and thus put a stop to cutthroat competition, all under the watchful eye of the government, were central concepts of Italian fascist corporatism in the 1920s and of the less formal but more effective German system of cartels in that period. The Nazis organized German industry along similar but more thoroughly regimented lines at about the same time as the NRA system was being set up in America. Great Britain also employed this tactic in the 1930s, albeit on a smaller scale. The British government allowed coal companies to limit and allocate production and to fix prices, and it encouraged similar practices by steel and textile manufacturers. The only major industrial power that did not adopt such a policy before the passage of the National Industrial Recovery Act was France. Later, in

1935, the Chamber of Deputies passed a measure that permitted competing companies to enter into "accords" with one another "in time of crisis." The measure would have allowed them to adjust, or put in order, the relations between production and consumption, which is essentially what NRA was supposed to make possible. This *projet Marchandeau* died in the French Senate, but some industries were encouraged to cooperate for this end by special decree.

But the area in which American historians of the Depression have been most myopic is New Deal agricultural policy. The extent to which the Agricultural Adjustment Act of 1933 evolved from the McNary-Haugen scheme of the Coolidge era and the Agricultural Marketing Act of the Hoover years has been universally conceded. Beyond these roots, however, historians have not bothered to dig. The stress on the originality of the AAA program has been close to universal. Arthur Schlesinger, Jr., put it clearly and directly when he wrote in his book *Coming of the New Deal* that "probably never in American history has so much social and legal inventiveness gone into a single legislative measure."

Schlesinger and the other historians who expressed this opinion have faithfully reflected statements made by the people most closely associated with the AAA at the time of its passage. Secretary of Agriculture Henry A. Wallace said that the law was "as new in the field of social relations as the first gasoline engine was new in the field of mechanics." President Roosevelt told Congress in submitting the bill that it was a new and untried idea.

In fact, Wallace and Roosevelt were exaggerating the originality of New Deal policy. The AAA did mark a break with the past for the United States. Paying farmers not to grow crops was unprecedented. Yet this tactic merely reflected the constitutional restrictions of the American political system; Congress did not have the power to fix prices or limit production directly. The strategy of subsidizing farmers and compelling them to reduce output in order to bring supplies down to the level of current demand for their products was far from original.

As early as 1906 Brazil had supported the prices paid its coffee growers by buying up surpluses in years of bountiful harvests and holding the coffee off the market. In the 1920s France had tried to help its beet farmers and wine makers by requiring that gasoline sold in France contain a percentage of alcohol distilled from French beets and grapes. More important in its effect on the United States, Great Britain had attempted in the 1920s to bolster the flagging fortunes of rubber planters in Britain's Asiatic colonies by restricting production and placing quotas on rubber exports. This Stevenson Plan, referred to in the American press as "the British monopoly," aroused the wrath of then Secretary of Commerce Herbert Hoover. It also caused Henry Ford and Harvey Firestone, whose factories consumed huge amounts of imported rubber, to commission their mutual friend Thomas A. Edison to find a latex-producing plant that could be grown commercially in the United States. (Edison tested more than ten thousand specimens and finally settled on goldenrod. Ford then bought a large tract in Georgia to grow the stuff, although it never became profitable to do so.)

After the Great Depression began, growers of staple crops in every corner of the globe adopted schemes designed to reduce output and raise prices. In 1930 British and Dutch tea growers in the Far East made an agreement to cut back on their production of cheaper varieties of tea. British and Dutch rubber planters declared a "tapping holiday" in that same year, and in 1931 Cuba, Java, and six other countries that exported significant amounts of cane sugar agreed to limit production and accept export quotas. Brazil began burning millions of pounds of coffee in 1931, a tactic that foreshadowed the "emergency" policy of the AAA administrators who ordered the plowing under of cotton and the "murder" (so called by critics) of baby pigs in 1933.

Far from being an innovation, the AAA was actually typical—one of many programs put into effect in countries all over the world in the depths of the Depression to deal with the desperate plight of farmers. The year 1933 saw the triumph nearly everywhere of a simple supply-and-demand kind of thinking that the French called "economic Malthusianism," the belief that the only way to raise prices was to bring output down to the level of current consumption. In February 1933, Indian, Ceylonese, and East Indian tea growers agreed to limit exports and prohibit new plantings for five years. A central committee of planters assigned and administered quotas limiting the exportation of tea. Dutch, British, French, and Siamese rubber growers adopted similar regulations for their product. In April 1933 representatives of nearly all the countries of Europe met in London with representatives of the major wheat-exporting nations, of which the United States, of course, was one of the largest. The gathering produced an International Wheat Agreement designed to cut production in hopes of causing the price of wheat to rise to a point where it would be profitable for farmers, yet still "reasonable" for consumers.

In addition to these international agreements, dozens of countries acted unilaterally in 1933 with the same goals in mind. Argentina adopted exchange controls, put a cap on imports, and regulated domestic production of wheat and cattle. The government purchased most of the 1933 wheat crop at a fixed price, then dumped the wheat abroad for whatever it could get. A Danish law of 1933 provided for government purchase and destruction of large numbers of low-quality cattle, the cost to be recovered through a slaughterhouse tax on all cattle butchered in Denmark. Declining demand caused by British restrictions on importation of Danish bacon led the Danish government to issue a specified number of "pig cards" to producers. Pigs sent to market with such cards brought one price, those without cards a lower one. The Dutch enacted similar restrictions on production of pork, beef, and dairy products.

Switzerland reduced milk production and limited the importation of feed grains in 1933, and Great Britain set up marketing boards that guaranteed dairymen a minimum price for milk. Sweden subsidized homegrown wheat and rye, and paid a bounty to exporters of butter. In 1933 France strengthened the regulations protecting growers of grapes and established a minimum price for domestic wheat. After Hitler came to power, the production, distribution, and sale of all foodstuffs was regulated. Every link from farmer to consumer was controlled.

Looking at the situation more broadly, the growers of staple crops for export were trying to push up prices by reducing supplies, ignoring the fact that higher prices were likely to reduce the demand still further. At the same time, the agricultural policies of the European industrial nations were making a bad situation worse. By reducing imports (and in some cases increasing domestic output) they were injuring the major food-producing countries and simultaneously adding to the costs of their own consumers.

It was, the British historian Sidney Pollard has written, "a world of rising tariffs, international commodity schemes, bilateral trade agreements and managed currencies." The United States was as much a part of Pollard's world as any other country.

One further example of the need to see American Depression policies in their world context is revealing. It involves the recession of 1937–38 and President Roosevelt's supposed responsibility for it. In early 1937 the American economy seemed finally to be emerging from the Depression. Unemployment remained high, but most economic indicators were improving. Industrial production had exceeded 1929 levels. A group of New Dealers who met at the home of the Federal Reserve Board chairman Marriner Eccles in October 1936 were so confident that the Depression was ending that their talk turned to how to avoid future Depressions. The general public was equally optimistic. "When Americans speak of the depression," the French novelist Jules Romains wrote after a visit to this country at that time, "they always use the past tense."

At this point Roosevelt, egged on by his conservative secretary of the treasury, Henry Morgenthau, warned the public in a radio speech that "the dangers of 1929 are again becoming possible." He ordered a steep cut in public works expenditures, and instructed the members of his cabinet to trim a total of $300 million from their departmental budgets. The President promised to balance the federal budget, and in fact brought the 1937 deficit down to a mere $358 million, as compared with a deficit of $3.6 billion in 1936. This reduction in federal spending, combined with the Federal Reserve's decision to push up interest rates and the coincidental reduction of consumer spending occasioned by the first collection of Social Security payroll taxes, brought the economic recovery to a halt and plunged the nation into a steep recession. The leading historian of the subject, K.D. Roose, called the recession a downturn "without parallel in American economic history."

Roosevelt had never been happy with deficits, and he was not much of an economist, but he was far from being alone in thinking that the time had come to apply the brakes to the economy. Economists who were far more knowledgeable than he saw the situation exactly as he did. Prices were still below 1929 levels in most countries, but they were rising rapidly. Using 1929 levels as an index, during 1937 prices jumped from 83 to 96 in Great Britain, from 80 to 93 in Italy, from 87 to 98 in Sweden, and from 80 to 86 in the United States.

These increases caused the grinding deflation of the years since 1929 to be forgotten. Fear of inflation resurfaced. The economist John Maynard Keynes had discounted the risks of inflation throughout the Depression. Inflation was a positive social good, he argued, a painless way to "disinherit" established wealth. But by January 1937 Keynes had become convinced that the British economy was beginning to overheat. He was so concerned that he published a series of articles in the *Times* of London on "How to Avoid a Slump." It might soon be necessary to "retard certain types of investment," Keynes warned. There was even a "risk of what might fairly be called inflation," he added. The next month the British government's

Committee on Economic Information issued a report suggesting a tax increase and the postponement of "road improvements, railway electrification, slum clearance," and other public works projects "which are not of an urgent character."

During this same period the Federal Reserve Board chairman Marriner Eccles, long a believer in the need to stimulate the economy, warned Roosevelt that "there is grave danger that the recovery movement will get out of hand, excessive rises in prices . . . will occur, excessive growth of profits and a boom in the stock market will arise, and the cost of living will mount rapidly. If such conditions are permitted to develop, another drastic slump will be inevitable."

It did not take much of this kind of talk to convince President Roosevelt. When Roosevelt's actions triggered the downturn, he reversed himself again, asking Congress for budget-busting increases in federal spending. The pattern elsewhere was similar. In the United States the money was spent on unemployment relief and more public works; in the major European countries the stimulus chiefly resulted from greatly increased expenditures on armaments. In 1939 World War II broke out, and the Great Depression came to a final end.

When viewed in isolation, the policies of the United States government during the periods when economic conditions were worsening seem to have been at best ineffective, at worst counterproductive. Those put into effect while conditions were getting better appear to have been at least partly responsible for the improvement. This helps to explain why the Hoover administration has looked so bad and the New Dealers, if not always good, at least less bad.

When seen in broader perspective, however, credit and blame are not so easily assigned. The heroes then appear less heroic, the villains less dastardly, the geniuses less brilliant. The Great Depression possessed some of the qualities of a hurricane; the best those in charge of the ship of state could manage was to ride it out without foundering.

Economists and politicians certainly know more about how the world economy functions than their predecessors did half a century ago. But the world economy today is far more complex and subject to many more uncontrollable forces than was then the case. A great depression like *the* Great Depression is highly unlikely. But a different great depression? Galbraith ended *The Great Crash* with this cynical pronouncement: "Now, as throughout history, financial capacity and political perspicacity are inversely correlated." That may be an overstatement. But then again, maybe not.

■ ■ ■ ■ ■ ■

FDR: The Man of the Century

Arthur Schlesinger, Jr.

That Franklin Roosevelt was the greatest American president of the twentieth century is generally accepted by Democrats and Republicans alike. Both the achievements of his New Deal in battling the Great Depression of the 1930s and his wartime leadership of the coalition that defeated Germany and Japan in World War II entitle him to that honor.

In this essay Arthur Schlesinger, Jr. concentrates on the latter aspect of Roosevelt's life. He traces his developing interests and experiences in foriegn matters before and during the first world war. But he concentrates on his role during World War II. Schlesinger has written extensively on Roosevelt and his times. He admires Roosevelt greatly but he recognizes that many of his wartime actions remain controversial. He still judges him to be the "man of the century."

■ ■ ■ ■ ■ ■ ■

After half a century it is hard to approach Franklin D. Roosevelt except through a minefield of clichés. Theories of FDR, running the gamut from artlessness to mystification, have long paraded before our eyes. There is his famous response to the newspaperman who asked him for his philosophy: "Philosophy? I am a Christian and a Democrat—that's all"; there is Robert E. Sherwood's equally famous warning about "Roosevelt's heavily forested interior"; and we weakly conclude that both things were probably true.

FDR's Presidency has commanded the attention of eminent historians at home and abroad for fifty years or more. Yet no consensus emerges, especially in the field of foreign affairs. Scholars at one time or another have portrayed him at every point across a broad spectrum: as an isolationist, as an internationalist, as an appeaser, as a warmonger, as an impulsive decision maker, as an incorrigible vacillator, as the savior of capitalism, as a closet socialist, as a Machiavellian intriguer plotting to embroil his country in foreign wars, as a Machiavellian intriguer avoiding war in order to let other nations bear the brunt of the fighting. As a gullible dreamer who thought he could charm Stalin into postwar collaboration and ended by selling Eastern Europe down the river into slavery, as a tightfisted creditor sending Britain down the road toward bankruptcy, as a crafty imperialist serving the interests of American capitalist hegemony, as a high-minded prophet whose vision shaped the world's future. Will the real FDR please stand up?

Two relatively recent books illustrate the chronically unsettled state of FDR historiography—and the continuing vitality of the FDR debate. In *Wind Over Sand* (1988) Frederick W. Marks III finds a presidential record marked by ignorance, superficiality, random prejudice, erratic impulse, a man out of his depth, not waving but drowning, practicing a diplomacy as insubstantial and fleeting as wind blowing over sand. In *The Juggler* (1991), Warren F. Kimball finds a record marked by intelligent understanding of world forces, astute maneuver, and a remarkable consistency of purpose, a farsighted statesman facing dilemmas that defied quick or easy solutions. One-third of each book is given over to endnotes and bibliography, which suggests that each portrait is based on meticulous research. Yet the two historians arrive at diametrically opposite conclusions. . . .

I suppose we must accept that human beings are in the last analysis beyond analysis. In the case of FDR, no one can be really sure what was going on in that affable, welcoming, reserved, elusive, teasing, spontaneous, calculating, cold, warm, humorous, devious, mendacious, manipulative, petty, magnanimous, superficially casual, ultimately decent, highly camouflaged, finally impenetrable mind. Still, if we can't as historians try to make sense out of what he *was*, we surely must as historians try to make sense out of what he *did*. If his personality escapes us, his policies must have some sort of pattern. . . .

How did FDR conceive the historical life-interests of the United States? His conception emerged from his own long, if scattered, education in world affairs. It should not be forgotten that he arrived in the White House with an unusual amount of international experience. He was born into a cosmopolitan family. His father knew Europe well and as a young man had marched with Garibaldi. His elder half-brother had served in American legations in London and Vienna. His mother's family had been in the China trade; his mother herself had lived in Hong Kong as a little girl. As FDR reminded Henry Morganthau in 1934, "I have a background of a little over a century in Chinese affairs."

FDR himself made his first trip to Europe at the age of three and went there every summer from his ninth to his fourteenth year. As a child he learned French and German. As a lifelong stamp collector he knew the world's geography and politics. By the time he was elected President, he had made thirteen trips across the Atlantic and had spent almost three years of his life in Europe. "I started . . . with a good deal of interest in foreign affairs," he told a press conference in 1939, "because both branches of my family have been mixed up in foreign affairs for a good many generations, the affairs of Europe and the affairs of the Far East."

Now much of his knowledge was social and superficial. Nor is international experience in any case a guarantee of international wisdom or even of continuing international concern. The other American politician of the time who rivaled FDR in exposure to the great world was, oddly, Herbert Hoover. Hoover was a mining engineer in Australia at twenty-three, a capitalist in the Chinese Empire at twenty-five, and a promoter in the City of London at twenty-seven. In the years from his Stanford graduation to the Great War, he spent more time in the British Empire than he did in the United States. During and after the war he supervised relief activities in Belgium and in Eastern Europe. Keynes called him the only man to emerge from the Paris Peace Conference with an enhanced reputation.

Both Hoover and Roosevelt came of age when the United States was becoming a world power. Both saw more of the world than most of their American contemporaries. But international experience led them to opposite conclusions. What Hoover saw abroad soured him on foreigners. He took away from Paris an indignant conviction of an impassable gap between his virtuous homeland and the European snake pit. Nearly twenty years passed before he could bring himself to set foot on the despised continent. He loathed Europe and its nationalist passions and hatreds. . . . The less America had to do with so degenerate a place, the Quaker Hoover felt, the better.

The patrician Roosevelt was far more at home in the great world. Moreover, his political genealogy instilled in him the conviction that the United States must at last take its rightful place among the powers. In horse breeder's parlance, FDR was by Woodrow Wilson out of Theodore Roosevelt. These two remarkable Presidents taught FDR that the United States was irrevocably a world power and poured substance into his conception of America's historic life-interests.

FDR greatly admired TR, deserted the Democratic party to cast his first presidential vote for him, married his niece, and proudly succeeded in 1913 to the office TR had occupied 15 years earlier, Assistant Secretary of the Navy. From TR and from that eminent friend of both Roosevelts, Admiral Mahan, Young Roosevelt learned the strategic necessities of international relations. He learned how to distinguish between vital and peripheral interests. He learned why the national interest required the maintenance of balances of power in areas that, if controlled by a single power, could threaten the United States. He learned what the defense of vital interests might require in terms of ships and arms and men and production and resources. His experience in Wilson's Navy Department during the First World War consolidated these lessons.

But he also learned new things from Wilson, among them that it was not enough to send young men to die and kill because of the thrill of battle or because of war's morally redemptive qualities or even because of the need to restore the balance of power. The awful sacrifices of modern war demanded nobler objectives. The carnage on the Western Front converted FDR to Wilson's vision of a world beyond war, beyond national interest, beyond balances of power, a world not of secret diplomacy and antagonistic military alliances but of an organized common peace, founded on democracy, self-determination, and the collective restraint of aggression.

Theodore Roosevelt had taught FDR geopolitics. Woodrow Wilson now gave him a larger international purpose in which the principles of power had a strong but secondary role. FDR's two mentors detested each other. But they joined to construct the framework within which FDR, who cherished them both, approached foreign affairs for the rest of his life.

As the Democratic vice presidential candidate in 1920, he roamed the country pleading for the League of Nations. Throughout the twenties he warned against political isolationism and economic protectionism. America would commit a grievous wrong, he said, of it were "to go backwards towards an old Chinese Wall policy of isolationism." Trade wars, he said, were "symptoms of economic insanity." But such sentiments could not overcome the disillusion and disgust with which Americans in the 1920s contemplated world troubles. As President Hoover told the Italian foreign minister in 1931, the deterioration of Europe had led to such "despair . . . on the part of the ordinary American citizen [that] now he just wanted to keep out of the whole business."

Depression intensified the isolationist withdrawal. Against the national mood, the new president brought to the White House in 1933 an international outlook based, I would judge, on four principles. One was TR's commitment to the preservation of the balance of world power. Another was Wilson's vision of concerted international action to prevent or punish aggression. The third principle argued that lasting peace required the free flow of trade among nations. The fourth was that in a democracy foreign policy must rest on popular consent. In this isolationist climate of the late 1930s, this fourth principle compromised and sometimes undermined the first three.

Diplomatic historians are occasionally tempted to overrate the amount of time Presidents spend in thinking about foreign policy. In fact, from Jackson to FDR, domestic affairs have always been, with a few fleeting exceptions—perhaps Polk, McKinley, Wilson—the presidential priority. This was powerfully the case at the start for FDR. Given the collapse of the economy and the anguish of unemployment, given the absence of obvious remedy and the consequent need for social experiment, the surprise is how much time and energy FDR did devote to foreign affairs in these early years.

He gave time to foreign policy because of his acute conviction that Germany and Japan were, or were about to be, on the rampage and that unchecked aggression would ultimately threaten vital interests of the United States. He packed the State Department and embassies abroad with unregenerate Wilsonians . . . He relished meetings with foreign leaders and found himself in advance of most of them in his forebodings about Germany and Japan. He invited his ambassadors, especially his political appointees, to write directly to him, and nearly all took advantage of the invitation.

His diplomatic style had its capricious aspects. FDR understood what admirals and generals were up to, and he understood the voice of prophetic statesmanship. But he never really appreciated the professional diplomat and looked with some disdain on the career Foreign Service as made up of tea drinkers remote from the realities of American life. His approach to foreign policy, while firmly grounded in geopolitics and soaring easily into the higher idealism, always lacked something at the middle level.

At the heart of Roosevelt's style in foreign affairs was a certain incorrigible amateurism. His off-the-cuff improvisations, his airy tendency to throw out half-baked ideas, caused others to underrate his continuity of purpose and used to drive the British especially wild, as minutes scribbled on Foreign Office dispatches make abundantly clear. This amateurism had its good points. It could be a source of boldness and creativity in a field populated by cautious and conventional people. But it also encouraged superficiality and dilettantism.

The national mood, however, remained FDR's greatest problem, Any U.S. contribution to the deterrence of aggression depended on giving the government power to distinguish between aggressors and their victims. He asked Congress for this authority, first in cooperating with the League of Nations sanctions in 1933, later in connection with American neutrality statutes. Fearing that aid to one side would eventually involve the nation in war, Congress regularly turned him down. By rejecting policies that would support victims against aggressors, Congress effectively nullified the ability of the United States to throw its weight in the scales against aggressors.

Roosevelt, regarding the New Deal as more vital for the moment than foreign policy and needing the support of isolationists for his domestic program, accepted what he could not change in Congressional roll calls. But he did hope to change public opinion and began a long labor of popular education with his annual message in January 1936 and its condemnation of "autocratic institutions that beget slavery at home and aggression abroad."

It is evident that I am not persuaded by the school of historians that sees Roosevelt as embarked until 1940 on a mission of appeasement, designed to redress German grievances and lure the Nazi regime into a constructive role in a reordered Europe. The evidence provided by the private conversations as well as by public pronouncements is far too consistent and too weighty to permit the theory that Roosevelt had illusions about coexistence with Hitler. Timing and maneuver were essential, and on occasion he tacked back and forth like the small boat sailor that Gaddis Smith reminds us he was. Thus, before positioning the United States for entry into war, he wanted to make absolutely sure there was no prospect of negotiated peace. . . . But his basic course seems pretty clear: one way or another to rid the world of Hitler.

I am even less persuaded by the school that sees Roosevelt as a President who rushed the nation to war because he feared German and Japanese economic competition. America "began to go to war against the Axis in the Western Hemisphere," the revisionist William Appleman Williams tells us, because Germany was invading U.S. markets in Latin America. The Open Door Cult recognizes no geopolitical concerns in Washington about German bases in the Western Hemisphere. Oddly, the revisionists accept geopolitics as an O.K. motive for the Soviet Union but deny it to the United States. In their view American foreign policy can never be aimed at strategic security but must forever be driven by the lust of American business for foreign markets.

In the United States, of course, as any student of history knows, economic growth has been based primarily on the home market, not on foreign markets, and the preferred policy of American capitalists, even after 1920, when the United States became a creditor nation, was protection of the home market, not freedom of trade. Recall Fordney-McCumber and Smoot-Hawley. The preference of American business for high tariffs was equally true in depression. When FDR proposed his reciprocal trade agreements program in 1934, the American business community, instead of welcoming reciprocal trade as a way of penetrating foreign markets, denounced the whole idea. Senator Vandenberg even called the bill "Fascist in its philosophy, Fascist in its objectives." A grand total of two Republicans voted for reciprocal trade in the House, three in the Senate.

The "corporatism" thesis provides a more sophisticated version of the economic interpretation. No doubt we have become a society of large organizations, and no doubt an associational society generates a certain momentum toward coordination. But the idea that exporters, importers, Wall Street, Main Street, trade unionists, and farmers form a consensus on foreign policy and impose that consensus on the national government is hard to sustain.

It is particularly irrelevant to the Roosevelt period. If Roosevelt was the compliant instrument of capitalist expansion, as the corporatism thesis implies, why did the leaders of American corporate capitalism oppose him so viciously? Business leaders vied with one another in their hatred of "that man in the White House." The family of J.P. Morgan used to warn visitors against mentioning Roosevelt's name lest fury raise Morgan's blood pressure to the danger point. When Averell Harriman, one of that rare breed, a pro-New Deal businessman, appeared on Wall Street, old friends cut him dead. . . .

What was at stake, as FDR saw it, was not corporate profits or Latin American markets but the security of the United States and the future of democracy. Basking as we do in the glow of democratic triumph. We forget how desperate the democratic cause appeared a half a century ago. The Great War had apparently proved that democracy could not produce peace; the Great Depression that it could not produce prosperity. By the 1930s contempt for democracy was widespread among elites and masses alike: contempt for parliamentary methods, for government by discussion, for freedoms of expression and opposition, for bourgeois individualism, for pragmatic muddling through. Discipline, order, efficiency, and all-encompassing ideology were the talismans of the day. Communism and fascism had their acute doctrinal differences, but their structural similarities—a single leader, a single body of infallible dogma, a single mass of obedient followers—meant that each in the end had more in common with each other than with democracy, as Hitler and Stalin acknowledged in August 1939.

The choice in the 1930s seemed bleak: either political democracy with economic chaos or economic planning with political tyranny. Roosevelt's distinctive contribution was to reject this either/or choice. The point of the New Deal was to chart and vindicate a middle way between laissez-faire and totalitarianism. When the biographer Emil Ludwig asked FDR to define his "political motive," Roosevelt replied, "My desire to obviate revolution . . . I work in a contrary sense to Rome and Moscow."

Accepting re-nomination in 1936, FDR spoke of people under economic stress in other lands who had sold their heritage of freedom for the illusion of a living. "Only our success," he continued, "can stir their ancient hope. They begin to know that here in America we are waging a great and successful war. It is not alone a war against want and destitution and economic demoralization. It is more than that: it is a war to save a great and precious form of government for ourselves and for the world."

Many people around the world thought it a futile fight. Let us not underestimate the readiness of Europeans, including leading politicians and intellectuals, to come to terms with a Hitler-dominated Europe. Even some Americans thought the downfall of democracy inevitable. As Nazi divisions stormed that spring across Scandinavia, the Low Countries, and France, the fainthearted saw totalitarianism, in the title of a poisonous little book published in the summer by Anne Morrow Lindbergh, a book that by December 1940 had rushed through seven American printings, as "the wave of the future." While her husband, the famous aviator, predicted Nazi victory and opposed American aid to Britain, the gentle Mrs. Lindbergh lamented "the beautiful things . . . lost in the dying of an age," saw totalitarianism as democracy's predestined successor, a "new, and perhaps even ultimately good, conception of humanity trying to come to birth," discounted the evils of Hitlerism and Stalinism as merely "scum on the wave of the future," and concluded that "the wave of the future is coming and there is no fighting it." For a while Mrs. Lindbergh seemed to be right. Fifty years ago there were only two democracies left on the planet.

Roosevelt, however, believed in fighting the wave of the future. He still labored under domestic constraints. The American people were predominantly against Hitler. But they were also, and for a while more strongly, against war. I believe that FDR himself, unlike the hawks of 1941—Stimson, Morganthau, Hopkins, Ickes, Knox—was in no hurry to enter the European conflict, He remembered what Wilson had told him when he himself had been a young hawk a quarter-century before: that a President could commit no greater mistake than to take a divided country into war. He also no doubt wanted to minimize American casualties and to avoid breaking political promises. But probably by the autumn of 1941 FDR had finally come to believe that American participation was necessary if Hitler was to be beaten. An increasing number of Americans were reaching the same conclusion. Pearl Harbor in any case united the country, and Hitler then solved another of FDR's problems by declaring war on the United States.

We accepted war in 1941, as we had done in 1917, in part because, as Theodore Roosevelt had written in 1910, if Britain ever failed to preserve the European balance of power, "the United Stated would be obliged to get in . . . in order to restore the balance." But restoration of the balance of power did not seem sufficient reason in 1941, any more than it had in 1917, to send young men to kill and die. In 1941 FDR provided higher and nobler aims by resurrecting the Wilsonian vision in the Four Freedoms and the Atlantic Charter and by proceeding, while the war was on, to lay the foundations for the postwar reconstruction of the world along Wilsonian lines. . . .

The war, he believed, would lead to historic transformations around the world. "Roosevelt," Harriman recalled, "enjoyed thinking aloud on the tremendous changes he saw ahead—the end of colonial empires and the rise of newly independent nations across the sweep of Africa and Asia." FDR told Churchill, "A new period has opened in the world's history, and you will have to adjust yourself to it." He tried to persuade the British to leave India and to stop the French from returning to Indochina, and he pressed the idea of UN trusteeships as the means of dismantling empires and preparing colonies for independence.

Soviet Russia, he saw, would emerge as a major power. FDR has suffered much criticism in supposedly thinking he could charm Stalin into postwar collaboration. Perhaps FDR was so naïve after all in concentrating on Stalin. The Soviet dictator was hardly the helpless prisoner of Marxist-Leninist ideology. He saw himself not as a disciple of Marx and Lenin but as their fellow prophet. Only Stalin had the power to rewrite the Soviet approach to world affairs; after all, he had already rewritten Soviet ideology and Soviet history. FDR was surely right in seeing Stalin as the only

FDR inspects General Eisenhower's troops in Sicily in 1943.

lever capable of overturning the Leninist doctrine of irrevocable hostility between capitalism and communism. As Walter Lippmann once observed, Roosevelt was too cynical to think he could charm Stalin. "He distrusted everybody. What he thought he could do was to outwit Stalin, which is quite a different thing."

Roosevelt failed to save Eastern Europe from communism, but that could not have been achieved by diplomatic methods alone. With the Red Army in control of Eastern Europe and a war still to be won against Japan, there was not much the West could do to prevent Stalin's working his will in countries adjacent to the Soviet Union. But Roosevelt at Yalta persuaded Stalin to sign American-drafted Declarations on Liberated Europe and on Poland - declarations that laid down standards by which the world subsequently measured Stalin's behavior in Eastern Europe and found it wanting. And FDR had prepared a fallback position in case things went wrong: not only tests that, if Stalin failed to meet them, would justify a change in policy but also a great army, a network of overseas bases, plans for peacetime universal military training, and the Anglo-American monopoly of the atomic bomb.

In the longer run Roosevelt anticipated that time would bring a narrowing of differences between democratic and Communist societies. He once told Sumner Welles that marking American democracy as one hundred and Soviet Communism as zero, the American system, as it moved away from laissez-faire, might eventually reach sixty, and the Soviet system, as it moved toward democracy, might eventually reach forty. The theory of convergence provoked much derision in the Cold War years. Perhaps it looks better now.

So perhaps does his idea of making China one of the Four Policemen of the peace. Churchill, with his scorn for "the pigtails," dismissed Roosevelt's insistence on China as the "Great American Illusion." But Roosevelt was not really deluded. As he said at Tehran, he wanted China there "not because he did not realize the weakness of China at present, but he was thinking farther into the future." At Malta he told Churchill that it would take "three generations of education and training . . . before China could become a serious factor." Today, two generations later, much rests on involving China in the global web of international institutions.

As for the United States, a great concern in the war years was that the country might revert to isolationism after the war just as it had done a quarter-century before—a vivid memory for FDR's generation. Contemplating Republican gains in the midterm election, Cordell Hull told Henry Wallace that the country was "going in exactly the same steps it followed in 1918." FDR himself said privately, "Anybody who thinks that isolationism is dead in this country is crazy."

He regarded American membership in a permanent international organization, in Charles Bohlen's words, as "the only device that could keep the United States from slipping back into isolationism." And true to the Wilsonian vision, he saw such an organization even more significantly as the only device that could keep the world from slipping back into war. He proposed the Declaration of the United Nations three weeks after Pearl Harbor, and by 1944 he was grappling with the problem that had defeated Wilson: how to reconcile peace enforcement by an international organization with the American Constitution. For international peace enforcement requires armed force ready to act swiftly in the command of the organization, while the Constitution requires (or, in better days, required) the consent of Congress before American troops can be sent into combat against a sovereign state. Roosevelt probably had confidence that special agreements provided for in Article 43 of the UN Charter would strike a balance between the UN's need for prompt action and Congress's need to retain its war-making power and that the great-power veto would further protect American interests.

He moved in other ways to accustom the American people to a larger international role—and at the same time to assure American predominance in the postwar world. By the end of 1944 he had sponsored a series of international conferences designed to plan vital aspects of the future. These conferences, held mostly by American initiative and dominated mostly by American agendas, offered the postwar blueprints for international organization (Dumbarton Oaks), for world finance, trade, and development (Bretton Woods), for food and agriculture (Hot Springs), for relief and rehabilitation (Washington), for civil aviation (Chicago). In his sweeping and sometimes grandiose asides, FDR envisaged plans for regional development with environmental protection in the Middle East and elsewhere, and his Office of the Coordinator for Inter-American affairs pioneered economic and technical assistance to developing countries. Upon his death in 1945 FDR left an imaginative and comprehensive framework for American leadership in making a better world—an interesting achievement for a President who was supposed to subordinate political to military goals.

New times bring new perspectives. In the harsh light of the Cold War some of FDR's policies and expectations were condemned as naïve or absurd or otherwise misguided. The end of the cold war may cast those policies in a somewhat different light.

FDR's purpose, I take it, was to find ways to safeguard the historic life-interests of the Republic—national security at home and a democratic environment abroad—in a world undergoing vast and fundamental transformations. This requires policies based on a grasp of the currents of history and directed to the protection of U.S. interests and to the promotion of democracy elsewhere. From the vantage point of 1994, FDR met this challenge fairly well. . . .

The world we live in today is Franklin Roosevelt's world. Of the figures who, for good or for evil, bestrode the narrow world half a century ago, he would be the least surprised by the shape of things at the end of the century. Far more than the rest, he possessed what William James called a "sense of futurity." For all his manifold foibles, flaws, follies, and there was a sufficiency of all of those, FDR deserves supreme credit as the twentieth-century statesman who saw most deeply into the grand movements of history.

■ ■ ■ ■ ■ ■ ▪

The Case of the Chambermaid and the "Nine Old Men"

William E. Leuchtenburg

The Supreme Court case described in this article, *West Coast Hotel Company* v. *Parrish,* is rightly described by Professor Leuchtenburg as the cause of a "constitutional revolution." It marked a great turning point in history, one in which the balance in the Court shifted from an anti–New Deal position to one supportive of New Deal reforms. Yet, like so many "landmark" constitutional cases, the litigants were not in themselves important; Elsie Parrish was a chambermaid, her employer the owners of the Cascadian Hotel in Wenatchee, Washington. The issue separating the two involved only a little more than two hundred dollars.

The case, however, resulted in a most improbable political alliance, bringing together as it did radical feminists and mossback constitutional conservatives, and it produced a deep division within the Democratic party only a few months after the Democrats had won an overwhelming victory in the 1936 elections.

Paradoxically, the decision was a tremendous victory for Franklin Roosevelt, but also a cause of the most stinging defeat of his presidency.

■　■　■　■　■　■　■

When, on a spring day in 1935, Elsie Parrish walked into the office of an obscure lawyer in Wenatchee, Washington, to ask him to sue the town's leading hotel for back pay, she had no idea she was linking her fate to that of exploited women in a Brooklyn laundry a whole continent away. Still less did she think that she was setting off a series of events that would deeply affect President Franklin D. Roosevelt's plans for his second term. Least of all did she perceive that she was triggering a constitutional revolution that, even today, remains the most significant chapter in the two centuries of existence of the United States Supreme Court. All that Elsie knew was that she had been bilked.

Late in the summer of 1933, Elsie Lee, a woman of about forty who would soon be Elsie Parrish, had taken a job as a chambermaid at the Cascadian Hotel in We-natchee, entrepôt for a beautiful recreation area reaching from the Columbia valley to the Cascades, and the country's foremost apple market. "Apples made We-natchee and apples maintain it," noted the WPA guide to Washington; "it is sur-rounded by a sea of orchards, covered in spring with a pink foam of blossoms, mile upon mile, filling the valleys and covering the slopes, the air of the town is sweet with the fragrance." Here, in the land of Winesaps and Jonathans, where "in summer and fall the spicy odor of apples is everywhere," Elsie worked irregularly over the next year and a half at cleaning toilets and sweeping rugs for an hourly wage of twenty-two cents, later raised to a quarter. When she was discharged in May

1935, she asked for back pay of $216.19, the difference between what she had received and what she would have gotten if she had been paid each week the $14.50 minimum wage required for her occupation under state law. The Cascadian, which was owned by the West Coast Hotel Company, offered to settle for a total of $17.00, but she would not hear of it. Instead, she, together with her husband, Ernest, brought suit for all that was due her.

Elsie and Ernest rested their case on the provisions of a statute that had been enacted by Washington State a quarter of a century before when, catching the contagion of reform from neighboring Oregon, the state legislature had taken steps to wipe out sweatshops. The 1913 act declared it "unlawful to employ women or minors . . . under conditions of labor detrimental to their health or morals; and . . . to employ women workers in any industry . . . at wages which are not adequate for their maintenance." To safeguard the welfare of female employees, the law established a commission that was authorized to call together employers, employees, and representatives of the public who would recommend a wage standard "not detrimental to health and morals, and which shall be sufficient for the decent maintenance of women." On receiving that recommendation, the commission was to issue an order stipulating the minimum wage that must be paid. For chambermaids, the weekly minimum was set at $14.50. Twice the statute had been challenged in the courts, and on both occasions the Washington Supreme Court had validated the act. Elsie Parrish appeared to have an airtight case.

Alas, any law student in the land could have told her that her case was hopeless, for, twelve years before, the United States Supreme Court had ruled, in a widely reported decision, *Adkins* v. *Children's Hospital,* that a minimum wage act for women was unconstitutional because it violated the liberty of contract that the Court claimed was guaranteed by the Constitution. Though the opinion by Justice George Sutherland commanded only five votes and elicited vigorous dissents, it reconfirmed a notion incorporated in constitutional doctrine only a generation before: that a great corporation and its employee—even someone as powerless as a chambermaid—each has an equivalent right to bargain about wages, a fantasy that Justice Oliver Wendell Holmes dismissed as "dogma" and the renowned commentator Thomas Reed Powell of Harvard Law School called "indefensible." *Adkins,* said one commentator, "makes forever impossible all other legislation along similar lines involving the regulation of wages." In principle Elsie's case was no different from *Adkins.* Any statute that deprived a person of life, liberty, or property, without due process of law, was disallowed. Though the Washington law remained on the books, it was presumed to be null and void. Hence, it startled no one when, in November 1935, after hearing Elsie's case, the presiding judge of the Superior Court of Chelan County, explaining that *Adkins* bound every court in the nation, ruled against her.

Surprisingly, the Supreme Court of the state of Washington took a different view. On April 2, 1936, it overturned the lower court's decision, thereby finding in Elsie Parrish's favor. To get around the huge obstacle of *Adkins,* the court pointed out that the U.S. Supreme Court had never struck down a *state* minimum wage law, which was true but irrelevant. The decision gave the Parrishes a moment of euphoria, but it hardly seemed likely that this opinion would, in the light of *Adkins* and the hostility of Justices such as Sutherland, survive a test in the United States Supreme Court.

Just eight weeks later the U.S. Supreme Court settled any doubt on that matter by a decision on a case that, three thousand miles from Wenatchee, had begun to wend its way through the judicial system while Elsie Parrish was still making beds in the Cascadian Hotel. It arose out of the hope of social reformers in New York, especially women active in the Consumers' League, that the Court, despite *Adkins,* might look favorably on a minimum wage law for women and minors if it was drafted to emphasize the value of the services rendered as well as the needs of women. To that end Felix Frankfurter of Harvard Law School and Benjamin Cohen, a former law clerk of Justice Brandeis, crafted a model law. New York State adopted it in 1933, during the fourth year of a great depression that had reduced some young women, paid starvation wages, to sleeping on subways. Frankfurter warned that it was "foolish beyond words" to expect the Court to reverse itself, but he hoped that the Justices might be willing to distinguish this statute, with its added feature of "value of services," from the one struck down in *Adkins.* "Every word" of the New York law, explained a prominent woman reformer, was "written with the Supreme Court of the United States in mind."

In accordance with the provisions of the model legislation, New York State obtained an indictment against Joseph Tipaldo, manager of the Spotlight Laundry in Brooklyn, who had been brutally exploiting his nine female employees, first by paying them far below the state minimum wage and then by pretending to pay the minimum but forcing the sweatshop laundresses to kick back the difference between what the state required and what he actually intended to pay. When Joe Tipaldo went to jail to stand trial on charges of disobeying the mandatory wage order and of forgery, the hotel industry (the same business that would be involved in the *Parrish* case) rushed to his side with an offer to bankroll a test of the constitutionality of the New York law. Since hotels were working their employees twelve hours a day, seven days a week, they had a high stake in the case. In fact, the state had already begun minimum wage proceedings against them. Consequently, each hotel put money in a kitty to finance Tipaldo's petition for a writ of habeas corpus to compel the warden of Brooklyn's city prison to release the laundry manager from custody. While his case was being prepared, Tipaldo, utterly shameless, renamed his firm the Bright Light Laundry and made a big investment in expanding his business. He explained, "I expect to get it back eventually on what I save in wages."

On June 1, 1936, the United States Supreme Court appeared to justify his optimism when, in a 5–4 decision, it struck down New York's minimum wage law. In a sweeping opinion by one of the most conservative Justices, the Court said that there was no meaningful difference between the New York statute and the D.C. act that had been invalidated in *Adkins,* for both violated the liberty of contract that safeguarded equally the rights of employer and employee to bargain about wages. After quoting from *Adkins* with obvious approval, the Court declared, in language that shocked champions of social reform, "The decision and the reasoning upon which it rests clearly show that the State is without power by any form of legislation to prohibit, change or nullify contracts between employers and adult women workers as to the amount of wages to be paid." Those words all but doomed Elsie Parrish's cause, and gave Joe Tipaldo the victory of a lifetime.

That victory, however, turned out to carry a very high price. "After the court decision, business looked good for a while," Joe told a reporter three months later. "I was able to undercharge my competitors a little on what I saved in labor costs." But then business started to fall off, then fell some more. "I think this fight was the cause of my trouble," he said. "My customers wouldn't give my drivers their wash." Before the summer was over, the Bright Light Laundry had folded and Joe Tipaldo was unemployed. "I'm broke now," he confessed. "I couldn't stand the gaff."

Elsie Parrish was made of sterner stuff. She was determined to carry on her struggle, though her prospects seemed bleak indeed. Given the precedent of *Adkins,* her case had never been promising. At one point the attorney for the West Coast Hotel Company asked the Washington Supreme Court judge who had written the opinion sustaining that state's minimum wage law in *Parrish* how he could possibly have done so in view of what the U.S. Supreme Court had said in *Adkins.* The judge replied, "Well, let's let the Supreme Court say it one more time." Now, in *Tipaldo,* the Court had stated unequivocally "one more time" that minimum wage laws for women were invalid. So gloomy was the outlook that, on the advice of Ben Cohen and Felix Frankfurter, the Consumers' League did not even file a brief in *Parrish.* "We are both rather pessimistic regarding its outcome," Cohen confided. Elsie Parrish had every reason to expect the worst.

The *Tipaldo* decision, though, engendered a powerful backlash, not least from some of the members of the Supreme Court. In a strongly worded dissent, Chief Justice Charles Evans Hughes upbraided the majority for failing to acknowledge either that the New York law differed from the statute in *Adkins* or that the state has "the power to protect women from being exploited by overreaching employers. . . ." Far more biting was the separate dissent filed by Justice Harlan Fiske Stone on behalf of himself and his fellow Justices Louis Brandeis and Benjamin Cardozo. In one of the most scathing criticisms ever uttered from the bench, Stone accused the Court of indulging its "own personal economic predilections," for he found "grim irony in speaking of the freedom of contract of those who, because of their economic necessities, give their services for less than is needful to keep body and soul together." In an impassioned warning to his brethren to exercise more self-restraint, Stone asserted, "The Fourteenth Amendment has no more embedded in the Constitution our preference for some particular set of economic beliefs than it has adopted, in the name of liberty, the system of theology which we may happen to approve."

Much of the nation shared Stone's sense of indignation about *Tipaldo.* Secretary of the Interior Harold Ickes noted angrily in his diary: "The sacred right of liberty of contract again—the right of an immature child or a helpless woman to drive a bargain with a great corporation. If this decision does not outrage the moral sense of the country, then nothing will." A Republican newspaper in upstate New York declared, "The law that would jail any laundry-man for having an underfed horse should jail him for having an underfed girl employee."

Only two groups applauded the decision. One was the press in a scattering of cheap-labor towns undismayed by the fact that, following the ruling, the wages of laundresses—mostly impoverished blacks and Puerto Rican and Italian migrants—were slashed in half. The other was a small faction of advanced feminists centered in Alice Paul's National Woman's Party. "It is hair-raising to consider how very close women in America came to being ruled inferior citizens," one of them wrote Justice Sutherland. Their argument was that there should be no special privileges for women—that putting them in a protected category was discriminatory and demeaning. Most women activists, though, were horrified by that view, which they believed reflected the dogmatism of upper-class ladies who had no familiarity with the suffering of workers. They were as devoted as Alice Paul to equal rights, and they must have shuddered at the paternalism implicit in earlier opinions sustaining separate treatment for women on the grounds that they were wards of the state. But they were sure that female employees required protection, and they knew that insistence on the principle of equal rights meant no minimum wage law whatsoever, since the Court, as constituted in FDR's first term, would never sanction social legislation for men. "Thus," the historian Mary Beard wrote Justice Stone, Alice Paul "plays into the hands of the rawest capitalists."

Stone, himself, had no doubt of the implications of *Tipaldo.* "We finished the term of Court yesterday," he wrote his sister, "I think in many ways one of the most disastrous in its history. . . . Our latest exploit was a holding by a divided vote that there was no power in a state to regulate minimum wages for women. Since the Court last week said this could not be done by the national government, as the matter was local, and now it is said that it cannot be done by local governments even though it is local, we seem to have tied Uncle Sam up in a hard knot."

Tipaldo, handed down on the final day of the term, climaxed an extraordinary thirteen months in which the Court struck down more important socioeconomic legislation than at any time in history. During that brief period it destroyed the two foundation stones of Roosevelt's recovery program, the National Industrial Recovery Act and the Agricultural Adjustment Act; turned thumbs down on a number of other New Deal laws and state reforms; and cavalierly rebuked the President and his appointees. The NIRA ruling had been unanimous, but almost all the others had come in split decisions, most often with the "Four Horsemen," Pierce Butler, James McReynolds, George Sutherland, and Willis Van Devanter, a quartet of adamantly conservative judges, joined in the spring of 1935 by the youngest member of the bench, Owen Roberts. At the end of the term, a nationally syndicated columnist wrote, "After slaughtering practically every New Deal measure that has been dragged before it, the Supreme Court now begins its summer breathing spell, ending a winter's performance which leaves the stage, as in the last act of a Shakespearean tragedy, strewn with the gory dead."

Despite the enormous setbacks the New Deal had sustained, Franklin Roosevelt gave every indication that he was accepting his losses virtually without complaint. Having been drubbed in the press for stating after the NIRA was struck down that the Court was returning the nation to a "horse and buggy" conception of interstate commerce, he had said nothing for the next year. *Tipaldo* moved him to break his silence to observe that the Court had created a "no-man's-land" where no government could function. But that was all he would say. While Elsie Parrish's feeble case was advancing toward its final reckoning in the United States Supreme Court, the

Justice George Sutherland, one of the conservative group known as the Four Horsemen.

President gave not the slightest indication that he had any plans whatsoever to make the Justices any less refractory, for it seemed to him altogether inadvisable in the 1936 presidential campaign to hand his opponents, who were hard put to find an issue, an opportunity to stand by the Constitution. As late as the end of January 1937, after FDR had delivered his State of the Union message and his Inaugural address, the editor of *United States Law Week* wrote that "last week it was made plain that he does not at the present time have in mind any legislation directed at the Court."

Less than two weeks later, on February 5, 1937, the President stunned the country by sending a special message to Congress that constituted the boldest attempt a Chief Executive has ever initiated to remold the judiciary. He recommended that when a federal judge who had served at least ten years waited more than six months after his seventieth birthday to resign or retire, the President could add a new judge to the bench. Since this was the most aged Court in history—they were referred to as the "nine old men"—Roosevelt would be able to add as many as six new Supreme Court Justices. He claimed he was presenting this proposal as a way of expediting litigation, but it was widely understood that what he really wanted was a more amenable tribunal. From the very first day, his program was saddled with a designation it could never shake off: the "Court-packing plan."

Though FDR's scheme provoked fierce protests, political analysts anticipated that it would be adopted. By winning in a landslide in 1936, Roosevelt had carried so many members of his party into Congress that the Republicans were left with only sixteen of the ninety-six seats in the Senate and fewer than one hundred of the more than four hundred seats in the House. So long as the Court continued to strike down New Deal reforms—and such vital legislation as the Social Security Act was still to be decided on—it was highly unlikely that enough Democrats would desert their immensely popular President to defeat the measure. The very first evidence of the attitude of the Court would come with its decision on Elsie Parrish's case, and there was every expectation that, acting not many months after *Tipaldo,* the Court would render an adverse ruling that would improve Roosevelt's already excellent chances. On the very day the *Parrish* decision was to be handed down, March 29, 1937, the president of the National Women's Republican Club declared, "I don't see how the President's bill can fail to get a majority."

March 29 came during the Easter holidays, always a gala season in Washington, D.C., and on that bright Monday morning in early spring, a host of camera-toting tourists and children carrying Easter baskets crowded the steps of the recently opened Supreme Court building and queued up in record numbers to enter the marble palace. The unusually protracted time of 103 days had elapsed since Elsie Parrish's case had been argued, and it was to be the first judgment handed down since FDR had suggested packing the Court. Some twelve thousand visitors flocked to the building in anticipation that this would be journey's end for the suit that had begun nearly two years earlier. An hour before the session was to start, at noon, four thousand visitors had already been admitted to the building, where many lined up two abreast from the courtroom doorway almost to the suite of Justice Stone in the idle hope of getting a peek at the proceedings. "There isn't room for them," said a police guard, "if they stood here all day long."

For some minutes it appeared that the spectators who were fortunate to get into the courtroom were also to be frustrated, for the proceedings began with a recital of an opinion on another case by one of the Four Horsemen that left the audience nearly numb with boredom. But when he finished, the Chief Justice leaned forward in his chair, picked up some sheets of paper, and announced, "This case presents the question of the constitutional validity of the minimum wage law of the State of Washington." This was to be Elsie Parrish's day after all, and the spectators stirred in anticipation. Hughes, fully aware of the effect he was having and surely conscious of his magnificent appearance (with his patrician features, sparkling eyes, and well-groomed beard, he was often likened to Jove), raised his voice to overcome the bustle, then paused and peered out over the crowded chamber for a moment before returning to his written opinion.

Not for some time did Hughes indicate what the Court had decided. Anxious minutes passed as he labored through a reprise of the facts in the case, and when he finally took up one of the arguments of Elsie Parrish's attorneys, he did so only to reject it disdainfully. It was "obviously futile," he said, for counsel to claim that the present case could be distinguished from *Adkins* on the grounds that Mrs. Parrish had worked for a "hotel and that the business of an innkeeper was affected with a public interest." As it happened, he noted, one of the cases *Adkins* had disposed of had dealt with a hotel employee. If the Washington State law was to survive the day, it would need a better justification than this rickety effort.

It took only a moment more for Hughes to reveal that the Court was prepared to meet *Adkins* head on. Unlike *Tipaldo,* where the U.S. Supreme Court had felt bound by the ruling of the Court of Appeals of New York that the New York minimum wage act could not be distinguished from the statute in *Adkins* and hence was invalid, *Parrish,* the Chief Justice declared, presented a quite different situation, for the highest tribunal of the state of Washington had refused to be guided by *Adkins* and had sanctioned the law in dispute. "We are of the opinion that this ruling of the state court demands on our part a reëxamination of the *Adkins* case," he continued. "The importance of the question, in which many States having similar laws are concerned, the close division by which the decision in the *Adkins* case was reached, and the economic conditions which have supervened, and in the light of which the reasonableness of the exercise of the protective power of the State must be considered, make it not only appropriate, but we think imperative, that in deciding the present case the subject should receive fresh consideration." To do so properly, he observed, required careful examination of the doctrine of freedom of contract that had bulked so large in *Adkins*.

"What is this freedom?" Hughes inquired, his voice rising. "The Constitution does not speak of freedom of contract." Instead, the Constitution spoke of liberty and forbade denial of liberty without due process of law. The Constitution did not recognize absolute liberty, however. "The liberty safeguarded is liberty in a social organization," he declared. "Liberty under the Constitution is thus necessarily subject to the restraints of due process, and regulation which is reasonable in relation to its subject and is adopted in the interests of the community is due process." As the Chief Justice spoke, members of the bar in the choice seats near the bench followed his every word as though transfixed, and Hughes's delivery of the opinion in "a clear, resonant voice," noted one correspondent, "electrified and held spellbound the spectators who crowded every corner of the majestic Supreme Court chamber."

The Court had long since established that the State had especial authority to circumscribe the freedom of contract of women, the Chief Justice continued. In *Muller* v. *Oregon* (1908), he pointed out, the Court had fully elaborated the reasons for accepting a special sphere of State regulation of female labor. In that landmark case the Court had emphasized, in the words of Justice David Brewer, that because a woman performs "maternal functions" her health "becomes an object of public interest and care in order to preserve the strength and vigor of the race." Hence, Brewer had gone on, a woman was "properly placed in a class by herself, and legislation designed for her protection may be sustained even when like legislation is not necessary for men and could not be sustained." The State could restrict her freedom of contract, the Court had determined, not merely "for her benefit, but also largely for the benefit of all."

The precedents established by *Muller* and several later rulings had led the dissenters in *Adkins* to believe that the D.C. minimum wage law should have been sustained, and with good reason, Hughes asserted. The dissenting Justices had challenged the distinction the majority in *Adkins* had drawn between maximum hours legislation (valid) and minimum wage statutes (invalid), and that challenge remained "without any satisfactory answer." The Washington State law was essentially the same as the D.C. act that had been struck down in *Adkins,* he acknowledged, "but we are unable to conclude that in its minimum wage requirement the State has passed beyond the boundary of its broad protective power." In that sentence, however convoluted, Hughes had said what for some minutes past it had been clear he was going to say: the Supreme Court was sustaining Washington's minimum wage law. Against all odds, Elsie Parrish had won.

Lest anyone miss the implication of the Court's reasoning, the Chief Justice spelled it out: "The *Adkins* case was a departure from the true application of the principles governing the regulation by the State of the relation of employer and employed." In short, *Adkins,* written by Sutherland and carrying the votes of a number of Hughes's other brethren, was being put to death in its fifteenth year. One could not possibly reconcile *Adkins,* Hughes maintained, with "well-considered" rulings such as *Muller.* "What can be closer to the public interest than the health of women and their protection from unscrupulous and overreaching employers?" he asked. "And if the protection of women is a legitimate end of the exercise of state power, how can it be said that the requirement of the payment of a minimum wage fairly fixed in order to meet the very necessities of existence is not an admissible means to that end?"

With an eloquence, even passion, few thought him capable of, the Chief Justice added: "The legislature of the State was clearly entitled to consider the situation of women in employment, the fact that they are in the class receiving the least pay, that their bargaining power is relatively weak, and that they are the ready victims of those who would take advantage of their necessitous circumstances. The legislature was entitled to adopt measures to reduce the evils of the 'sweating system,' the exploiting of workers at wages so low as to be insufficient to meet the bare cost of living, thus making their very helplessness the occasion of a most injurious competition."

Since many states had adopted laws of this nature to remedy the evil of sweatshop competition, the enactment of such legislation by the state of Washington could not be viewed as "arbitrary or capricious, and that is all we have to decide," Hughes said. "Even if the wisdom of the policy be regarded as debatable and its effects uncertain, still the legislature is entitled to its judgment." Delighted at what they were hearing, the New Deal lawyers in the chamber smiled broadly and nudged one another.

In his closing remarks the Chief Justice advanced an "additional and compelling" reason for sustaining the statute. The exploitation of "relatively defenceless" employees not only injured those women, he asserted, but directly burdened the community, because "what these workers lose in wages the taxpayers are called upon to pay." With respect to that reality, he said, the Court took "judicial notice of the unparalleled demands" the Great Depression had made upon localities. (That comment revealed how far he was reaching out, for the state of Washington had submitted no factual brief about any added responsibilities, and the statute in question had been enacted long before the Wall Street crash.) Hughes did not doubt that the state of Washington had undergone these tribulations, even if it had not troubled to say so, and that deduction led him to state, again with unexpected acerbity: "The community is not bound to provide what is in effect a subsidy for unconscionable employers. The community may direct its law-making power to correct the abuse which springs from their selfish disregard of the public interest." Consequently, the Chief Justice concluded, "The case of *Adkins* v. *Children's Hospital*

. . . should be, and it is, overruled," and the judgment of the Supreme Court of the state of Washington on behalf of Elsie Parrish "is affirmed." Some two years after she changed sheets in the Cascadian Hotel for the last time, the Wenatchee chambermaid was to receive her $216.19 in back pay.

It would require some time for Court watchers to grasp the full implications of Hughes's opinion in *Parrish*—to write of the "Constitutional Revolution of 1937"— but George Sutherland's dissent revealed that the Four Horsemen understood at that very moment that their long reign, going all the way back to *Adkins* and even before, with only slight interruption, had abruptly ended. When, having spoken the final words, the Chief Justice nodded to Justice Sutherland seated to his left, Sutherland surveyed the chamber silently, almost diffidently, before picking up the sheaf of papers in front of him and beginning to read. Sensing his day had passed, Sutherland appeared barely able to bring himself to carry out his futile assignment. He started off speaking in a curiously toneless murmur, and even those nearby had trouble at first catching his words. In the rear of the room, all was lost.

Consequently, not a few missed altogether Sutherland's first sentence, and even those who did hear it needed a moment to take in its full import. "Mr. Justice Van Devanter, Mr. Justice McReynolds, Mr. Justice Butler and I think the judgment of the court below should be reversed," Sutherland began. A commonplace utterance, yet it signaled a historic shift in the disposition of the Supreme Court. Once again, the Justices had divided 5–4, but this time Owen Roberts had abandoned the Conservative Four to compose a new majority that, on this day, and in the days and months and years to come, would legitimate the kind of social legislation that in FDR's first term had been declared beyond the bounds of governmental authority. The loss of Roberts did not go down easily. In the course of the afternoon, noted one captious commentary, "the Four Horsemen of Reaction whom he had deserted looked glum and sour."

After no more than a cursory paragraph saying that all the contentions that had just been advanced in *Parrish* had been adequately disposed of in *Adkins* and *Tipaldo,* Sutherland delivered a dissent that for quite some time constituted less a reply to Hughes and the majority in *Parrish* than to Justice Stone's 1936 calls for judicial restraint in cases such as *Tipaldo*. Undeniably, a Justice was obliged to consider the contrary views of his associates, Sutherland acknowledged, "but in the end, the question which he must answer is not whether such views seem sound to those who entertain them, but whether they convince him that the statute is constitutional or engender in his mind a rational doubt upon that issue." He added: "The oath which he takes as a judge is not a composite oath, but an individual one. And in passing upon the validity of a statute, he discharges a duty imposed upon *him,* which cannot be consummated justly by an automatic acceptance of the views of others which have neither convinced, nor created a reasonable doubt in, his mind. If upon a question so important he thus surrender his deliberate judgment, he stands forsworn. He cannot subordinate his convictions to that extent and keep faith with his oath or retain his judicial and moral independence."

Though Sutherland had been directing most of his barbs at Stone (Hughes's opinion had been all but forgotten), these last words may well have had a different target. His remarks, one writer conjectured, must have been intended as a rebuke

Justice Owen Roberts. His vote shifted the balance of the Supreme Court.

to Owen Roberts. Perhaps so, for the minority opinion did appear to be irritating Roberts, who, after looking toward Sutherland several times, raised a handkerchief to his mouth.

Sutherland, for his part, had hit full stride. After sipping some water, he seemed to gain strength, and his voice resounded throughout the chamber. Indeed, the Washington *Post* characterized the reading by the "usually mild-mannered Sutherland" as nothing less than "impassioned." The elderly judge, described in another account as "pale, grimlipped," even went so far as to rap his knuckles on the dais as he took issue with the President, though never by name; with Justice Roberts, no longer his ally; and even more vigorously, again without mentioning him directly, with Justice Stone. In rebuttal to the Chief Justice's assertion that the case before the Court required a fresh examination, in part because of the "economic conditions which have supervened," Sutherland stated bluntly, "The meaning of the Constitution does not change with the ebb and flow of economic events."

When, having read nearly five pages of his opinion, Sutherland finally turned to the case before the Court, he said little more than that *West Coast Hotel Co.* replicated the situation in *Adkins.* In every important regard, the two statutes involved had identical "vices," Sutherland maintained, "and if the *Adkins* case was properly decided, as we who join in this opinion think it was, it necessarily follows that the Washington statute is invalid." It was beyond dispute, he asserted, that the due process clause embraced freedom of contract, and Sutherland remained convinced, too, that women stood on an equal plane with men and that legislation denying them the right to contract for low-paying jobs was discriminatory. "Certainly a suggestion that the bargaining ability of the average woman is not equal to that of the average man would lack substance," he declared. "The ability to make a fair bargain, as everyone knows, does not depend upon sex."

But anybody who thought that those last sentences had a hint of jocularity quite misperceived Sutherland's mood. The *Parrish* decision blew taps for the nineteenth-century world, and Sutherland, born in England in 1862 and reared on the Utah frontier, knew it. Having had his say, he understood that there was no point in going on any longer. Wearily, he concluded, "A more complete discussion may be found in the *Adkins* and *Tipaldo* cases cited *supra*." His discourse at an end, he carefully laid his opinion on the dais and, stern-visaged, settled back in his chair.

When news of the momentous decision, relayed swiftly to every part of the nation over press association wires, reached Sutherland's supporters, they shared his sense of dismay. Conservatives were outraged. If FDR wanted a political court, said a disgruntled senator, he had one now, for the decision was blatantly political, a transparent effort to kill the Court-packing bill by demonstrating that the judges would no longer misbehave. Ardent feminists were no less incensed. One of them wrote Sutherland: "May I say that the minority opinion handed down in the Washington minimum wage case is, to me, what the rainbow was to Mr. Wordsworth? . . . You did my sex the honor of regarding women as persons and citizens."

Most reformers, though, women as well as men, hailed the *Parrish* ruling as a triumph for social justice and a vindication for FDR, who had been accorded an altogether unexpected victory in the most improbable quarter. One outspoken progressive, the columnist Heywood Broun, commented: "Mr. Roosevelt has been effective not only in forcing a major switch in judicial policy, but he has even imposed something of his style upon the majority voice of the court. There are whole sections in the document written and read by Chief Justice Hughes which sound as if they might have been snatched bodily from a fireside chat."

Partisans of the President jeered at the Court for its abrupt reversal of views on the validity of minimum wage legislation. Because of the "change of a judicial mind," observed the attorney general, Homer Cummings, sardonically, "the Constitution on Monday, March 29, 1937, does not mean the same thing that is meant on Monday, June 1, 1936." The head of one of the railway brotherhoods carried that thought a step further in noting, "On Easter Sunday, state minimum wage laws were unconstitutional, but about noon on Easter Monday, these laws were constitutional." That development perturbed some longtime critics of the Court ("What kind of respect do you think one can instill in law students for the process of the Court when things like this can happen?" Felix Frankfurter asked) but gave others no little satisfaction. A former United States senator from West Virginia wrote: "Suppose you have noticed that the untouchables, the infallible, sacrosanct Supreme Court judges have been forced to put upon the record that they are just a bundle of flesh and blood, and must walk upon the ground like the rest of human beings. I got quite a 'kick' out of reading that the Supreme Court said, right out loud in meeting, that it had been wrong. Like most of the wrongs done in life, there is no compensation for the great wrongs which that old court has been doing the country; but like all democrats, I am forgiving."

The performance of the Court proved especially embarrassing for the Chief Justice. Commentators, observing that Hughes had once said of a nineteenth-century decision that the "over-ruling in such a short time by one vote, of the previous decision, shook popular respect for the Court," pointed out that "now, within a period of only ten months, the Supreme Court had reversed itself on minimum wages, again by one vote." To be sure, Hughes did not admit that the Court had shifted, and years later Roberts claimed that he had voted with the Four Horsemen in *Tipaldo* only because New York had not presented the issue in the right manner. Furthermore, we now know that in *Parrish* Roberts had not been responding to the Court-packing threat since he had cast his vote before the plan was announced. However, scholars, who have the advantage of information not generally known in 1937, find Roberts's contention that he did not switch unpersuasive.

At the time, no one doubted that the Court, and more particularly Mr. Justice Roberts, had crossed over. "Isn't everything today exciting?" wrote one of the women who led the National Consumers' League. "Just to think that silly Roberts should have the power to play politics and decide the fate of Minimum Wage legislation. But, thank God he thought it was politically expedient to be with us." In a more whimsical vein, *The New Yorker* remarked: "We are told that the Supreme Court's about-face was not due to outside clamor. It seems that the new building has a soundproof room, to which justices may retire to change their minds."

Yet despite all the ridicule directed at the Court, Hughes read the opinion in Elsie Parrish's case with an unmistakable note of exultation in his voice. For by being able to show that he had won Roberts to his side in *Parrish,* he had gone a long way toward defeating the Court-packing scheme. Once Roosevelt had a 5–4 majority for social legislation, there no longer appeared to be an urgent need for a drastic remedy. "Why," it was asked, "shoot the bridegroom after a shotgun wedding?" Not for nearly four months would FDR's proposal be finally rejected, and it would retain substantial backing almost to the very end, but never was it as formidable a proposition as it had been on the eve of Elsie Parrish's case. Within days after the decision was handed down, Washington insiders were regaling one another with a saucy sentence that encapsulated the new legislative situation: "A switch in time saved nine."

The Court's shift in *Parrish* proved to be the first of many. On the very day that *Parrish* was decided, "White Monday," the Court also upheld a revised farm mortgage law (the original one had been struck down on "Black Monday," in 1935) as well as other reform statutes. Two weeks later, once more by 5–4 with Roberts in the majority, it validated the Wagner Act (the National Labor Relations Act) and in the following month it turned aside challenges to the Social Security Act. Indeed, never again did the Supreme Court strike down a New Deal law, and from 1937 to the present it has not overturned a single piece of significant national or state legislation establishing minimal labor standards. Many commentators even believe that the Court has forever abandoned its power of judicial review in this field. Little wonder then that analysts speak of the "Constitutional Revolution of 1937."

Battle-scarred veterans of the minimum wage movement found themselves in a universe remade. The seventeen states with minimum wage statutes on their books now took steps to enforce them, and New York made plans to enact new legislation to replace the law struck down in *Tipaldo.* Even more consequential were the implications of *Parrish* for the national government. Late in 1936 President Roosevelt had told newspapermen of an experience on the streets of New Bedford when his campaign car was mobbed by enthusiastic well-wishers, twenty thousand of them crowded into a space intended to hold a thousand:

"There was a girl six or seven feet away who was trying to pass an envelope to me and she was just too far away to reach. One of the policemen threw her back into the crowd and I said to my driver 'Get the note from that girl.' He got it and handed it to me and the note said this . . . 'Dear Mr. President: I wish you could do something to help us girls. You are the only recourse we have got left. We have been working in a sewing factory . . . and up to a few months ago we were getting our minimum pay of $11 a week. . . . Today the 200 of us girls have been cut down to $4 and $5 and $6 a week. You are the only man that can do anything about it. Please send somebody from Washington up here to restore our minimum wages because we cannot live on $4 or $5 or $6 a week.'

"That is something that so many of us found in the Campaign, that these people think that I have the power to restore things like minimum wages and maximum hours and the elimination of child labor. . . . And, of course, I haven't any power to do it."

Now, thanks to the constitutional revolution that the Wenatchee chambermaid had detonated, Congress was able to give him that power, and when the Fair Labor Standards Act of 1938 that set minimum wages and maximum hours for both men and women was challenged in the courts, a reconstituted Supreme Court found no difficulty in validating it.

Long before then Elsie Parrish had faded into the anonymity from which she had risen, and when more than thirty-five years later Adela Rogers St. Johns, a reporter who had won renown as the "sob sister" of the Hearst press, tracked her down in Anaheim, California, Mrs. Parrish expressed surprise that anyone would pay attention to her. Surrounded by grandchildren, looking much younger than her years, "dressed in something pink and fresh-washed and ironed," she said that she had gotten little notice at the time and "none of the women running around yelling about Lib and such have paid any since." But she was quietly confident that she had accomplished something of historic significance—less for herself than for all the thousands of women scrubbing floors in hotels, toiling at laundry vats, and tending machines in factories who needed to know that, however belatedly, they could summon the law to their side.

■　■　■　■　■　■　■

6

Postwar Politics

The Vietnam Memorial wall, bearing the names of those killed in action, was controversial when first installed, but soon became one of the most visited monuments in the nation's capitol.

Eisenhower as President

Steve Neal

The reputations of statesmen, like the reputations of artists, writers, and composers, tend to fluctuate over time. However, at least where statesmen are concerned, no mere shift in taste or fashion accounts for the changes that occur. In the first place, the passage of time can actually alter the significance of past events and thus change historians' judgments about the actors who shaped these events. Then too, new facts and new documents continually come to light, frequently suggesting more convincing explanations of what people did and why they behaved as they did, thus causing historians to change their minds.

No better recent example of the ups and downs of a major figure's reputation exists than that provided by the case of President Dwight D. Eisenhower. In the following essay Steve Neal, the chief political correspondent of the *Chicago Sun Times,* traces the way historians have viewed the Eisenhower presidency. Neal explains why most historians took a dim view of "Ike" in the late 1950s and early 1960s, a time when the public admired him extravagantly, and why the historians' opinion of him has changed so much in recent years. Neal is the author of *The Eisenhowers,* a kind of history of the Eisenhower family, of *Dark Horse: A Biography of Wendell Willkie,* and other books.

■ ■ ■ ■ ■ ■ ■

Early in 1952, Gen. Dwight David Eisenhower confided to a friendly Republican politician why he was reluctant to seek the Presidency: "I think I pretty well hit my peak in history when I accepted the German surrender."

Emerging from World War II as the organizer of the Allied victory, Eisenhower was America's most celebrated hero. Both major political parties sought to nominate him for the Presidency. And when Ike decided to risk his historical reputation, he captured the 1952 Republican presidential nomination and ended twenty years of Democratic rule. Ronald Reagan was among the millions of Democrats who crossed party lines to support the Republican general. Afterward, the badly beaten Democratic candidate, Adlai E. Stevenson, asked his friend Alistair Cooke: "Who did I think I was, running against George Washington?"

Not only did Eisenhower win two terms by margins of historic proportions, but he maintained his popularity throughout his Presidency. He left office in 1961 still revered by two-thirds of his countrymen, and the American public never stopped liking Ike.

But until recently it seemed that Eisenhower had lost his gamble with history. Like Ulysses S. Grant and Zachary Taylor, Eisenhower was frequently portrayed by historians and political scholars as a mediocre Chief Executive. Soon after Ike left the White House, a poll of leading scholars ranked him among the nation's ten worst Presidents.

Since then, however, Eisenhower's historical image has been dramatically reha-bilitated. In 1982 a similar poll of prominent historians and political scholars rated him near the top of the list of Presidents. Eisenhower is gaining recognition as one of the large figures of the twentieth century, not just for his role as Supreme Allied Commander in World War II, but also for his eight years as President of the United States.

One of the reasons for Eisenhower's comeback is nostalgia for an enormously popular President after an era of assassinations, political scandals, military defeat, and economic turmoil. Another factor in the reassessment is Eisenhower's record of eight years of peace and prosperity, which is unique among twentieth-century Presidents.

Eisenhower, a man of war, conducted his foreign policy with restraint and mod-eration. During the most turbulent era of the Cold War, he ended the Korean War, blocked British and French efforts to crush Arab nationalism, opposed military in-tervention in Southeast Asia, opened a new dialogue with the Soviet Union, and alerted the nation to the dangers of the expanding military-industrial complex. He was criticized for being too passive by the Cold Warriors Henry Kissinger and Gen. Maxwell Taylor, and the same critics berated him for a missile gap that turned out to be nonexistent. In retirement, Eisenhower said his most notable presidential achievement was that "the United States never lost a soldier or a foot of ground in my administration. We kept the peace."

In domestic affairs, Eisenhower also strove to maintain a peaceful equilibrium in handling such explosive issues as McCarthyism and segregation. While critics charged that Ike was spineless in his refusal to openly fight Sen. Joseph McCarthy, the President worked behind the scenes to reduce McCarthy's influence. Despite private doubts about a Supreme Court decision that outlawed segregation, he sent the 101st Airborne into Little Rock, Arkansas, when the state's governor defied the law. He also pushed through the first federal civil rights law since Reconstruction and established the United States Commission on Civil Rights.

Although Eisenhower's memoir of his first term was entitled *Mandate for Change,* his most notable achievement in domestic policy was the continuance of New Deal reforms initiated under President Roosevelt. For nearly a generation, congressional Republicans had been pledging to dismantle FDR's social programs. But Eisenhower had other ideas. "Should any political party attempt to abolish So-cial Security, unemployment insurance, and eliminate labor laws and farm pro-grams, you would not hear of that party again in our political history," he wrote to his brother Edgar, an outspoken conservative. During the Eisenhower era the num-ber of Americans covered by Social Security doubled, and benefits were increased. The Department of Health, Education, and Welfare was established as a domestic Pentagon. Eisenhower also launched the largest public-works project in American history by building the federal highway system, which turned out to be almost as important as the transcontinental railroad. Barry Goldwater denounced the Eisen-hower administration as a "dime-store New Deal," and another conservative critic, William F. Buckley, Jr., characterized Eisenhower's record as "measured socialism." But the Republican President's acceptance of the Roosevelt legacy effectively ended debate over the New Deal and meant that the reforms would endure.

The prosperity of the Eisenhower years was no accident. He produced three balanced budgets; the gross national product grew by over 25 percent; and inflation averaged 1.4 percent. To hold the line on inflation, Eisenhower made the tough choice to accept three recessions. The AFL-CIO president George Meany, who often criticized Ike's policies, nonetheless said that the American worker had "never had it so good."

Although he continued Roosevelt's social programs, Eisenhower's concept of presidential leadership was very different from FDR's. Ike's style was managerial with an orderly staff system and a strong cabinet. FDR was an activist who encouraged chaos and creative tension among his hyperactive staff and cabinet. Most political scholars shared Roosevelt's philosophy of government and viewed Eisenhower as an ineffectual board chairman. There were jokes about the Eisenhower doll; you wound it up and it did nothing for eight years. A memorable Herblock cartoon showed Ike asking his cabinet, "What shall we refrain from doing now?"

The early Eisenhower literature consisted of affectionate memoirs by World War II associates and adoring biographies by war correspondents. But as Chief Executive, Ike suddenly found a more independent panel of observers judging him by new and different standards.

Many of Ike's critics were Democratic partisans. A large factor in his low rating among scholars and liberal commentators was the extraordinary popularity among intellectuals of his major political rival, Adlai Stevenson. Stevenson's admirers were bitter that Eisenhower had twice routed their champion. In *Anti-Intellectualism in American Life,* the historian Richard Hofstadter described Stevenson as a "politician of uncommon mind and style" and Eisenhower as "conventional in mind, relatively inarticulate."

Arthur Larson, the University of Pittsburgh law dean who became an Eisenhower speech writer, recalled: "It was one of the paradoxes of my position in those days that the people I was most at home with, intellectually and ideologically, were more often than not bitterly critical of Eisenhower, if not downright contemptuous of him." Eisenhower did not improve his image in the academic community by flippantly remarking that an intellectual was someone "who takes more words than are necessary to tell more than he knows." As for the syndicated columnists, he declared that "anyone who has time to listen to commentators or read columnists obviously doesn't have enough work to do."

Eisenhower's poor showing in the poll taken shortly after he left office in which Arthur M. Schlesinger, Jr., got seventy-five historians to rate Ike's Presidency should not have been surprising: the participants included two of Stevenson's speech writers, a leader of the 1952 "Draft Stevenson" movement, and other Democratic partisans. Malcolm Moos, a political scholar and former Eisenhower speech writer, declined to participate in the survey, which he believed was stacked against Ike.

In the poll, Eisenhower finished twenty-second out of thirty-one Presidents, which placed him just between the White House mediocrities Chester Alan Arthur and Andrew Johnson. John F. Kennedy reportedly chuckled over Ike's low score in the Schlesinger survey. Eisenhower's associates were concerned that the negative rating might have staying power. "I'm very distressed at this tendency of academics to look down their noses at the Eisenhower administration," the former White

House chief of staff Sherman Adams acknowledged years later. "It's a common sort of thing with the intelligentsia. It's just typical. Look at Mr. Roosevelt. He's a great favorite with the academics, and he's probably a great man. But he lost a lot of battles, didn't he? . . . Well, we may not have done as much, may not have been as spectacular in terms of our willingness to break with the past, but we didn't lose a lot of battles either. A lot of our most important accomplishments were negative—things we avoided. We maintained a peaceful front and adjudicated a lot of issues that seemed ominous and threatening at the time."

Had Eisenhower served just one term, it is unlikely that his historical stock would have dropped so much. Near the end of his first term, his reputation looked fairly secure. A respected journalist, Robert J. Donovan, had written an authoritative history of Eisenhower's first term, which in many ways remains the best study of a sitting President, and which showed Ike firmly in charge. The Pulitzer Prize-winning historian Merlo Pusey had written a friendly treatment of the Eisenhower administration and predicted that Ike would be remembered as a great President, while the political scholar Clinton Rossiter wrote in *The American Presidency* (1956) that Eisenhower "already stands above Polk and Cleveland, and he has a reasonable chance to move up to Jefferson and Theodore Roosevelt."

But like most second terms, Eisenhower's last four years were less productive than his first. The nation was jolted when the Soviet Union launched Sputnik in 1957, and it took months to rebuild American confidence. The recession of 1958 marked the worst economic slide since the Great Depression; more than five million workers were jobless before the recovery began. Ike's 1957 stroke, his third major illness in three years, reinforced doubts about his health and capability to govern. His chief aide, Sherman Adams, became entwined in a political scandal and was forced to resign in 1958.

Eisenhower's 1960 Paris summit with Soviet premier Nikita Khrushchev and leaders of the Western alliance was ruined when an American reconnaissance aircraft, the U-2, was shot down over Central Russia and the pilot, Francis Gary Powers, was captured. Khrushchev stormed out of the summit, withdrawing his invitation for the President's scheduled June visit to the Soviet Union. Had Eisenhower followed his instincts, the U-2 fiasco might have been avoided. A year earlier, he had suggested that the spy flights be halted, but he relented when his National Security Council advisers objected. Later he personally approved Power's flight. In suggesting that Eisenhower might not have known of the secret mission over the Soviet Union, Khrushchev provided Ike with an alibi that might have salvaged the summit. Indeed, Sen. J. William Fulbright had urged Ike to disclaim responsibility. But Eisenhower told associates that denials would have been ineffectual because of the overpowering evidence. Furthermore, Eisenhower did not want to give credibility to the charge made by his detractors that he was not in control of his own administration.

In his critical 1958 portrait, *Eisenhower: Captive Hero,* the journalist Marquis Childs suggested that Ike was in the wrong job. "If his public record had ended with his military career, it seems safe to assume that a high place would be secure for him," Childs wrote. "But Eisenhower's performance in the presidency will count much more heavily in the final summing up." Childs offered the interpretation that

Eisenhower had been a weak and ineffective President, "a prisoner of his office, a captive of his own indecisiveness," another James Buchanan.

Striking a similar theme, the Harvard political scholar Richard Neustadt depicted Eisenhower as a passive, detached Chief Executive in his 1960 study, *Presidential Power.* According to Neustadt, Eisenhower became too isolated from his staff and should have been more involved in discussing policy options. "The less he was bothered," Neustadt quoted a White House observer, "the less he knew, and the less he knew, the less confidence he felt in his own judgment. He let himself grow stale."

In a revised 1960 edition of *The American Presidency,* Rossiter concluded that Eisenhower had been a disappointment. "He will be remembered, I fear, as the unadventurous president who held on one term too long in the new age of adventure." Without directly attacking Eisenhower, Kennedy suggested in his 1960 presidential campaign that the Republican incumbent was a tired old man, whose lack of leadership had weakened America's prestige in the world. Following his election, Kennedy privately acknowledged that he was struck by Eisenhower's vitality and ruddy health.

Eisenhower's own history of his Presidency was more authoritative but less provocative than those written by his critics, and it had little immediate impact on his reputation. The first volume, *Mandate for Change,* was published in late 1963, and *Waging Peace,* the second installment, came out two years later.

The former President's refusal to disclose his unvarnished opinions of political contemporaries or admit mistakes helped set a bland tone for both volumes. In *Mandate,* Eisenhower described a secret meeting at the Pentagon with a prominent Republican senator in the winter of 1951, without revealing the other man's identity. At the meeting Ike offered to renounce all political ambitions if the senator would make a public commitment to economic and military aid to Western Europe and American participation in the North Atlantic Treaty Organization. When the senator declined, Eisenhower began thinking much more seriously about running for the Presidency.

This meeting had been a turning point in modern American history because the senator Eisenhower neglected to identify in his memoirs was Robert A. Taft, the leading conservative contender for the 1952 Republican presidential nomination. Ike's memoirs would have been much more compelling reading if he had written what he told associates—that in the wake of their meeting he considered Taft a very stupid man. Had the Ohio senator accepted Eisenhower's offer at the Pentagon, it is more than likely that he would have been nominated for the Presidency and Eisenhower would have remained a soldier.

When Johns Hopkins University Press issued the first five volumes of Ike's papers in 1970, the former President's historical image received a boost almost overnight. John Kenneth Galbraith, who had been Stevenson's adviser and had once described the Eisenhower administration as "the bland leading the bland," wrote in *The Washington Post* that Ike's private writings demonstrated that he had been an "exceedingly vigorous, articulate, and clearheaded administrator, who shows himself throughout to have been also a very conscientious and sensible man."

With the opening of Eisenhower's private correspondence and other key documents of his administration to scholars in the seventies, experts were soon focusing attention on the primary source material, and a major reassessment of the Eisenhower Presidency was inevitable. Herbert S. Parmet, one of the first historians to make extensive use of newly declassified papers, made the argument in *Eisenhower and the American Crusades* (1972) that those who rated presidential greatness had overlooked Ike's importance in restoring confidence and building a national consensus in postwar America. To many erstwhile critics, Eisenhower's restrained style of leadership looked better in retrospect during the Vietnam War. At a time when thousands of Americans were dying in a long, bloody, fruitless struggle in Southeast Asia, there were new interpretations of the Eisenhower foreign policy. Murray Kempton's "The Underestimation of Dwight D. Eisenhower," which appeared in the September 1967 issue of *Esquire,* described how Ike had rejected the advice of Cold Warriors to seek military adventure in Vietnam. "He is revealed best, if only occasionally, in the vast and dreary acreage of his memoirs of the White House years," wrote Kempton. "The Eisenhower who emerges here . . . is the President most superbly equipped for truly consequential decision we may ever have had, a mind neither rash nor hesitant, free of the slightest concern for how things might look, indifferent to any sentiment, as calm when he was demonstrating the wisdom of leaving a bad situation alone as when he was moving to meet it on those occasions when he absolutely had to."

Other influential political analysts later expanded the same theme. On the left, I. F. Stone noted that Eisenhower, because of his confidence in his own military judgment, was not intimidated into rash action by the Pentagon.

Eisenhower's most enduring and prescient speech was his 1961 farewell address warning of the potential dangers of the military-industrial complex. "In the councils of government," he declared, "we must guard against the acquisition of unwarranted influence, whether sought or unsought, by the military-industrial complex. The potential for the disastrous rise of misplaced power exists and will persist."

Eisenhower's correspondence effectively demonstrates that his farewell address was an accurate reflection of his political philosophy. In an October 1951 letter to the General Motors executive Charles E. Wilson, Eisenhower wrote: "Any person who doesn't clearly understand that national security and national solvency are mutually dependent, and that permanent maintenance of a crushing weight of military power would eventually produce dictatorship, should not be entrusted with any kind of responsibility in our country." The White House press secretary James Hagerty wrote in his diary that Ike had confided, "You know, if you're in the military and you know about these terrible destructive weapons, it tends to make you more pacifistic than you normally have been."

Stephen E. Ambrose, a former editor of the Eisenhower papers and author of the most comprehensive Eisenhower biography, shows how Ike slowed the arms race and exerted firm leadership in rejecting the Gaither Commission's call for sharp increases in defense spending. "Eisenhower's calm, common-sense, deliberate response to [the Soviets launching of Sputnik] may have been his finest gift to the nation," wrote Ambrose, "if only because he was the only man who could have given it." Because of his military background, Eisenhower spoke with more authority about the arms race than his critics. In a 1956 letter to Richard L. Simon, president of Simon & Schuster, who had written him and enclosed a column urging a

Ike (second from left) conferred with Nikolai Bulganin of the Soviet Union, Edgar Faure of France, and Anthony Eden of Great Britain in Geneva in 1955. They were trying to promote détente by pushing for open exchange of military plans and aerial inspection of military bases.

crash program for nuclear missiles, Eisenhower replied, "When we get to the point, as we one day will, that both sides know that in any outbreak of general hostilities, regardless of the element of surprise, destruction will be both reciprocal and complete, possibly we will have sense enough to meet at the conference table with the understanding that the era of armaments has ended and the human race must conform its actions to this truth or die."

But while many recent historians have portrayed Eisenhower as a dove, a pioneer of détente, there are dissenters. Peter Lyon argued in his 1974 Eisenhower biography that the President's 1953 inaugural address was a "clarion" that "called to war," and that the general was a hawkish militarist. In her 1981 study *The Declassified Eisenhower,* Blanche Wiesen Cook says that Eisenhower used the CIA to launch a "thorough and ambitious anti-Communist crusade" that toppled governments on three continents.

Arthur Schlesinger, Jr., who had previously described Eisenhower as a weak, passive, and politically naïve executive, asserted in his 1973 book *The Imperial Presidency* that Ike went overboard in his use of presidential powers by introducing claims for "executive privilege" in denying government documents to Sen. Joseph McCarthy and by also approving the buildup of the CIA. Even so, Schlesinger now ranks Eisenhower with Truman and his former White House boss, John F. Kennedy, as the successful Presidents of the postwar era.

Another Eisenhower critic, William Leuchtenburg, insists that Ike was not so different from his more obviously hawkish successors. He points to Eisenhower's covert intervention in Iran and Guatemala, his threats to use nuclear weapons in Korea, and his war of words with China over the islands of Quemoy and Ma-tsu. Leuchtenburg also blames Eisenhower for neglecting major public issues, especially in the field of civil rights, "at a considerable cost." Even so, Schlesinger and Leuchtenburg both concede that Eisenhower was much more of a hands-on executive than was realized during his administration.

The records of the Eisenhower administration have ended the myth that the old soldier left foreign policy to his influential secretary of state, John Foster Dulles. A leading Eisenhower revisionist, Fred I. Greenstein, reported in his 1982 study *The Hidden-Hand Presidency* that Ike made the decisions and Dulles carried them out. Greenstein said that it was Eisenhower's international political strategy to be the champion of peace in his public statements, while his secretary of state acted as a Cold Warrior. Dulles once claimed that he, as secretary of state, had ended the Korean War by threatening the use of atomic weapons. But the diplomatic historian Robert A. Divine wrote in *Eisenhower and the Cold War* (1981) that Dulles had exaggerated his role. "It was Eisenhower, in his own characteristically quiet and effective way, who had used the threat of American nuclear power to compel China to end its intervention in the Korean conflict. . . ."

Eisenhower's decision not to intervene militarily in Vietnam is described by some revisionists as his finest hour. Nine years later Eisenhower explained in a private memorandum that he had not wanted to tarnish the image of the United States as the world's foremost anticolonial power. "It is essential to our position of leadership in a world wherein the majority of the nations have at some time or another felt the yoke of colonialism. Thus it is that the moral position of the United States was more to be guarded than the Tonkin Delta, indeed than all of Indochina."

Largely because of his White House staff structure and the authority that he delegated to ranking subordinates, Eisenhower was often characterized as a disengaged President. His chief of staff, Sherman Adams, wielded more power than any White House adviser since FDR's Harry Hopkins, and a popular joke of the fifties had the punch line: "What if Sherman Adams died and Ike became President?" But the memoirs of Adams, Richard M. Nixon, Henry Cabot Lodge, Hagerty, Emmet John Hughes, Milton and John Eisenhower have shown a President firmly in command.

Eisenhower's uneasy relationship with Nixon has also been distorted by some revisionist scholars. While Ike and Nixon were never close, some historians have demonstrated political naïveté in accepting Eisenhower's private criticism of his Vice-President at face value. If Eisenhower held such strong reservations about Nixon as they have suggested, it is unlikely that he would have retained him on the ticket in 1956 and supported him for the Presidency in 1960 and 1968. Eisenhower did not share Nixon's zest for Republican partisanship, but he considered him a loyal and capable Vice-President. Had one of Ike's personal favorites, such as his brother Milton or Treasury Secretary Robert Anderson, emerged as a potential heir, there is evidence that Eisenhower might have supported them over Nixon. But Ike definitely preferred his Vice-President over Nelson Rockefeller and Barry Goldwater.

Nothing damaged Eisenhower's standing with intellectuals more than his vague position on McCarthyism. Eisenhower historians are sharply divided over the President's role in ending the Wisconsin senator's reign of fear. Ambrose criticizes Eisenhower's "muddled leadership" and unwillingness to publicly condemn McCarthy and his abusive tactics. But Greenstein and William Bragg Ewald have made a strong argument that Eisenhower's behind-the-scenes efforts set the stage for McCarthy's censure by the Senate and destroyed his political influence. Eisenhower loathed McCarthy but believed that a direct presidential attack on him would enhance the senator's credibility among his right-wing followers. "I just won't get into a pissing contest with that skunk," Eisenhower told his brother Milton. The President's papers indicate that he never doubted his strategy against McCarthy, and in the end he felt vindicated.

Eisenhower is also still criticized for not showing sufficient boldness in the field of civil rights. The President was not pleased with the 1954 Supreme Court decision that overturned the "separate but equal" doctrine in public education, and he privately observed that the firestorm touched off by the *Brown v. Board of Education* decision had set back racial progress fifteen years. Despite his misgivings, Eisenhower never considered defying the Court, as his successors Gerald Ford and Ronald Reagan would do, over the volatile issue of school desegregation. Eisenhower enforced the Court's decision in sending federal troops into Little Rock, and he went on to establish a civil rights division in the Justice Department in 1957 that committed the federal government to defend the rights of minorities and provided momentum to the civil rights movement.

As a national hero, Eisenhower's popular appeal transcended his political party. According to a 1955 Gallup Poll, 57 percent of the nation's voters considered Eisenhower a political independent, which may have been why Eisenhower was unable to transfer his enormous popularity to the Republican party. Between 1932 and 1968, he was the only Republican elected to the White House. Ironically the GOP-controlled Eightieth Congress may have shortened the Eisenhower era five years before it began by adopting the Twenty-second Amendment, prohibiting any future President from serving more than two terms. Without the constitutional limit, John Eisenhower said his father would have run for a third term in 1960. Even Truman acknowledged that Eisenhower would have been reelected in another landslide.

Eisenhower restored confidence in the Presidency as an institution and set the agenda for the economic growth of the next decade. He understood public opinion as well as Roosevelt had, and he had a keener sense of military problems than any President since George Washington. As the failings of his successors became apparent, Eisenhower's Presidency grew in historical stature. A 1982 Chicago *Tribune* survey of forty-nine scholars ranked him as the ninth best President in history, just behind Truman and ahead of James K. Polk.

With the renewed appreciation of Eisenhower's achievements, Ambrose predicts that Ike may eventually be ranked ahead of Truman and Theodore Roosevelt, and just behind Washington, Jefferson, Jackson, Lincoln, Wilson, and FDR. "I'd put Ike rather high," the historian Robert Ferrell says, "because when he came into office at the head of an only superficially united party . . . he had to organize that heterogeneous group, and get it to cooperate, which he did admirably with all those keen political instincts of his."

"Whatever his failings," Robert J. Donovan wrote of Eisenhower in 1984, "he was a sensible, outstanding American, determined to do what he believed was right. He was a dedicated peacemaker, a president beloved by millions of people . . . and, clearly, a good man to depend on in a crisis. Of his high rank on the list of presidents there can be little doubt."

Henry Steele Commager, who was among Eisenhower's most thoughtful critics during his Presidency, said recently that he would now rank him about tenth from the top. Though Commager faults Eisenhower for not showing leadership against McCarthyism and on behalf of civil rights, he gives Ike high marks in foreign policy for not intervening in Vietnam and "having the sense to say 'no' to the Joint Chiefs of Staff."

Commager says that Eisenhower's election was the decisive factor in ending the Korean War. "Only a general with enormous prestige could have made peace in Korea. An outsider couldn't have done it." Even Adlai Stevenson told a reporter that the election of Eisenhower in 1952 had been good for the country. (He did not, however, feel the same way about Ike's second term.)

William Appleman Williams, the dean of revisionist historians, says that Eisenhower was far more perceptive in international politics than his predecessor or those who followed him. "He clearly understood that crusading imperial police actions were extremely dangerous," Williams notes, and he was determined to avoid World War III.

In the final months of his Presidency, Eisenhower made this private assessment of his managerial style: "In war and in peace I've had no respect for the desk-pounder, and have despised the loud and slick talker. If my own ideas and practices in this matter have sprung from weakness, I do not know. But they were and are deliberate or, rather, natural to me. They are not accidental."

■ ■ ■ ■ ■ ■ ■

The Education of John F. Kennedy

Richard Reeves

When he ran for president in 1960, John F. Kennedy profected himself as more forward looking, imaginative, and flexible than his predecessor, Republican Douglas D. Eisenhower. He promised to "get the country moving again" and suggested that the kindly and elderly "Ike" had been too bureacratic and precident bound, probably because of his military background.

In this essay, the journalist and historian Richard Reeves, author of President Kennedy: Profile of Power (1993) discusses Kennedy's method of administration during his tragically brief presidency. Although an admirer of Kennedy, Reeves points out the weaknesses of his informal way of gathering information and making decisions. Reeves concludes that Eisenhower's more organized method had much to recommend itself.

■　■　■　■　■　■　■

In early October of 1963, Rep. Clement Zablocki, a Wisconsin Democrat, led a House Foreign Affairs Committee fact-finding delegation to South Vietnam. Invited to the White House when he returned, Zablocki told President John F. Kennedy he thought that removing President Ngo Dinh Diem would be a big mistake, unless the United States had a successor in the wings. Remember Cuba, Zablocki said. "Batista was bad, but Castro is worse."

It was a little late for that. By then Kennedy was just about ready to sign off on the overthrow of Diem. In Saigon, Ambassador Henry Cabot Lodge and agents of the Central Intelligence Agency were aiding and encouraging the plots of various coup-minded Vietnamese generals. In Washington, schemers in the State Department, led by Averill Harriman, had persuaded the President that the fight against North Vietnamese communism was being lost because Diem was corrupt and foolish—and was not taking orders from his American sponsors and allies.

So Kennedy told Zablocki, "I hope you'll write an objective report and not put President Diem in a favorable light."

"Well, you know what the boss wants," Pierre Salinger remarked cheerfully as Zablocki left the White House.

"The boss will get what we think is right," the congressman said. "Somebody's giving the boss some bad information."

Somebody always seemed to be giving the President bad information in those days, a situation that appears to be repeating itself thirty years later in the Presidency of William Jefferson Clinton. The power at the center of American democracy is a function of what the President knows and when he knows it. And Presidents Kennedy and Clinton came to office sharing more than youth and membership in the Democratic party. Each wanted to open up the White House to new information, breaking up or dismantling the old bureaucracies and systems that they thought isolated their predecessors—the councils and committees and boards that channeled information into the President and then implemented and followed through on his orders.

In his turn Kennedy immediately replaced the rigid and formal organization of President Dwight Eisenhower's National Security Council with small ad hoc task forces, their number rising and falling with the President's perception of crises. Ideally the task forces would be unofficial, never permanent, never functioning long enough to generate their own bureaucracies or get around the direct control of the man at the center in the Oval Office.

Short conversations and long hours substituted for Ike's inflexible organization. The best way to reach Kennedy was to hang around the office of his secretary, Evelyn Lincoln. Periodically he would come out to look at newspapers and talk to whoever was standing there, Harriman, who had served, in his own way, two presidents before Kennedy, told his assistants that a man had seven seconds to make an impression on the boss. If the President looked your way, you seized the moment or it was lost forever.

After a couple of months in office, Kennedy invited NBC into the White House for a prime-time television special and described his no-meetings, hands-on management of the building, the country, and the world. It seemed spontaneous and flexible, a new management style, though some of his own men worried that there was more style than management. He had called only two cabinet meetings, he told NBC. "They're a waste of time." He repeated the line when he was asked why there had been no National Security Council meetings during his first months in office. "These general meetings are a waste of time," he said. "Formal meetings of the NSC are not as effective, and it is much more difficult to decide matters involving high national security if there is a wider group present."

Perhaps. On April 5, 1961, the President's national security adviser, McGeorge Bundy, sent Kennedy a memo under the title "Crisis Commanders in Washington," saying, in effect, that in the most important of ongoing foreign policy crises, no one was in charge: "Over and over since January 20th we have talked of getting 'task forces with individual responsible leaders' here in Washington for crisis situations. At the beginning, we thought we had task forces for Laos, the Congo, and Cuba. We did get working groups with nobody in particular in charge, but we did not get clearly focused responsibility. The reason was that the Department of State was not quite ready . . . these Assistant Secretaries, although men of good will, were not really prepared to take charge of the 'military' and 'intelligence' aspects—the government was in the habit of 'coordination' and out of the habit of the acceptance of individual executive leadership. More than once the ball has been dropped because no one person felt a continuing clear responsibility."

Two weeks after that, the ball and a lot more were dropped—on Kennedy's head. After a series of unstructured meetings with Secretary of State Dean Rusk, Secretary of Defense Robert McNamara, CIA Director Allen Dulles, and pretty much whoever else happened to be around, the President signed off on a CIA plan for an exile invasion of Fidel Castro's Cuba; fifteen hundred Cubans were landed at Castro's favorite fishing spot, the Bay of Pigs. Of course, Kennedy did not know about Castro's leisure habits, or much of anything else about the plan, because he never questioned whether or not the CIA knew what it was doing, and no one on his staff or in his cabinet or on the Joint Chiefs of Staff had any direct responsibility for the project. Kennedy himself never even saw the paperwork; at the end of each meeting he sat silently as the papers were collected by the operation's planner, the CIA's deputy director for operations, Richard Bissell, who took the only copies of the maps and such back to his office at agency headquarters in Langley, Virginia.

After the invasion, a perfect failure, Bundy wrote the President another memo, on May 16, this time dropping any pretense that the Executive problem was in the State Department.

"I hope you'll be in a good mood when you read this . . . ," he began. "Cuba was a bad mistake. But it was not a disgrace and there were reasons for it. . . .We do have a problem of management; centrally it is a problem of your use of time. What follows represents, I think, a fair consensus of what a good many people would tell you . . . We can't get you to sit still. . . . "

"The National Security Council, for example, really cannot work for you unless you authorize work schedules that do not get upset from day to day. Calling three meetings in five days is foolish—and putting them off for six weeks at a time is just as bad.

"Truman and Eisenhower did their daily dozens in foreign affairs the first thing in the morning, and a couple of weeks ago you asked me to begin to meet you on this basis. I have succeeded in catching you on three mornings, for a total of about 8 minutes, and I conclude that this is not really how you like to begin the day. Moreover, 6 of the 8 minutes were given not to what I had for you but what you had for me."

Bundy, the former dean of Harvard College, went on like that, scolding America's most important student: "Right now it is so hard to get to you with anything not urgent and immediate that about half of the papers and reports you personally ask for are never shown to you because by the time you are available you have clearly lost interest in them. . . . Above all you are entitled to feel confident that (a) there is no part of government on the national security area that is not watched over closely by someone from your own staff, and (b) there is no major problem of policy that is not out where you can see it and give a proper stimulus to those who should be attacking it."

Within a month, on June 13, the President heard the same thing again, this time in the top-secret 180-page Bay of Pigs investigation by retired Army Chief of Staff Maxwell Taylor and Attorney General Robert Kennedy. There was a single copy of the report; to prevent leaks, it could be read only in a locked room with an observer present to be sure no notes were taken. The document concluded with a dry summary of Kennedy's management: "The executive branch of the government was not organizationally prepared to cope with this kind of paramilitary operation. . . . There was no single authority short of the President capable of coordinating the actions of the CIA, State, Defense, and USIA. Top level direction was given through ad hoc meetings of senior officials without consideration of operational plans in writing and with no arrangement for recording conclusions and decisions reached."

In receiving the Bundy and Taylor memorandums, President Kennedy had also been unpleasantly surprised at home. He found out there was a revolution in his country by reading Th*e New York Times* on May 15, 1961. That Monday morning, under the headline, BI-RACIAL BUSES ATTACKED, RIDERS BEATEN IN ALABAMA, the paper published an Associated Press story that began: "Anniston, Ala.—A group of white persons today ambushed two buses carrying Negroes and whites who were seeking to knock down bus station racial barriers. A little later, sixty miles to the west, one of the buses ran into another angry crowd of white men at a Birmingham bus station. The interracial group took a brief but bloody beating, and fled. . . . They call themselves 'Freedom Riders.'"

The organizer of the rides, James Farmer, director of the Congress of Racial Equality, and black journalists, too, had tried without success to alert the President or Attorney General Robert Kennedy before the rides set off from the Greyhound and Trailways bus terminals a few blocks from the White House. But apparently their announcements and notes were lost somewhere in the channels President deliberately broke up when he took office. Ignorance of the rides, however, was not as personally embarrassing as his first meeting with British Prime Minister Harold Macmillan to discuss Britain's "Grand Design" for Europe. The prime minister hoped to develop a compromise power-sharing scheme on European security matters that was halfway between the United States' inclination to make unilateral decisions and French President Charles de Gaulle's insistence that France, Britain, and the United States must be equal partners in decision making. Kennedy had not read Macmillan's ideas; in fact, he had lost the papers. It took several hours to find them—in the bedroom of Kennedy's two-year-old daughter, Caroline.

One of the men in the Kennedy administration with extensive Executive experience, Undersecretary of State Chester Bowles, the former governor of Connecticut and a founder of the advertising agency BBO&O said: "Management in Jack's mind, I think, consists largely of calling Bob on the telephone and saying 'Here are ten things I want to get done. Why don't you go ahead and get them done.'" That judgment was often confirmed by the President himself, expressing his admiration for his brother-manager this way: "With Bobby, I don't have to think about organization. I just show up."

Management, in general, does not greatly interest politicians, but it happened that it was an important part of the two long conversations between Eisenhower and Kennedy during the 1960–61 transition period. As the President-elect began asking questions, Eisenhower quickly realized what was on Kennedy's mind, and he didn't like it. The new man's questions were about the structure of decision making on matters of national security and national defense. The senator obviously thought the Eisenhower White House structure was too complicated, too bureaucratic, too formal, and too slow—with too many decisions outside the President's reach and control. Ike thought Kennedy naïve, but he was not about to say that, so he began a long explanation of how and why he had built up what amounted to a military staff apparatus to methodically collect and feed information to the Commander in Chief and, at the same time, had created separate operations to coordinate and implement his decision making.

"No easy matters will come to you as President. If they are easy, they will be set-tled at a lower level," Eisenhower said. And Kennedy did not much like that idea.

"I did urge him to avoid any reorganization until he himself could become well acquainted with the problem," the President dictated to his secretary after Kennedy left. But it was obvious that the President-elect was not much interested in his orga-nization charts—or organization itself, for that matter. Ike's bent toward order was exactly the kind of passive thinking Kennedy wanted to sweep away. He had no use for the process of note making, minutes taking, and little boxes on charts showing the Planning Board and the Operations Coordinating Board. He did not think of himself as being on top of a chart; rather he wanted to be in the center, the center of all the action.

Ike, dictating for his journal, worried that the new man did not understand the complexity of the job, that Kennedy thought the Presidency was a personal thing, a question of getting the right people in a few jobs here and there.

That was just about right. Kennedy did believe that problem solving meant get-ting the right man into the right place at the right time—and, if things went wrong, putting in someone else. And he saw himself as the right man. Lines of power, he said, were supposed to be like the spokes of a wheel, all coming from him, all going to him. "It was instinctive at first," he said. "I had different identities, and this was a useful way of expressing each without compromising the others."

He preferred to work one-on-one — hallway meetings and telephone calls to desk officers in the State Department or to surprised professors and reporters. Anyone who had just been to countries in crisis or had written something the President had heard about was liable to be awakened by a Boston-accented voice saying: "This is Jack Kennedy. Can you tell me . . . ?" Some of them hung up on him, thinking it was a joke.

He wanted the action to be wherever he was: follow the body. At the far end-points of American policy, his policy, there would be young men like his own staff, hard-thinking patriots in chinos and work shirts, or Army berets or even native dress, ready to turn a crowd of demonstrating students or neutralize a Communist plot.

He was determined not to be trapped by establishment procedures. His bent was toward chaos; he was comfortable with a certain disorder around him; it kept his people off-balance, made them try a little harder. In dismantling Eisenhower's military-style national security bureaucracy, beginning with the Operations Control Board, a small unit responsible for systematically channeling foreign policy infor-mation to and from the President, Kennedy said, in an Executive Order: "We plan to work by maintaining direct communication with the responsible agencies, so that everyone will know what I have decided, while I in turn keep fully informed of the actions taken to carry out decisions." His use of the National Security Council itself was casual enough that when Gen. Earle Wheeler, the chief staff officer of the Joint Chiefs of Staff, was handed National Security Action Memorandum 22—the twenty-second formal national security order approved by the President—he real-ized he had never seen numbers 5 to 21. "The lines of control have been cut," Wheeler told his staff. "But no others have been established."

That cost Kennedy. The next time he saw Eisenhower was after the Bay of Pigs, at Camp David, named for Ike's grandson. It was the first time Kennedy had ever been to the place. The meeting of the two Presidents was part of a show of national unity after the capture of almost the entire exile brigade by Castro's waiting troops. Eisenhower supported Kennedy totally in public, but in private, as they walked the wooded paths of the Maryland mountain retreat, Ike gave Kennedy a tongue-lashing, saying, "Mr. President, before you approved this plan, did you have everybody in front of you debating the thing so you got the pros and cons yourself and then made the decision, or did you see these people one at a time?"

"Well, I didn't have a meeting. . . . I just approved a plan that had been recommended by the CIA and by the Joint Chiefs of Staff. I just took their advice."

"Mr. President, were there any changes in the plan . . . ?"

"Yes, there were. . . . We did want to call off one bombing sally."

"Why was that called off? Why did they change plans after the troops were already at sea?"

"Well," Kennedy said, "we felt it necessary that we keep our hand concealed in this affair; we thought that if it was learned that we were really doing this and not these rebels themselves, the Soviets would be very apt to cause trouble in Berlin."

"Mr. President, how could you expect the world to believe that we had nothing to do with it? Where did these people get the ships to go from Central America to Cuba? Where did they get the weapons? Where did they get all the communications and all the other things that they would need? How could you possibly have kept from the world that the United States had been involved?"

"No one knows how tough this job is until after he has been in it a few months," Kennedy said kind of ruefully.

"Mr. President," Eisenhower said, "If you will forgive me, I think I mentioned that to you three months ago."

"I certainly have learned a lot since," Kennedy said.

Certainly he did learn. A lot of that was just figuring out the right questions, as he showed only a week after the Bay of Pigs in questioning Gen. Lyman Lemnitzer, the chairman of the Joint Chiefs, about recommendations to airlift U.S. troops into Laos that spring of 1961.

"How will they get in there?"

"They can land at two airports," said the general. The places were named Savanaket and Peske. "How many can land at those airports?" Kennedy continued.

"If you have perfect conditions, you can land a thousand a day."

"How many Communist troops are in the area?"

"We would guess three thousand."

"How long will it take them to bring up four?"

"They can bring up five or six thousand, eight thousand, in four more days."

"What's going to happen," snapped the President, "if on the third day you've landed three thousand—and then they bomb the airport? And then they bring up five or six thousand more men! What's going to happen? Or if you land two thousand—and then they bomb the airport?"

Some histories of the Kennedy Presidency emphasize that kind of evidence of growth in the job, focusing on American domination of the Soviets during the Cuban missile crisis of 1962 and the Limited Nuclear Test Ban Treaty negotiated in the summer of 1963. But without gainsaying those achievements, it seems clear that after two years in office Kennedy was moving the United States into combat in South Vietnam in a slow and drawn-out replay of the Bay of Pigs invasion. He still seemed unable to sort through bad information. He focused on political appearance rather than military reality and continued to think the key to the problem was finding the right man—which meant eliminating the wrong one, Castro or Diem.

"Looking under bushes for the Vietnamese George Washington" was the way Gen. Maxwell Taylor privately described the process after Kennedy appointed him to succeed Lemnitzer as chairman of the Joint Chiefs. Twice Kennedy dispatched Taylor to South Vietnam, in October of 1961 and in again in September of 1963—two of more than a dozen fact-finding missions the President sent there, searching almost desperately for good information.

Taylor was one of the very few military men Kennedy trusted. Another was a Marine general, Victor Krulak. The President and that general had known each other since 1943, when they were a Navy lieutenant (junior grade) and a Marine lieutenant colonel. Kennedy's boat, *PT 109,* had rescued Marines under Krulak's command in the South Pacific, and Krulak had promised him a bottle of Three Feathers whiskey when they got home. He delivered it to the White House eighteen years later, as an inaugural gift. President Kennedy appointed Krulak as the Joint Chiefs' director of counter-insurgency, a job created by Kennedy in his devotion to the ideas presented by Eugene Burdick and William Lederer in their best-selling and extraordinarily influential novel *The Ugly American.*

The book, by Burdick, a political science professor, and Lederer, a captain in the U.S. Navy, sold more than five million copies during the 1960 presidential campaign, more than a few of them to Sen. John F. Kennedy. . . .

Krulak traveled to South Vietnam with a State Department officer named Joseph Mendenhall, whom Undersecretary of State Averill Harriman slipped aboard the plane just before it took off from Andrews Air Force Base near Washington. "The Crocodile," as Harriman was called because of his infighting skills, wanted to protect his own political view that Diem had to be removed against the Pentagon's concentration on military matters.

Krulak and Mendenhall reported back to Kennedy on September 10, 1963. Predictably the general said: "The shooting war is still going ahead at an impressive pace. . . . There is a lot of war left to fight. Particularly in the Delta, where the Viet Cong remains strong. . . . The Viet Cong war will be won if the current U.S. military and sociological programs are pursued, irrespective of the grave defects of the ruling regime."

Mandenhall disagreed: "I was struck be the fear that pervades Saigon, Hue and Da Nang. These cities have been living under a reign of terror. . . . " He said the war could not be won without changing the regime.

The President looked fron Krulak to Mendenhall and back, finally asking, "Did you two gentlemen visit the same country?"

The decision making in Kennedy's White House did, at times, lend itself to parody. . . .

Sometimes it seems this is the model for Bill Clinton, who met President Kennedy that month in the Rose Garden, when he was a seventeen-year-old dele-

A young Bill Clinton greets President John F. Kennedy in Washington in 1963.

gate from Arkansas to Boys Nation, an American Legion leadership program. Thirty years later President Clinton met "Brute" Krulak—the nickname is a compliment in his business—at a televised town meeting in San Diego. Krulak, who went on to become the president of the Copley newspaper chain, beat up on Clinton for military spending cuts, saying they would eventually produce "terrible fields of white crosses."

President Clinton took that, not having the vaguest idea who Krulak was. The same thing might have happened to Kennedy, because of another trait they shared: a reluctance to prepare and an absolute unwillingness to rehearse. They were both secure—or deluded—in the belief that they would prevail in any one-on-one encounter. That politicians' arrogance got Clinton, unprepared, into a room of hostile conservatives in San Diego led by Krulak—all on national television.

In his time it got President Kennedy into the bathroom. The first Medal of Freedom he awarded was to Paul-Henri Spaak, the retiring secretary-general of the North Atlantic Treaty Organization, in February of 1961. Kennedy, impatient as always, quickly read the proclamation, presented the medal, circled the Oval Office, shaking hands with various ambassadors, and stepped out the door. He had no idea where he was, saw another door, and went in—to the bathroom. He stayed there in solitary dignity until Spaak and the others left his office.

■ ■ ■ ■ ■ ■

Lyndon B. Johnson and Vietnam

Larry L. King

President Lyndon B. Johnson was the kind of politician people tend to tell tall stories about. He always had a strong—some would say an overpowering—personality. When he was placed by fate and an assassin's bullet in a position of enormous power, he came to project a larger-than-life image, to seem a kind of elemental, irresistible force that no mere mortal could successfully resist. He swiftly pushed through economic and social reforms that had appeared to paralyze his predecessor in the White House, the popular John F. Kennedy.

Although he could certainly be devious, Johnson was not a very subtle person and when, during the Vietnam war, he decided that the national honor and the safety of what he called the free world required that the United States pursue the conflict to victory, he devoted all his energies to the task. Of course he failed. Why he failed and how he reacted to failure is the subject of this article by Larry L. King. The account is one of the most graphic and tragic portraits we have of Johnson, or for that matter of any president. King is the author of a number of novels and also of *Confessions of a White Racist*. He was active in the 1960 and 1964 presidential campaigns.

■　■　■　■　■　■　■

He was an old-fashioned man by the purest definition. Forget that he was enamored of twentieth-century artifacts—the telephone, television, supersonic airplanes, spacecraft—to which he adapted with a child's wondering glee. His values were the relics of an earlier time; he had been shaped by an America both rawer and more confident than it later would become; his generation may have been the last to believe that for every problem there existed a workable solution: that the ultimate answer, as in old-time mathematics texts, always reposed in the back of the book. He bought the prevailing American myths without closely inspecting the merchandise for rips or snares. He often said that Americans inherently were "can-do" people capable of accomplishing anything they willed; it was part of his creed that Americans were God's chosen: why otherwise would they have become the richest, the strongest, the freest people in the history of man? His was a God, perhaps, who was a first cousin to Darwin: Lyndon B. Johnson believed in survival of the fittest, that the strong would conquer the weak, that almost always the big 'uns ate the little 'uns.

There was a certain pragmatism in his beliefs, a touch of fatalism, even a measure of common sense. Yet, too, he could be wildly romantic. Johnson truly believed that any boy could rise to become President, though only thirty-five had. Hadn't he—a shirt-tailed kid from the dusty hard-scrabble precincts of the Texas outback—walked with kings and pharaohs while reigning over what he called, without blushing, the Free World? In his last days, though bitter and withering in retirement at his rural Elba, he astonished and puzzled a young black teen-ager by waving his arms in windmill motions and telling the youngster, during a random encounter, "Well, maybe someday all of us will be visiting *your* house in Waco, because you'll be President and your home will be a national museum just as mine is. It'll take a while, but it'll happen, you'll see. . . ." Then he turned to the black teenager's startled mother: "Now, you better get that home of yours cleaned up spick-and-span. There'll be hundreds of thousands coming through it, you know, wanting to see the bedroom and the kitchen and the living room. Now, I hope you get that dust rag of yours out the minute you get home."

Doris Kearns, the Harvard professor and latter-day L.B.J. confidante, who witnessed the performance, thought it to be a mock show: "almost a vaudeville act." Dr. Johnson peddling the same old snake oil. Perhaps. Whatever his motives that day, Lyndon Johnson chose his sermon from that text he most fervently believed throughout a lifetime; his catechism spoke to his heart of American opportunity, American responsibility, American good intentions, American superiority, American destiny, American infallibility. Despite a sly personal cynicism—a suspicion of others, the keen, cold eye of a man determined not to be victimized at the gaming tables—he was, in his institutional instincts, something of a Pollyanna. There *was* such a thing as a free lunch; there *was* a Santa Claus; there *was,* somewhere, a Good Fairy, and probably it was made up of the component parts of Franklin Roosevelt, Saint Francis, and Uncle Sam.

These thoroughly American traits—as L.B.J. saw them—comprised the foundation stone upon which he built his dream castle; he found it impossible to abandon them even as the sands shifted and bogged him in the quagmire of Vietnam. If America was so wonderful (and it *was;* he had the evidence of himself to prove it), then he had the obligation to export its goodness and greatness to the less fortunate. This he would accomplish at any cost, even if forced to "nail the coonskin to the wall." For if Lyndon B. Johnson believed in God and greatness and goodness, he also believed in guts and gunpowder.

All the history he had read, and all he had personally witnessed, convinced him that the United States of America—if determined enough, if productive enough, if patriotic enough—simply could not lose a war. As a boy his favorite stories had been of the minutemen at Lexington and Concord, of the heroic defenders of the Alamo, of rugged frontiersmen who'd at once tamed the wild land and marauding Indians. He had a special affinity for a schoolboy poem proclaiming that the most beautiful sight his eyes had beheld was "the flag of my country in a foreign land." He so admired war heroes that he claimed to have been fired on "by a Japanese ace," though no evidence supported it; he invented an ancestor he carelessly claimed had been martyred at the Alamo; at the Democratic National Convention in 1956 he had cast his state's delegate votes for the Vice-Presidential ambitions of young John F. Kennedy, "that fighting sailor who bears the scars of battle."

On a slow Saturday afternoon in the 1950's, expansive and garrulous in his posh Senate majority-leader quarters, Johnson discoursed to a half dozen young Texas staffers in the patois of their shared native place. Why—he said—you take that ragtag bunch at Valley Forge, who'd have given them a cut dog's chance? There they were, barefoot in the snow and their asses hanging out, nothing to eat but moss and dead leaves and snakes, not half enough bullets for their guns, and facing the soldiers of the most powerful king of his time. Yet they sucked it up, wouldn't quit, lived to fight another day—and won. Or you take the Civil War, now: it had been so exceptionally bloody because you had aroused Americans fighting on *both* sides; it had been something like rock against rock, or like two mean ol' pit bull-dogs going at each other with neither of them willing to be chewed up and both of 'em thinking only of taking hunks out of the other. He again invoked the Alamo: a mere handful of freedom-loving men standing against the Mexican hordes, knowing they faced certain death, but they'd carved their names in history for all time, and before they got through with ol' General Santa Anna he thought he'd stumbled into a nest of stinging scorpions or bumble-bees.

Fifteen years later Johnson would show irritation when Clark Clifford suggested that victory in Vietnam might require a sustaining commitment of twenty to thirty years. No—L.B.J. said—no, no, the thing to do was get in and out quickly, pour everything you had into the fight, land the knockout blow: hell, the North Vietnamese *had* to see the futility of facing all that American muscle. If you really poured it on 'em, you could clean up that mess within six months. We had the troops, the firepower, the bombs, the sophisticated weaponry, the oil—everything we needed to win. Did we have the resolve? Well, the Texas Rangers had a saying that you couldn't stop a man who just kept on a-coming. And that's what we'd do in Vietnam, Clark, just keep on a-coming. . . .

Always he talked of the necessity to be strong; he invoked his father's standing up to the Ku Klux Klan in the 1920's, Teddy Roosevelt's carrying that big stick, F.D.R's mobilizing the country to beat Hitler and Tojo. He liked ol' Harry Truman—tough little bastard and his own man—but, listen, Harry and Dean Acheson had lost control when they failed to properly prosecute the Korean War. They lost the public's respect, lost control of General MacArthur, lost the backing of Congress, lost the *war* or the next thing to it. Next thing you know, they got blamed for losing China and then there was Joe McCarthy accusing them of being soft on communism and everybody believed it. Well, it wouldn't happen to him, nosir. *He* hadn't started the Vietnam war—Jack Kennedy had made the first commitment of out-and-out combat troops, don't forget—but *he* wouldn't bug out no matter how much the Nervous Nellies brayed. Kennedy had proved during the Cuban missile crisis that if you stood firm then the Reds would back down. They were playground bullies, and he didn't intend to be pushed around any more than Jack Kennedy had. When a bully ragged you, you didn't go whining to the teacher but gave him some of his own medicine.

Only later, in exile, when he spoke with unusual candor of his darker parts, did it become clear how obsessed with failure Lyndon Johnson always had been. As a preschool youngster he walked a country lane to visit a grandfather, his head stuffed with answers he knew would be required ("How many head of cattle you got, Lyndon? How much do they eat? How many head can you graze to the acre?") and fearing he might forget them. If he forgot them, he got no bright-red apple but received, instead, a stern and disapproving gaze. L.B.J.'s mother, who smothered him with affection and praise should he perform to her pleasure, refused to acknowledge his presence should he somehow displease or disappoint her. His father accused him of being a sleepyhead, a slow starter, and sometimes said every boy in town had a two-hour head start on him. Had we known these things from scratch, we might not have wondered why Lyndon Johnson seemed so blind for so long to the Asian realities. His personal history simply permitted him no retreats or failures in testings.

From childhood L.B.J. experienced bad dreams. As with much else, they would stay with him to the grave. His nightmares were of being paralyzed and unable to act, of being chained inside a cage or to his desk, of being pursued by hostile forces. These and other disturbing dreams haunted his White House years; he could see himself stricken and ill on a cot, unable even to speak—like Woodrow Wilson—while, in an adjoining room, his trusted aides squabbled and quarreled in dividing his power. He translated the dreams to mean that should he for a moment show weakness, be indecisive, then history might judge him as the first American President who had failed to stand up and be counted.

These deep-rooted insecurities prompted Lyndon Johnson always to assert himself, to abuse staff members simply to prove that he held the upper hand, to test his power in small or mean ways. Sometimes, in sending Vice President Hubert Humphrey off on missions or errands with exhortations to "get going," he literally kicked him in the shins. "Hard," Humphrey later recalled, pulling up his trouser leg to exhibit the scars to columnist Robert Allen. Especially when drinking did he swagger and strut. Riding high as Senate majority leader, Johnson one night after a Texas State Society function, at the National Press Club in Washington—in the spring of 1958—repaired to a nearby bar with Texas Congressmen Homer Thornberry and Jack Brooks. "I'm a powerful sumbitch, you know that?" he repeatedly said. "You boys realize how goddamn *powerful* I am?" Yes, Lyndon, his companions uneasily chorused. Johnson pounded the table as if attempting to crack stout oak: "Do you know Ike couldn't pass the Lord's Prayer in Congress without me? You understand that? Hah?" Yes, Lyndon. "Hah? Do you? Hah?" An observer thought he never had seen a man more desperate for affirmations of himself.

Johnson always was an enthusiastic Cold Warrior. He was not made uncomfortable by John Foster Dulles' brinkmanship rhetoric about "rolling back" communism or of "unleashing" Chiang Kai-shek to free the Chinese mainland. He was, indeed, one of the original soldiers of the Cold War, a volunteer rather than a draftee, just as he had been the first member of Congress to rush to the recruiting station following Pearl Harbor. Immediately after World War II he so bedeviled House Speaker Sam Rayburn about his fears of America dismantling its military machine that Rayburn appointed him to the postwar Military Policy Committee and to the Joint Committee on Atomic Energy. L.B.J. early had a preference for military assignments in Congress; he successfully campaigned for a seat on the House Naval Affairs Committee in the 1930's and, a decade later, the Senate Armed Services Committee. He eventually chaired the Senate Preparedness Committee and the Senate Space Committee. Perhaps others saw the exploration of outer space in scientific or peaceful terms. Johnson, however, told Senate Democrats that outer space offered "the ultimate position from which total control of the earth may be exercised. Whoever gains that ultimate position gains control, total control, over the earth."

Lyndon Johnson was a nagger, a complainer, a man not always patient with those of lesser gifts or with those who somehow inconvenienced him in the moment. Sometimes he complained that the generals knew nothing but "spend and bomb"; almost always, however, he went along with bigger military spending and, in most cases, with more bombing or whatever other military action the brass proposed. This was his consistent record in Congress, and he generally affirmed it as President.

On November 12, 1951, Senator Johnson rattled his saber at the Russians:

> We are tired of fighting your stooges. We will no longer sacrifice our young men on the altar of your conspiracies. The next aggression will be the last. . . . We will strike back, not just at your satellites, but at you. We will strike back with all the dreaded might that is within our control, and it will be a crushing blow.

Even allowing for those rhetorical excesses peculiar to senatorial oratory, those were not the words of a man preoccupied with the doctrine of peaceful coexistence. Nor were they inconsistent with Johnson's mind-set when he made a public demand—at the outbreak of the Korean War, in June, 1950—that President Truman order an all-out mobilization of all military reserve troops, national guard units, draftees, and even civilian manpower and industry. In a Senate debate shortly thereafter Senator Johnson scolded colleagues questioning the Pentagon's request for new and supplementary emergency billions: "Is this the hour of our nation's twilight, the last fading hour of light before an endless night shall envelop us and all the Western world?"

His ties with Texas—with its indigenous xenophobic instincts and general proclivities toward a raw yahooism—haunted him and, in a sense, may have made him a prisoner of grim political realities during the witch-hunting McCarthy era. "I'm damn tired," he said, "of being called a Dixiecrat in Washington and a Communist in Texas"; it perfectly summed up those schizophrenic divisions uneasily compartmentalizing his national political life and the more restrictive parochial role dictated by conditions back home. He lived daily with a damned-if-I-do-and-damned-if-I-don't situation. Texas was a particularly happy hunting ground for Senator Joe McCarthy, whose self-proclaimed anticommunist crusade brought him invitation after invitation to speak there; the Texas legislature, in the 1950's controlled beyond belief by vested interests and showing the ideological instincts of the early primates, whooped through a resolution demanding that Senator McCarthy address it despite the suggestion of State Representative Maury Maverick, Jr., that the resolution be expanded to invite Mickey Mouse. Both Johnson's powerful rightist adversaries and many of his wealthy Texas benefactors were enthusiastic contributors to the McCarthy cause.

Privately Johnson groused to intimates of McCarthy's reckless showboat tactics and particularly of the Texas-directed pressures they brought down on him: why, Joe McCarthy was just a damn drunk, a blowhard, an incompetent who couldn't tie his own shoelaces, probably the biggest joke in the Senate. But—L.B.J. reminded those counseling him to attack McCarthy—people believed him, they were so afraid of the Communists they would believe anything. McCarthy was as strong as horseradish. There would come a time when the hysteria died down, and then Mc-Carthy would be vulnerable; such a fellow was certain to hang himself in time. But right now anybody openly challenging McCarthy would come away with dirty hands and with his heart broken. "Touch pitch," he paraphrased the Bible, "and you'll be defiled." By temperament a man who coveted the limelight and never was bashful about claiming credit for popular actions, Johnson uncharacteristically remained in the background when the U.S. Senate voted to censure McCarthy in late 1954. Though he was instrumental in selecting senators he believed would be effective and creditable members in leading the censure effort, Johnson's fine hand was visible only to insiders.

Johnson believed, however—and probably more deeply than Joe McCarthy—in a worldwide, monolithic Communist conspiracy. He believed it was directed from Moscow and that it was ready to blast America, or subvert it, at the drop of a fur hat. L.B.J. never surrendered that view. In retirement he suggested that the Communists were everywhere, honeycombing the government, and he told surprised visitors that sometimes he hadn't known whether he could trust even his own staff. The Communists (it had been his first thought on hearing the gunshots in Dallas, and he never changed his mind) had killed Jack Kennedy; it had been their influence that turned people against the Vietnam war. One of L.B.J.'s former aides, having been treated to that angry lecture, came away from the Texas ranch with the sad and reluctant conclusion that "the Old Man's absolutely paranoid on the Communist thing."

In May, 1961, President Kennedy dispatched his Vice President to Asia on a "fact-finding" diplomatic trip. Johnson, who believed it his duty to be a team player, to reinforce the prevailing wisdom, bought without qualification the optimistic briefings of military brass with their charts and slides "proving" the inevitable American victory. "I was sent out here to report the *progress* of the war," he told an aide, as if daring anyone to give him anything other than good news. Carried away, he publicly endowed South Vietnam's President Ngo Dinh Diem with the qualities of Winston Churchill, George Washington, Andrew Jackson, and F.D.R. Visiting refugee camps, he grew angry at Communist aggressions "against decent people" and concluded: "There is no alternative to United States leadership in Southeast Asia. . . . We must decide whether to help to the best of our ability or throw in the towel . . . [and] . . . pull back our defenses to San Francisco and a 'Fortress America' concept." He believed then—and always would—in the "domino theory" first stated by President Eisenhower. Even after announcing his abdication, he continued to sing the tired litany: if Vietnam fell then the rest of Asia might go, and then Africa, and then the Philippines. . . .

When Lyndon Johnson suddenly ascended to the Presidency, however, he did not enter the Oval Office eager to immediately take the measure of Ho Chi Minh. Although he told Ambassador Henry Cabot Lodge that "I am not going to be the President who saw Southeast Asia go the way China went," he wanted, for the moment, to keep the war—and, indeed, all foreign entanglements—at arm's length. His preoccupation was with his domestic program; here, he was confident, he knew what he was doing. He would emulate F.D.R. in making people's lives a little brighter. To aides he eagerly talked of building schools and houses, of fighting poverty and attaining full employment, of heating the economy to record prosperity. The honeymoon with Congress—he said—couldn't last; he had seen Congress grow balky and obstinate, take its measure of many Presidents, and he had to assume it would happen again. Then he would lean forward, tapping a forefinger against someone's chest or squeezing a neighboring knee, and say: "I'm like a sweetheart to Congress right now. They love me because I'm new and courting 'em and it's kinda exciting, like that first kiss. But after a while the new will wear off. Then Congress will complain that I don't bring enough roses or candy and will accuse me of seeing other girls." The need was to push forward quickly: pass the Civil Rights bill in the name of the martyred John F. Kennedy, then hit Capitol Hill with a blizzard of domestic proposals and dazzle it before sentiment and enthusiasms cooled. Foreign affairs could wait.

Lyndon Johnson at that point had little experience in foreign affairs. Except for showcase missions accomplished as Vice President, he had not traveled outside the United States save for excursions to Mexico and his brief World War II peregrinations. He probably had little confidence in himself in foreign affairs; neither did he have an excessive interest in the field. "Foreigners are not like the folks I am used to," he sometimes said—and though it passed as a joke, his intimates felt he might be kidding on the level.

Ambassadors waiting to present their credentials to the new President were miffed by repeated delays—and then angrily astonished when L.B.J. received them in groups and clumps, seemingly paying only perfunctory attention, squirming in his chair, scowling or muttering during the traditional ceremonies. He appeared oblivious to their feelings, to their offended senses of dignity. "Why do *I* have to see them?" the President demanded. "They're Dean Rusk's clients, not mine."

Defense Secretary Robert McNamara was selected to focus on Vietnam while L.B.J. concocted his Great Society. McNamara should send South Vietnam equipment and money as needed, a few more men, issue the necessary pronouncements. But don't splash it all over the front pages, don't let it get out of hand, don't give Barry Goldwater Vietnam as an issue for the 1964 campaign. Barry, hell, he was a hip shooter; he'd fight Canada or Mexico—or, at least, give that impression—so the thing to do was sit tight, keep the lid on, keep all Vietnam options open. Above all, "Don't let it turn into a Bay of Pigs." Hunker down; don't gamble.

The trouble—Johnson said to advisers—was that foreign nations didn't understand Americans or the American way; they saw us as "fat and fifty, like the country-club set"; they didn't think we had the steel in our souls to act when the going got rough. Well, in time they'd find out differently. They'd learn that Lyndon Johnson was not about to abandon what other Presidents had started; he wouldn't permit history to write that he'd been the only American President to cut and run; he wouldn't sponsor any damn Munichs. But for right now—cool it. Put Vietnam on the back burner and let it simmer.

But the Communists—he later would say—wouldn't permit him to cool it. There had been the Gulf of Tonkin attack on the United States destroyer *Maddox*, in August of 19-and-64, and if he hadn't convinced Congress to get on record as backing him up in Vietnam, why, then, the Reds would have interpreted it as a sign of weakness and Barry Goldwater would have cut his heart out. And in February of

19-and-65, don't forget, the Vietcong had made that attack on the American garrison at Pleiku, and how could he be expected to ignore that? There they came, thousands of 'em, barefoot and howling in their black pajamas and throwing homemade bombs: it had been a damned insult, a calculated show of contempt. L.B.J. told the National Security Council: "The worst thing we could do would be to let this [Pleiku] thing go by. It would be a big mistake. It would open the door to a major misunderstanding." Twelve hours later American aircraft—for the first time—bombed in North Vietnam; three weeks later L.B.J. ordered continuing bombing raids in the north to "force the North Vietnamese into negotiations"; only a hundred and twenty days after Pleiku, American forces were involved in a full-scale war and seeking new ways to take the offensive. Eight Americans died at Pleiku. Eight. Eventually fifty thousand plus would die in Asia.

Pleiku was the second major testing of American will within a few months, in L.B.J.'s view. Then in the spring of 1965 rebels had attacked the ruling military junta in the Dominican Republic. Lives and property of U.S. citizens were endangered, as Johnson saw it, but—more—this might be a special tactic by the Reds, a dry run for bigger mischief later on in Vietnam. The world was watching to see how America would react. "It's just like the Alamo," he lectured the National Security Council. "Hell, it's like you were down at that gate, and you were surrounded, and you damn well needed somebody. Well, by God, I'm going to *go*—and I thank the Lord that I've got men who want to go with me, from McNamara right down to the littlest private who's carrying a gun."

Somewhat to his puzzlement, and certainly to his great vexation, Lyndon Johnson would learn that not everybody approved of his rushing the Marines into the Dominican Republic, and within days building up a twenty-one-thousand-man force. Attempting to answer criticism, he would claim thousands of patriots "bleeding in the streets and with their heads cut off," paint a false picture of the United States ambassador cringing under his desk "while bullets whizzed over his head," speak of howling Red hordes descending on American citizens and American holdings, and, generally, open what later became known as the Credibility Gap.

By now he had given up on his original notion of walking easy in Vietnam until he could put the Great Society across. Even before the three major testings of Tonkin Gulf, the Dominican Republic, and Pleiku, he had said—almost idly— "Well, I guess we have to touch up those North Vietnamese a little bit." By December, 1964, he had reversed earlier priorities: "We'll beat the Communists first, then we can look around and maybe give something to the poor." Guns now ranked ahead of butter.

Not that he was happy about it. Though telling Congress "This nation is mighty enough, its society is healthy enough, its people are strong enough to pursue our goals in the rest of the world while still building a Great Society here at home," he knew, in his bones, that this was much too optimistic an outlook. He privately fretted that his domestic program would be victimized. He became touchy, irritable, impatient with those who even timorously questioned America's increasing commitment to the war. Why should *I* be blamed—he snapped—when the Communists are the aggressors, when President Eisenhower committed us in Asia in 1954, when Kennedy beefed up Ike's efforts? If he didn't prosecute the Vietnam war now, then later Congress would sour and want to hang him because he hadn't—and would gut his domestic programs in retaliation. He claimed to have "pounded President Eisenhower's desk" in opposing Ike's sending two hundred Air Force "technicians" to assist the French in Indochina (though those who were present recalled that only Senators Russell of Georgia and Stennis of Mississippi had raised major objections). Well, he'd been unable to stop Ike that time, though he *had* helped persuade him against dropping paratroopers into Dien Bien Phu to aid the doomed French garrison there. And after all that, everybody now called Vietnam Lyndon Johnson's war. It was unfair. "The only difference between the Kennedy assassination and mine is that I am alive and it [is] more torturous."

Very well; if it was his war in the public mind, then he would personally oversee its planning. "Never move up your artillery until you move up your ammunition," he told his generals—a thing he'd said as Senate majority leader when impatient liberals urged him to call for votes on issues he felt not yet ripe. Often he quizzed the military brass, sounding almost like a dove, in a way to resemble courtroom cross-examinations. He forced the admirals and generals to affirm and reaffirm their recommendations as vital to victory. Reading selected transcripts, one might make the judgment that Lyndon Johnson was a most reluctant warrior, one more cautious than not. The evidence of Johnson's deeds, however, suggests that he was being a crafty politician—making a record so that later he couldn't be made the sole scapegoat. He trusted McNamara's computers, perhaps more than he trusted men, and took satisfaction when their print-outs predicted that X amount of bombing would damage the Vietcong by Y, or that X number of troops would be required to capture Z. Planning was the key. You figured what you had to do, you did it, and eventually you'd nail the coonskin to the wall.

He devoutly believed that all problems had solutions: in his lifetime alone we'd beaten the Great Depression, won two world wars, hacked away at racial discrimination, made an industrial giant and world power of a former agrarian society, explored outer space. This belief in available solutions led him, time and again, to change tactics in Vietnam and discover fresh enthusiasm for each new move; he did not pause, apparently, to reflect upon why given tactics, themselves once heralded as practical solutions, had failed and had been abandoned. If counterinsurgency failed, you bombed. If bombing wasn't wholly effective, then you tried the enclave theory. If *that* proved disappointing, you sent your ground troops on search-and-destroy missions. If, somehow, the troops couldn't find the phantom Vietcong in large numbers (and therefore couldn't destroy them), you began pacification programs in the areas you'd newly occupied. And if *this* bogged down, you beefed up your firepower and sent in enough troops to simply outmuscle the rice-paddy ragtags: napalm 'em, bomb 'em, shoot 'em. Sure it would work. It always had. Yes, surely the answer was there somewhere in the back of the book, if only you looked long enough. . . .

He sought, and found, assurances. Maybe he had only a "cow-college" education, perhaps he'd not attended West Point, he might not have excessive experience in foreign affairs. But he was surrounded by good men, what David Halberstam later would label "the best and the brightest," and certainly these were unanimous in their supportive conclusions. "He would look around him," Tom Wicker later said, "and see in Bob McNamara that [the war] was technologically feasible, in McGeorge Bundy that it was intellectually respectable, and in Dean Rusk that it was historically necessary." It was especially easy to trust expertise when the experts in their calculations bolstered your own gut feelings—when their computers and high-minded statements and mighty hardware all boiled down to reinforce your belief in American efficiency, American responsibility, American destiny. If so many good men agreed with him, then what might be wrong with those who didn't?

He considered the sources of dissatisfaction and dissent: the liberals—the "red-hots," he'd often sneeringly called them, the "pepper pots"—who were impractical dreamers, self-winding kamikazes intent on self-destruction. He often quoted an aphorism to put such people in perspective: "Any jackass can kick down a barn, but it takes a carpenter to build one." He fancied, however, that he knew all about these queer fellows. For years, down home, Ronnie Dugger and his *Texas Observer* crowd, in L.B.J.'s opinion, had urged him to put his head in the noose by fighting impossible, profitless fights. They wanted him to take on Joe McCarthy, slap the oil powers down, kick Ike's rear end, tell everybody who wasn't a red-hot to go to hell. Well, he'd learned a long time ago that just because you told a fellow to go to hell, he didn't necessarily have to go. The liberals didn't understand the Communists. Bill Fulbright and his bunch—the striped-pants boys over at the State Department and assorted outside pepper pots—thought you could *trust* the Communists; they made the mistake of believing the Reds would deal with you honorably when—in truth—the Communists didn't respect anything but force. You had to fight fire with fire; let them know who had the biggest guns and the toughest heart.

Where once he had argued the injustice of Vietnam being viewed as "his" war, Lyndon Johnson now brought to it a proprietary attitude. This should have been among the early warnings that L.B.J. would increasingly resist less than victory, no matter his periodic bombing halts or conciliatory statements inviting peace, because once he took a thing personally, his pride and vanity and ego knew no bounds. Always a man to put his brand on everything (he wore monogrammed shirts, boots, cuff links; flew his private L.B.J. flag when in residence at the L.B.J. ranch; saw to it that the names of Lynda Bird Johnson and Luci Baines Johnson and Lady Bird Johnson—not Claudia, as she had been named—had the magic initials L.B.J.), he now personalized and internalized the war. Troops became "my" boys, those were "my" helicopters, it was "my" pilots he prayed might return from their bombing missions as he paid nocturnal calls to the White House situation room to learn the latest from the battlefields; Walt Rostow became "my" intellectual because he was hawkish on L.B.J.'s war. His machismo was mixed up in it now, his manhood. After a cabinet meeting in 1967 several staff aides and at least one cabinet member—Stewart Udall, Secretary of the Interior—remained behind for informal discussions; soon L.B.J. was waving his arms and fulminating about his war. Who the hell was Ho Chi Minh, anyway, that he thought he could push America around? Then the President did an astonishing thing: he unzipped his trousers, dangled a given appendage, and asked his shocked associates: "Has Ho Chi Minh got anything like that?"

By mid-1966 he had cooled toward many of his experts: not because they'd been wrong in their original optimistic calculations so much as that some of them had recanted and now rejected *his* war. This Lyndon Johnson could not forgive:

they'd cut and run on him. Nobody had deserted Roosevelt, he gloomed, when he'd been fighting Hitler. McGeorge Bundy, deserting to head the Ford Foundation, was no longer the brilliant statesman but merely "a smart kid, that's all." Bill Moyers, quitting to become editor of *Newsday,* and once almost a surrogate son to the President, suddenly became "a little puppy I rescued from sacking groceries"— a reference to a part-time job Moyers held while a high-school student. George Ball, too, was leaving? Well, he'd always been a chronic belleracher. When Defense Secretary McNamara doubted too openly (stories of his anguish leaked to the newspapers), he found it difficult to claim the President's time; ultimately he rudely was shuttled to the World Bank. Vice President Hubert Humphrey, privately having second thoughts, was not welcomed back to high councils until he'd muffled his dissent and shamelessly flattered L.B.J. Even then Johnson didn't wholly accept his Vice President; Hubert, he said, wasn't a real man, he cried as easily as a woman, he didn't have the weight. When Lady Bird Johnson voiced doubts about the war, her husband grumbled that *of course* she had doubts; it was *like* a woman to be uncertain. *Has Ho Chi Minh got anything like that?*

Shortly after the Tet offensive began—during which Americans would be shocked by the Vietcong temporarily capturing a wing of the American embassy in Saigon—the President, at his press conference of February 2, 1968, made such patently false statements that even his most loyal friends and supporters were troubled. The sudden Tet offensive had been traumatic, convincing many Americans that our condition was desperate, if not doomed. For years the official line ran that the Vietcong could not hang on: would shrink by the attritions of battle and an ebbing of confidence in a hopeless cause; stories were handed out that captured documents showed the enemy to be of low morale, underfed, ill-armed. The Vietcong could not survive superior American firepower; the kill ratio favored our side by 7-to-1, 8-to-1, more. These and other optimisms were repeated by the President, by General Westmoreland, by this ambassador or that fact-finding team. Now, however, it became apparent that the Vietcong had the capability to challenge even our main lair in Asia—and there to inflict serious damage as well as major embarrassments.

It was a time demanding utmost candor, and L.B.J. blew it. He took the ludicrous position that the Tet offensive (which would be felt for weeks to come) had abysmally failed. Why, we'd known about it all along—had, indeed, been in possession of Hanoi's order of battle. Incredible. To believe the President one had also to believe that American authorities had simply failed to act on this vital intelligence, had wittingly and willingly invited disaster. The President was scoffed at and ridiculed; perhaps the thoughtful got goose bumps in realizing how far Lyndon Johnson now lived from reality. If there was a beginning of the end—of Johnson, of hopes of anything remotely resembling victory, of a general public innocence, of official razzmatazz—then Tet, and that press conference, had to be it.

Even the stubborn President knew it. His Presidency was shot, his party ruined and in tatters; his credibility was gone; he could speak only at military bases, where security guaranteed his safety against the possibility of mobs pursuing him through the streets as he had often dreamed. The nightmare was real now. Street dissidents long had been chanting their cruel "Hey, Hey, L.B.J./ How Many Kids Did You Kill

LBJ listens to a tape from his son-in-law, Marine Captain Charles Robb, describing action in Vietnam.

Today"; Senator Eugene McCarthy soon would capture almost half the vote in the New Hampshire primary against the unpopular President. There was nothing to do but what he'd always sworn he would not do: quit. On March 31, 1968, at the end of a televised speech ordering the end of attacks on North Vietnam in the hope of getting the enemy to the negotiation table, Johnson startled the nation by announcing: ". . . I do not believe that I should devote an hour or a day of my time to any personal partisan causes or to any duties other than the awesome duties of this office—the Presidency of your country. Accordingly, I shall not seek, and I will not accept, the nomination of my party for another term. . . "

"In the final months of his Presidency," former White House aide Eric Goldman wrote, "Lyndon Johnson kept shifting in mood. At times he was bitter and petulant at his repudiation by the nation; at times philosophical, almost serene, confidently awaiting the verdict of the future." The serenity always was temporary; he grew angry with Hubert Humphrey for attempting to disengage himself from the Johnson war policy and, consequently, refused to make more than a token show of support for him. He saw Richard Nixon win on a pledge of having "a secret plan" to end the war—which, it developed, he did not have.

In his final White House thrashings—and in retirement—Lyndon Johnson complained of unfinished business: he had wanted to complete Vietnam peace talks, free the crew of the *Pueblo,* begin talks with the Russians on halting the arms race, send a man to the moon. But the war—he would say in irritation—the war had ruined all that; the people hadn't rallied around him as they had around F.D.R. and Woodrow Wilson and other wartime Presidents; he had been abandoned—by Congress, by cabinet members, by old friends; no other President had tried so hard or suffered so much. He had a great capacity for self-pity and often indulged it, becoming reclusive and rarely issuing a public statement or making public appearances. Doris Kearns has said that she and others helping L.B.J. write his memoirs, *The Vantage Point,* would draft chapters and lay out the documentation—but even then Lyndon Johnson would say no, no, it wasn't like that, it was like *this;* and he would rattle on, waving his arms and attempting to justify himself, invoking the old absolutes, calling up memories of the Alamo, the Texas Rangers, the myths and the legends. He never seemed to understand where or how he had gone wrong.

■ ■ ■ ■ ■ ■ ■

Watergate

Walter Karp

In 1984, ten years after the resignation of President Richard M. Nixon, the editors of *American Heritage* asked the journalist Walter Karp and the novelist Vance Bourjaily to look back at the events that followed the "third-rate burglary" that we know of as "Watergate" and to write articles describing and explaining those events. Both produced fascinating accounts. Bourjaily's is primarily personal; Karp's is in the form of a narrative account of events and is better suited to the purposes of this volume. Karp takes a dim view of the courage and moral character not merely of the chief culprits and the other main characters in the drama he describes, but also of most of the members of Congress who, he argues, put off doing what in their hearts they knew they had to do for far too long. Whether or not one agrees with this judgment, Karp's account is both good history and eventually heartening, for it is a tale in which justice, after many trials and tribulations, finally triumphs.

■ ■ ■ ■ ■ ■ ■

Exactly ten years ago this August, the thirty-seventh President of the United States, facing imminent impeachment, resigned his high office and passed out of our lives. "The system worked," the nation exclaimed, heaving a sigh of relief. What had brought that relief was the happy extinction of the prolonged fear that the "system" might not work at all. But what was it that had inspired such fears? When I asked myself that question recently, I found I could scarcely remember. Although I had followed the Watergate crisis with minute attention, it had grown vague and formless in my mind, like a nightmare recollected in sunshine. It was not until I began working my way through back copies of The *New York Times* that I was able to remember clearly why I used to read my morning paper with forebodings for the country's future.

The Watergate crisis had begun in June 1972 as a "third-rate burglary" of the Democratic National Committee headquarters in Washington's Watergate building complex. By late March 1973 the burglary and subsequent efforts to obstruct its investigation had been laid at the door of the White House. By late June, Americans were asking themselves whether their President had or had not ordered the payment of "hush money" to silence a Watergate burglar. Investigated by a special Senate committee headed by Sam Ervin of North Carolina, the scandal continued to deepen and ramify during the summer of 1973. By March 1974 the third-rate burglary of 1972 had grown into an unprecedented constitutional crisis.

By then it was clear beyond doubt that President Richard M. Nixon stood at the center of a junto of henchmen without parallel in our history. One of Nixon's attorneys general, John Mitchell, was indicted for obstructing justice in Washington and for impeding a Securities and Exchange Commission investigation in New York. Another, Richard Kleindienst, had criminally misled the Senate Judiciary

Committee in the President's interest. The acting director of the Federal Bureau of Investigation, L. Patrick Gray, had burned incriminating White House documents at the behest of a presidential aide. Bob Haldeman, the President's chief of staff, John Ehrlichman, the President's chief domestic adviser, and Charles Colson, the President's special counsel, all had been indicted for obstructing justice in the investigation of the Watergate burglary. John Dean, the President's legal counsel and chief accuser, had already pleaded guilty to the same charge. Dwight Chapin, the President's appointments secretary, faced trial for lying to a grand jury about political sabotage carried out during the 1972 elections. Ehrlichman and two other White House aides were under indictment for conspiring to break into a psychiatrist's office and steal confidential information about one of his former patients, Daniel Ellsberg. By March 1974 some twenty-eight presidential aides or election officials had been indicted for crimes carried out in the President's interest. Never before in American history had a President so signally failed to fulfill his constitutional duty to "take care that the laws be faithfully executed."

It also had been clear for many months that the thirty-seventh President of the United States did not feel bound by his constitutional duties. He insisted that the requirements of national security, as he and he alone saw fit to define it, released him from the most fundamental legal and constitutional constraints. In the name of "national security," the President had created a secret band of private detectives, paid with private funds, to carry out political espionage at the urging of the White House. In the name of "national security," the President had approved the warrantless wiretapping of news reporters. In the name of "national security," he had approved a secret plan for massive, illegal surveillance of American citizens. He had encouraged his aides' efforts to use the Internal Revenue Service to harass political "enemies"—prominent Americans who endangered "national security" by publicly criticizing the President's Vietnam War policies.

The framers of the Constitution had provided one and only one remedy for such lawless abuse of power: impeachment in the House of Representatives and trial in the Senate for "high Crimes and Misdemeanors." There was absolutely no alternative. If Congress had not held President Nixon accountable for lawless conduct of his office, then Congress would have condoned a lawless Presidency. If Congress had not struck from the President's hands the despot's cudgel of "national security," then Congress would have condoned a despotic Presidency.

Looking through the back issues of The New York Times, I recollected in a flood of ten-year-old memories what it was that had filled me with such foreboding. It was the reluctance of Congress to act. I felt anew my fury when members of Congress pretended that nobody really cared about Watergate except the "media" and the "Nixon-haters." The real folks "back home," they said, cared only about inflation and the gasoline shortage. I remembered the exasperating actions of leading Democrats, such as a certain Senate leader who went around telling the country that President Nixon could not be impeached because in America a person was presumed innocent until proven guilty. Surely the senator knew that impeachment was not a verdict of guilt but a formal accusation made in the House leading to trial in the Senate. Why was he muddying the waters, I wondered, if not to protect the President?

It had taken one of the most outrageous episodes in the history of the Presidency to compel Congress to make even a pretense of action.

Back on July 16, 1973, a former White House aide named Alexander Butterfield had told the Ervin committee that President Nixon secretly tape-recorded his most intimate political conversations. On two solemn occasions that spring the President had sworn to the American people that he knew nothing of the Watergate cover-up until his counsel John Dean had told him about it on March 21, 1973. From that day forward, Nixon had said, "I began intensive new inquiries into this whole matter." Now we learned that the President had kept evidence secret that would exonerate him completely—if he were telling the truth. Worse yet, he wanted it kept secret. Before Butterfield had revealed the existence of the tapes, the President had grandly announced that "executive privilege will not be invoked as to any testimony [by my aides] concerning possible criminal conduct, in the matters under investigation. I want the public to learn the truth about Watergate. . . ." After the existence of the tapes was revealed, however, the President showed the most ferocious resistance to disclosing the "truth about Watergate." He now claimed that executive privilege—hitherto a somewhat shadowy presidential prerogative—gave a President "absolute power" to withhold any taped conversation he chose, even those urgently needed in the ongoing criminal investigation then being conducted by a special Watergate prosecutor. Nixon even claimed, through his lawyers, that the judicial branch of the federal government was "absolutely without power to reweigh that choice or to make a different resolution of it."

In the U.S. Court of Appeals the special prosecutor, a Harvard Law School professor named Archibald Cox, called the President's claim "intolerable." Millions of Americans found it infuriating. The court found it groundless. On October 12, 1973, it ordered the President to surrender nine taped conversations that Cox had been fighting to obtain for nearly three months.

Determined to evade the court order, the President on October 19 announced that he had devised a "compromise." Instead of handing over the recorded conversations to the court, he would submit only edited summaries. To verify their truthfulness, the President would allow Sen. John Stennis of Mississippi to listen to the tapes. As an independent verifier, the elderly senator was distinguished by his devotion to the President's own overblown conception of a "strong" Presidency. When Nixon had ordered the secret bombing of Cambodia, he had vouchsafed the fact to Senator Stennis, who thought that concealing the President's secret war from his fellow senators was a higher duty than preserving the Senate's constitutional role in the formation of United States foreign policy.

On Saturday afternoon, October 20, I and millions of other Americans sat by our television sets while the special prosecutor explained why he could not accept "what seems to me to be non-compliance with the court's order." Then the President flashed the dagger sheathed within his "compromise." At 8:31 P.M. television viewers across the country learned that he had fired the special prosecutor; that attorney general Elliot Richardson had resigned rather than issue that order to Cox; that the deputy attorney general, William Ruckelshaus, also had refused to do so and had been fired for refusing; that it was a third acting attorney general who had finally issued the order. With trembling voices, television newscasters reported that the President had abolished the office of special prosecutor and that the FBI was standing guard over its files. Never before in our history had a President, setting law at defiance, made our government seem so tawdry and gimcrack. "It's like living in a banana republic," a friend of mine remarked.

Now the question before the country was clear. "Whether ours shall continue to be a government of laws and not of men," the ex-special prosecutor said that evening, "is now for the Congress and ultimately the American people to decide."

Within ten days of the "Saturday night massacre," one million letters and telegrams rained down on Congress, almost every one of them demanding the President's impeachment. But congressional leaders dragged their feet. The House Judiciary Committee would begin an inquiry into *whether* to begin an inquiry into possible grounds for recommending impeachment to the House. With the obvious intent, it seemed to me, of waiting until the impeachment fervor had abated, the Democratic-controlled committee would consider whether to consider making a recommendation about making an accusation.

Republicans hoped to avoid upholding the rule of law by persuading the President to resign. This attempt to supply a lawless remedy for lawless power earned Republicans a memorable rebuke from one of the most venerated members of their party: eighty-one-year-old Sen. George Aiken of Vermont. The demand for Nixon's resignation, he said, "suggests that many prominent Americans, who ought to know better, find the task of holding a President accountable as just too difficult. . . . To ask the President now to resign and thus relieve Congress of its clear congressional duty amounts to a declaration of incompetence on the part of Congress."

The system was manifestly not working. But neither was the President's defense. On national television Nixon bitterly assailed the press for its "outrageous, vicious, distorted" reporting, but the popular outrage convinced him, nonetheless, to surrender the nine tapes to the court. Almost at once the White House tapes began their singular career of encompassing the President's ruin. On October 31 the White House disclosed that two of the taped conversations were missing, including one between the President and his campaign manager, John Mitchell, which had taken place the day after Nixon returned from a Florida vacation and three days after the Watergate break-in. Three weeks later the tapes dealt Nixon a more potent blow. There was an eighteen-and-a-half-minute gap, the White House announced, in a taped conversation between the President and Haldeman, which had also taken place the day after he returned from Florida. The White House suggested first that the President's secretary, Rose Mary Woods, had accidentally erased part of the tape while transcribing it. When the loyal Miss Woods could not demonstrate in court how she could have pressed the "erase" button unwittingly for eighteen straight minutes, the White House attributed the gap to "some sinister force." On January 15, 1974, court-appointed experts provided a more humdrum explanation. The gap had been produced by at least five manual erasures. Someone in the White House had deliberately destroyed evidence that might have proved that President Nixon knew of the Watergate cover-up from the start.

At this point the Judiciary Committee was in its third month of considering whether to consider. But by now there was scarcely an American who did not think the President guilty, and on February 6, 1974, the House voted 410 to 4 to authorize the Judiciary Committee to begin investigating possible grounds for impeaching the President of the United States. It had taken ten consecutive months of the most damning revelations of criminal misconduct, a titanic outburst of public indignation, and an unbroken record of presidential deceit, defiance, and evasion in order to compel Congress to take its first real step. That long record of immobility and feigned indifference boded ill for the future.

The White House knew how to exploit congressional reluctance. One tactic involved a highly technical but momentous question: What constituted an impeachable offense? On February 21 the staff of the Judiciary Committee had issued a report. Led by two distinguished attorneys, John Doar, a fifty-two-year-old Wisconsin Independent, and Albert Jenner, a sixty-seven-year-old Chicago Republican, the staff had taken the broad view of impeachment for which Hamilton and Madison had contended in the *Federalist* papers. Despite the constitutional phrase "high Crimes and Misdemeanors," the staff report had argued that an impeachable offense did not have to be a crime. "Some of the most grievous offenses against our Constitutional form of government may not entail violations of the criminal law."

The White House launched a powerful counterattack. At a news conference on February 25, the President contended that only proven criminal misconduct supplied grounds for impeachment. On February 28, the White House drove home his point with a tightly argued legal paper: If a President could be impeached for anything other than a crime of "a very serious nature," it would expose the Presidency to "political impeachments."

The argument was plausible. But if Congress accepted it, the Watergate crisis could only end in disaster. Men of great power do not commit crimes. They procure crimes without having to issue incriminating orders. A word to the servile suffices. "Who will free me from this turbulent priest," asked Henry II, and four of his barons bashed in the skull of Thomas à Becket. The ease with which the powerful can arrange "deniability," to use the Watergate catchword, was one reason the criminal standard was so dangerous to liberty. Instead of having to take care that the laws be faithfully executed, a President, under that standard, would only have to take care to insulate himself from the criminal activities of his agents. Moreover, the standard could not reach the most dangerous offenses. There is no crime in the statute books called "attempted tyranny."

Yet the White House campaign to narrow the definition of impeachment met with immediate success. In March one of the members of the House of Representatives said that before voting to impeach Nixon, he would "want to know beyond a reasonable doubt that he was directly involved in the commission of a crime." To impeach the President for the grave abuse of his powers, lawmakers said, would be politically impossible. On the Judiciary Committee itself the senior Republican, Edward Hutchinson of Michigan, disavowed the staff's view of impeachment and adopted the President's. Until the final days of the crisis, the criminal definition of impeachment was to hang over the country's fate like the sword of Damocles.

The criminal standard buttressed the President's larger thesis: In defending himself he was fighting to protect the "Presidency" from sinister forces trying to "weaken" it. On March 12 the President's lawyer, James D. St. Clair, sounded this theme when he declared that he did not represent the President "individually" but rather the "office of the Presidency." There was even a National Citizens Committee for Fairness to the Presidency. It was America's global leadership, Nixon insisted, that made a "strong" Presidency so essential. Regardless of the opinion of some members of the Judiciary Committee, Nixon told a joint session of Congress, he would do nothing that "impairs the ability of the Presidents of the future to make the great decisions that are so essential to this nation and the world."

I used to listen to statements such as those with deep exasperation. Here was a President daring to tell Congress, in effect, that a lawless Presidency was necessary to America's safety, while a congressional attempt to reassert the rule of law undermined the nation's security.

Fortunately for constitutional government, however, Nixon's conception of a strong Presidency included one prerogative whose exercise was in itself an impeachable offense. Throughout the month of March the President insisted that the need for "confidentiality" allowed him to withhold forty-two tapes that the Judiciary Committee had asked of him. Nixon was claiming the right to limit the constitutional power of Congress to inquire into his impeachment. This was more than Republicans on the committee could afford to tolerate.

"Ambition must be made to counteract ambition," Madison had written in *The Federalist.* On April 11 the Judiciary Committee voted 33 to 3 to subpoena the forty-two tapes, the first subpoena ever issued to a President by a committee of the House. Ambition, at last, was counteracting ambition. This set the stage for one of the most lurid moments in the entire Watergate crisis.

As the deadline for compliance drew near, tension began mounting in the country. Comply or defy? Which would the President do? Open defiance was plainly impeachable. Frank compliance was presumably ruinous. On Monday, April 29, the President went on television to give the American people his answer. Seated in the Oval Office with the American flag behind him, President Nixon calmly announced that he was going to make over to the Judiciary Committee—and the public—"edited transcripts" of the subpoenaed tapes. These transcripts "will tell it all," said the President; there was nothing more that would need to be known for an impeachment inquiry about his conduct. To sharpen the public impression of presidential candor, the transcripts had been distributed among forty-two thick, loose-leaf binders, which were stacked in two-foot-high piles by the President's desk. As if to warn the public not to trust what the newspapers would say about the transcripts, Nixon accused the media of concocting the Watergate crisis out of "rumor, gossip, innuendo," of creating a "vague, general impression of massive wrongdoing, implicating everybody, gaining credibility by its endless repetition."

The next day's *New York Times* pronounced the President's speech "his most powerful Watergate defense since the scandal broke." By May 1 James Reston, the newspaper's most eminent columnist, thought the President had "probably gained considerable support in the country." For a few days it seemed as though the President had pulled off a coup. Republicans on the Judiciary Committee acted accordingly. On the first of May, 16 of the 17 committee Republicans voted against sending the President a note advising him that self-edited transcripts punctured by hundreds upon hundreds of suspicious "inaudibles" and "unintelligibles" were not

Nixon with the transcripts of the Watergate tapes, in their forty-two loose-leaf binders.

in compliance with the committee's subpoena. The President, it was said, had succeeded in making impeachment look "partisan" and consequently discreditable.

Not even bowdlerized transcripts, however, could nullify the destructive power of those tapes. They revealed a White House steeped in more sordid conniving than Nixon's worst enemies had imagined. They showed a President advising his aides on how to "stonewall" a grand jury without committing perjury: "You can say, 'I don't remember.' You can say, 'I can't recall. I can't give any answer to that, that I can recall.'" They showed a President urging his counsel to make a "complete report" about Watergate but to "make it very incomplete." They showed a President eager for vengeance against ordinary election opponents. "I want the most comprehensive notes on all those who tried to do us in. . . . They are asking for it and they are going to get it." It showed a President discussing how "national security grounds" might be invoked to justify the Ellsberg burglary should the secret ever come out. "I think we could get by on that," replies Nixon's counsel.

On May 7 Pennsylvania's Hugh Scott, Senate Republican Minority Leader, pronounced the revelations in the transcript "disgusting, shabby, immoral performances." Joseph Alsop, who had long been friendly toward the President in his column, compared the atmosphere in the Oval Office to the "back room of a second-rate advertising agency in a suburb of hell." A week after Nixon's seeming coup Republicans were once again vainly urging him to resign. On May 9 the House Judiciary Committee staff began presenting to the members its massive accumulation of Watergate material. Since the presentation was made behind closed doors, a suspenseful lull fell over the Watergate battleground.

Over the next two months it was obvious that the Judiciary Committee was growing increasingly impatient with the President, who continued to insist that, even in an impeachment proceeding, the "executive must remain the final arbiter of demands on its confidentiality." When Nixon refused to comply in any way with a second committee subpoena, the members voted 28 to 10 to warn him that "your refusals in and of themselves might constitute a ground for impeachment." The "partisanship" of May 1 had faded by May 30.

Undermining these signs of decisiveness was the continued insistence that only direct presidential involvement in a crime would be regarded as an impeachable offense in the House. Congressmen demanded to see the "smoking gun." They wanted to be shown the "hand in the cookie jar." Alexander Hamilton had called impeachment a "National Inquest." Congress seemed bent on restricting it to the purview of a local courthouse. Nobody spoke of the larger issues. As James Reston noted on May 26, one of the most disturbing aspects of Watergate was the silence of the prominent. Where, Reston asked, were the educators, the business leaders, and the elder statesmen to delineate and define the great constitutional issues at stake? When the White House began denouncing the Judiciary Committee as a "lynch mob," virtually nobody rose to the committee's defense.

On July 7 the Sunday edition of the *New York Times* made doleful reading. "The official investigations seem beset by semitropical torpor," the newspaper reported in its weekly news summary. White House attacks on the committee, said the *Times,* were proving effective in the country. In March, 60 percent of those polled by Gallup wanted the President tried in the Senate for his misdeeds. By June the figure had fallen to 50 percent. The movement for impeachment, said the *Times,* was losing its momentum. Nixon, it seemed, had worn out the public capacity for righteous indignation.

Then, on July 19, John Doar, the Democrats' counsel, did what nobody had done before with the enormous, confusing mass of interconnected misdeeds that we labeled "Watergate" for sheer convenience. At a meeting of the Judiciary Committee he compressed the endlessly ramified scandal into a grave and compelling case for impeaching the thirty-seventh President of the United States. He spoke of the President's "enormous crimes." He warned the committee that it dare not look indifferently upon the "terrible deed of subverting the Constitution." He urged the members to consider with favor five broad articles of impeachment, "charges with a grave historic ring," as the *Times* said of them.

In a brief statement, Albert Jenner, the Republicans' counsel, strongly endorsed Doar's recommendations. The Founding Fathers, he reminded committee members, had established a free country and a free Constitution. It was now the committee's momentous duty to determine "whether that country and that Constitution are to be preserved."

How I had yearned for those words during the long, arid months of the "smoking gun" and the "hand in the cookie jar." Members of the committee must have felt the same way, too, for Jenner's words were to leave a profound mark on their final deliberations. That I did not know yet, but what I did know was heartening. The grave maxims of liberty, once invoked, instantly took the measure of meanness and effrontery. When the President's press spokesman, Ron Ziegler, denounced the committee's proceedings as a "kangaroo court," a wave of disgust coursed through Congress. The hour of the Founders had arrived.

The final deliberations of the House Judiciary Committee began on the evening of July 24, when Chairman Peter Rodino gaveled the committee to order before some forty-five million television viewers. The committee made a curious spectacle: thirty-eight strangers strung out on a two-tiered dais, a huge piece of furniture as unfamiliar as the faces of its occupants.

Chairman Rodino made the first opening remarks. His public career had been long, unblemished, and thoroughly undistinguished. Now the representative from Newark, New Jersey, linked hands with the Founding Fathers of our government. "For more than two years, there have been serious allegations, by people of good faith and sound intelligence, that the President, Richard M. Nixon, has committed grave and systematic violations of the Constitution." The framers of our Constitution, said Rodino, had provided an exact measure of a President's responsibilities. It was by the terms of the President's oath of office, prescribed in the Constitution, that the framers intended to hold Presidents "accountable and lawful."

That was to prove the keynote. That evening and over the following days, as each committee member delivered a statement, it became increasingly clear that the broad maxims of constitutional supremacy had taken command of the impeachment inquiry. "We will by this impeachment proceeding be establishing a standard of conduct for the President of the United States which will for all time be a matter of public record," Caldwell Butler, a conservative Virginia Republican, reminded his conservative constituents. "If we fail to impeach . . . we will have left condoned and unpunished an abuse of power totally without justification."

There were still White House loyalists of course; men who kept demanding to see a presidential directive ordering a crime and a documented "tie-in" between Nixon and his henchmen. Set against the great principle of constitutional supremacy, however, this common view was now exposed for what it was: reckless trifling with our ancient liberties. Can the United States permit a President "to escape accountability because he may choose to deal behind closed doors," asked James Mann, a South Carolina conservative. "Can anyone argue," asked George Danielson, a California liberal, "that if a President breaches his oath of office, he should not be removed?" In a voice of unforgettable power and richness, Barbara Jordan, a black legislator from Texas, sounded the grand theme of the committee with particular depth of feeling. Once, she said, the Constitution had excluded people of her race, but that evil had been remedied. "My faith in the Constitution is whole, it is complete, it is total and I am not going to sit here and be an idle spectator to the diminution, the subversion, the destruction of the Constitution."

On July 27 the Judiciary Committee voted 27 to 11 (six Republicans joining all twenty-one Democrats) to impeach Richard Nixon on the grounds that he and his agents had "prevented, obstructed, and impeded the administration of justice" in "violation of his constitutional oath faithfully to execute the office of President of the United States and, to the best of his ability, preserve, protect, and defend the Constitution of the United States, and in violation of his constitutional duty to take care that the laws be faithfully executed."

On July 29 the Judiciary Committee voted 28 to 10 to impeach Richard Nixon for "violating the constitutional rights of citizens, impairing the due and proper administration of justice and the conduct of lawful inquiries, or contravening the laws governing agencies of the executive branch. . . ." Thus, the illegal wiretaps, the sinister White House spies, the attempted use of the IRS to punish political opponents, the abuse of the CIA, and the break-in at Ellsberg's psychiatrist's office—misconduct hitherto deemed too "vague" for impeachment—now became part of a President's impeachable failure to abide by his constitutional oath to carry out his constitutional duty.

Lastly, on July 30 the Judiciary Committee, hoping to protect some future impeachment inquiry from a repetition of Nixon's defiance, voted 21 to 17 to impeach him for refusing to comply with the committee's subpoenas. "This concludes the work of the committee," Rodino announced at eleven o'clock that night. Armed with the wisdom of the Founders and the authority of America's republican principles, the committee had cut through the smoke screens, the lies, and the pettifogging that had muddled the Watergate crisis for so many months. It had subjected an imperious Presidency to the rule of fundamental law. It had demonstrated by resounding majorities that holding a President accountable is neither "liberal" nor "conservative," neither "Democratic" nor "Republican," but something far more basic to the American republic.

For months the forces of evasion had claimed that impeachment would "tear the country apart." But now the country was more united than it had been in years. The impeachment inquiry had sounded the chords of deepest patriotism, and Americans responded, it seemed to me, with quiet pride in their country and themselves. On Capitol Hill, congressional leaders reported that Nixon's impeachment would command three hundred votes at a minimum. The Senate began preparing for the President's trial. Then, as countless wits remarked, a funny thing happened on the way to the forum.

Back on July 24, the day the Judiciary Committee began its televised deliberations, the Supreme Court had ordered the President to surrender sixty-four taped conversations subpoenaed by the Watergate prosecutor. At the time I had regarded the decision chiefly as an auspicious omen for the evening's proceedings. Only Richard Nixon knew that the Court had signed his death warrant. On August 5 the President announced that he was making public three tapes that "may further damage my case." In fact they destroyed what little was left of it. Recorded six days after the Watergate break-in, they showed the President discussing detailed preparations for the cover-up with his chief of staff, Bob Haldeman. They showed the President and his henchman discussing how to use the CIA to block the FBI, which was coming dangerously close to the White House. "You call them in," says the President. "Good deal," says his aide. In short, the three tapes proved that the President had told nothing but lies about Watergate for twenty-six months. Every one of Nixon's ten Judiciary Committee defenders now announced that he favored Nixon's impeachment.

The President still had one last evasion: on the evening of August 8 he appeared on television to make his last important announcement. "I no longer have a strong enough political base in Congress," said Nixon, doing his best to imply that the resolution of a great constitutional crisis was mere maneuvering for political advantage. "Therefore, I shall resign the Presidency effective at noon tomorrow." He admitted to no wrongdoing. If he had made mistakes of judgment, "they were made in what I believed at the time to be in the best interests of the nation."

On the morning of August 9 the first President ever to resign from office boarded Air Force One and left town. The "system" had worked. But in the watches of the night, who has not asked himself now and then: How would it all have turned out had there been no White House tapes?

■ ■ ■ ■ ■ ■ ▪

7

Social Change

For many, the 1969 Woodstock rock music festival marked the "dawning of the age of Aquarius."

Levittown: The Buy of the Century

Alexander O. Boulton

When World War II ended, many feared that the sudden disruption of the production of planes, tanks, and other weapons as well as the return of millions of soldiers and sailors in search of civilian employment would create another Great Depression. Instead, after a brief period of adjustment, came a great boom.

Of the many causes of this boom was the revolution in the way houses were constructed. This housing revolution was organized by Alfred and William Levitt in suburban Long Island, east of New York City. As the architectural historian Alexander O. Boulton explains, in a little more than a decade beginning in 1947, the Levitts designed, built, and sold more than 17,000 single-family homes, thus creating a new community–Levittown.

This Sprawlig settlement and others like it built by the Levitts and their competitors changed the face of postwar America and altered the way countless Americans lived and thought. Not all these changes were salutary, as Boulton points out, for the residents of the new communities or even for the Levitts.

■ ■ ■ ■ ■ ■ ■

Years later, after the fall of his financial empire, William Levitt remembered with some satisfaction the story of a boy in Levittown, Long Island, who finished his prayers with "and God bless Mommy and Daddy and Mr. Levitt." Levitt may well have belonged in this trinity. When he sold his company in 1968, more Americans lived in suburbs than in cities, making this the first suburban nation in history, and his family was largely responsible for that.

Jim and Virginia Tolley met William Levitt in 1949 after waiting in line with three thousand other ex-GIs and their families to buy houses. Bill Levitt pointed to a plot on a map spread out on a long table and advised the Tolleys to buy the house he would build on that spot. Thanks to a large picture window with an eastern exposure, the Tolley's home, Levitt promised, would have sunshine in the coldest months of winter, and its large overhanging eaves would keep them cool in the summer. The Tolleys, who lived in a three-room apartment in Jackson Heights, bought the unbuilt house.

Their story was shared by the more than 3.5 million Americans who had lacked new housing in 1946, housing that had not been built during the Depression and the war. People kept marrying and having babies, but for almost two decades nobody was building new homes.

In providing affordable housing for thousands of Americans after the war, the Levitts were following a basic American success formula; they were at the right place at the right time. Abraham, the patriarch of the family, had been a real estate lawyer in Brooklyn. His two sons, William and Alfred, briefly attended New York

University before they began to buy land and design and build houses on a small scale. Alfred was the architect, learning his trade by trial and error, while William was the salesman and became the more public figure. The Second World War transformed their business. Encouraged by wartime contracts for large-scale housing projects, they followed the same mass-production principles that earlier in the century had been developed to build automobiles and that in wartime made ships and airplanes, tanks and guns.

Levittown, Long Island, thirty miles east of New York City, was the first of their postwar projects. Levittown was not the earliest planned in the country, but it was certainly the biggest, and it is still considered the largest housing project ever assembled by a single builder. Between 1947 and 1951 the Levitts built more than seventeen thousand houses, along with seven village greens and shopping centers, fourteen playgrounds, nine swimming pools, two bowling alleys, and a town hall, on land that had once been potato farms. In addition, the company sold land for schools at cost and donated sites for churches and fire stations.

Following the course of other American industries, the Levitts expanded both horizontally and vertically. They purchased timberland in California and a lumber mill, they built a nail factory, they established their own construction supply company to avoid middlemen, and they acquired a fleet of cement trucks and grading equipment. Instead of the product moving along a production line, however, the Levitt house stood stationary while men, materials, and equipment moved around it. At its peak of efficiency the Levitt organization could complete a house every fifteen minutes. Although these were not prefabricated houses all the materials, including the preassembled plumbing systems and precut lumber, were delivered to the site ready for construction. Twenty-seven steps were required to build a Levittown house, and each work crew had its specialized task. One man did nothing but move from house to house bolting washing machines to the floor. William Levitt liked to say his business was the General Motors of the housing industry. Indeed, the automobile seems to have inspired many of Levitt's practices. He even produced new house models each year, and a few Levittown families would actually buy updated versions, just as they bought Detroit's latest products.

The first style, a four-and-a-half room bungalow with steeply pitched roof, offered five slight variations on the placement of doors and windows. The result, according to a 1947 *Architectural Forum,* was "completely conventional, highly standardized, and aptly described in the public's favorite adjective, 'cute.'" A couple of years later the same publication moderated its tone of easy scorn to pronounce the style "a much better-than-average version of the darling of the depression decade—builder's Cape Cod."

Levittown houses were not what the popular 1960s song called "little boxes of ticky-tacky." They were exceptionally well built, the product of some of the most innovative methods and materials in the industry. Taking a page from Frank Lloyd Wright's Usonian houses, Levittown homes stood on concrete slab foundations (they had no basements), in which copper coils provided radiant heating. The Tolleys were among the first customers for the 1949 ranch-style houses that replaced the earlier Cape Cod design. The ranches featured Thermopane glass picture windows, fireplaces opening into two rooms, and carports instead of garages. In addi-

Although later mocked as "little boxes made of ticky-tacky," Levittown houses allowed many to realize the dream of owning their own home.

tion, they had built-in closets and bookcases and swinging shelf units that acted as walls to open up or close the space between kitchen, living room, and entry passage. At twenty-five by thirty-two, the houses were also two feet longer than the earlier models, and they offered as standard features built-in appliances that were only just coming into general use; many houses contained Bendix washing machines and Admiral television sets. The fixed price of $7,990 allowed the Levitts to advertise "the housing deal of the century." It was probably true. Levitt and his sons seemed to be practically giving homes away. Thousands of families bought into new Levittowns in Pennsylvania, New Jersey, Illinois, Michigan, and even Paris and Puerto Rico. The techniques that the Levitts initiated have been copied by home builders throughout the country ever since.

Despite its immediate success, from the earliest days Levittown also stood as a metaphor for all the possible failings of postwar America. The architectural critic Lewis Mumford is said to have declared the tract an "instant slum" when he first saw it, and he certainly was aiming at Levittown when he condemned the postwar

American suburb for its "multitude of uniform, unidentifiable houses, lined up inflexibly, at uniform distances, on uniform roads, in a treeless communal waste, inhabited by people of the same class, the same age group, witnessing the same television performances, eating the same prefabricated foods, from the same freezers, conforming in every inward and outward respect to the same common mold." Some of the early rules, requiring the neighbors to mow their lawns every week, forbidding fences, or banning the hanging out of laundry on weekends, did indeed speak of the kind of regimentation Mumford snobbishly abhorred.

Today's visitor to the original Long Island Levittown might be surprised by many of those early criticisms. Now almost fifty years old, most of the houses have been so extensively remodeled that it is often difficult to distinguish the basic Cape Cod or ranch inside its Tudor half-timbering or postmodern, classical eclecticism. Greenery and shade trees have enveloped the bare landscape of the 1950s and Japanese sand gardens, Renaissance topiary, and electrically generated brooks and waterfalls decorate many of Levittown's standard sixty-by-one-hundred-foot plots. The place now seems not the model of mass conformity but a monument to American individualism.

Probably Levittown was never the drab and monotonous place its critics imagined. For many early residents it allowed cultural diversity to flourish. Pre-war inner-city neighborhoods often had ethnic divisions unknown in Levittown. Louis and Marylin Cuviello, who bought a one-bathroom house in 1949 and reared eleven children there, found themselves moving in a wider world than the one they had known in the city. She was a German-American married to an Italian-American, and in their Levittown neighborhood most of the householders were Jewish. During their first years there the Cuviellos took classes in Judaism at the local synagogue, and they often celebrated both Passover and Christmas with their neighbors.

But this American idyll was not for everyone. In 1949, after Gene Burnett, like his fellow veteran Jim Tolley, saw advertisements for Levittown in several New York newspapers, he drove to Long Island with his fiancée. The Levittown salesman refused to give him an application form. "It's not me," the agent said. "The builders have not at this time decided to sell to Negroes." This pattern of racial exclusion was set in 1947, when rental contracts prohibited "the premises to be used or occupied by any person other than a member of the Caucasian race." In 1992 Gene Burnett, now a retired sergeant in the Suffolk County, Long Island, Police Department, told a reporter, "I'll never forget the ride back to East Harlem."

There were other such episodes. Bill Cotter, a retired auto mechanic, and his family sublet a house in Levittown in 1953. When his sublet expired, he was informed that he would not be allowed either to rent or to own a house in Levittown. Despite the protests of friendly neighbors, who launched a petition drive in their behalf, Cotter, his wife, and their five children were forced to vacate. These racial policies persisted. As late as the 1980s real estate agents in the area assured white home buyers that they did not sell to blacks, and in 1990 the census revealed that .03 percent of Levittown's population—127 out of more than 400,000—was African-American.

Levittown has been both celebrated and denounced as the fruit of American laissez-faire capitalism. In fact, it may more accurately be described as the successful result of an alliance between government and private enterprise. Levittown and the rise of American suburbia in general could not have happened without attractive loan packages for home buyers guaranteed by the FHA and the VA. Tax breaks, such as the deductibility of mortgages, encouraged suburbanites, who were also helped by a burst of federally funded highway construction. For almost half a century after World War II, the government has played a major role in helping consumers obtain the products of industry—washing machines, television sets, cars, and, especially, houses. For most of us it's been a great ride.

For Bill Levitt it's been a roller coaster. Things started to go sour for him after the sale of his company to ITT in 1968. He received about fifty million dollars in ITT stock and launched a spending spree that did not stop until the courts stepped in. Levitt's agreement with ITT prohibited him from building projects in the United States for ten years, so he turned elsewhere: housing in Nigeria and Venezuela, oil drilling in Israel, and housing and irrigation in Iran—just before the fall of the shah. He invested in rotary engines, recording companies, and pharmacies. Most of the projects failed. Meanwhile, the ITT stock that was his major capital asset plummeted from $104 to $12 a share in the first four years.

Levitt re-entered the housing market in the United States in 1978 with projects in Orlando and Tampa, Florida. Construction and sales moved quickly at first but soon slowed as contractors began to sue for payment. More than two thousand people, some of them original Levittowners who were now ready to retire, paid deposits for houses in the Florida Levittowns that were never built. Levitt, it was later discovered, had been using the funds from his Florida projects to support his expensive habits. Along the way he had removed more than ten million dollars from a charitable foundation that his family had established. These legal and financial problems have made Bill Levitt a virtual hermit, and today he lives in seclusion not far from the Long Island Levittown that bears his name.

Levittown residents have mixed feelings about their unique heritage. Periodically some of them have attempted to redraw the boundaries of their town line so they could have more elegant addresses. More recently, proud members of the Levittown Historical Society have worked to encourage a new appreciation for their community. They are pushing to establish historic landmark districts while they try to preserve the few houses that have remained relatively unchanged over the years. They are also casting a wide net among their neighbors and former neighbors to gather artifacts and memorabilia for a museum. Recently the Smithsonian Institution announced that it was looking for an original Levittown house to add to its American domestic-life collection. Some African-American groups continue to question the virtue of memorializing a policy of exclusion, but the history-minded residents are pressing ahead, and Eddie Bortell, the Historical Society's vice president, is optimistic. If the work of the historical society has helped bring attention to some of these painful questions, he says, then that in itself is a reward for its efforts.

■ ■ ■ ■ ■ ■ ■

Desegregating the Schools

Liva Baker

Any list of major events in American history and any account of the shifting course of race relations in the United States is bound to include the Supreme Court case known officially as *Brown* v. *the Board of Education of the City of Topeka.* The importance of key Supreme Court decisions has already been pointed out in my article on the case of *Marbury* v. *Madison* and in Alan F. Westin's essay "Ride-In." In 1896, in the case known as *Plessy* v. *Ferguson,* the Court had decided that blacks could be segregated from whites in railroad cars (and by implication in schools) provided that their facilities were equal in quality to those of whites. Over the years this "separate but equal" rule determined how the Court dealt with racial questions. Segregation was broken down to some extent, but only after it had been conclusively demonstrated that the facilities provided for blacks were inferior to those available to whites.

Liva Baker's account of how the Court reached the contrary conclusion in *Brown* v. *Board of Education* begins with an earlier case involving voting (*Smith* v. *Allwright,* 1944). She goes on to show how the members of the Court finally came to conclude that separate was inherently unequal and therefore unconstitutional. Beyond this, she explains how the justices dealt with the socially explosive question, "*how* and *when* was desegregation to be achieved?" Baker is the author of *Felix Frankfurter,* a biography of a key actor in the drama she describes here.

■ ■ ■ ■ ■ ■ ▪

On May 17, 1954, the Supreme Court of the United States destroyed the legal basis for racial segregation in public schools. As it almost had to be in a case that stirred elemental passions, the decision was unanimous. It was also, as Chief Justice Earl Warren had told the other justices ten days earlier it must be, "short, readable by the lay public, non-rhetorical, unemotional, and, above all, non-accusatory."

As the Chief Justice read the historic and potentially divisive opinion the nine justices—Justice Robert H. Jackson had left his hospital bed to be present—sat expressionless and calm, the rare picture of august solidarity belying three years of judicial soul-searching that had led to this moment.

. . . The 1954 desegregation decision, which still is attended by controversy, not only altered the nation's educational patterns but also eroded a way of life and touched people's most sensitive nerves.

Like most cases that come to the Supreme Court, *Brown* v. *Board of Education* was begun in a small way by quite ordinary people. Linda Brown, of Topeka, Kansas, in 1951 a fourth-grade student at a public elementary school for Negroes a long walk and a bus trip from her home, wanted to attend a nearby public elementary school for white children. She was turned away. Her father, the Reverend Oliver Brown, and twelve other parents sued the Topeka Board of Education in the

Linda Brown of Topeka, Kansas, posed for the camera in 1953. She was turned away from her neighborhood white elementary school, an action that set in motion the events leading to the momentous Brown v. Board of Education decision.

local federal court. A special three-judge panel heard the case and decided that since Negro and white schools in Topeka were substantially equal, the Negroes were not discriminated against and they could not attend white schools. The Browns and the other parents appealed to the Supreme Court.

Since the Constitutional Convention of 1789 the issue of race had either been compromised or evaded, except during Reconstruction. No branch of government had been willing to confront it squarely, and as Justice Jackson commented during the oral argument of *Brown*, "I suppose that realistically the reason this case is here is that action couldn't be obtained from Congress." Beginning in the late 1930's, the Supreme Court had begun gradually but steadily desegregating American life; restrictive covenants that insured residential segregation, the white primary, segregated education in graduate schools, Jim Crow laws—these and others had collapsed before the Supreme Court. Now the court was forced to face the most explosive issue of all: segregation in public elementary schools.

The justices were not unworldly men, however avidly they sometimes seemed to cultivate an aura of monasticism. Before appointment to the Supreme Court each of them had held some public office. During their deliberations they were grimly aware that their decisions—whether they would hear the case or not hear it; whether, if they did hear it, they declared racial segregation in public schools constitutional or unconstitutional—presaged resentment at best, and probably resistance, from a large segment of the population.

They spent an extraordinary amount of time discussing the problem, examining it from historical, legal, political, and social perspectives. When the Brown case first reached the Supreme Court late in 1951, the justices spent seven months discussing whether they would even hear it. Finally, on June 7, 1952, they agreed that the court could note *probable* jurisdiction. . . .

Once that jurisdictional obstacle was hurdled, however, the court added other school segregation cases and combined them for argument until they had a total of five cases: one from the border state of Kansas, one each from rural Virginia and South Carolina, one from North-oriented Delaware, and one from federally administered District of Columbia. Together these cases gave the Supreme Court a detailed picture of racial segregation by law in American public schools. (At the time, state constitutional provisions and laws or local ordinances required the schools of seventeen southern and border states and the District of Columbia to be segregated; in four other states—Arizona, Kansas, New Mexico, and Wyoming—segregated schools were legally permitted on an optional basis.)

The court that was to hear these five segregation cases argued in December, 1952, was judicially unpredictable. At one end were two liberal activists: justices Hugo L. Black, former United States senator from Alabama, and William O. Douglas, former Yale law professor and chairman of the Securities and Exchange Commission. Appointed to the Supreme Court by President Franklin D. Roosevelt, both were quick to use the power of the court in the name of "social justice."

The rest of the court was enigmatic on the issue of racial segregation in public schools. Indianian Sherman Minton had been an administrative aide to President Franklin D. Roosevelt and a close friend of Harry S. Truman, with whom he entered the Senate in 1935. He was appointed to the Supreme Court by President Truman in 1949. Nothing in his writings indicated his position in these segregation cases.

The *New York Times* described Justice Harold H. Burton, on his appointment to the Supreme Court in 1945, as a "liberal of marked independence." As a justice, however, he seemed to lean toward a conservative stance; on civil rights he had voted both ways.

Justice Jackson, Solicitor General and Attorney General under Roosevelt, vigorous prosecutor of war criminals at Nuremberg, assumed the mantle of judicial restraint when he was appointed to the Supreme Court in 1941; he was hesitant to overrule state and federal enactments, believing, like his frequent judicial ally Justice Frankfurter, that undesirability could not be equated with unconstitutionality.

At the Senate hearings on his appointment to the Supreme Court in 1949, Justice Tom C. Clark, a Texas protégé of Senator Tom Connally and Representative Sam Rayburn, had been denounced by Negro groups for failing to protect Negro civil rights when he was Attorney General. Yet it was under Clark's stewardship that the Justice Department began to file amicus curiae (friend of the court) briefs defining the administration's legal positions; these consistently argued against racial discrimination and became a significant part of later civil-rights litigation. Clark had also, as president of the Federal Bar Association, demanded admission of Negro lawyers, and in 1950 had written a concurring opinion when the Supreme Court quashed a criminal indictment of a Negro on the grounds that Negroes had been discriminated against in the selection of grand jury panels. Clark's record looked "liberal" in 1952; however, he had not yet had to face the question whether racial segregation in public schools denied "equal protection of the laws."

Justice Stanley F. Reed came from the border state of Kentucky and had been Solicitor General under Roosevelt, arguing for the validity of NRA, TVA, the Wagner Act, and other of the President's measures. Appointed to the Supreme Court in 1938, he had become somewhat conservative but had also written a vigorous defense of Negro voting rights in 1944. How Reed came to write that 1944 opinion reveals not a little of the political consideration that goes into a major decision of the Supreme Court.

At conference on January 15, 1944, the Supreme Court decided to declare the Texas exclusion of Negroes from primary elections unconstitutional. Felix Frankfurter was assigned to write the opinion. The case was called *Smith* v. *Allwright*.

". . . That afternoon," a Frankfurter memorandum reads, "Bob Jackson came to see me. . . . He thought it was a very great mistake to have me write the *Allwright* opinion. For a good part of the country the subject—Negro disenfranchisement—was in the domain of the irrational and we have to take account of such facts. At best it will be very unpalatable to the South and should not be exacerbated by having the opinion written by a member of the Court who has, from the point of view of Southern prejudice, three disqualifications: 'You are a New Englander, you are a Jew and you are not a Democrat—at least not recognized as such.'" Frankfurter replied that he saw Jackson's point; Jackson was free, Frankfurter said, to suggest to the Chief Justice—Harlan Fiske Stone at that time—that the opinion be reassigned. When Stone later asked Frankfurter to suggest a name, Frankfurter declared that "the job required, of course, delicacy of treatment and absence of a raucous voice and that I thought of the Southerners Reed was the better of the two for the job. He agreed to that. . . ."

Thus, on April 3, 1944, in the case of *Smith* v. *Allwright*, the Texas white primary was invalidated. Justice Reed—Southerner, Protestant, and Democrat—spoke for the majority: "The United States is a constitutional democracy. Its organic law grants to all citizens a right to participate in the choice of elected officials without restriction by any State because of race."

In 1952, in addition to these seven justices, there were two crucial men on the court that was to hear the school segregation cases: Chief Justice Fred M. Vinson and Felix Frankfurter. But Vinson died before the school segregation cases were decided, and so what he would have done can only be a matter of speculation.

He was succeeded by Earl Warren, three-term governor of California and Republican candidate for Vice President in 1948. A hearty, amiable man on the surface, he was expected to be, as one of his biographers put it, "the colorless manager of a team of all-stars." No one, including President Dwight D. Eisenhower, who appointed him, expected a courageous, reforming chief justice. Justice Frankfurter wrote his impressions of Warren to a young English friend at the time of the appointment:

> . . . He has not had an eminent legal career, but he might well have had had he not been deflected from the practice of law into public life. He brings to his work that largeness of experience and breadth of outlook which may well make him a very

good Chief Justice provided he has some other qualities which, from what I have seen, I believe he has. First and foremost, complete absorption in the work of the Court is demanded. That is not as easy to attain as you might think, because this is a very foolish and distracting town. Secondly, he must have great industry because . . . for about nine months of the year it is a steady grind. Further, he must have the capacity to learn, he must be alert to the range and complexities of the problems that come before this Court. . . . One more requisite. . . . Intent, open-minded, patient listening is a surprisingly rare faculty even of judges. The new Chief Justice has it, I believe, to a rare degree.

Warren seemed, like most of the court, judicially unpredictable. He had never been able to live down his major role as California attorney general in sending Japanese and Japanese-Americans in the state to detention camps at the outbreak of World War II. But beyond this questionable moment in his career, there was a bold record as crusading district attorney in Alameda County and a progressive governorship during which Warren battled annually against a hostile legislature for social legislation and reforms.

The other crucial man on the Supreme Court in 1952 was Felix Frankfurter. Appointed to the Supreme Court in 1939 by Roosevelt, Justice Frankfurter had eagerly joined in the decisions invalidating legal segregation prior to the Brown case. He had, however, consistently laid a light restraining hand on his brethren.

He was a sworn enemy of racial discrimination; he had served on the legal committee of the NAACP from 1929 until he was appointed to the Supreme Court (when he scrupulously severed connections with all organizations). He was, however, aware of the potential for divisiveness in racial discrimination cases before the court. He wrote in a note to Justice Wiley B. Rutledge regarding a 1948 case of racial discrimination on an excursion boat: ". . . Considerable practical experience with problems of race relations led me to the conclusion that the ugly practices of racial discrimination should be dealt with by eloquence of action but with austerity of speech. . . ." Likewise, when Chief Justice Vinson's draft opinion in a 1950 case involving segregation in graduate schools was circulated among the justices for suggestions—as is customary on the court—Frankfurter urged restraint in the rhetoric. The opinion, he said, ought to accomplish "the desired result without needlessly stirring the kind of feelings that are felt even by truly liberal and high-minded southerners. . . . One does not have to say everything that is so. . . . The shorter the opinion, the more there is an appearance of unexcitement and inevitability about it, the better. . . ."

The school desegregation decisions of 1952–1955 were broken into two parts. The first was *whether* racial segregation in public schools was constitutional or unconstitutional; inherent in this question was whether it was the business of the court or the business of Congress to deal with the problem. The court struggled nearly a year before making up its mind on that question.

The second part of the decisions was the question of remedy: *How* and *when* was desegregation to be achieved? This question was not answered for a full year after the court declared racial segregation in public schools unconstitutional, in May of 1954. The delay—which gave the South a breathing spell—was used to forge a compromise between immediate wholesale desegregation and gradual adjustment to the court's decision; between Negro rights and southern hostility. That year was full of judicial pondering and introspection that scotch any notion that the court arbitrarily exerted its power.

The segregation cases had been argued the first time in December, 1952. Lawyers—mostly from the NAACP—argued for the Negro plaintiffs that state school segregation laws denied to Negroes the equal protection guaranteed under the Fourteenth Amendment of the Constitution. Attorneys for the southern school districts countered that school segregation involved no constitutional rights; it was, they said, strictly a state legislative matter. The court listened, waited six months, and then in June, 1953, scheduled the cases for reargument the following term, with counsel for both sides instructed this time to address themselves to five specific questions.

The first three questions concerned the original intent of the framers of the Fourteenth Amendment regarding racial segregation in public schools.

That amendment, passed by a Republican Congress in 1866 in the heat of post-Civil War passion, says nothing about racial segregation in public schools; but neither does it say anything about housing or transportation or juries, areas in which the Supreme Court had, by 1953, already used it to invalidate discriminatory practices. Like the rest of the Constitution, the Fourteenth Amendment is a vessel into which judges had, over the years, poured many meanings. Its crucial first section merely said: "No State shall . . . deny to any person within its jurisdiction the equal protection of the laws." Section 5 gives Congress the power to enforce the amendment's provisions "by appropriate legislation."

Now in 1953 the Supreme Court wanted to know: Did the authors of the Fourteenth Amendment in fact intend desegregation of public schools either at the time of their writing or in the future? Exhaustive research by the court and the contending parties never revealed a clear answer to that.

Questions four and five asked how desegregation might be achieved, prompting observers to speculate that the court—still headed by Chief Justice Vinson—had already decided to declare racial segregation in public schools unconstitutional.

For the scheduled rehearing the court extended an invitation to the Attorney General of the United States to participate in oral arguments. A Frankfurter memorandum of June 8, 1953, explained that the new administration under Eisenhower "may have the responsibility of carrying out a decision full of perplexities; it should therefore be asked to face that responsibility as part of our process of adjudication. . . ." When the rearguments were heard in December, 1953, their significant portions turned out to be those dealing with the question of a remedy for segregation if deemed warranted.

NAACP lawyers, led by Thurgood Marshall, later to be appointed to the Supreme Court himself, urged immediate admission of Negro children to the schools of their choice, but reluctantly acknowledged that the Supreme Court had the power to effect instead a gradual adjustment. The southern states, whose chief attorney was John W. Davis, 1924 Democratic Presidential candidate, argued that the Supreme Court had the power to order a gradual process, but no effective way of mandating the details. "Your Honors do not sit, and cannot sit, as a glorified

Board of Education for the State of South Carolina or any other State," John Davis declared.

At this stage of the proceedings the government's position was anomalous. The brief filed by the Eisenhower administration did not urge the court to hold public school segregation unconstitutional, although its overall tenor supported such a holding. Some of the lawyers who worked on it have said that an original version did include a direct call for the court to declare public school segregation unconstitutional but that it was diluted by either Attorney General Herbert Brownell or President Eisenhower. Brownell has denied this, saying that the brief never contained such a call. But he agreed—and advised Eisenhower—that if J. Lee Rankin, the Assistant Attorney General who was to argue for the government in court, was asked during oral argument for the administration's position, he would answer that the court should hold public school segregation unconstitutional—which was what Rankin actually did.

On the question of how desegregation could be accomplished, the government suggested remanding the cases to the lower courts, where, in the light of local conditions, decrees would be formulated and a gradual adjustment be made.

Shortly after this December reargument and four months before the Supreme Court would officially declare public school segregation unconstitutional, Justice Frankfurter addressed himself, in a memorandum for his associates, to the questions of *how* and *when*. He explained, in a covering note, that he was thinking out loud and that "sometimes one's thinking, whether good or bad, may stimulate good thoughts in others." He added parenthetically that "the typewriting was done under conditions of strictest security."

Whether the court was already thinking in terms of two decisions rather than one and had reached unanimity is not known. The memorandum's cautious restraint seems to indicate, however, that Frankfurter, in an attempt to achieve unanimity, was articulating the concerns of whatever recalcitrant justices remained, and perhaps trying to point out that implementation, while it had major difficulties, was not impossible. Because it introduces the concept of "with all deliberate speed," it is one of the most important pieces of writing on the segregation cases prior to their being decided.

Although, Frankfurter told his brethren, the court had before it only five individual cases, "we are asked in effect to transform state-wide school systems in nearly a score of states," and it was not going to be easy. First the court must define, Frankfurter wrote, exactly what the required result was. For the first time in the written discussions, the word *integration* was used; it has since become the heart of much of the controversy surrounding school racial problems. "Integration," Frankfurter said, "that is, 'equal protection,' can readily be achieved by lowering the standards of those who at the start are, in the phrase of George Orwell, 'more equal'. . . . It would indeed make a mockery of the Constitutional adjudication designed to vindicate a claim to equal treatment, to achieve 'integrated' but lower educational standards."

As to the time factor, the court does its duty, he explained, "if it gets effectively under way the righting of a wrong. When the wrong is a deeply rooted state policy the court does its duty if it decrees measures that reverse the direction of the un-

Thurgood Marshall (center), then special counsel of the NAACP, with the two other attorneys who successfully argued the landmark case. Marshall was later appointed to the Supreme Court in 1967.

constitutional policy so as to uproot it 'with all deliberate speed.'" This was a phrase Frankfurter had used previously in at least three decisions. Like *integration*, it became a controversial issue in the desegregation process.

Tentatively, Frankfurter preferred some gradual process of desegregation. "The Court does not know," he wrote, "that a simple scrambling of the two school systems may not work. It surely cannot assume that scrambling is all there is to it. . . . One is surely entitled to suspect that spreading the adjustment over time will more effectively accomplish the desired end. . . ."

However, he warned, before the court could fashion a decree, it faced an enormous and complex fact-finding task, made more difficult by the various interpretations that could be applied to facts "different in kind than courts usually consider" and "embedded in deep feeling."

"Physical, educational, budgetary, and time factors" must be considered; there would be problems for both teachers and students, and "problems caused by shifts in population which these readjustments may well induce." All these must be ascertained in a complex framework where "the spread of differences in the ratios of white to colored population among the various counties in different States is very considerable."

Awareness of these difficulties accounts for the fact that a remedy for segregated schools did not appear in the May 17, 1954, decision. The justices simply declared racially segregated schools unconstitutional, and the last paragraph of the unanimous opinion read:

> Because these are class actions, because of the wide applicability of this decision, and because of the great variety of local conditions, the formulation of decrees in these cases presents problems of considerable complexity. We have now announced that such segregation is a denial of the equal protection of the laws. In order that we may have the full assistance of the parties in formulating decrees, the cases will be restored to the docket, and the parties are requested to present further argument on questions 4 and 5 [the questions of *how*] previously propounded by the Court for the reargument this Term.

The Attorney General of the United States as well as the attorneys general of the states requiring or permitting segregation in public education were invited to participate as amici curiae. Undoubtedly the court hoped that by inviting participation of the states—most of them southern—that permitted or required segregation, the South itself, at least on an official level, would accept the inevitability of change and join in devising an acceptable remedy.

The justices knew they had touched sensitive nerves, but they were probably not prepared for the widespread resistance their decision drew, largely in the South. Emotion outran reason; invective submerged valid legal debate. Deep South prosegregationist states such as Alabama, Georgia, and Mississippi did not accept the court's invitation to participate in reargument lest they endow the May 17, 1954, decision with recognition. Vacationing in Massachusetts, Frankfurter mused on the problem and, in a letter to Warren, recommended that the court gather data on what "administrative, financial, commonsensical and other considerations legitimately enter" the normal school-districting process so as to have some frame of reference in dealing with southern redistricting. "The Southern States are fever patients. Let us find out, if we can, what healthy bodies do about such things in order to guard against attributing to the fever conduct and consequences that are not fairly attributable to fever. . . ."

Following Frankfurter's suggestion, Chief Justice Warren circulated among the justices in November, 1954, a seventy-nine-page Segregation Research Report containing background information to be referred to by the justices in thinking about implementing their decision of the past May. It included a survey of normal school-districting practices, a summary of southern reaction to the May 17 decision, analyses of previously desegregated schools, proposed plans to abolish public schools, discussion of court jurisdiction over school districting, and maps of school districts showing distribution of white and Negro students. The report pointed up the complexity of the *how* problem facing the Supreme Court: How could nine justices, sitting in their marble palace in Washington, with their limited knowledge of local problems, devise a formula that could be applied to such a diversified collection of school districts? The *when* was equally a problem: "'Forthwith' would either be given a meaning short of immediacy or introduce a range of leeway to render it imprecise," Frankfurter said in a memorandum of February 10, 1955. "And it would most certainly provoke resentment. Yet any limitation allowing a specific number of years in which to achieve compliance could well be treated as a grace period during which nothing need be done."

The segregation cases were reargued from April 11 to 14, 1955. On the last of those days, Frankfurter wrote to his colleagues: "Hamilton Basso is, as I dare say you know, a very perceptive Southern writer, and carries weight, I believe, both North and South. A letter of his in last Sunday's *New York Times* has for me the persuasiveness not of novelty but of emphasis."

Basso's letter, which Frankfurter reproduced, was an urgent *cri de coeur* for understanding of the South's present defiant temper. Segregation, it said, like slavery the century before, "was the foremost preoccupation of the Southern mind" in the press and in conversation. Out of a confusion of opinion, ranging from "logical argument to irrational bitterness," Basso wrote, "that which most clearly emerges is a feeling of deep resentment over what is looked upon as outside pressure. . . . It [the South] has gone far toward convincing itself that it is going to be 'pressured' in a quick reorganization of its whole society . . . and that the rest of the country is almost callously indifferent to the difficulties implicit in such a course."

Two days later, on April 16, 1955, the justices met in conference, still searching—against the background of angry resistance—for answers to the questions they had asked in court. Chief Justice Warren opened the discussion with his admission that he himself had not reached a fixed opinion; perhaps the brethren could talk it over, as they had the original desegregation decision.

There were, Warren began, some things the court should not do. The Supreme Court ought not to tell the lower courts what to do; it should not fix a definite date for completion of desegregation nor even suggest to a lower court that that court should set a date, nor should the Supreme Court dictate any procedural requirement. Clearly, Their Honors were not going to sit as a "super school board."

What appealed to Warren at the time, rather than a formal decree, was an opinion citing factors for the lower courts to consider, with some Supreme Court guidance; it would, he explained, be rather cruel to shift back and let them flounder. There were two ground rules to be observed: (1) these were class actions—that is, as the May 17, 1954, decision had declared, they affected everyone similarly situated, not only the plaintiffs—and (2) the lower courts should be entitled to consider physical factors but not psychological attitudes.

Adhering to conference protocol, the other justices spoke in turn, from the most senior (Black) to the most junior (John Marshall Harlan, who had replaced Robert Jackson on Jackson's death). There was little agreement among them except as to the fact that the final opinion should be unanimous. Justice Black expressed the feeling when he declared that if a unanimous opinion were humanly possible, he would do everything he could to achieve it. Nonetheless, the Alabaman differed with Chief Justice Warren. He knew, he said, every southern district judge on anyone's list, and not one of them was going to be for desegregation. Black advised saying and doing as little as possible; nothing was more important than that the Supreme Court should not issue what it could not enforce. He advised reiterating the unconstitutionality of racial segregation in public schools, formulating a decree affecting only the five cases before the court, and enjoining school boards from refusing to admit these specific Negro students.

Perhaps no one except the justices themselves will ever know exactly how the Warren-Black points of view were reconciled. However, the unanimity so necessary to this kind of decision was in some way achieved, and six weeks after the April 16 conference, on May 31, 1955, Chief Justice Earl Warren read the Supreme Court's unanimous opinion, outlining that court's plan for desegregating the nation's schools. It was very much a Warren opinion, conforming to the points he had made in the April 16 conference.

The court showed that *it* was not "callously indifferent" to the difficulties of reorganizing southern society, as Hamilton Basso had said the South believed most of the nation was. The decision in fact gave every opportunity to the South to itself solve whatever problems accompanied desegregation—and in its own good time.

As the 1954 decision had been clearly for the Negro plaintiffs, this 1955 decision was clearly for the defendant school boards. Together, the two decisions were an attempt to balance the claims of the two parties, to reconcile "public and private needs."

The court solved the *how* of desegregation by attempting to be neither so vague as to invite "confusion and evasion" nor so specific that the court would become the nation's school board. The burden of desegregating was placed on the local school boards, with the lower courts required to consider "whether the action of school authorities constitutes good faith implementation of the governing constitutional principles."

But the lower courts were not left to flounder. As Warren had suggested in the April 16 conference, they were given general guidelines: they were to adjust and reconcile "public and private needs"; they could consider "problems related to administration, arising from the physical conditions of the school plant, transportation system, personnel, revision of school districts and attendance areas into compact units to achieve a system of determining admission to the public schools on a non-racial basis"; and there was to be no gerrymandering. However, as Chief Justice Warren had also said in the April 16 conference, psychological factors were to be disallowed, and the opinion reaffirmed it: "the vitality of these constitutional principles cannot be allowed to yield simply because of disagreement with them."

The crucial question of *when* was reserved until the last paragraph. It was not going to be the beginning of the next school term, as NAACP lawyers had urged.

Frankfurter had warned the court in a memorandum against requiring a deadline, because, he said, it would have to be an arbitrary deadline and would be considered "an imposition of our will without the ascertainment . . . of the local situation. And it would tend to alienate instead of enlist favorable or educable local sentiment." Instead, the phrase in Frankfurter's January, 1954, memorandum appeared in the final decision: "the cases are remanded to the District Courts to take such proceedings and enter such orders and decrees consistent with this opinion as are necessary and proper to admit to public schools on a racially nondiscriminatory basis with all deliberate speed the parties to these cases. . . ."

In the years since the desegregation decisions most observers have credited Chief Justice Warren with welding the various individuals together to achieve unanimity. Warren modestly denies it: "It was the most self-effacing job ever written there. . . . Everyone there was so cooperative and so helpful" he has said, going on to give credit to the three Southerners on the court—Clark, Reed, and Black—"not because they developed the legal philosophy of it, but because they had the courage to do what was done." It was, Warren points out, "tough for them to go home" for a time.

Justice Frankfurter had made the same observation, but with an added dimension, in a note he wrote to Justice Reed three days after the 1954 decision. It read:

> History does not record dangers averted. I have no doubt that if the *Segregation* cases had reached decision last Term there would have been four dissenters—Vinson, Reed, Jackson and Clark—and certainly several opinions for the majority view. That would have been catastrophic. And if we had not had unanimity now inevitably there would have been more than one opinion for the majority. That would have been disastrous.
>
> It ought to give you much satisfaction to be able to say, as you have every right to say, "I have done the State some service." I am inclined to think, indeed I believe, in no single act since you have been on this Court have you done the Republic a more lasting service. I am not unaware of the hard struggle this involved in the conscience of your mind and in the mind of your conscience. I am not unaware, because all I have to do is look within.
>
> As a citizen of the Republic, even more than as a colleague, I feel deep gratitude for your share in what I believe to be a great good for our nation.

■ ■ ■ ■ ■ ■ ■

The Housework Revolution

Ruth Schwartz Cowan

The writing of the history of past events is greatly influenced by the present in several ways, some obvious, some subtle. The modern women's movement, for example, has led historians to investigate the role and activities of women in previous periods, and since the movement has resulted in more women entering the work force and seeking to become professionals of every sort, it has led to a rapid increase in the number of women historians. These historians, in turn, have both been drawn to the study of women's history and been influenced in how they interpret the past by their personal experiences as women.

This essay by Professor Ruth Schwartz Cowan of the State University of New York at Stony Brook illustrates these points. She specializes in women's history, but also in the history of science and technology. So in dealing with the impact of household appliances such as vacuum cleaners and washing machines, she is interested not only in how these "laborsaving" appliances worked but also in how they affected the lives of the women who used them. The automobile, which presumably has made life freer and easier, is for anyone running a household, Professor Cowan explains, just another mechanical appliance, a necessary tool for getting the job done. Perhaps a male historian might have arrived at this conclusion, but Cowan makes clear that personal experience lay behind her insight.

■ ■ ■ ■ ■ ■ ■

Things are seldom what they seem. Skim milk masquerades as cream. And laborsaving household appliances often do not save labor. This is the surprising conclusion reached by a small army of historians, sociologists, and home economists who have undertaken, in recent years, to study the one form of work that has turned out to be most resistant to inquiry and analysis—namely, housework.

During the first half of the twentieth century, the average American household was transformed by the introduction of a group of machines that profoundly altered the daily lives of housewives; the forty years between 1920 and 1960 witnessed what might be aptly called the "industrial revolution in the home." Where once there had been a wood- or coal-burning stove there now was a gas or electric range. Clothes that had once been scrubbed on a metal washboard were now tossed into a tub and cleansed by an electrically driven agitator. The dryer replaced the clothesline; the vacuum cleaner replaced the broom; the refrigerator replaced the icebox and the root cellar; an automatic pump, some piping, and a tap replaced the hand pump, the bucket, and the well. No one had to chop and haul wood any more. No one had to shovel out ashes or beat rugs or carry water; no one even had to toss egg whites with a fork for an hour to make an angel food cake.

And yet American housewives in 1960, 1970, and even 1980 continued to log about the same number of hours at their work as their grandmothers and mothers had in 1910, 1920, and 1930. The earliest time studies of housewives date from the very same period in which time studies of other workers were becoming popular—the first three decades of the twentieth century. The sample sizes of these studies were usually quite small, and they did not always define housework in precisely the same way (some counted an hour spent taking children to the playground as "work," while others called it "leisure"), but their results were more or less consistent: whether rural or urban, the average American housewife performed fifty to sixty hours of unpaid work in her home every week, and the only variable that significantly altered this was the number of small children.

A half-century later not much had changed. Survey research had become much more sophisticated, and sample sizes had grown considerably, but the results of the time studies remained surprisingly consistent. The average American housewife, now armed with dozens of motors and thousands of electronic chips, still spends fifty to sixty hours a week doing housework. The only variable that significantly altered the size of that number was full-time employment in the labor force; "working" housewives cut down the average number of hours that they spend cooking and cleaning, shopping and chauffeuring, to a not insignificant thirty-five—virtually the equivalent of another full-time job.

How can this be true? Surely even the most sophisticated advertising copywriter of all times could not fool almost the entire American population over the course of at least three generations. Laborsaving devices must be saving something, or Americans would not continue, year after year, to plunk down their hard-earned dollars for them.

And if laborsaving devices have not saved labor in the home, then what is it that has suddenly made it possible for more than 70 percent of the wives and mothers in the American population to enter the work force and stay there? A brief glance at the histories of some of the technologies that have transformed housework during the twentieth century will help us answer some of these questions.

The portable vacuum cleaner was one of the earliest electric appliances to make its appearance in American homes, and reasonably priced models appeared on the retail market as early as 1910. For decades prior to the turn of the century, inventors had been trying to create a carpet-cleaning system that would improve on the carpet sweeper with adjustable rotary brushes (patented by Melville Bissell in 1876), or the semiannual ritual of hauling rugs outside and beating them, or the practice of regularly sweeping the dirt out of a rug that had been covered with dampened, torn newspapers. Early efforts to solve the problem had focused on the use of large steam, gasoline, or electric motors attached to piston-type pumps and lots of hoses. Many of these "stationary" vacuum-cleaning systems were installed in apartment houses or hotels, but some were hauled around the streets in horse-drawn carriages by entrepreneurs hoping to establish themselves as "professional housecleaners."

In the first decade of the twentieth century, when fractional-horsepower electric motors became widely—and inexpensively—available, the portable vacuum cleaner intended for use in an individual household was born. One early model—

invented by a woman, Corrine Dufour—consisted of a rotary brush, an electrically driven fan, and a wet sponge for absorbing the dust and dirt. Another, patented by David E. Kenney in 1907, had a twelve-inch nozzle attached to a metal tube attached to a flexible hose that led to a vacuum pump and separating devices. The Hoover, which was based on a brush, a fan, and a collecting bag, was on the market by 1908. The Electrolux, the first of the canister types of cleaner, which could vacuum something above the level of the floor, was brought over from Sweden in 1924 and met with immediate success.

These early vacuum cleaners were hardly a breeze to operate. All were heavy, and most were extremely cumbersome to boot. One early home economist mounted a basal metabolism machine on the back of one of her hapless students and proceeded to determine that more energy was expended in the effort to clean a sample carpet with a vacuum cleaner than when the same carpet was attacked with a hard broom. The difference, of course, was that the vacuum cleaner did a better job, at least on carpets, because a good deal of what the broom stirred up simply resettled a foot or two away from where it had first been lodged.

Whatever the liabilities of early vacuum cleaners may have been, Americans nonetheless appreciated their virtues; according to a market survey taken in Zanesville, Ohio, in 1926, slightly more than half the households owned one. Later improvements in design made these devices easier to operate. By 1960 vacuum cleaners were found in 70 percent of the nation's homes.

When the vacuum cleaner is viewed in a historical context, however, it is easy to see why it did not save housewifely labor. Its introduction coincided almost precisely with the disappearance of the domestic servant. The number of persons engaged in household service dropped from 1,851,000 in 1910 to 1,411,000 in 1920, while the number of households enumerated in the census rose from 20.3 million to 24.4 million. Moreover, between 1900 and 1920 the number of household servants per thousand persons dropped from 98.9 to 58.0, while during the 1920s the decline was even more precipitous as the restrictive immigration acts dried up what had once been the single most abundant source of domestic labor.

For the most economically comfortable segment of the population, this meant just one thing: the adult female head of the household was doing more housework than she had ever done before. What Maggie had once done with a broom, Mrs. Smith was now doing with a vacuum cleaner. Knowing that this was happening, several early copywriters for vacuum cleaner advertisements focused on its implications. The vacuum cleaner, General Electric announced in 1918, is better than a maid: it doesn't quit, get drunk, or demand higher wages. The switch from Maggie to Mrs. Smith shows up, in time-study statistics, as an increase in the time that Mrs. Smith is spending at her work.

For those—and they were the vast majority of the population—who were not economically comfortable, the vacuum cleaner implied something else again: not an increase in the time spent in housework but an increase in the standard of living. In many households across the country, acquisition of a vacuum cleaner was connected to an expansion of living space, the move from a small apartment to a small house, the purchase of wall-to-wall carpeting. If this did not happen during the difficult 1930s, it became more possible during the expansive 1950s. As living quarters grew larger, standards for their upkeep increased; rugs had to be vacuumed every week, in some households every day, rather than semiannually, as had been customary. The net result, of course, was that when armed with a vacuum cleaner, housewives whose parents had been poor could keep more space cleaner than their mothers and grandmothers would have ever believed possible. We might put this everyday phenomenon in language that economists can understand: The introduction of the vacuum cleaner led to improvements in productivity but not to any significant decrease in the amount of time expended by each worker.

The history of the washing machine illustrates a similar phenomenon. "Blue Monday" had traditionally been, as its name implies, the bane of a housewife's existence—especially when Monday turned out to be "Monday . . . and Tuesday to do the ironing." Thousands of patents for "new and improved" washers were issued during the nineteenth century in an effort to cash in on the housewife's despair. Most of these early washing machines were wooden or metal tubs combined with some kind of hand-cranked mechanism that would rub or push or twirl laundry when the tub was filled with water and soap. At the end of the century, the Sears catalog offered four such washing machines, ranging in price from $2.50 to $4.25, all sold in combination with hand-cranked wringers.

These early machines may have saved time in the laundering process (four shirts could be washed at once instead of each having to be rubbed separately against a washboard), but they probably didn't save much energy. Lacking taps and drains, the tubs still had to be filled and emptied by hand, and each piece still had to be run through a wringer and hung up to dry.

Not long after the appearance of fractional-horsepower motors, several enterprising manufacturers had the idea of hooking them up to the crank mechanisms of washers and wringers—and the electric washer was born. By the 1920s, when mass production of such machines began, both the general structure of the machine (a central-shaft agitator rotating within a cylindrical tub, hooked up to the household water supply) and the general structure of the industry (oligopolistic—with a very few firms holding most of the patents and controlling most of the market) had achieved their final form. By 1926 just over a quarter of the families in Zanesville had an electric washer, but by 1941 fully 52 percent of all American households either owned or had interior access (which means that they could use coin-operated models installed in the basements of apartment houses) to such a machine. The automatic washer, which consisted of a vertically rotating washer cylinder that could also act as a centrifugal extractor, was introduced by the Bendix Home Appliance Corporation in 1938, but it remained expensive, and therefore inaccessible, until after World War II. This machine contained timing devices that allowed it to proceed through its various cycles automatically; by spinning the clothes around in the extractor phase of its cycle, it also eliminated the wringer. Although the Bendix subsequently disappeared from the retail market (versions of this sturdy machine may still be found in Laundromats), its design principles are replicated in the agitator washers that currently chug away in millions of American homes.

Both the early wringer washers and their more recent automatic cousins have released American women from the burden of drudgery. No one who has ever tried to launder a sheet by hand, and without the benefits of hot running water,

Early washers took some drudgery out of housework, but modern ones have simply made the housewife a laundress.

would want to return to the days of the scrub board and tub. But "labor" is composed of both "energy expenditure" and "time expenditure," and the history of laundry work demonstrates that the one may be conserved while the other is not.

The reason for this is, as with the vacuum cleaner, twofold. In the early decades of the century, many households employed laundresses to do their wash; this was true, surprisingly enough, even for some very poor households when wives and mothers were disabled or employed full-time in field or factory. Other households—rich and poor—used commercial laundry services. Large, mechanized "steam" laundries were first constructed in this country in the 1860s, and by the 1920s they could be found in virtually every urban neighborhood and many rural ones as well.

But the advent of the electric home washer spelled doom both for the laundress and for the commercial laundry; since the housewife's labor was unpaid, and since the washer took so much of the drudgery out of washday, the one-time expenditure for a machine seemed, in many families, a more sensible arrangement than continuous expenditure for domestic services. In the process, of course, the time spent on laundry work by the individual housewife, who had previously employed either a laundress or a service, was bound to increase.

For those who had not previously enjoyed the benefits of relief from washday drudgery, the electric washer meant something quite different but equally significant: an upgrading of household cleanliness. Men stopped wearing removable collars and cuffs, which meant that the whole of their shirts had to be washed and then ironed. Housewives began changing two sheets every week, instead of moving the top sheet to the bottom and adding only one that was fresh. Teen-agers began changing their underwear every day instead of every weekend. In the early 1960s, when synthetic no-iron fabrics were introduced, the size of the household laundry load increased again; shirts and skirts, sheets and blouses that had once been sent out to the dry cleaner or the corner laundry were now being tossed into the household wash basket. By the 1980s the average American housewife, armed now with an automatic washing machine and an automatic dryer, was processing roughly ten times (by weight) the amount of laundry that her mother had been accustomed to. Drudgery had disappeared, but the laundry hadn't. The average time spent on this chore in 1925 had been 5.8 hours per week; in 1964 it was 6.2.

And then there is the automobile. We do not usually think of our cars as household appliances, but that is precisely what they are, since housework, as currently understood, could not possibly be performed without them. The average American housewife is today more likely to be found behind a steering wheel than in front of a stove. While writing this article I interrupted myself five times: once to take a child to field-hockey practice, then a second time, to bring her back when practice was finished; once to pick up some groceries at the supermarket; once to retrieve my husband, who was stranded at the train station; once for a trip to a doctor's office. Each time I was doing housework, and each time I had to use my car.

Like the washing machine and the vacuum cleaner, the automobile started to transform the nature of housework in the 1920s. Until the introduction of the Model T in 1908, automobiles had been playthings for the idle rich, and although many wealthy women learned to drive early in the century (and several participated in well-publicized auto races), they were hardly the women who were likely to be using their cars to haul groceries.

But by 1920, and certainly by 1930, all this had changed. Helen and Robert Lynd, who conducted an intensive study of Muncie, Indiana, between 1923 and 1925 (reported in their famous book *Middletown*), estimated that in Muncie in the 1890s only 125 families, all members of the "elite," owned a horse and buggy, but by 1923 there were 6,222 passenger cars in the city, "roughly one for every 7.1 persons, or two for every three families." By 1930, according to national statistics, there were roughly 30 million households in the United States—and 26 million registered automobiles.

What did the automobile mean for the housewife? Unlike public transportation systems, it was convenient. Located right at her doorstep, it could deposit her at the doorstep that she wanted or needed to visit. And unlike the bicycle or her own two feet, the automobile could carry bulky packages as well as several additional people. Acquisition of an automobile therefore meant that a housewife, once she had learned how to drive, could become her own door-to-door delivery service. And as more housewives acquired automobiles, more businessmen discovered the joys of dispensing with delivery services—particularly during the Depression.

To make a long story short, the iceman does not cometh anymore. Neither does the milkman, the bakery truck, the butcher, the grocer, the knife sharpener, the seamstress, or the doctor. Like many other businessmen, doctors discovered that their earnings increased when they stayed in their offices and transferred the responsibility for transportation to their ambulatory patients.

And so a new category was added to the housewife's traditional job description: chauffeur. The suburban station wagon is now "Mom's Taxi." Children who once walked to school now have to be transported by their mothers; husbands who once walked home from work now have to be picked up by their wives; groceries that once were dispensed from pushcarts or horse-drawn wagons now have to be packed into paper bags and hauled home in family cars. "Contemporary women," one time-study expert reported in 1974, "spend about one full working day per week on the road and in stores compared with less than two hours per week for women in the 1920s." If everything we needed to maintain our homes and sustain our families were delivered right to our doorsteps—and every member of the family had independent means for getting where she or he wanted to go—the hours spent in housework by American housewives would decrease dramatically.

The histories of the vacuum cleaner, the washing machine, and the automobile illustrate the varied reasons why the time spent in housework has not markedly decreased in the United States during the last half-century despite the introduction of so many ostensibly laborsaving appliances. But these histories do not help us understand what has made it possible for so many American wives and mothers to enter the labor force full-time during those same years. Until recently, one of the explanations most often offered for the startling increase in the participation of married women in the work force (up from 24.8 percent in 1950 to 50.1 percent in 1980) was household technology. What with microwave ovens and frozen foods, washer and dryer combinations and paper diapers, the reasoning goes, housework can now be done in no time at all, and women have so much time on their hands that they find they must go out and look for a job for fear of going stark, raving mad.

As every "working" housewife knows, this pattern of reasoning is itself stark, raving mad. Most adult women are in the work force today quite simply because they need the money. Indeed, most "working" housewives today hold down not one but two jobs; they put in what has come to be called a "double day." Secretaries, lab technicians, janitors, sewing machine operators, teachers, nurses, or physicians for eight (or nine or ten) hours, they race home to become chief cook and bottle washer for another five, leaving the cleaning and the marketing for Saturday and Sunday. Housework, as we have seen, still takes a lot of time, modern technology notwithstanding.

Yet household technologies have played a major role in facilitating (as opposed to causing) what some observers believe to be the most significant social revolution of our time. They do it in two ways, the first of which we have already noted. By relieving housework of the drudgery that it once entailed, washing machines, vacuum cleaners, dishwashers, and water pumps have made it feasible for a woman to put in a double day without destroying her health, to work full-time and still sustain herself and her family at a reasonably comfortable level.

The second relationship between household technology and the participation of married women in the work force is considerably more subtle. It involves the history of some technologies that we rarely think of as technologies at all—and certainly not as household appliances. Instead of being sheathed in stainless steel or porcelain, these devices appear in our kitchens in little brown bottles and bags of flour; instead of using switches and buttons to turn them on, we use hypodermic needles and sugar cubes. They are various forms of medication, the products not only of modern medicine but also of modern industrial chemistry: polio vaccines and vitamin pills; tetanus toxins and ampicillin; enriched breads and tuberculin tests.

Before any of these technologies had made their appearance, nursing may well have been the most time-consuming and most essential aspect of housework. During the eighteenth and nineteenth centuries and even during the first five decades of the twentieth century, it was the woman of the house who was expected (and who had been trained, usually by *her* mother) to sit up all night cooling and calming a feverish child, to change bandages on suppurating wounds, to clean bed linens stained with excrement, to prepare easily digestible broths, to cradle colicky infants on her lap for hours on end, to prepare bodies for burial. An attack of the measles might mean the care of a bedridden child for a month. Pneumonia might require six months of bed rest. A small knife cut could become infected and produce a fever that would rage for days. Every summer brought the fear of polio epidemics, and every polio epidemic left some group of mothers with the perpetual problem of tending to the needs of a handicapped child.

Cholera, diphtheria, typhoid fever—if they weren't fatal—could mean weeks of sleepless nights and hard-pressed days. "Just as soon as the person is attacked," one experienced mother wrote to her worried daughter during a cholera epidemic in Oklahoma in 1885, "be it ever so slightly, he or she ought to go to bed immediately and stay there; put a mustard [plaster] over the bowels and if vomiting over the stomach. See that the feet are kept warm, either by warm iron or brick, or bottles of hot water. If the disease progresses the limbs will begin to cramp, which must be prevented by applying cloths wrung out of hot water and wrapping round them. When one is vomiting so terribly, of course, it is next to impossible to keep medicine down, but in cholera it must be done."

These were the routines to which American women were once accustomed, routines regarded as matters of life and death. To gain some sense of the way in which modern medicines have altered not only the routines of housework but also the emotional commitment that often accompanies such work, we need only read out a list of the diseases to which most American children are unlikely to succumb today, remembering how many of them once were fatal or terribly disabling: diphtheria, whooping cough, tetanus, pellagra, rickets, measles, mumps, tuberculosis, smallpox, cholera, malaria, and polio.

And many of today's ordinary childhood complaints, curable within a few days of the ingestion of antibiotics, once might have entailed weeks, or even months, of full-time attention: bronchitis; strep throat; scarlet fever; bacterial pneumonia; infections of the skin, or the eyes, or the ears, or the airways. In the days before the introduction of modern vaccines, antibiotics, and vitamin supplements, a mother who was employed full-time was a serious, sometimes life-endangering threat to the health of her family. This is part of the reason why life expectancy was always low and infant mortality high among the poorest segment of the population—those most likely to be dependent upon a mother's wages.

Thus modern technology, especially modern medical technology, has made it possible for married women to enter the work force by releasing housewives not just from drudgery but also from the dreaded emotional equation of female employment with poverty and disease. She may be exhausted at the end of her double day, but the modern "working" housewife can at least fall into bed knowing that her efforts have made it possible to sustain her family at a level of health and comfort that not so long ago was reserved only for those who were very rich.

■ ■ ■ ■ ■ ■ ■

Cigarettes and Cancer

John A. Meyer

When the first tobacco was shipped to England from Virginia by the Jamestown settlers, King James I himself denounced smoking as a "stinking" custom "dangerous to the lungs." But large numbers of his subjects quickly acquired the smoking habit and tobacco was soon one of the main colonial exports to the mother country and indirectly to the rest of Europe. Most Europeans smoked tobacco in pipes (American Indians preferred cigars or a primitive cigarette, wrapped in a corn husk). By the time of the Civil War, cigarettes were becoming popular and after the development of machines that could mass produce them, demand increased rapidly.

During this period few people considered smoking harmful and those who did were usually considered old fashioned. Children were told that smoking would stunt their growth, and conservatives considered women who smoked wantons or at least ladylike, but decade by decade through the twentieth century, per capita consumption of cigarettes soared.

How the harmful effects of tobacco were discovered and what was done about this knowledge is the subject of this essay by John A. Meyer. Dr. Meyer, a professor of thoracic surgery, is the author of *Lung Cancer Chronicles*.

■ ■ ■ ■ ■ ■ ■

The patient at Barnes Hospital in St. Louis, in 1919, might have wondered during his last days why all the physicians were so peculiarly interested in his case. When the man died, Dr. George Dock, chairman of the department of medicine, asked all third- and fourth-year medical students at the teaching hospital to observe the autopsy. The patient's disease had been so rare, he said, that most of them would never see it again. The disease was lung cancer.

Dr. Alton Ochsner, then one of the students, wrote years later, "I did not see another case until 1936, seventeen years later, when in a period of six months, I saw nine patients with cancer of the lung. Having been impressed with the extreme rarity of this condition seventeen years previously, this represented an epidemic for which there had to be a cause. All the afflicted patients were men who smoked heavily and had smoked since World War I. . . . I had the temerity, at that time, to postulate that the probable cause of this new epidemic was cigarette use."

At the beginning of this century, most smokers chose cigars; the cigarette was seen as somewhat effete and faintly subversive. Smoking was an almost wholly male custom. In 1904 a New York City policeman arrested a woman for smoking a cigarette in an automobile and told her, "You can't do that on Fifth Avenue!" Smoking by female schoolteachers was considered grounds for dismissal. At an official White House dinner in 1910, Baroness Rosen, wife of the Russian ambassador, asked President Taft for a cigarette. The embarrassed President had to send his military aide, Maj. Archie Butt, to find one; finally the bandleader obliged.

The commercial manufacture of cigarettes had been a cottage industry until 1881, when James A. Bonsack invented a cigarette-making machine. In 1883 James Buchanan Duke, who had inherited his father's tobacco business in Durham, North Carolina, bought two of Bonsack's machines. Within five years Duke's company was selling nearly a billion cigarettes annually, far more than any other manufacturer.

Until World War I, cigarette production in America remained stable. But after the United States entered the conflict, in 1917, Duke's company and the National Cigarette Service Committee distributed millions of cigarettes free to the troops in France, and they became so powerful a morale factor that General Pershing himself demanded priority for their shipment to the front. The war began to fix the cigarette habit on the American people: between 1910 and 1919 production increased by 633 percent, from fewer than ten billion a year to nearly seventy billion. Contemporary literature reflected the change. O. Henry's carefully observed turn-of-the-century stories almost never mention cigarettes. But by the time of Ernest Hemingway's expatriates in *The Sun Also Rises,* published in 1926, men and women alike smoke constantly.

It was the consequences of this growing habit that physicians began to notice in the 1930s. As the first cases of lung cancer began to appear, doctors struggled to find ways to cope with the disease. . . . In 1950 [Dr. Evarts A.] Graham and a medical student named Ernst Wynder published a landmark study of the disease in the *Journal of the American Medical Association.* They found that practically all the victims had been long-time heavy cigarette smokers. An association between lung cancer and smoking had already been suggested by a number of other researchers, and a 1932 paper in the *American Journal of Cancer* had accurately blamed the tars in cigarettes for the formation of cancer. But this was the first major study to make the connection. In 1953 it was followed by the Sloan-Kettering Report, in which researchers at the Memorial Sloan-Kettering Cancer Center, in New York City, announced that they had produced skin cancers in mice by painting the tars from tobacco smoke on their backs.

Graham himself had been a cigarette smoker for more than twenty years, but he quit after his 1950 study and devoted himself after retirement in 1951 to research on the mechanisms of cancer production by tobacco tars. The remainder of the story is one of sad irony. In 1957 he was found to have lung cancer himself, of an especially malignant type called small-cell carcinoma. Graham died that same year; his patient Dr. Gilmore survived him by more than half a decade.

Long before the dangers of smoking became evident, cigarette companies were implying that it was actually beneficial. In 1927 the American Tobacco Company launched an advertising campaign claiming that "11,105 physicians" endorsed Lucky Strikes as "less irritating to sensitive or tender throats than any other cigarettes." Physicians' groups responded angrily, but they were more offended by the commercialization of professional opinion than by the specific claims involved.

In 1946 the R. J. Reynolds Tobacco Company launched its campaign featuring the "T-Zone Test" ("Taste and Throat") with a claim that "more doctors smoke Camels than any other cigarette!" Of course, many more doctors did smoke then than now, and Camels were extremely popular. In 1949 Camel advertised its "30-day

The figures quoted have been checked and certified to by LYBRAND, ROSS BROS. AND MONTGOMERY, Accountants and Auditors

The comforting presence of a doctor ratifies Lucky's claim to smoothness in a 1930 advertisement.

Test" with a group photograph of "noted throat specialists" who had found "not one case of throat irritation due to smoking Camels!" By the early 1950s, however, as medical studies began demonstrating close links between cigarette smoking and ill health, the manufacturers stopped claiming that smoking was healthful and began instead to insist that no connection with disease had been proved.

In the meantime, cases of—and deaths from—lung cancer among American men had begun a dizzying climb. In 1930 the death rate from lung cancer among men was less than 5 per 100,000 population per year. By 1950 it had quintupled to more than 20; today it is above 70. The numbers of new cases and of deaths have never been very far apart; even today not quite 10 percent of all lung-cancer patients can be cured. In 1989 there were an estimated 155,000 new cases of lung cancer in the United States and 142,000 deaths from the disease, making it far and away the leading cause of cancer deaths in our society, and cigarette smoking is responsible for an estimated 85 percent of the cases. The death rate still continues to rise, but there are definite signs that among men its rate of increase is diminishing, as more men give up smoking.

The rise of lung cancer among women lagged behind that among men by about thirty years. Heavy smoking remained relatively unacceptable socially for women until around World War II. Today women's lung-cancer death rates are sky-rocketing the way men's did twenty or thirty years ago. A number of studies indicate that it may be harder for women to quit than for men, and it has been predicted that by the year 2000 more women than men will be dying of lung cancer.

World War II, like World War I, gave cigarette smoking an enormous boost. Cigarettes were sold at military-post exchanges and ships' stores tax-free and virtually at cost—usually for a nickel a pack—and they were distributed free in the forward areas and were packaged in K rations.

The 1950s were the golden age of cigarettes on television. Arthur Godfrey would sign off at the end of his Chesterfield-sponsored variety show, saying, "This is Arthur 'Buy-'em-by-the-carton' Godfrey!" (The message was dropped in 1959 when Godfrey himself was found to have lung cancer. He underwent removal of the lung followed by radiation therapy, made a remarkable recovery, and lived for twenty-four years afterward.) When John Cameron Swayze anchored "The Camel News Caravan" in the early days of television, the sponsor required him to have a burning cigarette visible whenever he was on camera. Likewise, Edward R. Murrow was never seen on air without a cigarette; he died of lung cancer in 1965. But during the 1960s the tide turned against cigarettes on TV.

The change had begun in 1955, when Surgeon General Leroy E. Burney invited representatives of the National Cancer Institute, the National Heart Institute, the American Cancer Society, and the American Heart Association to establish a study group to assess the mounting evidence of links between cigarette smoking and lung cancer. The group concluded that a causal relationship did indeed exist, and late in 1959 Dr. Burney published an article in the *Journal of the American Medical Association* stating the Public Health Service's position: Cigarette smoking caused cancer.

The reports received little notice at the time, but as the 1960s got under way, agitation began to grow for the adoption of an official government position on smoking and health. In May 1962 an enterprising reporter pressured President John F. Kennedy on the subject at a press conference. The President plainly was caught off guard: "The—that matter is sensitive enough and the stock market is in sufficient difficulty without my giving you an answer which is not based on complete information, which I don't have, and therefore perhaps we could—I'd be glad to respond to that question in more detail next week."

Not long afterward Kennedy announced that he was assigning his surgeon general, Dr. Luther Terry, the responsibility for a study of smoking and health. He assured Dr. Terry that he expected an expert scientific review and would allow no political interference.

In July 1962 the surgeon general and his staff met with representatives of various medical associations and volunteer organizations, the Food and Drug Administration, the Federal Trade Commission, the Departments of Agriculture and Commerce, the Federal Communications Commission, the President's Office of Science and Technology, and the industry-backed Tobacco Institute. The representatives were given a list of 150 eminent biomedical scientists, none of whom had taken a major public position on smoking; from this list they were to propose a committee of ten members and to strike any name to which they objected for any reason.

All of the first ten scientists contacted agreed to serve; three were cigarette smokers. They began meeting in November 1962 and worked for fourteen months before submitting their formal report, which was released at a press conference on January 11, 1964. Known ever after as the Surgeon General's Report, it indicted smoking as a major cause of lung cancer in men and as a contributing cause of many forms of chronic lung disease.

After the report came out, the Federal Trade Commission issued the Trade Regulation Rules on Cigarette Labeling and Advertising, which, as of January 1, 1966, required that all cigarette packages carry a warning ("Caution, Cigarette Smoking May Be Hazardous to Your Health"), that cigarette advertising not be directed at people under twenty-five or at schools or colleges, and that no claims be made for the healthfulness of filters or cigarette products.

The industry's Tobacco Institute protested the new rules: "We respectfully submit that in these Trade Regulation Rules the Commission is . . . plainly legislating." Few could deny the substance of the allegation, but a tradition of "delegated authority" had long been emerging between Congress and its administrative agencies, so the legal question became one of the limits of that delegation. It has largely been resolved in favor of the agencies.

The tobacco companies received a further blow in 1970, when after two years of lobbying, the Federal Trade Commission persuaded Congress to pass the Public Health Cigarette Smoking Act. The bill had two main provisions: a stronger warning was to appear not only on cigarette packages but in print advertisements as well ("Warning: The Surgeon General Has Determined That Cigarette Smoking Is Dangerous to Your Health"), and all cigarette advertising was to be banned from radio and television. This time Congress itself issued the restrictive ruling. Challenged in the courts by the tobacco industry, the legislation was upheld by the Supreme Court in 1972. In 1984 the warning was made stronger again, establishing today's four alternating messages: "Cigarette Smoke Contains Carbon Monoxide"; "Quitting Smoking Now Greatly Reduces Serious Risks to Your Health"; "Smoking by Pregnant Women May Result in Fetal Injury, Premature Birth, and Low Birth Weight"; and "Smoking Causes Lung Cancer, Heart Disease, Emphysema, and May Complicate Pregnancy."

In the summer of 1987 the First U.S. Circuit Court of Appeals in Boston ruled that these warnings on cigarette packages are sufficient to protect the tobacco companies against lawsuits claiming injury or death from smoking; the ruling dismissed the case of *Palmer* v. *Liggett Group,* filed in 1983 and seeking damages for $3 million for the death of Joseph C. Palmer from lung cancer in 1980. In the case of *Cipollone* v. *Liggett Group, Lorillard, Inc., and Philip Morris, Inc.,* concluded in New Jersey in 1988, the plaintiff herself was found "80 percent responsible" for her illness and its course, and the Liggett Group "20 percent responsible." The verdict required Liggett to pay the plaintiff's family an award of $400,000. The jury concluded that Liggett had failed to warn of health risks and had misled the public with its advertising slogans prior to 1966, when the first warning-label rule took effect, but the tobacco companies were exonerated of having conspired to misrepresent the dangers of smoking. The defense called the award "an expression of sympathy by the jury"; it was voided on appeal in January 1990, and then went to the United States Supreme Court. The Supreme Court ruled in June of this year that warning labels did not pre-empt all damage suits, and opened the way for a retrial of the Cipollone case. Moreover, by ruling that Congress had "offered no sign that it wished to insulate cigarette manufacturers from longstanding rules governing fraud," the court threw the door wide open for future damage suits alleging that tobacco companies concealed information about the dangers of smoking or otherwise deceived smokers.

The biggest change in cigarettes themselves since the 1964 Surgeon General's Report has been the proliferation of low-tar, low-nicotine filtered cigarettes. Filters were first added to cigarettes long before there was public concern about the dangers of smoking. Viceroy advertised them in 1939: "AT LAST . . . a cigarette that filters each puff clean! . . . No more tobacco in mouth or teeth." After Wynder and Graham's 1950 report and the 1953 Sloan-Kettering Report, filters came into progressively greater public demand, and by the 1960s they had practically taken over the market.

Unfortunately, the advantages of low-tar and low-nicotine "light" cigarettes have proven to be largely illusory for several reasons: first, while nicotine and tars can be reduced, carbon monoxide is a product of burning, and as long as cigarettes burn, they will produce it; second, confirmed smokers tend to increase their cigarette consumption after switching to lighter brands; and third, studies have found that the risk of heart attack increases with the number of cigarettes smoked per day and does not decline when milder ones replace full-strength brands.

Cigarette manufacturers counter by pointing out that a precise chain of events leading from smoking to cancer has never been established, and that no statistical study of smokers and cancer has been able to rule out every other possible variable—factors such as diet, environment, and alcohol consumption. The industry continues to maintain that its product does not harm its users' health and that it provides pleasurable relaxation. This latter point, at least, is inarguable. Jean Nicot de Villemain, a French ambassador to Lisbon in the late sixteenth century, is said to have sent seeds of the tobacco plant to Catherine de Médicis, Queen of France, around 1556. The product had been brought to Europe from the New World first by Spanish and Portuguese explorers, but it was Nicot who presented it to Catherine and who later achieved immortality when Linnaeus used his name to christen the plant the seeds came from, *Nicotiana tabacum.* Later the active chemical alkaloid in its leaves was named nicotine.

This is the primary addicting substance in tobacco, and it is readily absorbed into the bloodstream from tobacco smoke in the lungs or from smokeless tobacco in the mouth or nose. Once in the blood, nicotine is rapidly distributed to the brain, where it binds to chemical receptors located throughout the nervous system to quicken the heartbeat, raise the blood pressure, relax skeletal muscles, and affect nearly all the endocrine glands.

In regular tobacco users, nicotine levels accumulate in the body during the day and persist at declining levels overnight; as a result, users maintain some degree of exposure to the drug practically around the clock.

For decades there have been organizations that try to help smokers quit, but successive surgeon generals' reports have found that most ex-smokers have quit spontaneously and on their own. A 1985 national survey estimated that of the 41 million Americans who quit smoking, 90 percent had done so without formal treatment programs or smoking-cessation devices. . . .

Surgical removal of the lung, or an appropriate part of it, remains the only real potential cure for lung cancer, and then only when the cancer has not yet begun to spread. Unfortunately, spreading cancer cells may be impossible to identify before the operation and afterward can give rise to recurrence or metastasis, the transmission of the disease to a new site. As a result the surgeon can speak of having effected a cure only in terms of the passage of time. Lung cancer will generally recur within three years or less if it is to recur at all. Among all patients with a new diagnosis of lung cancer, not quite one in ten will live five years. . . .

Probably no other human affliction besides AIDS depends so completely on prevention. Having risen from obscurity in our own century, lung cancer remains the number-one killer among all cancers.

The New Indians

Fergus M. Bordewich

Early in this essay, Fergus M. Bordewich asks: are Native Americans so fundamentally different from other Americans that they occupy a special category to which conventional American values and laws should not apply?" That question has been argued by both Indians and other Americans repeatedly over the years.

Some Indians see themselves primarily as Americans with certain special values and traditions, more or less like those of, say Irish Americans or Italian Americans. Others, however, insist that they belong to independent nations existing within the United States.

Bordewich, author of *Killing the White Man's Indian* (1996) traces the history of U.S. Indian policy and Indian reactions to it from the 1880s to the present day. He sympathizes with those who support the more radical groups but feels they should not become "isolated islands" within American society.

■ ■ ■ ■ ■ ■ ■

Micki's Café is, in its modest way, a bulwark against the encroachment of modern history and a symbol, amid the declining fortunes of prairie America, of the kind of gritty (and perhaps foolhardy) determination that in more self-confident times used to be called the frontier spirit. To Micki Hutchinson, the problem in the winter of 1991 seemed as plain as the grid of streets that white homesteaders had optimistically laid out in 1910, on the naked South Dakota prairie, to create the town of Isabel in the middle of what they were told was no longer the reservation of the Cheyenne River Sioux Tribe. It was not difficult for Hutchinson to decide what to do when the leaders of the tribal government ordered her to purchase a $250 tribal liquor license: She ignored them.

"They have no right to tell me what to do. I'm not Indian!" Hutchinson told me a year and a half later. She and other white businesspeople had by then challenged the tribe's right to tax them in both tribal court and federal district court and had lost. The marks of prolonged tension showed on her tanned, angular, wary face. "If this were Indian land, it would make sense. But we're a non-Indian town. This is all homestead land, and the tribe was paid for it. I can't vote in tribal elections or on anything else that happens on the reservation. What they're talking about is taxation without representation."

When I visited, everyone in Isabel still remembered the screech of the warning siren that someone had set off on the morning of March 27, 1991, when the tribal police reached the edge of town, as if their arrival were some kind of natural disaster, like a tornado or fire. The convoy of gold-painted prowl cars rolled in from the prairie and then, when they came abreast the café, swung sideways across the road. Thirty-eight tribal policemen surrounded the yellow brick building. The tribe's police chief, Marvin LeCompte, told Hutchinson that she was in contempt of tribal court. Officers ordered the morning crowd away from their fried eggs and coffee. Then they went back into the pine-paneled bar and confiscated Hutchinson's stock of beer and liquor—"contraband," as LeCompte described it—and drove off with it to the tribal government's offices at Eagle Butte.

A few days before I met Hutchinson, I had interviewed Gregg J. Bourland, the youthful chairman of the Cheyenne River Sioux Tribe. Bourland is widely reckoned to be one of the most effective tribal chairmen in the region and, with a degree in business from the state college in Spearfish, also one of the best educated. "Let them talk about taxation without representation," Bourland told me dismissively. "We're not a state. We're a separate nation, and the only way you can be represented in it is to be a member of the tribe. And they can't do that. They're not Indians. These folks are trespassers. They are within reservation boundaries, and they will follow reservation law. They've now had one hundred years without tribal authority over them out here. Well, that's over."

More than Micki Hutchinson or than any of the other angry whites in their declining prairie hamlets, it was Bourland who understood that what was at stake was much more than small-town politics. The tax, the ostentatious convoy, and the lawsuit were part of a much larger political drama that was unfolding across the inland archipelago of reservations that make up modern Indian Country. They symbolized the reshaping of the American West, indeed of the United States itself. By the 1990s, almost unnoticed by the American public or media, a generation of legislation and court actions had profoundly remade Indian Country, canonizing ideas about tribal autonomy that would have shocked the lawmakers who a century before had seen the destruction of the reservations as the salvation of the American Indian. If Bourland was right, Micki Hutchinson and the white residents of Isabel were living in a sovereign tribal state. They were tolerated guests with an uncertain future.

Until the 1870s, reservations were established throughout the Dakota Territory and other parts of the West with the promise that they would be reserved in perpetuity for the Indians' exclusive use. Those promises were broken almost everywhere when reservations were opened to homesteading at the end of the century, usually with only perfunctory consultation with the tribes or none at all. As I listened to Gregg Bourland, it was easy to sympathize with the tribe's striving for some kind of control over forces that were felt to have invaded their land and undermined their culture. Bourland justified the tax as a means both to raise revenue and to control alcohol consumption on a reservation where more than 60 percent of the adults were unemployed and 53 percent were active alcoholics.

But promises that had been made a century ago to the ancestors of settlers like Micki Hutchinson were now being broken too. From the 1880s until the 1930s, the cornerstone of Federal Indian policy had been the popular program known as allotment, the systematic breaking up of most of the nation's reservations into private holdings. In its day allotment seemed the perfect panacea to resolve at a single stroke the perennial problems of white settlers' insatiable desire for new land and Indians' growing dependency on the federal government. Sen. Henry L. Dawes, the idealistic architect of the Allotment Act of 1881, which set the pattern for a generation of similar legislation, ringingly proclaimed that as a result of allotment, the Indian "shall be one of us, contributing his share to all that goes to make up the strength and glory of citizenship in the United States."

The means of the Indian's salvation was to be the family farm, which most people at the time regarded as the ultimate repository of American individualism and the democratic spirit. Each Indian allottee would receive 160 acres of land and eventual citizenship, along with money for seed, tools, and livestock. The "excess," or leftover, land would be offered to white settlers, who would be free to form their own municipal governments. The promise of the allotment policy was twofold: that the nation would integrate Indians into white society and that non-Indian settlers would never be subject to tribal regimes.

At the time, the Commissioner of Indian Affairs dismissed notions of separate Indian nationality as mere sentimentality: "It is perfectly clear to my mind that the treaties never contemplated the un-American and absurd idea of a separate nationality in our midst, with power as they may choose to organize a government of their own." To maintain such a view, the commissioner added, was to acknowledge a foreign sovereignty on American soil, "a theory utterly repugnant to the spirit and genius of our laws, and wholly unwarranted by the Constitution of the United States."

As I left Isabel, I wondered who really was the victim here and who was the victimizer. Behind that nagging question lurked still more difficult ones that occupied me for many months, from one end of the United States to the other, in the course of researching what was to become *Killing the White Man's Indian*, an investigation into the political and cultural transformation of modern Indian Country. Are Native Americans so fundamentally different from other Americans that they occupy a special category to which conventional American values and laws should not apply? Or are they simply one more American group, whose special pleading is further evidence that the United States has become a balkanized tangle of ghettos and ethnic enclaves? Do we discriminate against Indians by failing to blend them more effectively into the national mainstream? Or is the very notion of "mainstreaming" Indians so inherently racist that it should not even be contemplated as a component of national policy? Are Indian reservations and the way of life they preserve a precious national resource that must be maintained without the taint of contact with white America? Or is tribal self-determination creating a new form of segregation that merely freezes decayed tribal cultures like ghettoized versions of Colonial Williamsburg? Who, ultimately, are Indians in the 1990s? What are they to other Americans, and the others to them?

Killing the White Man's Indian represented a return to familiar country. As a youth in the 1950s and early 1960s, I often accompanied my mother, who was the executive director of the Association on American Indian Affairs, in her travels around reservations, part of her tireless effort to prod the federal government into improving tribal economies, education, health care, and law and order. Vivid experiences were plentiful: participating in a nightlong peyote rite in a tepee on the Montana prairie; a journey by pirogue deep into the Louisiana bayous to meet with a forgotten band of Houmas who wanted Washington to take notice of their existence; walking the Little Bighorn Battlefield with an aged Cheyenne who, as a boy, had witnessed the annihilation of Custer's command. Poverty shaded almost every experience. Staying with friends often meant wind fingering its way through gaps in the walls, a cheese and bologna sandwich for dinner, sleeping three or four in a bed with broken springs. It seemed there was always someone talking about an uncle who, drunk, had frozen to death on a lonely road or about a cousin already pregnant at sixteen. More generally those years left me with a sense of the tremendous diversity of the lives and communities that lay submerged within the catchall label of "Indians" and a recognition that Native Americans were not mere vestiges of a mythic past but modern men and women struggling to solve twentieth-century problems.

In the course of four years' research on my book, I visited reservations from upstate New York to southern California and from Mississippi to Washington State, meeting with tribal leaders, educators, and hundreds of ordinary men and women, both Indian and white. In Michigan I sailed Lake Superior with waterborne Chippewa police, searching for poachers on tribal fisheries on the lake. In Oregon I hiked the Cascades with professional foresters from the Warm Springs Tribe, which with its several hydroelectric dams and thriving timber industry is one of Indian Country's great success stories. I sweated with a group of recovering Navajo alcoholics in a traditional sweat lodge in the New Mexico desert. I also spent many a night in dust-blown reservation towns where, as an old South Dakota song puts it, "There's nothing much to do except walk up and down." In a few places, as a result of childhood connections, I was welcomed as a friend. More frequently I met with suspicion rooted in the widespread belief that curiosity like mine was just a form of exploitation and that whites are incapable of writing about Indians with objectivity and honesty.

My original intention had been to use the lives of several men and women whom I had known in the 1950s as a microcosm and through them to chart the changes that had been wrought in Indian Country during the intervening years. But I soon realized that such a focus would be far too narrow, for it had become clear to me that a virtual revolution was under way that was challenging the worn-out theory of Indians as losers and victims and was transforming tribes into powers to be reckoned with for years to come. It encompassed virtually every aspect of Indian life, from the revival of moribund tribal cultures and traditional religions to the development of aggressive tribal governments determined to remake the relationship between tribes and the United States. The ferment was not unalloyed, however. Alongside inspired idealism, I also found ethnic chauvinism, a crippling instinct to mistake isolation for independence, and a habit of interpreting present-day reality through the warping lens of the past.

In the 1970s, in a reversal of long-standing policies based on the conviction that Indians must be either persuaded or compelled to integrate themselves into mainstream America, the United States enshrined the concept of tribal sovereignty at the center of its policy toward the nation's more than three hundred tribes. In the watershed words of Richard Nixon, federal policy would henceforth be guided "by Indian acts and Indian decisions" and would be designed to "assure the Indian that he can assume control of his own life without being separated from the tribal group."

In 1975 the Indian Self-Determination and Education Assistance Act amplified this principle, calling for a "transition from Federal domination of programs for and services to Indians to effective and meaningful participation by the Indian people." This has been reflected in a national commitment to the strengthening of tribal governments and to more comprehensive tribal authority over reservation lands. More ambiguously, it has also led to the increasing development of a new sphere of political power that rivals, or at least claims to rival, that of the states and the national government and for which there is no foundation in the Constitution. In the mid-1990s I found tribal officials invoking "sovereign right" in debates over everything from highway maintenance and fishing quotas to law and order, toxic-waste disposal, and the transfer of federal services to tribal administrations, not to mention the rapid proliferation of tribally run gambling operations. Reflecting the sentiments of many tribal leaders, Tim Giago, the publisher of *Indian Country Today*, the most widely read Indian newspaper in the United States, likened the state legislation that affects Indians to "letting France make laws that also become law in Italy."

To people like Micki Hutchinson, it often seems that Indians were playing an entirely new game, and that no one but the Indians knew the rules. In Connecticut, and elsewhere, tribes were exploiting a principle of sovereignty unknown to the average American in order to build casinos that sucked colossal sums of money from neighboring regions. New Mexicans found that they were equally helpless in the face of the Mescalero Apaches' determination to establish a nuclear-waste facility on their reservation outside Alamogordo. In Wisconsin and in Washington State, recurrent violence had accompanied the judicially mandated enlargement of Indian fishing rights in accordance with nineteenth-century treaties. In Nevada farmers found themselves on the brink of failure as the Paiutes of Pyramid Lake gained political leverage over the watershed of the Truckee River.

In some states Indian demands for the return of sacred lands posed significant threats to local economies, including, most prominently, the Black Hills region of South Dakota. Nor was science exempt. Tribal claims on ancestral bones and artifacts were depleting many of the most valuable anthropological collections in the country.

Strangely enough, these conflicts—widespread, often bitter, and with profound ramifications for American institutions—seemed to be happening beyond the ken of most Americans, for whom Indians remain a people of myth and fantasy. Like no other inhabitants of the United States, Indians have nourished our imagination, weaving in us a complex skein of guilt, envy, and contempt; yet when we imagine we see "the Indian," we often see little more than the distorted reflection of our own fears, fancies, and unhappy longings. This was vividly brought home to me on a visit to the reservation of the two-hundred member Campo Band of Mission Indians, in the arid hills an hour's drive east of San Diego. This reservation landscape is a profoundly discouraging one. It offers nothing to comfort the eye, produces nothing of value, and provides almost nothing to sustain life as it is enjoyed by most Americans today. The single resource that the Campos possess is wasteland. In 1987 the band learned that the city of San Diego had named the reservation as one of several potential dump sites for the city's refuse.

"We just need this one little thing to get us started," the band's chairman, Ralph Goff, told me as we walked through the redshank and yucca and ocher sand where the first trenches had been cut for the new landfill. "With it we can create our own destiny." Goff, a formidably built man with little formal education, grew up in the 1940s, when the only work available was as a cowhand or day laborer for whites. When there was no work, people went hungry. "You just had to wait until there was some more food." In the 1960s most of the unskilled jobs disappeared, and nearly every Campo family went on welfare. "We needed it, but it really wrecked us as people. It created idleness. People didn't have anything to do in order to get money."

If the Campos have their way, by the end of the decade daily freight trains will be carrying loads of municipal waste to a three-hundred-acre site on a hilltop at the southern end of the reservation. For the privilege of leasing the band's land, a waste-management firm will pay the Campos between two and five million dollars a year. Goff argued that the dump would put an end to the band's dependence on federal largesse. It would create jobs for every adult Campo who is willing to work, provide long-term investment capital for the band, supply money for full college scholarships for every school-age member of the band, and finance new homes for the families that now live in substandard housing. The dump would, in short, give the Campos financial independence for the first time in their modern history.

The landfill would be one of the most technically advanced in the United States; to regulate it, the Campos enacted an environmental code more stringent than the State of California's. Nevertheless, the dump generated fierce opposition in towns near the reservation, where thousands of non-Indians live. Geologists hired by the dump's opponents have suggested, but not proved, that seepage from the dump might contaminate the water supply of ranches beyond the reservation boundary. Environmentalists accused the band of irresponsibility toward the earth and charged that the Campos had been targeted by an "assault" on reservations by "renegade" waste-dumping companies. A bill was even introduced in the California legislature that would have made it a crime to deliver waste to the Campo landfill. Goff shrugged away the protests. "It's a sovereignty issue. It's our land, and we'll do what we want with it."

"How can you say that the economic development of two hundred people is more important than the health and welfare of all the people in the surrounding area?" an angry and frustrated rancher, whose land lay just off the reservation, asked me. "It's hard making a living here. The fissures will carry that stuff right through here. We'll have all that stuff in our water and blowing down on us off the hills. If our water is spoiled, then everything's spoiled."

There were predictable elements to her rage: the instinctive resistance of most Americans to any kind of waste dump anywhere near their homes and the distress of many white Americans when they realize the implications of tribal sovereignty for the first time and find themselves subject to the will of a government in which they have no say. But there was something more, a sort of moral perplexity at Indians' having failed to behave according to expectation, an imputation that they were guilty of self-interest. Revealingly, I thought, on the wall of the rancher's trailer there was a poster decorated with Indian motifs. Entitled "Chief Seattle Speaks," it began, in words that are becoming as familiar to American schoolchildren as those of the Gettysburg address once were: "How can you buy or sell the sky, the warmth of the land?" Here, in sight of the dump, the so-called testament of Chief Seattle was a reproach to the Campos, an argument rooted in what the rancher presumably believed to be the Indians' profoundest values. "Before all this I had this ideal about Indian people and all they've been through," she told me, "I used to think they had this special feeling about the land."

More than any other single document, Seattle's twelve-hundred-word "testament" lends support to the increasingly common belief that to "real" Indians any disruption of the earth's natural order is a kind of sacrilege and that the most moral, the most truly "Indian" relationship with the land is a kind of poetic passivity. Having been translated into dozens or languages and widely reproduced in school texts, the "testament" has attained a prophetic stature among environmentalists: In 1993 Greenpeace used it as an introduction to a scarifying report on toxic dumping, calling it "the most beautiful and profound statement on the environment ever made." Unfortunately, like much literature that purports to reveal the real nature of the Indians, the "testament" is basically a fiction. Seattle was indeed a historical figure, a slave-owning chief of the Duwamishes who sold land to the United States in the mid-1850s and welcomed the protection of the federal government against his local enemies. However, the "testament," as it is known to most Americans, was created from notes allegedly made thirty years after the fact by a white doctor who claimed to have been present when Seattle spoke, and which then were extravagantly embroidered by a well-meaning Texas scriptwriter by the name of Ted Perry as narration for a 1972 film on the environment, produced by the Southern Baptist Radio and Television Commission. How is it, I wondered, that Americans have so readily embraced such a spurious text not only as a sacred creed of the ecology movement but also as a central document of "traditional" Native American culture?

Increasingly it became clear to me that to be able to describe the realities of modern Indian life and politics, I would have to strip away the myths that whites have spun around Native Americans ever since Columbus arbitrarily divided the peoples he encountered into noble Arawaks and savage Caribs, conflating European fantasies with presumed native reality and initiating a tradition that would eventually include Montesquieu, Locke, Hobbes, and Rousseau, as well as a vivid popular literature stretching from *The Last of the Mohicans* to *Dances With Wolves*. Untamable savage, child of nature, steward of the earth, the white man's ultimate victim: each age had imagined its own mythic version of what the historian Robert F. Berkhofer, Jr., termed the "white man's Indian."

Typically the Denver *Post* could declare, not long ago, in an editorial attacking the University of Arizona for a plan to build an observatory atop an allegedly sacred mountain: "At stake is the very survival of American Indian cultures. If these sacred places are destroyed, then the rituals unique to those places will no longer be performed and many tribes simply may cease to exist as distinct peoples." Such logic implies both that only Native Americans who profess to live like pre-Columbians are true Indians and that Indians are essentially hopeless and helpless and on the brink of extinction. Apparently it never occurred to the paper's editorialist that the religion of the great majority of Indians is not in fact some mystical form of traditionalism but a thriving Christianity.

In keeping with our essentially mythic approach to the history of Indians and whites, Americans were generally taught until a generation or so ago to view their national story as a soaring arc of unbroken successes, in which the defeat of the Indians reflected the inevitable and indeed spiritual triumph of civilization over barbarism. More recently, but not so differently, numerous revisionist works like Kirkpatrick Sale's *The Conquest of Paradise: Christopher Columbus and the Columbian Legacy* and Richard Drinnon's *Facing West: The Metaphysics of Indian-Hating and Empire Building* have tended to portray the settlement of North America as a prolonged story of unredeemed tragedy and failure, in which the destruction of the Indians stands as proof of a fundamental ruthlessness at the heart of American civilization. Such beliefs have steadily percolated into the wider culture—to be embodied in New Age Westerns like *Dances With Wolves* and popular books like the best-selling *Indian Givers: How the Indians of the Americas Transformed the World,* which purports to show how practically every aspect of modern life from potatoes to democracy derives from the generosity of American Indians—and into the consciences of journalists, clergy, and others who shape public opinion.

On the whole the complex and intricate relationship between whites and Indians has been presented as one of irreconcilable conflict between conqueror and victim, corruption and innocence, Euro-American "materialism" and native "spirituality." The real story, of course, is an often contradictory one, disfigured by periods of harsh discrimination and occasional acts of genocide but also marked by considerable Indian pragmatism and adaptability as well as by the persistent, if sometimes shortsighted, idealism of whites determined to protect Indians from annihilation and find some place for them in mainstream America.

For instance, in contradiction of the notion that Indians were innocent of even the most elementary business sense, it was clear during negotiations over the Black Hills in the 1870s that Sioux leaders had a perfectly good grasp of finance and that indeed they were determined to drive the best bargain they could. "The Black Hills are the house of Gold for our Indians," Chief Little Bear said at the time. "If a man owns anything, of course he wants to make something out of it to get rich on." Another chief, Spotted Tail, added: "I want to live on the interest of my money. The amount must be so large as to support us." Similarly, in contrast with the popular belief that the United States government was committed to a policy of exterminating the Indian (no such policy ever existed, in fact), Senator Dawes publicly described the history of Indians in the United States as one "of spoliation, of wars, and of humiliation," and he firmly stated that the Indian should be treated "as an individual, and not as an insoluble substance that the civilization of this country has been unable, hitherto, to digest."

Indeed, the impulse behind the allotment of tribal lands and the national commitment to Indians was dramatically (and, in hindsight, poignantly) acted out in a rite of citizenship that after 1887 was staged at Timber Lake, in the heart of the Cheyenne River Sioux country, and at many other places in the freshly allotted lands of other tribes. In the presence of representatives of the federal government,

Residents of the Torres Martinez Indian Reservation south of Los Angeles demonstrate outside the Los Angeles County Hall of Administration to protest the dumping of sewage sludge on land within the reservation.

new allottees stood resplendent in the feathers and buckskins of a bygone age. One by one, each man stepped out of a tepee and shot an arrow to symbolize the life he was leaving behind. He then put his hands on a plow and accepted a purse that indicated that he was to save what he earned. Finally, holding the American flag, the Indian repeated these words: "Forasmuch as the President has said that I am worthy to be a citizen of the United States, I now promise this flag that I will give my hands, my head, and my heart to the doing of all that will make me a true American citizen." It was the culminating, transformative moment of which Senator Dawes had dreamed.

It is true enough, however, that, as so often in the Indian history, reality failed to live up to good intentions. Unscrupulous speculators soon infested the allotted reservations, offering worthless securities and credit in return for land. Within a few years it was found that of those who had received patents to their land at Cheyenne River, 95 percent had sold or mortgaged their properties. When the Allotment Act was passed in 1881, there were 155 million acres of Indian land in the United States. By the time allotment was finally brought to a halt in 1934, Indian Country had shrunk by nearly 70 percent to 48 million acres, and two-thirds of Indians were either completely landless or did not have enough land left to make a living from it. In the mid-1990s Indian Country as a whole is still a daunting and impoverished landscape whose inhabitants are twice as likely as other Americans to be murdered or commit suicide, three times as likely to die in an automobile accident, and five times as likely to die from cirrhosis of the liver. On some reservations unemployment surpasses 80 percent, and 50 percent of young Indians drop out of high school, despite progressively increased access to education.

Is the tribal-sovereignty movement a panacea for otherwise intractable social problems? In the cultural sphere, at least, its importance cannot be underestimated. "Our people live in a limbo culture that is not quite Indian and not quite white either," said Dennis Hastings, surrounded by books, gazing out toward the Iowa plains through the window of the sky blue trailer where he lives in a cow pasture. Hastings, a burly former Marine and the tribal historian of the Omaha Nation, which is in northeastern Nebraska, has almost single-handedly led an effort to recover tribal history as a foundation for community renewal that is probably unmatched by any other small tribe in the United States. "It's like living in a house without a foundation. You can't go back to the old buffalo days, stop speaking English and just use our own language, and ignore whites and everything in white culture. If we did that, we'd become dinosaurs."

Teasing small grants and the help of volunteer scholars from institutions around the country, Hastings has initiated an oral-history project to collect memories of fading tribal traditions. "We go into each family, get an anthropologist to record everything right from how you wake up in the morning," he said. Hundreds of historic photographs of early reservation life have been collected and deposited with the State Historical Society, in Lincoln. A friendly scholar from the University of Indiana recovered a trove of forgotten Omaha songs recorded in the 1920s on wax cylinders. Another at the University of New Mexico undertook a collective genealogy that would trace the lineage of more than five thousand Omahas back to the eighteenth century. Hastings explained, "Until now everything was oral. Some people knew the names of their ancestors, and some knew nothing at all. There was a loss of connection with the past. Now people can come back and find out who their ancestors were." In sharp contrast with the combative chauvinism of some tribes, the Omahas invited scientists from the University of Nebraska and the Smithsonian Institution to examine repatriated skeletons to see what they could discover about the lives of their ancestors. In 1989, astonishing perhaps even themselves, tribal leaders brought home Waxthe'xe, the True Omaha, the sacred cottonwood pole that is the living embodiment of the Omaha people, which had lain for a hundred years in Harvard's Peabody Museum; at the July powwow that year, weeping hundreds bent to touch it as if it were the true cross or the ark of the covenant.

"We want the benefits of modern society," Hastings told me in his nasal Midwestern draw. "But America is still dangerous for us. The question is then, How do we take the science that America used against us and make it work for us? The answer is, we try to build on the past. It's like a puzzle. First you see where the culture broke and fragmented. Then you try to build on it where people have been practicing it all along. Then people start to think in a healthy way about what they were in the past. If you can get each person to be proud of himself, little by little, you can get the whole tribe to become proud. We're going to dream big and be consistent with that dream."

In its broadest sense the tribal sovereignty movement is demonstrating that the more than three hundred Indian tribes in the lower forty-eight states (more than five hundred if you count Alaskan native groups) are distinct communities, each with its unique history, traditions, and political environment, for whom a single one-size-fits-all federal policy will no longer suffice. Greater autonomy will surely enable well-governed and economically self-sufficient tribes—mostly those located near big cities and those with valuable natural resources—to manage their own development in imaginative ways. For many others, however, far from airports and interstate highways, populated by ill-trained workers and governed, in some cases, by politicians who do not abide by the most democratic rules, the future is much less assured.

There is nothing abstract about such concerns in Timber Lake, South Dakota, which lies a short drive east from Isabel across the rolling plains of the Cheyenne River Sioux Reservation. Like Isabel, Timber Lake has been battered by the general decline of a region that is hemorrhaging jobs and people. Timber Lake is one of the relatively lucky places, kept alive by the presence of the Dewey County offices, the rural electric co-op, the central school, and a cheese factory. Even so, one hundred of the six hundred people who lived there a decade ago have moved away to places with better prospects and more hope. Isabel's population has dropped by half, to three hundred. Trail City has shrunk from three hundred and fifty to thirty, Firesteel to a single general store, and Landeau has disappeared completely. Entire towns have lost their doctors, banks, and schools. From a certain angle of vision, Sioux demands for the restoration of the reservation to its original nineteenth-century limits are simply an anticlimax.

The people of Timber Lake—the mechanics, the teachers, the co-op clerks, the men who work at the grain elevator, the retired farmers—are the human fruit of allotment, the flesh-and-blood culmination of the cultural blending that Senator Dawes envisioned. "Everyone here has relatives who are Indian," said Steve Aberle, a local attorney whose Russian-Jewish father married into the Ducheneaux, a prominent clan of Cheyenne River Sioux. Aberle, who is thirty-five, is one eighth Sioux; he is a voting member of the tribe and served for two and a half years as chairman of the tribal police commission. Nevertheless he shares the unease of non-Indians who feel themselves slipping toward a kind of second-class citizenship within the reservation's boundaries. "It would be better in a situation where everybody works together and deals with people as people, but it's hard to do that when people know they pay taxes but are excluded from benefits and services," Aberle told me. "When my grandparents came from Russia, the United States government told them they would be full citizens if they moved out here. Now I see people being told that they can't even take part in a government that wants to regulate them. Something is inherently wrong when you can't be a citizen where you live because of your race. It just doesn't fit with the traditional notion of being a U.S. citizen. At some point there has to be a collision between the notion of tribal sovereignty and the notion of being United States citizens. Anytime you have a group not in the political process they will be discriminated against. There's going to be more and more friction. It's going to hurt these communities. People start looking for jobs elsewhere."

The Sioux were the victims of nineteenth-century social engineering that decimated their reservation. But the descendants of the adventurous emigrants who settled the land are also the victims of an unexpected historical prank, the trick of the disappearing and now magically reappearing reservation. Reasonably enough, the rhetoric of tribal sovereignty asks for tribes a degree of self-government that is taken for granted by other Americans. However, the achievement of a sovereignty that drives away taxpayers, consumers, and enterprise may be at best a Pyrrhic victory over withered communities that beg for cooperation and innovation to survive at all.

With little debate outside the parochial circles of Indian affairs, a generation of policymaking has jettisoned the long-standing American ideal of racial unity as a positive good and replaced it with a doctrine that, seen from a more critical angle, seems disturbingly like an idealized form of segregation, a fact apparently invisible to a nation that has become increasingly accustomed to looking at Indians only through the twin lenses of romance and guilt and in an era that has made a secular religion of passionate ethnicity. Much of the thinking that underlies tribal sovereignty seems to presuppose that cultural purity can and ought to be preserved, as if Indian bloodlines, economies, and histories were not already inextricably enmeshed with those of white, Hispanic, and black Americans.

Such concerns will be further exacerbated in the years to come as Indian identity grows increasingly ambiguous. Virtually all Indians are moving along a continuum of biological fusion with other American populations. "A point will be reached . . . when it will no longer make sense to define American Indians in generic terms [but] only as tribal members or as people of Indian ancestry or ethnicity," writes Russell Thornton, a Cherokee anthropologist and demographer at the University of Southern California, in *American Indian Holocaust and Survival*, a study of fluctuations in native populations. Statistically, according to Thornton, Indians are marrying outside their ethnic group at a faster rate than any other Americans. More than 50 percent of Indians are already married to non-Indians, and Congress has estimated that by the year 2080 less than 8 percent of Native Americans will have one-half or more Indian blood.

How much ethnic blending can occur before Indians finally cease to be Indians? The question is sure to loom even larger for coming generations, as the United States increasingly finds itself in "government-to-government" relationships with tribes that are becoming less "Indian" by the decade. Within two or three generations the nation will possess hundreds of "tribes" that may consist of the great-great-grandchildren of Indians but whose native heritage consists mainly of autonomous governments and special privileges that are denied to other Americans.

Insofar as there is a political solution to the Indian future, I have come to believe that it lies in the rejection of policies that lead to segregation and in acknowledgment of the fact that the racially and ethnically variegated peoples whom we call "Indian" share not only a common blood but also a common history and a common future with other Americans. The past generation has seen the development of a national consensus on a number of aspects of the nation's history that were long obscured by racism or shame; there is, for instance, little dispute today among Americans of any ethnic background over the meaning of slavery or of the internment of Japanese-Americans during the Second World War. There is as yet no such consensus as to the shared history of Indians and whites, who both still tend to see the past as a collision of irreconcilable opposites and competing martyrdoms.

That history was not only one of wars, removals, and death but also one of calculated compromises, mutual accommodation, and deliberately chosen risks, a story of Indian communities and individuals continually remaking themselves in order to survive. To see change as failure, as some kind of cultural corruption is to condemn Indians to solitary confinement in a prison of myth that whites invented for them in the first place. Self-determination gives Indian tribes the ability to manage the speed and style of integration but not the power to stop it, at least not for long. Integration may well mean the eventual diminishing of conventional notions of "tribal identity," but it must also bring many new individual opportunities, along with membership in the larger human community. "People and their cultures perish in isolation, but they are born or reborn in contact with other men and women, with men and women of another culture, another creed, another race," the Mexican novelist Carlos Fuentes has written. Tribes will survive, if anything, as stronger entities than they have been for many generations. The question is whether they will attempt to survive as isolated islands or as vital communities that recognize a commonality of interest and destiny with other Americans.

TEXT CREDITS

"Why They Impeached Andrew Johnson" by David Herbert Donald, *American Heritage,* December 1956: 20–25, 102–103. Copyright © 1956 by American Heritage, a division of Forbes, Inc.

"Ride-in" (reprinted under the title "Ride-in: A Century of Protest Begins") by Alan F. Westin, *American Heritage,* August 1962: 57–64. Copyright © 1962 by American Heritage, a division of Forbes, Inc.

"The Reluctant Conquerors: How the Generals Viewed the Indians" (reprinted under the title "Reluctant Conquerors: American Army Officers and the Plains Indians") by Thomas C. Leonard, *American Heritage,* 27, 5, August 1976: 34–40. Copyright © 1976 by American Heritage, a division of Forbes, Inc.

"The Grand Acquisitor" (reprinted under the title "John D. Rockefeller: America's Fist Billionaire") by Robert L. Heilbroner, *American Heritage,* December 1964: 20–25, 80–85. Copyright © 1964 by American Heritage, a division of Forbes, Inc.

"A Little Milk, A Little Honey" (reprinted under the title "The Diaspora in America: A Study of Jewish Immigration") by David Boroff, *American Heritage,* October 1966: 12–21, 74–81. Copyright © 1966 by American Heritage, a division of Forbes, Inc.

"The Age of the Bosses" by William V. Shannon, *American Heritage,* 20, 4, June 1969: 26–31. Copyright © 1969 by American Heritage, a division of Forbes, Inc.

"The Myth of the Happy Yeoman" from *The Age of Reform* by Richard Hofstadter. Copyright © 1955 by Richard Hofstadter. Reprinted by permission of Albert A. Knopf, Inc.

"Saint Jane and the Ward Boss" (reprinted under the title "Jane Addams: Urban Crusader") by Anne Firor Scott, *American Heritage,* December 1960: 12–17, 94–99. Copyright © 1960 by American Heritage, a division of Forbes, Inc.

"Inventing Modern Football" (reprinted under the title "Reforming College Football") by John S. Watterson, *American Heritage,* 39, 6, September/October 1988: 102–113. Copyright © 1988 by American Heritage, a division of Forbes, Inc.

"'I Was Arrested, Of Course . . .'" (reprinted under the title "The Fight for Women's Suffrage: An Interview with Alice Paul") by Robert S. Gallagher, *American Heritage,* 25, 2, February 1974: 16–24, 92–94. Copyright © 1974 by American Heritage, a division of Forbes, Inc.

"Father of the Forests" (reprinted under the title "Gordon Pinchot: Father of the Forests") by T. H. Watkins, *American Heritage,* 42, 1, February/March 1991: 86-98. Copyright © 1991 by American Heritage, a division of Forbes, Inc.

"The Needless War with Spain" by William Leuchtenburg, *American Heritage,* February 1957: 32-45, 95. Copyright © 1957 by American Heritage, a division of Forbes, Inc.

"The Enemies of Empire" by Harold A. Larrabee, *American Heritage,* June 1960: 28-33, 76-80. Copyright © 1960 by Harold Larrabee.

"Yesterday, December 7, 1941 . . ." (reprinted under the title "Pearl Harbor: The 'Day of Infamy'") by Richard M. Ketchum, *American Heritage,* 40, 7, November 1989: 52–72. Copyright © 1989 by Richard M. Ketchum.

"The Biggest Decision: Why We Had to Drop the Bomb" by Robert James Maddox, *American Heritage,* May/June 1995: 71–77. Copyright © 1995 by American Heritage, a division of Forbes, Inc.

"The Days of Boom and Bust" (reprinted under the title "The Causes of the Great Depression") by John Kenneth Galbraith, *American Heritage,* August 1958: 28–33, 101–103. Copyright © 1958 by John Kenneth Galbraith. Reprinted by permission of Alfred A. Knopf, Inc.

"The Big Picture of the Great Depression" by John A. Garraty, *American Heritage,* 37, 4, August/September 1986: 90–97. Copyright © 1986 by American Heritage, a division of Forbes, Inc.

"FDR: The Man of the Century" by Arthur Schlesinger, Jr., *American Heritage,* May/June 1995: 83–93. Copyright © 1994 by American Heritage, a division of Forbes, Inc.

"The Case of the Chambermaid and the 'Nine Old Men'" by William E. Leuchtenburg, *American Heritage,* 38, 1, January/February 1987. Copyright © 1987 by American Heritage, a division of Forbes, Inc.

"Eisenhower as President" by Steve Neal, *American Heritage,* December 1985. Copyright © 1985 by American Heritage, a division of Forbes, Inc.

"The Education of John F. Kennedy" by Richard Reeves, *American Heritage,* September 1993: 59–66. Copyright © 1993 by American Heritage, a division of Forbes, Inc.

"Machismo in the White House: Lyndon B. Johnson and Vietnam" (reprinted under the title "Lyndon B. Johnson and Vietnam") by Larry L. King, *American Heritage,* August 1976: 8–13, 98–101. Copyright © 1976 by Larry L. King.

"The Hour of the Founders" (reprinted under the title "Watergate") by Walter Karp, *American Heritage,* 1984. Copyright © 1984 by American Heritage, a division of Forbes, Inc.

"The Buy of the Century" (reprinted under the title "Levittown: The Buy of the Century") by Andrew O. Boulton, *American Heritage,* July/August 1993: 62–69. Copyright © 1993 by American Heritage, a division of Forbes, Inc.

"With All Deliberate Speed" (reprinted under the title "Desegregating the Schools") by Liva Baker, *American Heritage,* 24, 2, February 1973: 42–48. Copyright © 1973 by American Heritage, a division of Forbes, Inc.

"Less Work for Mother?" (reprinted under the title "The Housework Revolution") by Ruth Schwartz Cowan, *American Heritage,* 38, 6, September/October 1987: 68–76. Copyright © 1987 by American Heritage, a division of Forbes, Inc.

"Cigarette Century" (reprinted under the title "Cigarettes and Cancer") by John A. Meyer, *American Heritage,* 43, 8, January 1993: 72–80. Copyright © 1993 by American Heritage, a division of Forbes, Inc.

"Revolution in Indian Country" (reprinted under the title "The New Indians") by Fergus M. Bordewich, *American Heritage,* July/August 1996: 34–46. Copyright © 1996 by American Heritage, a division of Forbes, Inc.

ILLUSTRATION CREDITS

The abbreviations T, C, B, R, and L stand for Top, Center, Bottom, Right, and Left, repectively.

261   Wally McNamee/Woodfin Camp & Associates
267   Elliot Landy/Magnum Photos
270   Bernard Hoffman/Life Magazine, ©Time, Inc.
274   Carl Iwasaki, Life Magazine, © Time, Inc.
280   AP/Wide World Photos
289   Library of Congress
296   New York Public Library, Astor, Lenox, and Tilden Foundation
309   Ana E. Fuentes/Los Angeles Times Syndicate
309   Nick Ut/AP/Wide World Photos

#7